HYDRAULIC CITY

HYDRAULIC CITY

Water and the Infrastructures of Citizenship in Mumbai

NIKHIL ANAND

Duke University Press   Durham and London   2017

© 2017 Duke University Press
All rights reserved
Printed in the United States of America on acid-free paper ∞
Designed by Courtney Leigh Baker
Typeset in Arno Pro and League Gothic

Library of Congress Cataloging-in-Publication Data
Names: Anand, Nikhil, [date] – author.
Title: Hydraulic city : water and the infrastructures of citizenship in Mumbai /
Nikhil Anand. Description: Durham : Duke University Press, 2017. |
Includes bibliographical references and index.
Identifiers: LCCN 2016038105 (print) | LCCN 2016039150 (ebook)
ISBN 9780822362548 (hardcover : alk. paper)
ISBN 9780822362692 (pbk. : alk. paper)
ISBN 9780822373599 (e-book)
Subjects: LCSH: Water security—India—Mumbai. | Water-supply—India—Mumbai. |
Infrastructure (Economics)—India—Mumbai. | Marginality, Social—India—Mumbai. |
Social integration—India—Mumbai. | India—Social conditions—21st century.
Classification: LCC TD304.M86 A53 2017 (print) | LCC TD304.M86 (ebook) |
DDC 363.6/10954792—dc23
LC record available at https://lccn.loc.gov/2016038105

COVER ART: *River of Pipes*, photo by Nikhil Anand.

Contents

Preface: Water Stories—vii
Acknowledgments—xi

INTRODUCTION. Water Works—1

   Interlude. A City in the Sea—25

1. SCARE CITIES—29

   Interlude. Fieldwork—61

2. SETTLEMENT—65

   Interlude. Renewing Water—95

3. TIME PÉ (ON TIME)—97

   Interlude. Flood—127

4. SOCIAL WORK—131

   Interlude. River/Sewer—159

5. LEAKS—161

   Interlude. Jharna (Spring)—191

6. DISCONNECTION—193

   Interlude. Miracles—219

CONCLUSION—223

Notes—239
References—265
Index—289

Preface: Water Stories

Rain, floods, rivers, pipes, tides, and springs. Water is moving and is moved. Humans have experienced water as the giver of life and death. They have imagined it as three atoms or one of four elements, springing from the head of the divine, or floating under his son's feet. Human histories can be characterized by the search for and control of water. Wells, canals, aqueducts, lakes. Cities and civilizations have withered in its absence; others have risen through their control of the oceans. The social life of water has a deep, complex, and remarkable history that quickly traverses social, natural, and political boundaries.[1]

This book addresses the way water is made and managed by cities in a period of dramatic environmental change. In particular, it explores the everyday uncertainty with which water is accessed by those living on the margins of the state *and* the market in Mumbai, India. As states increasingly seek to distribute things through market mechanisms, this research asks why water continues to be demanded as a public good, *particularly* by settlers (also called slum dwellers) who are marginalized by public institutions.[2] The city and its citizens are made and unmade by the everyday practices around water provisioning—practices that are as much about slaking thirst as they are about making durable forms of belonging in the city. Yet this is only one of many stories about this city of water. The city, surrounded by the sea, irrigated by a river-sewer, and annually flooded by the monsoons, is soaked in water stories. They constantly disrupt the stories and arguments I tell in this book.

In a wonderful essay about the power and promise of stories, K. Sivaramakrishnan and Arun Agrawal (2003) point out that stories have multiple vocalities and multiple sites of production. Unlike discourses, stories are particularly attendant to the diverse locations at which human agency is thwarted or dreams are partially realized. Stories are unstable. Stories are the stuff with which cities are made (Calvino 1972). They present other ways for the world to be known. Unfortunately, while Mumbai is filled with stories of water, many of these stories are now submerged in a new wave of crisis narratives about water, its politics, and its urban state. As policy experts proclaim a future of water wars, scientists warn of imminent changes to our climate, and government officials, politicians, and researchers proclaim new emergencies around the state of cities; these emergency narratives often work to subdue and suppress the multivalence of water and its storytellers in the city.[3] They obscure how, for many residents of large cities, the uncertainties around critical resource provision are already an ongoing, almost mundane feature of everyday life.[4]

The telling of stories is always a political act. Ethnographers have been famously uneasy with the ways in which our stories silence others. In recent years, however, infrastructures of the Internet, of mobile phones and mobile audio and video technologies, have changed the landscape of possibility for those long silenced by the political economy of writing. If writing has never been too far from projects to administer structural violence on the poor, as Akhil Gupta (2012) has poignantly argued, part of the excitement around new communications technologies has to do with the way in which they have reinvigorated popular oral and visual circuits of storytelling. They also promise to democratize the ways in which stories are told, circulate, and, as such, affect political structures (Appadurai 2006).[5] They permit the ethnographer an opportunity to have the stories we tell through ethnography destabilized by other storytelling projects, entangled as they often are with our own.[6]

In a modest and somewhat accidental effort, I worked with youth in two community organizations, Akansha Sewa Sangh and Agaz, and an artist organization, CAMP, to produce *Ek Dozen Paani* (One Dozen Waters), a series of twelve short films about water in the city while conducting fieldwork in 2007–8. I had been hosting weekend seminars on the city and citizenship for members of the two youth groups in the settlement where I worked, using water as a heuristic to do so. Through our conversations in these meetings, I was struck by the profound memories and experiences my volunteers-friends-students had around water. To them, water was neither dull nor merely politics. Instead, it animated their social memories of settlement, environment, and the city. Together, we agreed to archive these memories through a collaborative video documentary project. Members of our small collective shot video and contributed their footage into a shared archive. A series of ten storytellers then composed and assembled a montage of audio and video footage to tell their own stories, narrated through the relationships between water and its infrastructures. The films are freely available online and lie alongside the stories I tell in this book. In addition, some of these stories are featured in the book as interludes. Like the other interludes in the book, they sit with and sometimes interrupt life that I describe in these pages. Water, like many other things we pretend to know and control, leaks from and undermines the stories we tell. It saturates, soaks, and erodes the stability of the world we know.

Supriya Polmuri's film in the collection, *The Question* (*Prashna*), is one example that demonstrates not only the power of stories but also the phenomenal power of water to order and render human life precarious and possible. The film begins with Polmuri looking out a window into the relentless monsoon rain. As she does so, she remembers how this cyclical, temporary, and yet prolific storm is so essential for the possibility of human life. She narrates an Akbar Birbal story.

As parables circulating through oral traditions, Akbar Birbal stories have long been told to children on the Indian subcontinent. These stories would always teach children to be thoughtful and a little irreverent in the world. Here, Polmuri draws on one Akbar Birbal story to remind us that while the world has long been ruled by great powers, they too are ultimately dependent on water to survive.

> Akbar asked his brother-in-law, "Tell me, what will remain in this world if we take away the ten *nakshatra*[7] of the monsoon?" The brother-in-law said, "I am not a little child to be asking me such questions. Naturally, seventeen constellations will remain." Akbar said, "That is incorrect." Akbar then asked Birbal the same question. Birbal answered: "Zero." Everybody in the *darbar* started whispering, "How can it be zero? . . ." Birbal said, "If the rain's constellations go away, what will remain in the world? If it does not rain, how will the crops ripen? Human life itself depends on water. If the rain's constellations are taken away, all life forms will disappear." (Supriya Polmuri 2008)

In telling this story, Supriya describes how Akbar, one of India's most powerful rulers, was nonetheless aware of water's necessity to the earth and to life. By telling the story with *nakshatra*—lunar constellations that are used to compose the calendar year—the story illuminates how water does not "just" make life possible. It also marks time and gives life meaning.

Yet even as we recollect water's powers, engineering projects to control water frequently presume we can rule over it and make its flows predictable, continuous, and ordered. Of course, as stories in this book demonstrate, pretenses of human control are routinely swept away in times of drought and deluge, or when the technologies of concrete and steel yield to water's steady, patient pressure. Nevertheless, hydraulic projects continue to reanimate the city in an always incomplete effort to make environments predictable and reliable. As we enter times beyond the grasp of human history, we now need to confront the very real possibility that modernist modes of hydraulic government may no longer be sufficient for stabilizing our worlds.[8]

Indeed, in his life, Akbar would realize that despite ruling over much of the Indian subcontinent, he could not control its waters as effectively. In the late sixteenth century, Akbar decided to move his capital from Agra to Fatehpur Sikri so that he could live closer to the Sufi saint Salim Chisti. The capital city, specially constructed for the purpose, took fifteen years to build. Constructed out of red sandstone, its royal durbars, large columns, and impressive gates together are believed to compose one of the finest examples of Mughal architecture. Yet just fourteen years after it was completed, this fine city had to be abandoned when its nearby lakes suddenly dried up. Salman Rushdie recounts the event in his novel *The Enchantress of Florence*:

> The destruction of Fatehpur Sikri had begun. . . . Slowly, moment by moment, retreating at a man's walking pace, the water was receding. [The emperor] sent for the city's leading engineers but they were at a loss to explain the phenomenon. . . . Without the lake the citizens who could not afford Kashmiri ice would have nothing to drink, nothing to wash or cook with, and their children would soon die. . . . Without the lake the city was a parched and shriveled husk. The water continued to drain away. The death of the lake was the death of Sikri as well.
>
> *Without water we are nothing. Even an emperor, denied water, would swiftly turn to dust. Water is the real monarch and we are all its slaves.*
>
> "Evacuate the city," the emperor Akbar commanded. (Rushdie 2008, 344–45)

Acknowledgments

This research on Mumbai's water took me home to a world I did not know. Like many in Mumbai, I had for a long time lived in the city without needing to be conscious of the tremendous work of its social and material infrastructures. Through fieldwork, I learned of the extraordinary quotidian labor of employees of the city's hydraulic engineering department and those that live in the city's auto-constructed settlements, just to make water appear every day in city taps. And so it is with this more mundane book. Its appearance as a discrete thing conceals the generosity and work that has been invested in it by many others, just to make it appear in the world.

As residents, friends, and experts of the city I love, I would like to thank Vasant Ambore, Shaina Anand, Amisha Birje, Durga Gudilu, Devika Mahadevan, Shahnawaz Pathan, Urmila Salunkhe, Shali Shaikh, Sitaram Shelar, Ashok Sukumaran, and Satish Tripathi. I am both touched and honored that they shared their cities and their lives with me, and value their continued friendship. I am also grateful to so many residents of Jogeshwari, who gave me time they did not have to talk to me about water. Thanks to Mr. Borse, Mr. Gondalia, Mr. Joshi, Mr. Shah, and Mr. Virkar of Mumbai's Hydraulic Engineers Department, for their many years of thankless service to the hydraulic city. With a generosity I came to associate with the city's public servants, they patiently shared their experience, practices, and even their lunch with me.

This project began over ten years ago at Stanford University. I am most grateful to James Ferguson, who, through his teaching, advising, and mentoring, has inspired me to be puzzled about the world. I aspire to carry his lucid insights, rigor, and generosity with me in the years ahead. Akhil Gupta has been a most wonderful guide, and has consistently urged me to step back and think of the larger questions that animate our work as researchers, and as persons. I am also indebted to Sylvia Yanagisako, for her careful reading, sharp analysis, and indefatigable energy, good humor, and spirit. My dearest friends and fellow travelers through graduate school, Hannah Appel, Elif

Babul, Mon Young Cho, Maura Finkelstein, Tomas Matza, Ramah McKay, Robert Samet, Rania Sweis, and Austin Zeiderman, continue to be my most careful, generous, and critical readers.

For encouraging me to think about cities even before I was a graduate student, and their support through fieldwork, I am grateful to Arjun Appadurai and Carol Breckenridge. In the periods both prior to and following fieldwork, K. Sivaramakrishnan (Shivi) and Anne Rademacher have inspired me to think about the strange environments in and around cities. I am thankful to Liisa Malkki, Paulla Ebron, and Purnima Mankekar, who enthused me about the worlds of anthropology and South Asian studies in my formative years in the anthropology department at Stanford. I would also like to thank Amita Baviskar and Thomas Blom Hansen for their gentle encouragement through the many papers and chapters they read. In different ways, they reminded me that the worlds between India and the United States are not as far as they initially seemed.

I complete this book working amid wonderful and supportive colleagues in the Department of Anthropology at the University of Pennsylvania. In particular, I would like to thank Adriana Petryna, Deborah Thomas, Greg Urban, Lisa Mitchell, and Asif Agha for many stimulating conversations and engagements that animate this book. In workshops and seminars at the University of Minnesota, Bruce Braun, David Chang, Kate Derickson, Vinay Gidwani, Michael Goldman, George Henderson, Karen Ho, Jean Langford, Sarah Nelson, David Pellow, Shaden Tageldin, Karen-Sue Taussig, and David Valentine have enriched this book. My thanks to them. In the salubrious and tranquil environments of the Institute for Advanced Study at Princeton, I am grateful for the keen attentions of Didier Fassin and Joan Scott, as well as Lisa Davis, Omar Dewachi, Jeff Flynn, Joe Hankins, Joe Masco, Ramah McKay, Manuela Picq, Noah Solomon, Sverker Sorlin, Ellen Stroud, and Richard York, who provided generative comments on the introduction and the chapter on leaks. Thanks also to Nishita Trisal, Matthew Hull, and the graduate students of the South Asia reading group at the University of Michigan for their helpful comments on the introduction and the first chapter. Arjun Appadurai, Hannah Appel, Jessica Barnes, Joao Biehl, Carol Greenhouse, Shaila Seshia, Jesse Shipley, and Austin Zeiderman have each helped me work through other chapters of the book, for which I am grateful.

Soon after returning from my initial fieldwork in 2009, I was most privileged to have sections of this work resonate with scholars pursuing an anthropology of infrastructure. For conversations, provocations, and collaborative projects begun, ongoing, and sometimes finished, I have learned from Hannah

Appel, Jessica Barnes, Laura Bear, Geof Bowker, Dominic Boyer, Ashley Carse, Cassie Fennell, Akhil Gupta, Penelope Harvey, Kregg Hetherington, Brian Larkin, Shaylih Muehlmann, Natasha Myers, Antina von Schnitzler, and Christina Schwenkel. Thanks also to Sarah Besky, Sapana Doshi, Asher Ghertner, Alex Nading, and Malini Ranganathan. I have learned from our conversations sparked by their work on cities and political ecology over the last decade.

Fellowships and grants have been critical to both the fieldwork and the writing of this project. I would like to thank the Wenner-Gren Foundation, the Social Science Research Council, and the National Science Foundation for supporting the field research for this project. Writing grants and Fellowships from the University of Minnesota Press IAS Quadrant Fellowship, the Institute for Advanced Study at Princeton, and the Wenner-Gren Foundation Hunt Fellowship permitted me an unusual amount of time to devote to sharpening the text. Some text in the chapters presented here appeared in an early format in previous publications, including *Antipode, Cultural Anthropology, Ethnography,* and *Public Culture,* as well as in edited volumes such as *A Companion to the Anthropology of India* and *Urban Navigations.* I thank the editors and reviewers of these articles. Their comments were helpful in focusing the contributions of this book.

I am grateful to Ken Wissoker, Elizabeth Ault, and Susan Albury at Duke University Press. From our very first conversations nearly six years ago, Ken has helped me sharpen my arguments in the book, and nurtured its interventions. Elizabeth and Susan have been splendid to work with as well, moving the book quickly and reliably from its initial submission through production, and into the world. Rachel Jones, Amy Summer, and Sheila McMahon have carefully and diligently copyedited the manuscript and patiently delivered on its impossible deadlines at diffferent stages of its preparation. My thanks to Jake Coolidge for his careful work on the maps and illustrations, and Celia Braves for her skillful work with the index.

I would most of all like to thank my families—both in India and the United States. My siblings, Rahul and Nisha, and their partners, Tasmai and Anand, have been an infrastructure of care that sustains my life in Mumbai. My gratitude to Jill and Ron McKay, a lovely family I have more recently been granted, They have ensured that we are yet to have a childcare crisis on account of traveling for work. From our time in California, and through our several oscillations between the Mid-Atlantic and the Upper Midwest, Ramah McKay has been a joy with whom to share my life, our moving boxes, and this book. I delight in sharing every day with her, and our beautiful children, Kabir and

Neel. Their smiles nourish these pages. Finally, I would like to acknowledge my parents, Roshni and Surinder Anand. It has been a long journey since when, with little more than a prayer and a leap of faith, they ventured to send me to college on the other side of the world. While things did not quite work out as they expected (I never did become an engineer), I have received only their most unconditional love and support. It is to them, and to their indefatigable optimism and spirit that I dedicate this book.

INTRODUCTION. Water Works

Every day, engineers working in Mumbai's Hydraulic Engineering Department source and distribute 3.4 billion liters of water through over three thousand miles of pipe to the city's residents and businesses. Residents receive
this water for a few hours a day, according to a schedule made by engineers
and planners. Working between the ward and zonal offices, engineers decide
when, and for how long, each of the city's 110 hydraulic zones gets water. The
schedule is then operationalized by a small army of *chaviwallas* (key people),
who ride in municipal vans on crowded city roads to turn eight hundred valves
on and off with a series of specialized cranks and levers (known as keys). As
they turn valves at the rate of one for every minute of the day, their rather
mundane work produces dynamic and temporary pulses of water pressure in
city pipes that hydrate the lives of over thirteen million residents. Their work,
together with the five hundred water engineers and seven thousand laborers of
the Hydraulic Engineering Department, is absolutely necessary to produce a
vital matter of city life: water.[1]

Yet, despite all of this phenomenal labor and engineering, the hydraulic
city is leaking profusely. During the hours of water supply, some pressured
water hydrates the lives of known publics. The rest silently seeps out of pipes
to unknown (human and nonhuman) others. As a result, the water infrastructure is full of contests and controversies. Residents are always shouting,
complaining and protesting for more water.[2] When groups protest in their
offices or on the streets, engineers sometimes respond by trying to rearrange
the water pressures and the hours of supply. They try to give more water to
protesting publics by providing them water for "more time." However,

FIGURE 1. Chaviwallas turning a valve on city streets. All photos are by the author unless otherwise credited.

because the amount of water the city gets every day is finite and materialized by valve operations, to give one hydraulic zone more water is also to give another zone less.

Residents, meanwhile, are not always content with waiting for the city to act. They often work with plumbers to redirect pipes without the permissions of the water department. As they do so, the city's water flows become difficult to control and know through centralized technologies. Instead, as water is constantly being redirected between and within city wards, that a neighborhood or a household has water in the present does not necessarily mean that it will continue to have water in the future.

Less than half a mile from a valve that chaviwallas turn on the evening shift, Alka tai, a longtime resident of Jogeshwari, Mumbai, told me about her daily work of water collection.[3] Despite the chaviwallas' routines, some residents of Meghwadi—the settlement in which she lived—no longer received water with sufficient pressure. Established over thirty years prior, Meghwadi was now categorized by the state as a "recognized slum." As such, its residents, unlike those of more recent settlements, were eligible for municipal services such as electricity, water, and garbage collection. Yet, in my previous meetings at the community center, Alka tai had been very vocal about the water problems in the settlement, and particularly in her home. "Water comes out of the pipe like a child's piss," one of her neighbors told me, gesturing with her little finger to indicate the fickleness and inadequacy of the service. The water department's impotency, she seemed to suggest, required many residents to spend their time laboring for water.

To see what she and her neighbors were experiencing firsthand, Alka tai invited me to her home. We stepped out of the community center, which sat on the main road, and walked into the settlement. With neatly painted brick walls, grilled windows, and electricity, Meghwadi's houses looked quite solid and reliable. They were arranged neatly on a grid. Children played in the alleys, skipping deftly away from those returning from work at the end of the day. Potted plants lined the alley. The neighborhood's "beautification" was a poignant reminder not only of the settlers' achievements but also of their aspirations for urban environments.[4]

As we walked through the paved alleys and right by open wells of Alka tai's neighborhood, we stopped a few doors just before her home, by a tap near a small provision store. She turned it on to show me that indeed there was water—that it was the area's scheduled water time.

Alkai tai's home was just around the corner. It was larger than I expected, with a staircase leading to an upper floor. Downstairs, the tiled front room was separated from the kitchen by a fading curtain. Its walls were painted bright pink. Her house had water infrastructure built into its design. Both her kitchen and bathroom had concealed plumbing, taps, and drainage. To my surprise, I also saw an overhead water storage tank sitting above the washing room. The water infrastructure in Alka tai's home looked a lot like the one I grew up with, twenty kilometers away in the high-rises of a neighborhood in central Mumbai.   *author*

Yet, for Alka tai, the overhead tank was no longer of much use. Her family had installed the tank when there was good water pressure. Now, there was so little water pressure that she could barely fill the small drums and buckets that packed the washing area. It was one thing to have water infrastructure, I thought to myself, and quite another to have water at home. Alka tai explained to me that her water problems did not have to do with a lack of water in her pipes. "There is water!" she insisted. To demonstrate this, she began sucking water out of the pipe in the washing room—a human pump. In a few seconds, the fickle water began flowing, hesitant at first, and then consistently, quietly. "See," she said, "whenever I want water I have to do this." I marveled at the mundane yet physical way in which she needed to use her own labor to physically draw water out of municipal pipes. Sympathetic toward her water difficulties, I wondered where her problem was located. Was it because the valves of the water department were not sufficiently turned? Or might the problem be nearer her home, in the piped network of her neighborhood? Where the blockage was physically located would determine whether the responsibility for its repair was a private or public matter.[5]

It was only after she demonstrated her difficulties that Alka tai welcomed me as a guest in her home and offered to make me a cup of chai. As I sat down to wait in the living room, I was surrounded by four children doing their homework. They, in turn, were surrounded by their schoolbooks, neatly encased in laminated, brown paper covers. One of them had an assignment in English. A few minutes later, Alka tai brought me some peanut *chikki* and tea and sat down to chat. "*Sab kuch hai,*" she said. "We have everything." Her husband had a stable job with the railways, her kids were being educated in English at private schools, and she spent her afternoons working with her women's savings group. Indeed, her home and her household infrastructure had all the marks of upward mobility. "*Sab kuch hai, par paani nahi hai,*" she continued. "If we don't have water, what is the use of all this?" She gestured around her home, at the painted walls, the electrified ceiling, and the books of her children.

Perhaps because it was still early in my fieldwork, my evening in Alka tai's home was formative to the questions that frame this book. I had not expected her home to be so ordinary—that it would have painted walls, tiled floors, internal plumbing, and be full of children going to private school.[6] As I sat in her home, waiting for tea, I was compelled to reconsider many preconceived ideas that I had about life in the "slums," having grown up next to them in Mumbai, and having read about them as a graduate student in California. Through these memories and texts, I had learned a fair amount about slums as "informal" and marked by different kinds of absence—the absence of planning, formal civil associations, concrete houses, laws, and city infrastructure.[7] I had learned that slums were popularly imagined to be structures built without the permissions, recognitions, and licenses of the state, on property that belonged to someone else. In the documents of the state, "slums" are not marked by their legality but instead signify places of nuisance, dangers to public health, and also potential sites for the extension of urban services.[8] Several Bollywood films depict slums as places filled with rural immigrants, criminals, or enterprising heroes.[9] And finally, a range of popular texts on slums in the Global South have recently described them simultaneously as places of sparse living conditions and places of potentiality and revolutionary action.[10]

Alka tai's home, meanwhile, did not have a place in these accounts, saturated as they are with structural accounts of precarity, displacement, and absence. Nor did her home fit neatly into sensationalist and entrepreneurial renditions of slum life. As I sat under a fan in her spotless, electrified, *pucca* home, in a paved, clean neighborhood, sipping tea and looking at her derelict water network, I confronted the very *ordinary* ways in which her family had, within a generation, cemented their lives in the city despite tremendous odds, even as she struggled to access water. If her home seemed exceptional it was not because it was marked by the qualities carried by the word *slum*. What seemed remarkable instead was that Alka tai had inhabited her home without the permission of the state and had, within a generation, improved it substantively. Her household was now seen by the state as one that *could* receive state services.

Accordingly, in this book I try to avoid using the terms *slum* and *slum dweller*. As many have by now pointed out, these terms carry images and ideas (of danger, vice, disorder, and filth) that did not characterize my experience in homes like Alka tai's.[11] Instead, I use the terms *settlement* and *settler* to identify the ways in which residents built and inhabited particular kinds of homes prior to formal state recognition. While these terms also have their troubling histories,[12] they better describe the material and political processes by which homes like Alka tai's have been built and claimed in the city. Where I do occasionally use the term *slum* or *slum dweller* it is to reference the state categories through which settlements are known.

How did Alka tai's family make life in the city possible? Her house and neighborhood were well connected to many urban services—electricity, schools, water, and hospitals. That fact that her children went to private school revealed not only the state of public education in the city but also her family's ability to transcend it and realize their aspirations for children who spoke English. Later in our conversations, she spoke about the ways in which her *mahila mandal* (women's organization) helped others access health services in hospitals or gain school admissions. She was able to ensure that her garbage was regularly collected, that she could live in material and social comfort. Nevertheless, despite her work, and the work of the city's water department, she had water problems that made daily life rather difficult. As she went on to describe the graduated and discretionary means by which she accessed city services, I noted that her access to urban services—water, housing, food, electricity–did not come as an indivisible package of rights, borne out of her formal legal status, nor was she outside these infrastructural regimes. Instead, they were discretely entailed and materialized through diverse recognitions of technology, law, and state practice in the city.

This book follows the iterative, discreet, and incremental ways in which marginal groups establish their lives in the city by attending to the fickle flow of water through municipal pipes. Noting the ordinary and extraordinary work that it takes to make water flow from rain-fed dams to the homes of the city's marginalized residents, I focus on how cities, citizens, and their political authorities are mediated and made through the everyday government of hydraulic infrastructure. This infrastructure is a living, breathing, leaking assemblage of more-than-human relations.[13] It is composed as much of steel and cement as "nature," laws, social histories, and political practices. The surfeit materialities and socialities that have accreted around modern water distribution infrastructures in the city not only assist in but also perforate, interrupt, and sit alongside powerful efforts to constitute liberal cities and subjects in Mumbai.

In making this argument I draw on the work of postcolonial historian Dipesh Chakrabarty, who has urged an attention to the way that the multiple "politics of human belonging and diversity" at times assist and (at other times) interrupt the performances of capitalism.[14] These forms of social and natural belonging—"History 2s," as Chakrabarty calls them—are neither external to nor are they subsumed by capitalism (Chakrabarty 2000, 66). They "live in intimate and plural relation to capital, from opposition to neutrality" (66). By designating several possible "History 2s" in this way, Chakrabarty seeks to draw attention to multiplicities of life worlds that persistently have ambivalent relations with capital formation.[15] While capitalism is powerful, it is also a contingent process full of instabilities, improvisations, and unanticipated articulations (see Mitchell 2002; Tsing 2015).[16]

In this book I draw on Chakrabarty's argument to theorize the social life of infrastructure in Indian cities. In demonstrating how Mumbai's hydraulic infrastructure is powerful, and yet is full of leaks and always falling apart, I suggest that infrastructure is a social-material assemblage that not only constitutes the form and performance of the liberal (and neoliberal) city but also frequently punctures its performances. Infrastructure entangles liberal rule in lifeworlds that its administrators have long sought to transform and transcend.

Historians and geographers of the liberal city have traced its formation to the rise and administration of sanitary infrastructures in Europe in the late eighteenth and early nineteenth centuries.[17] As proponents of liberal rule rose to prominence during this period, they sought to give liberalism form by "freeing" political subjects and objects from the "primitive" entanglements of social and political life. It is difficult to overemphasize the role of infrastructure in this project. The infrastructures that were rapidly produced, extended, and renovated in this time—roads, sanitary infrastructures, and marketplaces—were not only productive of liberal expertise but also enabled a series of constitutive divisions necessary for the operation of liberal rationalities in everyday life.[18] These included the separation of the technical domain from the political, the material and natural from the social, and the private from the public. Promising to enable states to rationally govern subjects from a distance (see Foucault 1988), infrastructures have since been key sites for the administration of life.[19] Through their extension, management, and repair, infrastructures make life and liberal rule possible.[20]

Nevertheless, the promises of liberalism (and for that matter, neoliberalism)—of the free, continuous flows of people, ideas, and things—have long been elusive particularly (but not just) in the postcolonial city.[21] In Mumbai, liberal rule has been troubled by colonial histories, fickle natures, and restive publics. Colonial histories of limited liberal government, a technopolitical regime that is beholden to regular annual rainfall in a distant (but relatively small) watershed, and present neoliberal modes of governing infrastructures have instead constituted the city's infrastructures as unstable forms that continuously leak, break down, *and* operate as background in everyday life. While infrastructures occasionally produce and enable the movement of some political subjects or things, they also continue to stall, stick, and bind projects of liberal and neoliberal reform in the city. In these pages, I focus on the excesses of Mumbai's hydraulic infrastructure to demonstrate how its materialities, histories, and socialities have ambivalent relations with the production of liberal rule. I argue that water infrastructures are generative of a multiple, entangled, nonconstitutive outside to the form and performance of the liberal city.

Following this larger argument, I make three subsidiary arguments that pertain to how the hydraulic city and its citizens are made. First, hydraulic citizenship (or substantive membership in the city's water distribution regime) is not a singular, historical event in the linear time of liberal polities. Instead, it is an incremental, intermittent, and reversible process that is composed of multiple temporalities. Second, as citizens are formed through the historic, political, and material relations they make with water pipes, these relations constantly have political effects that exceed human intentionality, thought, and action. As such, we need to more carefully account for the material politics of infrastructure in readings of postcolonial history and theorizations of government. Finally, I draw attention to excesses of Mumbai's water infrastructure—the leaks of water and authority—because such forms of wasted authority and uncontrolled flow are why water systems remain public. Despite being marginalized through these infrastructures, settlers desire public infrastructures precisely because "bloated" public systems provide many more points of access through which settlers can incrementally and tenuously establish reliable homes in the city. In the following sections, I work through each of these arguments in more detail.

Hydraulic Citizenship

Over the last two decades, anthropologists have demonstrated how citizenship is not simply a formal category of membership that guarantees its bearer equal membership in a national polity.[22] Citizenship is a flexible and contingent form of political subjectification that emerges through iterative (and constitutive) performances between the state and its subjects (Ong 1996). It is claimed through formal practices of voting, everyday performances of social belonging, and also through demands for the resources of states—water services, schools, and health care.[23] While formal citizenship promises equality among citizens, the distribution of substantive civil, political, socioeconomic, and cultural rights among citizens has long been unequal (Holston and Appadurai 1996; see also Holston 2008). Anthropologists have shown how social and cultural difference have often been the grounds for both the denial and the accommodation of citizenship claims, as marginalized groups—immigrants, minorities, indigenous groups, and the poor—are often seen and treated as second-class citizens by their nation-states.[24] The graduated forms of membership and belonging that ensue demonstrate how citizenship can be inclusive, yet also dramatically unequal (Holston 2008).

In this book, I draw on this work on citizenship to explore how the materiality of the socionatural world matters to citizenship forms. By attending to the iterative relations between Mumbai's residents, and their relations to pipes and municipal engineers, I argue that hydraulic citizenship—the ability of residents to be recognized by city agencies through legitimate water services—is an intermittent, partial, and multiply constituted social and material process. Hydraulic citizenship is not a linear process that is realized through the accreted recognitions of city laws, documents, and policies, or the outcome of political protest or social recognition. Hydraulic citizenship

is a cyclical, iterative process that is highly dependent on social histories, political technologies, *and* the material-semiotic infrastructures of water distribution in the city.

Residents in Mumbai are only too aware of the ways that the promises of
citizenship are only fitfully delivered, even to those who have all the necessary documents that establish their claims to the city. For instance, Alka
tai's story made clear that her everyday experiences of the entitlements of
her citizenship were only tenuously related to her formal status as an Indian
citizen or her governmental status as being eligible for water services. While
she was a formal citizen—for instance, she was recognized as a voting citizen
by both the federal and municipal governments—she received only *some* of
the promises and guarantees of this citizenship.

Residents of the city are discretely hailed by different city agencies in the
provisioning of their daily needs. While different state services are related to
each other, they do not "arrive" at residents' homes consistently, or together,
when they are "recognized" as urban citizens.[25] Alka tai recognized her cyclical and patchy experiences of substantive citizenship when she gestured to
the anachronistic state of her water network together with her family's other
tangible accomplishments. She and her family now lived in a house that, while
unauthorized, was recognized by the city administration to be fit and deserving of its governmental services—garbage collection, electricity, water.
Her house was protected from the arbitrary demolition exercises of the state.
Accordingly, her family had invested in internal plumbing and overhead storage tanks. This infrastructure and its commitments (hardware, pipes, finance) suggest that she felt reasonably stable in her home and that she had
received high-pressure water from the city. As such, she was not just a formal
citizen—with the papers and pipes marking the ways in which her home
was recognized by the state. The infrastructures of her home also indexed
the ways in which she was seen and treated as a substantive citizen by the
city's electricity utility, education department, health services, and the water
department.

Yet these achievements were belied by the difficulties she had recently
begun to face. When I visited Alka tai, she no longer received water with a
pressure she had come to expect.[26] Instead, she was compelled to draw the
state and its water into her home using her own bodily labor, by sucking water
out of the pipes.

The nonlinear relation between her past connections, everyday experiences
with other public infrastructures, and expectations for the future—here instantiated by a fickle water line—illuminates how hydraulic citizenship in

the city, like other forms of belonging, is not an event that is turned on and off like a switch, nor is it secured with the recognitions of land tenure or other papers and policies of urban belonging.[27] Instead, hydraulic citizenship emerges through diverse articulations between the technologies of politics (enabled by laws, plans, politicians, patrons, and social workers) and the politics of technology (enabled by the peculiar and situated forms of plumbing, pipes, and pumps). It depends on the fickle and changing flows of water, the social relations through which everyday political claims are recognized, and the materials that enable residents to connect to and receive reliable water from the urban government. It takes a significant amount of work to become *and remain* a hydraulic citizen. As settlers and other residents constantly evaluate and respond to the dynamic flow of water pressure in the city, their water connections not only form and constitute their social and political urban communities but also elucidate and differentiate the ways in which residents are able to claim and live in them.[28]

How did Alka tai once get reliable water with so much pressure that she could fill an overhead tank? And why could she no longer do so? When Alka tai gestured to her water infrastructure as she spoke, she suggested that the likelihood of her being counted once again among the city's hydraulic citizens related to not only to the conditions of her belonging to the city's polity but also to the material conditions of the water infrastructure. These conditions depended on the life of the installed pipes, as well as daily maintenance work of city engineers, chaviwallas, and the various political and technical intermediaries (councilors and plumbers) that connected her home to the city's public system. To reliably retrieve water through her pipes again, she was now required to do vital maintenance work in order to restore her claims to water pressure from the city's water department.[29]

The Matter of Government

In Mumbai, and indeed in many other cities, residents understand that their access to water services is both productive and reflective of their relationship to state institutions.[30] Water services, as such, not only describe the substantive ways in which residents are seen and treated as deserving subjects of state authority, of ways they are seen by the state (Scott 1998). Water services also are means through which subjects "see the state" (Corbridge et al. 2005). The pipes and pressures of the water network are a key site through which the legitimacy of state officials and their institutions is evaluated and claimed by residents of the hydraulic city.

In recent years, scholars have drawn on Michel Foucault's formulation of biopolitics to theorize the entailments, limits, and possibilities of modern, liberal forms of government that emerged through Europe's relations with its colonies in the late eighteenth century.[31] Biopolitics is understood as a modality of rule that works through the administration of goods and resources (like water) that people need to live. It "refers to a taken-for-granted (though not necessarily very well conceptualized) fact: that all modern governments are concerned with managing the biological, social, and economic life of their subjects" (Collier 2011, 17). Indeed, as thousands of miles of water pipes connect the legal regimes and political resources of the municipal state to the intimate habits of life in Mumbai's households—quenching thirst, cooking food, and washing bodies—the everyday management of these infrastructures is a political technology constantly bringing states, cities, and subjects into being (see Barry 2001, 2013).

Nevertheless, if Foucauldian scholarship has drawn attention to how human imaginaries, social categories, and politics have been embedded in technologies, less clear is the manner in which the peculiar materialities of technologies matter to the form and formation of government.[32] That is to say, if different technologies—of water, health, or energy—are extended by a governmental regime, do they produce different kinds of subjects, or do they each have similar effects? For instance, is a hydraulic citizen the same as an electric (or energetic) citizen? Does the hydraulic state produce the same forms of political subjectivity as the electric (or energetic) state?[33]

There has been an active and long-standing debate in science and technology studies (STS) as to whether and how artifacts and objects may "have" a politics (see Star 1999; Winner 1999; Woolgar and Cooper 1999). In this book I demonstrate how the materials and technologies of water infrastructures are not politically neutral, subject to the powerful political rationalities of government officials or World Bank reform projects. Nor do different modernist infrastructures in the city produce similar kinds of political subjectivity. Water, electric, cellular, and media infrastructures emerge from, produce, and permit different (but related) forms of political subjectivity in the city.[34] Mobilized by both their semiotics and their material affordances, these infrastructures call out and enable forms of everyday management that are reducible neither to the political rationalities of administrators or politicians nor to the material technologies that engineers mobilize in the city. Instead, they are unsteady accretions of different and dispersed social and material relations.[35] They are brought into being out of a multiplicity of historical forms and technopolitical relations that, while bound together, seldom fully cohere. Slowly formed over time, infrastructures are made by and constitutive of diverse political rationalities, past and present. Finally, infrastructures are not smooth surfaces that perform as planned; instead, they are flaky, falling-apart forms that constantly call out for projects of management, maintenance, and repair that challenge projects of human knowledge and control.

This is why pipes connecting Alka tai's home to the state's large reservoirs and dams acted in ways that often confused her, plumbers, and the city's water engineers alike. The "eventful" politics of pipes, storage reservoirs, and valves—formed through relations between humans and nonhumans—all too frequently leaked through and permeated projects to govern this vital resource (see Braun and Whatmore 2011). At times, these political effects participate in or challenge projects of government. At others, they lay beyond systems of human thought, control, and action, constantly troubling the form and formation of life in the city.

In returning our attentions to the vitality and activity of the material worlds we live with, this book does not suggest that our political structures are determined and regulated by material conditions.[36] Instead, as already assembled infrastructures constantly break down, they reveal how our material, imaginative, discursive, and legal worlds are held together through unstable relations that rapidly and frequently transcend those of politics and technology, of the human and nonhuman, of nature, matter, and ideology. As infrastructures need to be maintained and renewed, they are constantly open to forming and reforming new kinds of cities and citizens.

For example, Alka tai's home made abundantly clear that her water problems were not only the effect of physical arrangements—the hardware of the network. Indeed, the thin pipes she was permitted to use were more fragile and liable to blockage. Yet these pipes were not just described by the diameters of steel, or the various qualities of steel pipe that are more or less liable to rust and rupture. Here water problems were also constituted through "soft" systems—legal regimes that deny water to recent settlers, department policies that permit settlers like Alka tai water lines no larger than a half inch in diameter, the plans of water distribution that direct lower-pressure water to her neighborhood, and the diffuse and decentralized everyday practices of residents, plumbers, and chaviwallas who live in the city. As such, the hydraulic system that emerges here is not a centralized formation of power and knowledge—the hydraulic state—that Karl Wittfogel imagined half a century ago.[37] Instead, the network that emerges here is controlled by a variety of residents, engineers, and administrators that move water in the city. It is an infrastructure that leaks almost as much water as it delivers according to plan. Residents and governmental experts do not rule over Mumbai's water infrastructures. Instead they are made to live through its fickle and multiple leaks and breakdowns in an environment of social, political, and material uncertainty.[38]

Therefore, in describing Mumbai's water network, I theorize infrastructure not as a fixed set of material *things* that are functioning in the background until they break down in visible ways.[39] Infrastructures are neither ontologically prior to politics nor are they merely effects of social organization. Infrastructures are flaky accretions of sociomaterial *processes* that are brought into being through relations *with* human bodies, discourses, and other things (sewage, soil, water, filtration plants). They are processes always in formation and, as Alka tai found, always coming apart.

Thinking about Mumbai's water infrastructures as a process, one that is and yet is always becoming (see Biehl and Locke 2010), allows us to recognize the ways in which it structures the present and yet is also contingent on the imaginations and labor performed in a technological and political moment.[40] As such, infrastructures accrete different temporalities.[41] As new technologies, socialities, and politics are always emergent, they sometimes bring into being new infrastructures, whose moralities are appended onto already existing infrastructures. When new reform regimes are grafted onto already existing gatherings of steel, water, engineering, and politics, the resulting forms sometimes evade the structures and regimes of government (see Collier 2011). By drawing attention to the intransigence of water pipes and the ways in which their pressures, leakages, and weight matter, I show how, despite a deep history of state control, by no means has water been successfully encompassed by technopolitics. As water leaks, despite efforts to conserve it for human use, its materiality is not only constitutive of the political field but also always exceeds it, destabilizing its different regimes with a significant degree of uncertainty.

Postcolonial Infrastructure

Research on water infrastructures, energy networks, housing, and roads has demonstrated how political subjectivities and authorities are made through projects to manage infrastructure, the connections and disconnections they enable, and the ways in which they materialize and rescale geographies.[42] In his generative review of the literature, Brian Larkin has pointed out that "infrastructures are matter that enable the movement of other matter. . . . They are things and also the relation between things" (2013, 329). They are political structures and cultural forms that have, for some time, been associated as symbols, promises, and vectors of modernity. In both social theory and political life, infrastructures have served as temporal markers for what distinguishes the developed from the developing world, a telos upon which the wealth of nations and the modern time of their cultures have been mapped and assessed.[43]

Infrastructures and technologies have long circulated around the world as political technologies to govern populations. Since it was first installed in 1860, Mumbai's water system is, in many ways, as old, complex, and extensive as those in several other global cities, including New York, Paris, and London. Built in the same era as the large public hydraulic works in these other cities, colonial Mumbai's modern water infrastructure was formed in close conversation with experts, engineers, and bureaucrats in Europe. As in those cities, Mumbai's water projects too were formed amid conversations around urban modernity and liberalism.[44]

Nevertheless, because infrastructural forms also depend on the political and social milieu in which they are assembled (Hughes 1983), it is significant that the city's hydraulic infrastructure was first established and extended during its time as a colonial city. If hydraulic engineers shared the technologies and arts of constructing a modern system between London and Mumbai, their expertise was subject to restrictions in the colony. Colonial administrators in Mumbai were subject to particularly rigid fiscal constraints because their supervisors in London questioned whether the city and its subjects were deserving of the fiscal investments entailed by a modern water system (see Dossal 1991, 2010). When the provincial government finally received permission to build and finance Mumbai's water infrastructure, it was first extended to secure the needs of the city's military cantonment and its wealthy native merchant communities.

Therefore, if production of a water system was inextricably tied to the making of a liberal citizen and a circulating public in London or Manchester (see Joyce 2003), the production of a water system in colonial Mumbai was designed to discriminate between those who were deserving of membership in the colonial city and those for whom the promises of liberal citizenship were deferred or denied.[45] As such, in Mumbai (and indeed in many other postcolonial cities), splintered urban forms are not merely an effect of neoliberal restructuring. Mumbai's water system has been splintered and technopolitical from its earliest days as a colonial city.[46] As such, the, installation of the water system in colonial Bombay served at once to institute the colonial state as the leading patron of water delivery in the city, shift the costs of this delivery onto residents, and, by doing so, establish a biopolitical system of *limited* liberal governance in an emerging center of empire.

There is little record of the colonial or the early postcolonial government extending water services to those who lived in the city's auto-constructed settlements.[47] While water services would eventually be extended to those living in the working-class housing blocks of the city, this was done slowly and incrementally. To this day, these social differences are reproduced by the accreted laws, policies, and techniques that govern water in the postcolonial city. For instance, the historic alignment of water mains continues to favor the wealthier upper classes that live in the southern parts of the city, as do different kinds of laws that continue to tie water access to property claims. Nevertheless, the political forms of government have also changed over the last seventy years. Today, the laws and practices of differentiation and marginalization are constantly contested by settlers and other marginalized residents who mobilize both technical expertise and the political claims of citizenship, kinship, and clientship to demand a more inclusive regime of government in the city.

That many of those living in settlements have historically *not* been considered substantive citizens of government poses a problem for scholars of global cities, who sometimes assume the ubiquity of the liberal subject in their critiques of neoliberalism and citizenship.[48] Owing to the political histories of the postcolonial city, liberal citizenship has not been the dominant political location from which subjects make political claims.

In fact, settlers work hard to mobilize water connections precisely *because* these are also helpful in establishing their citizenship in the city. Legal water connections deliver more than water in Mumbai. The bills and pipes that legal connections also deliver are critical in demonstrating to other branches of city government that their subjects are good, recognized citizens. Thus, to be seen as deserving urban citizens in the country's most capitalist city, settlers meticulously mobilize the correct languages, papers, materials, and practices that document their presence in the city, so that they may get a legal water connection.[49] They mobilize various governmental and political practices—crossing the boundaries between liberalism and illiberalism, patronage and citizenship—to establish both access to water and, with it, documentary evidence that they "belong" to the city.[50]

In paying close attention to these kinds of political practices, Partha Chatterjee has suggested that the space of negotiation for marginalized groups takes place not through the procedures of civil society but through those of political society. Marginalized populations, Chatterjee argues, "make their claims on government, and in turn are governed, not within the framework of stable constitutionally defined rights and laws, but rather through tempo-rary, contextual and unstable arrangements arrived at through direct political negotiations. . . . All of this makes the claims of people in political society a matter of constant political negotiation and the results are never secure or permanent. Their entitlements, even when recognized, *never quite become rights*" (2008, 57–58; emphasis added).

Chatterjee's framing of political society describes a powerful way to ex-amine how settlers have improved their homes and their infrastructure in Mumbai—through relationships with policemen, municipal officers, and political leaders (see chapter 2). Yet settlers do not only mobilize the claims and demands of political society as subjects of humanitarian care in Mumbai. They are recognized as formal citizens through temporary yet critical civil rituals such as elections, public consultations, or human rights training pro-grams (chapter 4). They also work hard to be counted, recognized, mea-sured, and mapped in government surveys as legitimate citizens. With these compromised and multiple techniques, settlers in Mumbai have effected a critical shift in the terms and means of belonging to the urban polity over the last three decades, where their politics of life are *sometimes* framed in terms of a politics of rights. Like many other more privileged residents of the city, their political practices—of claiming rights and favors—emerge from the political situation formed by their relations with friends, families, and other infrastructures of life, including the water network.[51]

Thus, the social histories of Alka tai's neighborhood are full of different stories of protest marches to the offices of the water department, and of peti-tions and special requests made at the offices of city councilors. Residents animatedly describe how they control their water system despite the lethargy of state officials. Their stories are also populated by prosaic and tedious appli-cation forms, proofs of address, and plumber work orders. Residents care for these papers actively, and through them claim and call out for the programs and protections of government, performing what anthropologist Arjun Ap-padurai has called "governmentality from below" (2002, 35; see also Zeider-man 2013). Accordingly, these improvement projects are not only extended "down" to the settlements from the offices of the city municipal corporation. Settlers also often tugged, pulled, and vociferously demanded these connec-tions to their homes.

In Mumbai, wealthy and poor residents alike do not get individual household connections, but share their water connections with their neighbors. As such, the water department generates and holds together social collectives that mediate relations between the state and individual households.[52] For instance, for Alka tai to get a water connection in accordance with the municipal rules, her household was required to form a cooperative society with ten other neighboring households and apply as a group for a single shared "standpost" connection at the water office. Since obtaining this connection, Alka tai and other "members" have made their own investments in the network and designed the water infrastructures from the city water main to their homes.

Because her water pipes were shared with her neighbors, Alka tai also shared with them her water problems as well as her strategies for managing them.[53] As soon as we finished our tea, she took me to a neighbor's house. Like Alka tai's husband, Jadhav was gainfully employed. He ran a lathe above his home and was busy doing small machining works on contract. Like Alka tai, he too complained of an unreliable supply. Hearing us discussing water outside his home, another neighbor who worked in the postal service came out to talk with us. Yes, water was a problem, he said, but it was not something to fuss about. His friend had commissioned a city councilor's plumber to clean the pipes. He would take 1,000 rupees (US$20) from each household to do the work and guaranteed success. Instead of doing this *kit-pit* (complaining) with a useless researcher, perhaps they could try him? The suggestion sounded good to both Alka tai and her neighbor. The amount of money did not seem to bother them too much, and they agreed to call the plumber to see if he could fix the errant pipes.

Public Reforms

In much of the development literature, the crumbling, visible, decrepit water infrastructures that Alka tai lived with are suggested to be emblematic of cities in the Global South. Against the normative expectations of infrastructure's invisibility, the hypervisibility of infrastructure in cities of the Global South is often taken—by scholars and administrators alike—as evidence of pathological breakdown, of "not-quite" modernity.[54] In recent years, however, a series of infrastructural disasters and mundane infrastructural disrepair in the Global North has challenged our imagined geographies of breakdown, abandonment, and infrastructural development. As stories of infrastructural breakdown increasingly permeate newspapers and research projects in the United States, the production of smooth and spectacular infrastructures has been taken up most actively in developing countries like Brazil, India, and

China as evidence of their global ambitions.[55] It is through the active production and extension of hypermodern infrastructures that countries like India and China seek to join the "developed" world.

In this landscape, the Jawaharlal Nehru National Urban Renewal Mission (NURM), launched over a decade ago, was India's most significant urban intervention in the country's history. The NURM was directed at the production and extension of infrastructures in its cities.[56] Through this program, over US$11 billion was been allocated to improve urban infrastructure and restructure municipal government in sixty-seven Indian cities. Yet, unlike previous moments in which infrastructure was planned, financed, and constructed by state agencies, the NURM follows the neoliberal turn in development planning, in both form and content. When allocating funding to (primarily large) cities, the Ministry of Urban Development reviewed not only the funding proposal (made by cities for infrastructure projects) but also the extent to which the city requesting funds fulfilled its reform commitments (see Kundu 2014; Kundu and Samanta 2011). Had the city formulated a development plan? Did it follow its stated timeline for the implementation of urban reforms? The content of the specific reforms required was substantive and wide ranging. The NURM required cities to reform their property tax structures and systems of accounting. It recommended that cities abolish their rent control and urban land ceiling laws, toward the creation of liberal property markets. The policy reforms recommended also included full cost recovery of urban services, encouraging public–private partnerships for the delivery of urban services, and, somewhat paradoxically, ensuring the tenurial security of all residents "at affordable prices."

Yet, even as the federal government sought to introduce funding incentives to compel municipal authorities to encourage the privatization of different infrastructures (roads, electricity networks, etc.), water networks in India, like those in other parts of the world, have consistently troubled privatization. In contemporary India, while the state has declared its commitment to neoliberal policies and operationalized its commitments through programs like the NURM, water projects continue to be managed by public institutions. How might we understand the persistence of public water programs in a state that constantly proposes and avows the principles of neoliberal government? What makes water particularly resistant to commodification? By situating this research amid a water privatization project in Mumbai, the pages of this book begin to answer these questions.

In part because of its deep history as a state-saturated water supply system, projects to directly privatize water distribution in Mumbai were not proposed until relatively recently. In 2004 the Public Private Infrastructure Advisory Facility (PPIAF), a World Bank program, worked with the Ministry of Urban Development in Delhi to fund a study toward recommending and overseeing structural reforms necessary to "improve" Mumbai's water supply in K-East ward, one of the largest wards in the city. Still recovering from the very public opposition and subsequent collapse of World Bank–supported water privatization projects in Delhi and Bangalore, both the World Bank and their consultants repeatedly tried to assure people that the Water Distribution Improvement Project (WDIP) was just a "study" focused on improvement and *not* a privatization project. Nevertheless, critics of the project pointed to drafts of bid documents and a "transition team" formulated *prior* to the study to argue that it was only a legitimizing exercise for an already determined process of privatization.

Expecting protests and opposition to the plan, I arrived at Mumbai's water system particularly because I was interested in learning how and why the project to privatize urban water distribution would run into trouble in subsequent years. It was a stimulating time to be doing fieldwork. Stories of water often feature in the city's newspapers. Yet the considerable talk and controversy around the privatization project allowed for even more exciting headlines about the city's pipes and distribution regimes. Between 2006 and 2009, activists, water department engineers, and NGOs in Mumbai organized a moderately effective opposition to the WDIP by arguing that water was a human right and not a commodity. Their claims were countered by the World Bank consultants proposing reforms, who pointed to the fact that the poor are already paying with their time for water of poor quality in the public system, and that they would likely be willing to pay more for better service.

Yet such a framing of the difference between public and private systems was neither theoretically productive nor useful to residents like Alka tai.[57] Settlers are disadvantaged through *both* private and public management of city infrastructures. On the one hand, purchasing water as a private commodity is prohibitively expensive. On the other hand, state agencies, particularly in urban areas, often do not consider the poor as equal citizens. Therefore, settlers in Mumbai tend to cope with water scarcity by making multiple sets of claims. To access water, they engage not only with formal states and markets but also with a wide range of political and sometimes illegal social arrangements that include kin, local politicians, municipal plumbers, and social workers. These everyday practices of accessing water suggest we need to rethink the perils and potential of both rights and commodities for marginalized subjects living in the city.

In this book I argue that settlers demand public water systems not because public systems deliver reliable supplies to all. Settlers desire public systems because, relative to private infrastructures, these "bloated," "inefficient" public systems are known systems that offer many more points of access (officials, politicians, social workers, and leaky pipes) through which settlers can be connected to the hydraulic city. Settlers also desire water through the public system because its documents (printed on government stationary) allow them to claim and access *other* public urban services and substances of citizenship—like housing, health, and education. Because public water infrastructures are constituted by city engineers, councilors, plumbers, and pipes, residents have learned the diverse social and political ways they may pressure these actors to make water flow to them, even when the rules, laws, and policies of the city preclude their access (Anand 2011). In short, relative to private systems, public systems are known systems that are more accommodating of vital forms of leakage that nourish those marginalized by states and markets in the city. Public infrastructures are more amenable to hidden, partly known, materialized arrangements through which millions of residents access water and live in the city.

Settlers in Mumbai recognize, and recognize very well, that the laws and norms of states are made by those more powerful. While conducting fieldwork, residents of Jogeshwari incessantly pointed out how water distribution was consistently unequal, favoring the wealthier populations living in the southern reaches of the city. They recognized that city officials were more beholden to the needs of wealthier residents in South Mumbai. They were aware that their complaints would only seldom be attended to if made through the "proper" channels. Accordingly, they often sought to make their claims on the city's water through infrapolitics—unobtrusive, invisible, and often illicit kinds of connections, often made with sympathetic officials, to the city's network (Scott 1990).[58]

After all, it was because she had seen me as a potential fixer of her trenchant water pipe that Alka tai invited me to her home to see her water network. She was hoping that I would be a known social relation who might help her solve her water difficulties or, at the very least, diagnose her water problem.[59] Recognizing different markers of my class (like those of NGO workers who frequented the area), Alka tai was not incorrect in making this assumption. Indeed, the impatience of her second neighbor in talking with us stemmed from the same recognition. Living in Meghwadi for as long as he did, he was familiar with both the intentions and effectiveness of those who descend on "slums" to save them. He was also aware of a more quotidian, more situated way in which their water problem could be solved—by talking with local experts who knew others who would help pressure the water pipe again. He successfully urged his neighbors to hire a plumber to clean, maintain, and reinstall their water pipe. When a plumber finally worked on the problem, he cleaned and fixed the pipe, all without the knowledge or the intervention of the city's water department.

THE CHAPTERS OF THIS book are full of mundane stories of social and material connection that describe the hidden and yet tremendously vital ways in which Mumbai's residents (and particularly its settlers) have been able to establish their lives in the city. This is not to say that settlement is an easy or a durable process, nor is it to say that infrapolitics is always effective. As researchers of South Asian cities have recently shown, marginalized residents are confronting a revanchist urban administration that has worked with powerful real estate developers to intensely remake cities to serve the needs of the "world class."[60] I do not intend to underplay these processes, which have been dramatically remaking the neighborhoods of Jogeshwari as well, sometimes violently.[61] Yet even as these exclusionary processes are ongoing, we know less about how and why the processes of gentrification and displacement have consistently been troubled and slowed.[62] Connections—here made through and with attempts to secure access to water—demonstrate how residents are able to live in the city despite the predations of states and markets.

This book is based on ethnographic fieldwork conducted over eight years, most of it performed in eighteen uninterrupted months between 2007 and 2009. During this time, I followed the work of water department engineers as they moved water through the city, and that of settlers in the settlements of Jogeshwari who mobilized pipes, plumbers, and politicians to access it. Living in one of Jogeshwari's settlements for nine months, I learned how my neighbors responded to these difficulties and worked to restore reliable connections to their homes. I also interviewed vital intermediaries in this hydraulic system—city councilors, plumbers, and social workers—and explored how they traversed the boundaries of the law to produce their authority in the settlements. Together with my research assistant, I carefully perused between six and eight newspapers (in English, Hindi, and Marathi) for twelve months, to attend to the ways in which the city's water crisis was being written about and read in the city. These news stories percolate the text of the book. By featuring these news stories within and between most chapters, I wish to demonstrate how the hydraulic city is constantly being discursively constructed in the city's media (Gupta 1995). This way of knowing Mumbai's water has important political consequences in the city (see chapter 1).

As I was conducting fieldwork at the same time as the water privatization project was being actively explored in the same municipal ward, my fieldwork was enhanced and enriched with the work of several experts, officials, and activists (themselves often at odds with each other). I interviewed a range of planners, engineers, and technical experts charged with conducting a study of the ward and implementing a pilot water privatization project. They were generous (and always a little wary) to share their research, their documents, and their surveys with me. At the same time, I attended meetings with the Water Rights Campaign—a network of NGOs and community groups protesting privatization—sharing my readings of water privatization in other cities of the world. Finally, to understand how the reform efforts were situated in a national (and international) conversation around urban water reforms, I participated in national workshops on the topic that were organized for administrators and municipal water engineers from all over the country. These workshops were intended to teach municipal experts the arts of water reform, and how to manage pipes and publics during the transition period. Yet, for both attending urban engineers and me, the workshops also provided an opportunity to learn about attempts at water reforms in different parts of the country, and the difficulties that reform projects encountered.

While the book seeks to make a contribution to debates about neoliberalism, it is not centered and organized around the privatization initiative in Mumbai. In the book, and indeed in the city, privatization projects arrived both tenuous and late, as a contingent, compromised, and fitful effort to restructure the city's ongoing history of hydraulic settlement and government. I am interested in how hydraulic infrastructures structure, and are structured by, the diverse ways residents and experts imagine, live with, and manage water in the city (see Larkin 2015). Having been continuously constituted over the last 150 years, Mumbai's public water system is formed with the regular appearances of water stories in the city's news, the imbrication of ever-changing state policies, hydrology, technology, and a medley of different political and social relations that are enabled by the materiality of water and the politics of the democratic state. These relationships not only make a certain *kind* of water but also produce particular kinds of hydraulic subjects—those who are conscious and anxious of water's cyclical temporality—and their illiberal, modern, democratic, considerate, and coercive technopolitical experts: engineers and city councilors.

Finally, while I focus on the water that courses through the treatment plants and water pipes of the Mumbai water department, this is not the only kind of water in the city. Indeed, both researchers and residents of the swampy city are not allowed to forget that different waters are everywhere in Mumbai. Thousands of wells and many sinkholes perforate a city that is surrounded by the sea. Every year, the torrential monsoons, together with the flooded sea, inundate the city, halting the movement of things and people through it. The Mithi river-sewer travels the length of much of the city, before slowly pouring its mysterious liquid material into Mahim Bay. These different waters percolate through this book as interludes. As interludes, they sometimes mix with, sometimes disrupt, and at other times just lie alongside a tidier ethnographic story I tell about piped water supply in the chapters. The interludes remind us that stories of water scarcity and anxiety are just some of many liquid stories residents know and live with in this sodden city.[63]

Chapter 1 begins by showing how rainfall in an agrarian district one hundred kilometers from the city is made Mumbai's through labor, technology, and narratives of water scarcity. Drawing on scholarship in political ecology that has been especially attendant to the politics of environmental crisis, I show how the discursive rendering of water scarcity unmakes both rural and urban residents, and makes water generative of an anxious and xenophobic urban public.

In chapter 2, I engage the urban studies literature on capitalist transformation by showing the discretionary processes through which settlers have established themselves in Mumbai. To do so, I provide a brief history of a settlement in the neighborhood of Jogeshwari, examining how its residents have made critical improvements to their water infrastructure through a series of liberal and illiberal claims. Most residents are now able to apply for public water connections following incremental and graduated processes of state recognition. These processes of recognition, paradoxically, continue to require and proliferate illiberal technologies of government in the city.

Today, Jogeshwari's residents, like other residents in Mumbai, receive water on a water supply schedule, for a few hours every day. Chapter 3 is an ethnographic account of how water time punctuates the rhythms of social life in the household, figuring and producing gendered and classed subjects through it.

Chapter 4 draws on fieldwork in a community organization to focus attention on the unstable and unsteady ways in which settlers manage diverse regimes of subjectification and citizenship in the city. I focus on the dangerous situation that emerged when community groups in the area demanded water as a right, while continuing to depend on "good relations" with the elected city councilor. When these diverse forms of subjectivity were revealed to the councilor at a water reform consultation, his response showed how political leaders exert sovereign and disciplinary power to rule their populations despite the power of elections and the promises they bring.

In recent years, consultants at the World Bank and India's Ministry of Urban Development have sought to restructure public distribution systems to provide not staggered but continuous (24/7) water supply to all urban residents. Yet efforts to make water available 24/7 have been strongly compromised by the prolific leakages of water from the city's underground network. Chapter 5 shows how, amid the heterogeneous physical and social demands of the network, engineers are unable to stop water from "leaking." These leakages not only nourish settlers but are also critical to the reproduction of the hydraulic state. As engineers struggle to address unknown quantities of physical and social leakage, staggered water supply becomes a critical way for engineers to reassert control over a public system.

Where the previous chapters show how settlers have made critical and incremental claims to the city's water network, chapter 6 explores how Muslim settlers in Premnagar have been rendered an abject population through the cultural rhetorics and practices of water engineers. The ability of Premnagar's residents to live in the city despite municipal abjection shows how Mumbai's water constantly and consistently escapes technocratic control. As Premnagar's settlers draw water from bore wells and other hidden sources, they mark a critical way in which water's leakages and subterranean flows permit abject hydraulic subjects to live in the city.

Amid spectacular infrastructural breakdowns in recent years, and their increasing regularity in times of climate change, the book concludes by drawing attention to the ordinary lives of crumbling infrastructures, and the processes and politics with which they are put together again. As scholars of anthropology, geography, politics, and science studies attend to the infrastructures that mediate relations between environments, engineered landscapes, and politics in the contemporary period, the book concludes with four provisional contributions to these literatures that emerge from a study of the social life of water in Mumbai.

Relative to the towns of Surat in the north and Goa in the south, the swampy amphibious mixture that was Bombay was not of much interest to either the Marathas or Bahadur Shah, the ruler of the Sultanate in Gujarat in the sixteenth century. In 1534 Bahadur Shah, weakened by a series of wars, yielded the temporary mixtures of earth and sea that was the city to the Portuguese (Tindall 1982). More than a century later, in 1661, the Portuguese crown, in a customary gesture of imperial arrogance, gifted Bombay to the British to commemorate the wedding of Catherine of Braganza to Charles II.

While there can be little dispute that Bombay was gifted, the Portuguese and English got into a bitter dispute about what Bombay was. The islands, appearing contiguous at certain times of day (during low tide) and scattered islets at others, confused surveyors of both the East India Company and the Portuguese Crown, who were in disagreement about where the gifted city ended and the remaining Portuguese islands began. Each made their own maps, to verify their own truths. Anuradha Mathur and Dilip da Cunha describe the confusion in their book *Soak*: "The many configurations of Mumbai in the seventeenth and eighteenth century have been attributed to poor mapping techniques, deliberate misrepresentation for the sake of gaining territory, or the temporality of a terrain where landforms are subject to tidal variations. Few challenge the inadequacies of the notion of island in a place which was so fluid and dynamic that it could at times be largely under the sea, and at other time become part of the mainland" (2009, 14).

After years of bitter dispute, the English came to control the seven or so islands in the southern reaches of the city, and the Portuguese controlled the larger island of Salsette to the North. Eager to solidify (their claims to) the city, the British connected their islands with causeways and breakwaters to make the ring of several islands that circled a large area of mud flats into single island city (see map 1). As such, the ground of the city has been made whole and one through infrastructure works that have drained the

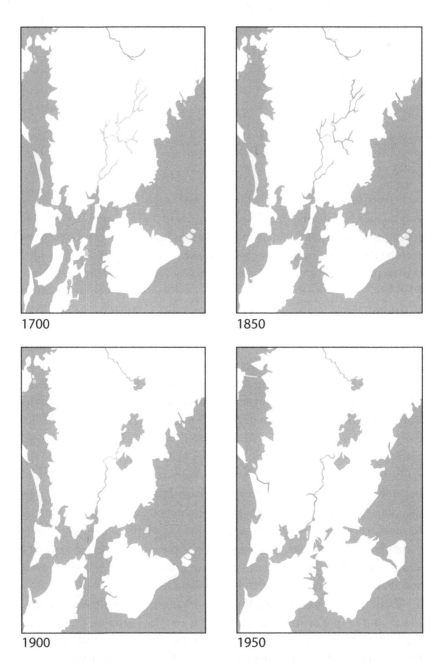

1700

1850

1900

1950

MAP 1. The making of Bombay. The British made the many islands of Bombay (in the south) into an "Island City" through large engineering works conducted in the eighteenth and nineteenth centuries. Note the creation of Vihar, Tulsi, and Powai "lakes" in the late nineteenth century on Salsette Island. Jogeshwari, a former village on Salsette Island, lies just southwest of the lakes. Images redrawn by Jake Coolidge, reproduced with permission from *Soak: Mumbai in an Estuary*, an exhibition at the National Gallery of Modern Art and book by Anuradha Mathur and Dilip da Cunha (New Delhi: Rupa, 2009).

wetlands of the sea that had, until recently, occupied them for at least part of every day. As Gyan Prakash (2010) poignantly reminds us, Mumbai has been made through a "double colonization". The British ruled Bombay by capturing territory from both native residents and the sea. While this is so, the making of Bombay was also contingent on the colonization of lands and oceans that exceeded the city's geography.

From its earliest days as a colonial city, the city in the sea has been made a critical center in world systems of commerce, colonialism, and empire. Until the late eighteenth century, most trade in the Arabian Sea was controlled by non-Europeans: Parsi and Muslim merchants based in Surat, a trading city to the north of the marshland that later became Bombay. In an effort to make Bombay a center of commerce in the region, colonial officials offered attractive financial terms to ship builders to move their operations from Surat to Bombay (Furber 1965). At the same time that they sought to make the city the primary port in Western India, the British began exercising control over the Arabian Sea. Amid the decline of the Ottoman and Safavid empires in the eighteenth century, the British began to exert their influence on the Arabian Sea, demanding protection money from maritime merchants to "save" their ships from British pirates (Farooqui 2006). Over time, as the company consolidated control of the seas, they instituted a system of compulsory licensing and taxation for ship operators, the proceeds of which came to fund the construction of the city's road and rail infrastructure.

The city, having long struggled to be fiscally sound, became a profitable node of empire through the opium trade (and the Opium Wars) with China in the late eighteenth and early nineteenth centuries. The opium trade enriched the city's Parsi merchants and the city's colonial municipal government alike (Furber 1965). The city was also fed by commodity circuits that fueled the Atlantic slave trade in the eighteenth century. Cotton textiles made in the hinterlands of Mumbai were traded by colonial officials for slaves in West Africa to endow sugar plantations in the Caribbean (Kobayashi 2013; Mintz 1985).

Enriched by the profits they made in maritime commerce, Indian capitalists set up the city's first large cloth mills, drawing hundreds of thousands of workers from the southern coast of the province. Staffed with cheap migrant labor, the mills were lucrative. They enriched the city with windfall profits in the late nineteenth century when cotton exports from the United States to Europe were interrupted on account of the U.S. civil war (Hazareesingh 2001). The opening of the Suez Canal during this period stimulated a great demand for Mumbai's industrial goods in Europe. By fulfilling this demand, the city's merchants and laborers made the city one of the most significant industrial centers in South Asia, a status that persists to this day.

This is a brief history of Mumbai in the world. It is a wheeling-dealing city, built in and on its relations with the sea and, through it, the world. Mumbai has always been a world city, a city that has been built on and with relations made through water.

1. SCARE CITIES

Study a city and neglect its sewers and power supplies (as many have), and you miss essential aspects of distributional justice and planning power. —SUSAN LEIGH STAR, "The Ethnography of Infrastructure"

It was at the very end of the monsoon of 2008—another spectacular, torrential, ordinary monsoon—that I was able to meet with Ravindra Waikar, then the leader of the Standing Committee of Mumbai's municipal council. A local politician who had risen through the ranks of the Shiv Sena, a nativist political party based in Mumbai and the state of Maharashtra, Waikar was now the head of the legislative branch of the city council and had been key to several projects to "improve" the city's water supply.[1] When I met him at the council headquarters, Waikar was prepared for the interview. A hydraulic engineer was on his right, and several planning documents related to the city's supply were arranged on his large, glass-topped desk. Photos of Shivaji provided blessings from one side of the office, while his party patriarch, Bal Thackeray, looked down from the other.

Situated between plans, engineers, politicians, and historical kings, it was clear that Waikar drew on several sources of sovereignty and power to maintain his authority. Yet, when I inquired into the city's water problems, Waikar explained the situation with numbers, a method commonly employed by city engineers. With a population of 17 million residents, the city required approximately 4,000 million liters of water per day (MLD), and received approximately 3,300 MLD, he told me. A new dam, currently in the works, would provide an additional 450 MLD but this would only partly solve the problem.

My head swirling with figures, I asked him to clarify what the numbers and quantities he presented were meant to suggest.[2] By foregrounding the city's population and its water demands, did he think that population was mainly responsible for the city's water problem? He replied: "Yes, because of the population. That is why we want whatever population comes to Bombay, we want it [the number] to settle. How many people can Bombay bear? We are saying that the country's rule—that in a democracy people can go anywhere, stay anywhere, that is good. But really, stay *anywhere*?! On the footpath, on RG [recreational ground], on PG [playground] land, on lakes, and pipes, near the sea, in the wetlands and on the drains? All this must be stopped. Only then can Mumbai be saved."

In explaining his position, Waikar quickly moved from talking about the quantities of water and people to the qualities of a particular kind of resident—the urban migrant. I was not surprised by this. Over the last four decades, his political party had built its reputation as a party that was firmly opposed to migration to the city, a position it made clear through ritualistic and systematic performances of violence.[3] Waikar was pointing out that migrants trouble the city not just because they take the *jobs* meant for the "sons of the soil," or Marathi-speaking residents (Hansen 2001). Migrants trouble the viability of the city also because of the demands they place on the city's water system. Waikar was not opposed to all migrants. The dangerous migrants were not ones who lived in one of the city's high-rises and worked in its growing information technology industry. Their numbers posed no danger. The dangerous ones were, in particular, those who "live anywhere," violating the plans of the city, choking the city's systems, and causing water scarcities for the city's public.

It would be easy to dismiss Waikar's (or the Shiv Sena's) fear of migrants as a particularly conservative and parochial response to processes of migration. Yet anxieties about human migration in what is now called an urban century are not restricted to leaders of conservative or nativist political parties but are also produced and reproduced in the worlds of urban planning and policy in India and in the world more generally.

In these national and global stories of migration, Mumbai has a special place. For instance, in a recent interview, the curator of the BMW Guggenheim Lab—a traveling urban think tank that previously worked in Berlin and New York—argued that "migration is the basis of many of Mumbai's problems" (*Indian Express*, December 17, 2012). Similarly, experts speaking at the 2009 World Water Forum in Istanbul urged an attention to cities where "human thirst is most intensely concentrated" by pointing specifically to the "300 rural migrants [that] swell Mumbai each day" (*Xinhua*, March 20, 2009).

Migrants and the attendant population increases they manifest have also long haunted environmental scholarship. In his memorable 1968 treatise, *The Population Bomb*, Paul Ehrlich famously described how he and his wife Linda came to "emotionally" understand overpopulation "one stinking hot night in Delhi" as they returned home in a taxi: "As we crawled through the city, we entered a crowded slum area. The temperature was well over 100, and the air was a haze of dust and smoke. The streets seemed alive with people. People eating, people washing, people sleeping. People visiting, arguing and screaming. People thrusting their hands through the taxi window, begging. People defecating and urinating ... People, people, people, people. ... Would we ever get to our hotel? All three of us were, frankly, frightened. It seemed that anything could happen" (Ehrlich 1968, 1). Articulating both the anxieties that Thomas Malthus (1798) had about carrying capacity and those that Robert Kaplan would later have about cultural others in "The Coming Anarchy" (1994) nearly two hundred years later, Ehrlich's influential work described a future jeopardized by growing numbers of people on the planet.

Four decades after the publication of Ehrlich's book, its concerns about population growth now afflict the literature in urban studies. For instance, in *Planet of Slums*, Mike Davis evokes an ongoing emergency that is unfolding with the rapid growth of urban populations around the world; an urban population explosion, he reveals, is occurring because of migration from the farms to the factories in cities of the Global South. Davis, like geographer David Harvey (2008) and others, warns that we are witnessing processes of planetary urbanization that produce severe inequalities reminiscent of the cities of nineteenth-century Europe (see also Dawson and Edwards 2004). Citing a slew of figures, Davis warns that "the dynamics of Third World urbanization both recapitulate and confound the precedents of nineteenth- and early twentieth-century Europe and North America" (Davis 2006, 11).

These teleological and often apocalyptic accounts of growth in cities of the Global South, which rely on projections of ensuing resource scarcity—of postcolonial "lacks"—are troubling (Chakrabarty 2000; Sundaram 2010). As urban scholars have recently pointed out, it is an open question as to whether models or theories of urbanization, centered on a handful of cities—Paris, London, New York, or Chicago—can explain ongoing processes of urbanization in cities of the Global South (Robinson 2002, 2011; Ananya Roy 2009).[4] Second, scholarship that warns of an ensuing emergency in cities of the Global South often assumes a Malthusian relationship between populations and resources, and tends to overlook the everyday ways in which populations are made and differentiated through the everyday administration of environmental resources (like water) in the city (see, e.g., Dawson and Edwards 2004).

In this chapter, I focus on the ways in which populations are imagined, planned, and governed through pronouncements and projects to manage water and alleviate water scarcity in Mumbai. How do numbers, projections, and imaginations of scarcity inform the politics and programs that govern the flow of vital resources? Scarcity is not a given geophysical condition that animates and structures urban politics. As Jessica Barnes (2014) has explained in her study of the Nile, scarcity is *made* through discursive and material practices.[5] Through an analysis of city newspaper reports, planning documents, and interviews with city engineers, I show how concerns over water scarcity structure the city's politics. I argue that in Mumbai, a manufactured discourse around the insufficient *quantities* of water regularly appears in the city's newspapers to produce particular *qualities* of municipal water—a kind of water that is simultaneously saturated with concerns and fears of migrants and migration. To consume water made by scarcity talk, I suggest, is to consume the social and political anxiety that constitutes it; it is to imbibe a toxic anxiety that produces the city's politics. Mobilized and made by discourses of scarcity, Mumbai's water system in turn produces anxious, xenophobic, and limited *municipal* publics—publics that are rendered unequal both within the city and in the region.

Today, Mumbai's water department mobilizes over 3.3 billion liters of water to flow to Mumbai daily. This prodigious movement of liquid material over one hundred kilometers does not only occur "by gravity," as engineers suggest, but also requires a series of policy and financial structures, and is also helped along by the topography of the capital (and capitalist) city in its state.[6] By moving water from proximate and distant watersheds to the city, Mumbai's engineered water projects are technopolitical processes, deeply implicated in projects of urban being and belonging in the city.[7]

In his work on engineering, Michel Callon has urged us to note the ways in which infrastructures and technologies are brought into being by relations between not just social actors but also "a mass of silent others"—human and nonhuman—and their enabling environments. Engineers, he argues, are only too aware of the ways in which "technical, scientific, social, economic and political considerations are inextricably bound up" (Callon 1989, 84). As such, Mumbai's water infrastructure depends not only on a combination of policy documents and popular politics but also on the cooperation of nonhuman actors in order to work. The city requires a reliable monsoon around its dam sites, pipes that resist pilferage or corrosion, and urban ground water that needs to be overlooked. When monsoons fail or floods occur, these events frequently destabilize and reveal the precarious silences and stories of scarcity upon which Mumbai's water supply depends.

I begin this chapter with a history of the creation of Mumbai's Hydraulic Engineering Department, and its paradigm of water distribution. Created shortly after the consolidation of Mumbai as the primary port city in western India, the department was founded when the colonial government confronted water scarcity in a rapidly growing city. In the second section of this chapter, I focus on how the city's newspapers play a key role in generating discourses of water scarcity and participate in the production and extension of the city's dam-driven water infrastructure. Discourses of scarcity, I show in the following section, efface and silence knowledge about the availability of other kinds of water in Mumbai on the one hand, and possible claimants to its piped water on the other. Finally, I conclude by describing the afterlives of scarcity discourses in Mumbai. As water that is collected over ninety kilometers away is made the city's, its settler populations are made *not of the city* through a series of legal and extralegal techniques. They are frequently unmade, by pointing to the water demands they place on the city. These contradictory processes—of urban ingestion on the one hand, and disconnection on the other—are constitutive of the city of Mumbai and its municipally constituted public.

Hydraulic Histories

Matthew Gandy has evocatively suggested that the history of cities can be read as the history of water (Gandy 2002, 22). Simultaneously subject to annual rains and daily tides, much of what is now considered Mumbai was in fact wetlands until the late nineteenth and early twentieth centuries. Tidal swamps connected and periodically flooded the city's seven islands (Dwivedi and Mehrotra 1995; Mathur and da Cunha 2009). Yet British colonization, a hospitable harbor, and a supply of potable fresh water also made the city a suitable place to live.

In her careful histories of the city, Mariam Dossal (1991, 2010) details growth of Mumbai as a colonial city from the sixteenth century.[8] The Portuguese administered the territories that now constitute Mumbai from 1534 to 1661. In 1661 the Portuguese crown gifted the island to the English to commemorate the wedding of the king of England to a Portuguese princess, Catherine of Braganza. As the town grew slowly through the eighteenth century, the

Bombay government—controlled intermittently by the British Crown and the East India Company—incrementally consolidated the islands of the city through large-scale engineering works and military campaigns securing its hinterlands. Control over both the city and its outlying regions had been secured by the early nineteenth century, and a series of land surveys established a reliable, if contentious, revenue system upon which the city's colonial rulers and also its local middlemen thrived.

For most of the city's history, Bombay's residents have lived on the water provided by lakes and wells, managed by wealthy philanthropists and merchants. Contrary to contemporary assumptions, there is little evidence in these accounts to indicate private water distribution was morally objectionable. However, as Bombay grew rapidly in the nineteenth century following the consolidation of British control, these sources came under considerable strain. By the 1820s, Bombay had a population of more than 300,000, making it the world's sixth largest city (Gandy 2014, 116). Commercial activity quadrupled between 1813 and 1858 and the population continued to grow exponentially through the later half of the nineteenth century.[9] Faced with growing urban populations that were increasingly restive over the quality and quantity of water in the stressed wells and tanks of the city, the colonial government began considering ways to augment the city's water supply.

In 1850 J. H. G. Crawford, an officer of the East India Company, drew up plans to supply water to Mumbai by damming the Vihar valley in Salsette.[10] Yet the ability of Mumbai's government to construct a modern system was constantly compromised by uncommitted and fiscally conservative mercantile (and subsequently colonial) governments in London and Calcutta. Colonial officials questioned whether the city—as a colonial outpost—was deserving of substantive investments in its water infrastructure. City merchants were opposed to paying higher taxes for a system that would primarily benefit the city's colonial elite (Doshi 2004; Dossal 1991). Led most vocally by Jamsetjee Jejeebhoy, the merchants raised the objection that, unlike opening the tanks to the public, the construction of the Vihar water project "was no one-time act of charity" to permit access to water but a mechanism to perpetually increase the natives' tax burden (Dossal 1991, 102).

Thus, Crawford's plan was shelved and gathered dust for years, and would have likely remained an unrealized plan but for a series of political and ecological events that made the large water supply project a matter of life and death in the city. Following a debilitating drought in 1855, the city's wells were not able to provide water for Mumbai's rapidly growing population. Under duress, the government constituted a Water Committee to manage supplies in all the wells and tanks and to pass rules against "excessive" water use. Cattle and their pastures were removed from the city so that more water could be directed to the city's human populations. Even as water was imported in train cars to slake the city's thirst, a series of significant political events including the Revolt of 1857 struck at the heart of colonial exploitation of the subcontinent. Fearing the loss of control over India's civilian populations as a consequence of the East India Company's excesses, the British crown began to directly administer the subcontinent and recognize the need for different welfare projects to placate local populations. Colonial engineers were called to London to prepare plans for Mumbai's first water project—the damming of Vihar valley beyond the then-boundaries of the city and the piping of water to privileged populations living in the colonial town. When the project was completed in 1860, it became Bombay's—and urban India's—first municipal water project.

With the construction of the Vihar project in 1860, Mumbai's water system was in transition: from the hundreds of tanks and wells that sustained the swampy city to that of modern dams, pipes, and reservoirs that would be administered by a state water authority for the well-being of its favored populations. The shift not only required political power. It also required the cooperation of the city's topography, the event of the drought, its merchants and their taxes, and the interests and aspiration of its colonial government following a popular revolt.[11]

That Bombay's water infrastructure has its roots in the government of a colonial city continues to matter to this day. Planners and administrators of the colonial city were subject to financial restrictions that administrators in neither Paris nor London were subject to as they addressed urban publics through infrastructure provision.[12] Thus, when municipal infrastructures (water, sanitation, roads, electricity, housing) were commissioned in Bombay in the late nineteenth and early twentieth centuries by the city's colonial administration, these did not address the needs of an expansive urban public (as they did in Europe and the United States).[13] As colonial historian Sandeep Hazareesingh (2000, 2001) demonstrates, strident demands of a more expansive and inclusive citizenship made by town planners like Patrick Geddes were carefully and steadily ignored.[14] The policies and practices of government in colonial urban India were "dominated by the economic, political and social needs of a small demographic minority"—here the city's colonial rulers and a small native elite (Hazareesingh 2001, 254). The colonial model of citizenship—of constituting and distinguishing between service for a *limited* domain of liberal citizens (as recognized property owners who were entitled to civic services) and remaining subjects (who are placed beyond liberal regimes of state care)—continue to this day in the postcolonial city.[15] Part of how these discriminations continue to be legitimized and performed are through the everyday management and maintenance of infrastructures amid a state of water scarcity in the city.

Enduring Scarcity

The concern over insufficient water supplies has been a persistent condition through which Bombay and Mumbai's water department has been made and extended over the last one and a half centuries. Soon after the Vihar Dam was completed, a municipal report confirmed that water from the dam would be inadequate to meet the city's growing needs (see Kidambi 2007, 39). Engineers proposed a variety of source augmentation projects around the dam site. Adjacent to Vihar, the Tulsi project, completed in 1879, provided another 15 million liters per day. The Powai project, completed in 1891, supplied another 4 million liters per day of low quality water. When these dams *still* did not provide enough water, engineers planned the ambitious Tansa project, the first dam that would be located beyond the city limits of Mumbai, in the neighboring Thane district.

The Tansa Dam was constructed between 1892 and 1948 and provided an additional 420 million liters per day. Built approximately ninety kilometers from the incorporated city of Bombay, the water from Tansa joined the water from more proximate sources to increase the supply of water to the city by 400 percent (see Municipal Engineers Association et al. 2006). Yet again, even as the large Tansa Dam was being completed, newspaper reports continued to predict a shortfall in the water necessary to meet the city's needs.

And so it continues to this day. Both prior to *and following* the construction of every dam in Mumbai's history—the Tansa, Modak Sagar, Bhatsa, and, most recently, the upper Vaitarna—the shortfall between Mumbai's water demand and supply has, according to the city water department, never been bridged. The city's enduring water scarcity has continued to be highlighted over the entire history of the city's water department. Take, for example, the introductory lines of a news article that foretells of an imminent and continuous state of scarcity: "The water-starved Mumbai will feel the heat in the coming years. The development plan for the city for 2005–2025 predicts city's water demand to shoot up to 5048 million litres daily (mlds)—a good 898 mlds more than the demand of 4150 mlds now" (Ashar and Vyas 2007).[16] Both in the city's newspaper reports *and* in the city's planning documents, the case for water scarcity is made by mobilizing numbers that are stabilized and received as objective facts by the city's publics through endless repetition (see Hacking 1990; Poovey 1998).[17] The gap between demand and supply has never been bridged in the city's history (see figure 2). It only "narrows," continuing to call for a proliferation of new dams for the city's future. Accordingly, new projects—at Pinjal, Gargai, and Shai—are currently being planned in the city to satiate the city's water needs, both in the current moment and in the future.

Every planning document consistently reaffirms the discourse of water scarcity. For instance, Mumbai's hydraulic engineering department plans the distribution of water on the basis of the *Report of the Expert Committee (Water Planning) on Bombay's Future Water Resources and Improvement in Present Water Supply Scheme* (Municipal Corporation of Greater Mumbai 1994). Known informally as the Chitale Committee Report (named after its chairman), the study is a detailed planning document that orients the city's water department toward providing for the city's needs until 2021. Department officials routinely cite figures from the Chitale report to describe the city's water shortage. A closer examination of the report reveals how the case of water scarcity is carefully crafted and made by overestimating the city's water demand.

Demand is calculated as the product of the city's population and per capita consumption levels. Both of these figures are overestimates. To calculate the anticipated population in the city in the coming years, the report extrapolates from census trends in the past. As the report itself points out, the city's population projections are an *overestimate*. More recent figures suggest that Mumbai is not growing as rapidly as it previously has (see figure 2). Nevertheless, the report continues to use these inflated numbers because "it is very difficult to state positively that this phenomenon [of decreasing populations] will repeat in the subsequent decades" (Bombay Municipal Corporation 1994, 3–5).

Similarly, the planning report also inflates the quantity of water it claims each resident of the city requires. Calculating the daily demand of every urban resident is difficult work, in part because it is difficult to distinguish between how much people use and how much people really need. Water use is both a marker of and productive of social class. Further, what people in settlements and high-rises demand is based on how much water they are actually given by the city. Nevertheless, the city homogenizes all of its residents to produce a single figure for per capital water demand, determined not by actual use but instead by extrapolation. Based in part on studies in

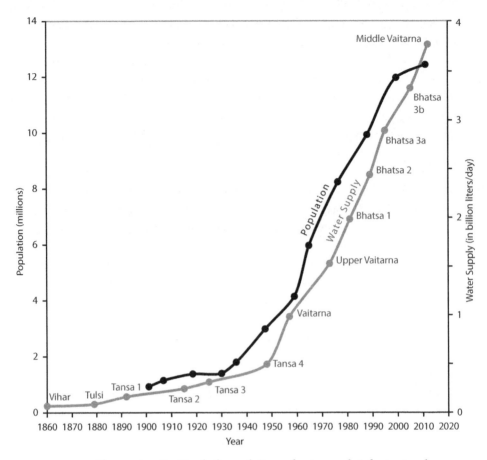

FIGURE 2. The growing city. Mumbai's population and water supply infrastructure has grown steadily over the last 150 years.

other cities and in part on what is "actually observed" in Greater Bombay, the report wills the *existing* per capita consumption of a Mumbai resident to be 240 liters per day—an amount that compares to the per capita water use in London and Paris.[18]

Thus, in its planning documents, the city uses inflated numbers for both its population and its per capita water demand, allowing engineers to demonstrate its water demand to be 3310 million liters per day (MLD) for domestic consumers and 700 MLD for industrial and commercial users. In addition, it assumes 863 MLD is "lost" in the system.[19] Taken together, the Chitale report calculates the daily water demand in Mumbai was approximately 5043 million liters in 2011. This is the figure that was frequently bandied about by hydraulic department officials in press conferences and meetings concerning the insufficiency of the city's water supply, even as new dams constantly proliferate in the hinterlands of the city.

The concerns around this shortfall get particularly animated in the media during the summer months, just prior to the arrival of the monsoons every year. As the reservoir levels dip, the time is marked by anxious meetings between the chief hydraulic engineer and city municipal commissioners, daily updates in the offices of planning and control, and attention in every one of Mumbai's many newspapers. *Every year,* as the summer begins, for as long as I can remember, engineers and administrators have held press conferences to nervously announce the danger of failing monsoons and the likelihood of water cuts. Every year, the front page in several city newspapers features a small graphic indicating the water levels in each of the city's five dams, often measured against their maximum (or overflow levels). Some also prominently display, in days, the amount of water Mumbai has left. These figures produce a great deal of public anxiety and concern. Newspapers such as the *Economic Times* report this scare faithfully, carefully highlighting the imminent crisis and the likelihood of water cuts for the city's residents:

> The financial capital of the country may face water cuts if the ongoing dry spell continues for a few more days, the civic body chief said on Friday.
>
> "If the dry spell continues for another 10–15 days, it is a cause of worry and we may have to think of water cuts," said Jairaj Phatak, the Municipal Commissioner. . . . Presently there is enough water available to meet the needs of the city for the next 60 days, he said. ("Mumbai to Face Water Crisis if Dry Spell Continues," *Economic Times,* June 20, 2008)

While highlighting this ritualized alarm, I do not suggest that the city is not dependent on the three months of monsoon rains to supply its annual water requirement, nor that engineers and the media are playing up what is otherwise a mundane matter of weather. What I wish to highlight instead are the kinds of institutions, politics, and subjectivities that the talk of water scarcity produces, and the kinds of relations, politics, and waters it suppresses, disguises, or makes invisible.[20]

The Productive Life of Scarcity

The discursive and public renderings of water scarcity are productive of state institutions.[21] As Samer Alatout argues in his study of water in Israel, "water scarcity and the strong centralized state were produced in the same technopolitical process" (2008, 962).[22] In fact, scarcity narratives around Bombay/Mumbai's water systems have been remarkably consistent throughout the colonial and postcolonial period. Through both the city's colonial and postcolonial history, scarcity talk has been the key strategy through which the city's hydraulic state has been continuously extended.[23]

Scarcity talk, therefore, serves to animate a series of material and discursive practices in the city that make and remake the city's municipal state—both within and beyond its geographies. As the city's control over water resources rescales its geographies, scarcity talk produces the boundary between the country and the city. It permits the city water department to demand that more water be moved from proximate rural rivers to the city. Scarcity talk also comes to govern water within city limits. By insisting that there is neither enough water pressure nor volume for meeting every resident's demands, the city water department does not keep its water distribution lines pressured for twenty-four hours a day but rations water in the city, distributing calculated and differentiated daily allocations of water to residents in the city for a few hours every day.

The temporary appearance of water in households materializes water scarcity in everyday life. It produces significant concern among the city's residents who rush through their daily routines of provisioning water for the household—not necessarily because there is not enough water in the city but instead because this water is not available at any time. As the summer begins every year, this concern is only exacerbated. Residents "feel the heat" as concomitant water cuts, together with a relentless incantation of water scarcity in the city's newspapers, produce a social anxiety around water supplies in the city. These worries produce urban subjects who are constantly aware of the limits and shortages of water in the city. To live in the city—often regardless of class—is to be concerned (or at least mindful) about water shortages.

Many city engineers are only too aware of what all the talk of scarcity and water cuts does. A former chief engineer, long familiar with these proclamations, made the point explicitly to me in a conversation we had in June 2009, just before the failed monsoons of that year: "These things are just announced to make the public feel like they should save. The real cut will be less than 5 percent. The water budget is prepared every year, with provisions for supply without rain until June 30. There is no problem with the sources." According to the chief engineer, talk of water scarcity was directed to encourage Mumbai's public to save water. In a dramatic (and unsubstantiated) flourish to underscore his point, the engineer told me that in case of emergency, the dams held enough water for an additional year. Indeed, when pressed, he could not remember the last time the city was in a position so precarious that it did not receive water. He flagged 1987 as a bad year, but even then, the reservoirs overflowed, he said. He pointed out that there were no problems with the sources of water, with insufficient rainfall, or with the dams. The problems, he seemed to suggest, lay further down the city's serpentine water lines—lines that leaked profusely.

The chief engineer is not alone in recognizing that there is enough water entering Mumbai to meet the needs of all its residents. In public and private conversations, the city's water engineers confess that there is more than enough water entering the city to meet the demands of every urban resident (see, e.g., Jain 2014). Indeed, a closer scrutiny of the differentiated figures in the city's planning reports suggests this to be the case. To the extent there is water scarcity in Mumbai, it is not because of insufficient water supply from the city's impounded rivers and reservoirs. If the city's residents receive insufficient water, this has more to do with the material politics of distribution and leakage *after* water is secured from distant watersheds and delivered to the city (see chapter 5).

Silence

In his work on the production of historical narrative and the making of the Haitian nation, anthropologist Michel-Rolph Trouillot reminds us that narratives are contingent not only on the management and proliferation of facts, but also through the management of silences. "The presences *and absences* embodied in sources or archives are neither natural nor neutral," Trouillot argues; rather, "they are created" (Trouillot 1995, 48; emphasis added). These silences are irrevocably intertwined in and around the stories we know, tell, and use to make sense of the world we inhabit. For Trouillot, silences are not remnants. They are not stories that lie on the cutting room floor of history's powerful actors. Silences continuously need to be produced and managed. Trouillot's work is particularly generative for understanding water scarcity in Mumbai, particularly because it draws our attention to the ways in which the excesses both of water and of politics need to be "silenced" so that narratives of scarcity can remain powerful and productive.

The particular kind of water that Mumbai's residents live on requires at least three kinds of silencing. First, for narratives of scarcity to call on the emergencies they do, they require a particular silence around the everyday inequalities of water distribution within the city. Second, city engineers need

FIGURE 3. Water mains, Mumbai. Large steel pipes, approximately seven feet in diameter, today join its rural water sources to its urban reservoirs.

to silence (or fail to account for) the rich (and not so deep) history of potable urban water that continues to lie under the city's building foundations. Finally, for Mumbai's stories of scarcity to matter, they require planners and urban residents not to account for the inequalities of water distribution between the city and the areas it makes its hinterlands.

Urban Inequalities

The calculation of the singular figure that represents the city's water demand—5,043 million liters required per day—black boxes residents of the city into a singular political unit. City and state politicians never fail to point out that Mumbai—as India's most vital economic center—*needs* five thousand million (or 5 billion) liters of water per day to maintain its populations, and it does this by estimating that each resident requires 240 liters per person per day. Indeed, the figure plays its part in making Mumbai a singular, postcolonial city—one that demands more resources than its government is able to provide.

Of course, even if this would be Mumbai's daily water demand, one would be hard pressed to explain why (and how) 240 liters of water is *needed* every day, by every citizen. The demand for water is tremendously elastic and also contingent on how much water is being supplied. Moreover, the use of this figure for *all* the city's residents obscures the inequalities in the process of water supply *between* different kinds of residents in the city. Indeed, *some* residents get water services in quantities (but not times) comparable to residents in New York or London, as the city's water demand figures predict. Yet, unsurprisingly, residents living in settlements, accounting for approximately 60 percent of the city's total population, get far less than 240 liters per day. They receive less water than upper-class residents in buildings not by accident but by *design*. The water department consistently works to deliberately distribute less water to settlers than they do to those living in authorized buildings. While there are implicit discriminations at work here that divide the city for its water engineers (see chapter 6), city engineers justified the inequality in distribution by pointing to the national norms established by the federal Ministry of Urban Development.

Following the standards established by the *Manual on Water Supply and Treatment* (1999), issued by the Central Public Health and Environmental Engineering Organisation, Mumbai's field engineers design the city's water network to deliver only 90 liters per capita per day to those living in settlements, and nearly twice that quantity to those living in the city's high-rises. The manual suggests that smaller allocations of water are required for those living in "untoileted structures."

Data from the Brihanmumbai Municipal Corporation's (BMC) own water consumption studies and water bills demonstrate this inequality.[24] In a survey report of per capita consumption conducted by the BMC in 1999, those living in planned buildings consumed 231 liters per capita—close to the figure of water demand used by the city water department. Those living in rehabilitated chawls and recognized settlements consumed less than half that amount—approximately 113 liters per capita (Municipal Corporation of Greater Mumbai, and Hydraulic Engineers Department 1999, 34). Even more precarious settlers that do not have homes recognized by the city administration are likely consuming even less water because engineers, as well as the BMC's water consumption surveys, neither account for nor formally provision water to these residents. Taken together then, over half the city's population gets significantly less than half of the 240 liters per day budgeted in its planning documents.

The disjuncture between the figures used by the city to project water demand and those that more precisely indicate the smaller quantities of water
delivered to residents living in urban settlements reveals how the city department is intimately involved in the production and management of difference
among urban bodies in the city. By controlling the quantities of water directed
into different neighborhoods and rationing this water by time, city water engineers are constantly adjudicating the value of urban residents by responding
(or not responding) to their demands for more water. Nevertheless, both in
planning documents and in their representations and press conferences for
the city's news media, the water department is silent about its differentiated
distributive practices. Instead, the city uses a single figure of water demand to
discursively produce water scarcity in newspapers and planning documents.

WATER UNDERGROUND

In December 2008 I met with Mr. Gupte, a senior hydraulic engineer at
Mumbai's water department. He had invited me to his field office to see a new
water tunnel project whose construction he had recently been deputed to su-
pervise. I was eager to take a look at the tunnel, and he was happy to oblige. I
talked with Gupte for a while before his assistant outfitted me in a safety hat
and boots and sent me down a long elevator shaft deep into the belly of the
earth. The elevator stopped more than twenty stories below the ground. The sky
was but a small circle at one end of the shaft. The tunnel was three and a half
meters in diameter. Along its horizontal axis, two rail tracks carried a wagon,
which ran back and forth carrying the debris generated by the large drill bit
at one end of the tunnel. Men in construction hats of different colors moved
back and forth along its length.

    As my eyes adjusted to the artificial light, I was surprised to find that,
deep within the tunnel, it was pouring rain. The earth above the water tunnel
was releasing a prodigious amount of water into it. Engineers walked around
under open umbrellas, sporting rain gear. Moreover, this was not a light subterranean shower but one that was relentless, continuous, and prolific. When
Gupte saw my amazement at the shower, he volunteered: "This is nothing. In
some places it rains like it did on July 26."[25] The downpour in the tunnel was
a temporary condition, he assured me. The tunnel would eventually be lined
with a one-foot-thick wall of reinforced concrete to prevent "seepage" from
the ground above. When the tunnel was completed, Gupte told me, only
water from the distant Tansa Dam would be permitted to travel through its
passages and into the bodies of the city's residents. Groundwater would have
to find somewhere else to hide.

Built out of the sea, and yet having a remarkably deep history of providing potable water, Mumbai's stories of water scarcity have always stood on porous ground. After all, for three months every year, the heaviest monsoon showers inundate the city, and engineers work hard to bury and expel this water from the city through various storm water drainage projects. At the same time, they also work hard to ensure that buried water does not reappear in the designs, plans, and policies of the water department. Continuous with the narratives, practices, and programs of its colonial predecessor, the city's postcolonial administration refuses to account for groundwater in its plans to provision water to the city.[26]

Still, it is not that subterranean water is *not* being used. It is. In an economy of water rationing, Mumbai's underground water serves both those living in luxury apartments and urban settlers denied access to the public system. It is just that this water is not being managed, counted, and distributed by the city's water department. Much of this water is drawn from privately owned wells in the city.[27] For example, close to where I did my fieldwork, a middle-class housing colony in Andheri (E) is said to draw water from bore wells. Close to this housing colony, the residents of Premnagar, a resettlement colony, have also recently renovated their wells (some of which are close to one hundred years old) to help meet their water needs (Shaikh 2008; see also chapter 5).

Those who do not have direct access to wells, often buy this water from the city's flourishing private water tanker network. The cost of tanker water fluctuates wildly, depending on the demand for water and the class of customers being serviced. It often costs at least ten times more than piped water from the public system. Running entirely on an unregulated cash economy (with some of this cash filling the pockets of municipal workers), tankers lubricate a thriving business for Mumbai's buried water.

Despite the prolific use of ground water, engineers in Mumbai are not interested in managing its distribution regimes. When I was conducting fieldwork, several city engineers waved away suggestions for rainwater harvesting or bore-well water extraction by insisting that the city's ground water is polluted, contaminated, and dirty.[28] They pointed to the dangers of percolation and pollution of the city's water table by industrial and human waste, especially because of the city's partial and leaky sewerage system. Anxious about the unseen mixing of polluted water with drinking water, one water engineer in an interview exclaimed, "I wouldn't even touch it [ground water] with my bare hands!" Pending water testing, I do not wish to challenge the validity of the engineers' claims here. Suffice it to say that these claims justify and allow engineers to focus on the public, dam-dependent paradigm of water supply and "forget" more proximate sources of water.

Yet, if forgetting and silencing are effects of power and politics and are central to projects of rule, they are dependent on the cooperation of geophysical and material actors. Engineers were unequivocally dismissive about well water when I spoke to them between 2007 and 2008 because they had been accustomed to an annual monsoon that, despite cyclical anxieties, has generally succeeded in filling the city's dam-reservoirs to their maximum level.

The monsoon of 2009, however, changed things. While the rains were "normal" in Mumbai, they were deficient in Shahpur, where most of the city's large dams were located. The dams did not fill that year, which generated panic in the city and the state administration. Pressed by the media, administrators and politicians began to furtively and furiously look for other water sources to feed the city's demand. Some politicians began promising desalination plants to irrigate the city's population. Others chastised the government for not doing enough to bring water from different sources. Confronting this pressure, the city's municipal commissioner could not be silent about the wells or leave them forgotten. Before long, wells surfaced in the city's news media as a viable alternative to dam water.

Just prior to the monsoon that year, in June 2009, the city's municipal commissioner had said at a press conference that he had knowledge of only 4,000 wells in the city. Yet, when confronted with a deficient monsoon just one month later, the water department "found" 12,351 wells, more than three times the number that the commissioner had reported in the previous month. The *Times* of India reported the story:

> MUMBAI: It takes a water crisis—like the one looming large over the city at present—for the BMC to get its numbers right.
>
> BMC officials, until a fortnight ago, had felt that there were 4,000 wells in the city. But, the insecticide department, which keeps a record of these figures to curb the spread of mosquitoes, pegged the number at 12,351. Incidentally, this report is submitted to the BMC's water department every year. But it seems as if the civic administration has paid attention to it only now in the face of water shortage. (Lewis 2009)

The safety of water, thus, is not just the result of its inherent qualities and quantities. Well water emerges as a safe and viable alternative in a particular political and environmental conjuncture. It was only because the monsoon failed in Shahpur that well water became interesting to city government in

2009. Despite earlier warnings from engineers regarding their dangers, wells were suddenly deemed to be good enough to use after a little maintenance. Leaders of political parties pressured the civic administration to clean and maintain its forgotten wells. As leaders from a range of political parties, including the Congress, Shiv Sena, and Maharashtra Navnirman Sena (MNS), all began demanding well water to alleviate scarcity, the civic administration invested larger sums of money in their maintenance.

Yet the interest in (and funds for maintaining) wells was temporary, lasting only until the monsoon of the following year. Following a normal monsoon in 2010, regular water supply was restored and wells were again pressed into the background. Nevertheless, their temporary and critical emergence in 2009 not only ruptured the carefully constructed silence around wells; it also showed that, given the right conditions, subterranean water did not necessarily need to be hidden away, nor was it too dirty to use. Groundwater from many wells could feasibly be used (and in fact is being used) with a little maintenance work.

AGRARIAN PUBLICS

As water is made to travel, it rescales space and challenges social scientific research that is often grounded in particular places and polities. As water infrastructures stretch across local and regional (and sometimes national) scales, they challenge researchers to describe their effects across distant geographies. Researchers (and indeed administrators) often focus on particular sites to document the effects of water infrastructures. For instance, stimulated and articulated through opposition to the large dam projects—particularly the Narmada and Tehri Dams—critics in India have published important scholarship on the dangers and detriments of large dams.[29] Yet, while this work has drawn much-needed attention to the displacements of millions on the rural margins, it is often silent on the ways in which these dams make urban life possible. In turn, urban sociologists and geographers have not always engaged regional political and economic infrastructures that make urban life possible.[30] A review of the academic scholarship reinforces this separation. Studies of water and the marginalizations produced by large dams have been sequestered in the environmental studies literature.[31] The unequal politics of water distribution within cities have remained in the field of urban sociology and urban geography.[32] Nevertheless, as its prodigious pipe networks connect Mumbai's riverine hinterlands to urban publics, these assemblages of machines, nature, and humans are not only productive of cyborg cities and citizens.[33] These infrastructures also produce

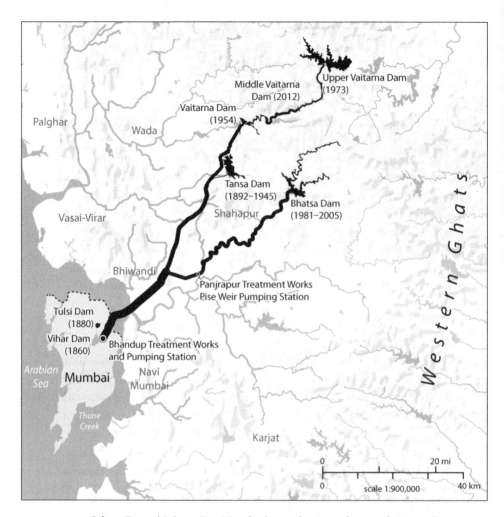

MAP 2. Cyborg Rivers/Cyborg City. Map displaying the rivers, dams, and pipe works that are managed by the Municipal Corporation to hydrate the city. The width of each line is scaled to the volume of water it carries daily. The dates below each dam indicate when these were completed. Because the Bhatsa and Tansa Dams were large projects, they were extended and completed in stages over several years.

cyborg waterscapes enrolled in the production and sustenance of urban life (Baviskar 2007; Gandy 2005).

Water infrastructures produce hydraulic regimes that rescale geographies and produce discrete regions and their polities. The polities of the country, the city, and even national borders are often constituted through a delicate organization of water resources and their material infrastructures.[34] Mumbai is no exception. The city is deeply situated within and heavily dependent on the hydrological resources of its hinterlands—the geographic territory that lies next to, yet just beyond, the city. In fact, the urban hinterland has, in large part, been made as such by the development of the city's phenomenal water infrastructure.

Starting with the development of the Tansa watershed in 1927, the city began to successively and successfully appropriate the waters of rivers in Shahpur taluk (Thane district), nearly one hundred kilometers away. As of 2016, Mumbai draws over 90 percent of its water from Shahpur taluk by controlling five dams on the Tansa, Bhatsa, and Vaitarna rivers. The dams collect and store water through the monsoons, and direct it into pipes to hydrate the city. As the water crisis in 2009 demonstrated, the city is more dependent on the rains in Shahpur district than the rains within the city. As municipal pipes, engineers, and technologies extend beyond the city to control, manage, and maintain these water resources on a daily basis, they reveal how the hydraulic future of the city is dependent on ongoing processes of social, spatial, and ecological colonization beyond its margins.

The marginalization of Shahpur's residents is made possible by relentless discourses about the vulnerability of the city on its tenuous water sources. Regularly manifest in newspapers, the ritualized concern over adequate rainfall serves to both obfuscate and produce silence around the social and technical effects of this massive technopolitical system on its proximate and marginalized agrarian populations. For instance, schoolchildren in the city learn that Mumbai gets its water from five "lakes": Vihar, Tansa, Vaitarna, Bhatsa, and Tulsi. That these lakes are built on the debris of agrarian fields and villages flooded by the construction of large dams is concealed by these stories. Thus, while both news media and school curricula acknowledge the extent of hydraulic infrastructures that the city depends on, they silence the kinds of violence and injustice on which these infrastructures are based, by emptying their landscapes of competing interests, human bodies, and livelihoods.

As I tacked between the city and its dam sites, I noted the extraordinary work required to maintain and manage this silence with existing systems of provisioning the city. City water engineers managing the dams were well aware of their role in managing life, in both the country and the city. They often spoke humbly of the power of the monsoons—a phenomenon that, despite their technological skill and infrastructure, they were unable to control and manage. When they worked in Shahpur, or in many other places, they spoke of how their work was more than just a job. They took seriously their commitment to public service. They also recognized that this service was always liable to be compromised by "natural" events that could easily exceed their control.

For instance, I discussed the annual cycles of water scarcity with Mr. Rao, a highly experienced field engineer who had spent most of his professional life managing the dams. Rao, unlike other engineers, was pleased to be working well outside the city. His decision to work in Shahpur had little to do with either the salary or the prestige of his position on the urban margins. It is easy to make money, but hard to be happy in the city, he told me one afternoon. He said he liked it more in Shahpur. "*Kuch lagaav hona chahiye,*" he told me. "There has to be some attachment." Rao felt proud of his efforts at the dam, organizing water for Mumbai. The city lived because he was delivering the resources it required. Yet, while he was a powerful municipal engineer, he also highlighted how his work was contingent not only on technology and urban power but also providence. Despite all of his technical work to ensure the city's water supply, Rao was cognizant of the fact that his success was contingent on the annual appearance of the monsoons. "The dam is nothing but an accumulator," he told me. "You can accumulate water, but there is a limit [you cannot create water]. So if it doesn't rain in June, we can manage for one and a half months after that. Not more. But God is a kind God. He is not unkind. So every year we get enough water."

While Rao was an engineer with faith in technology and science, he also recognized that the life of the city remains dependent on a "kind God" for its water. Yet Rao did not seem to be very worried about the arrival of the monsoons. Indeed, when I interviewed Rao in 2008, he spoke of how they had never, in his experience, "failed."[35] When Rao speaks of success or failure, he is speaking of the success of the water infrastructure (dams, pipes, conveyance systems) to deliver sufficient quantities of water to Mumbai, contingent on the performance of the monsoon. His assessment of success or failure had little to do with the ways in which the dam had failed the rural populations in Shahpur taluk (subdistrict) that lived nearer its catchments and floodplains.

For most of the year, the residents of Shahpur's villages live in semiarid conditions and are granted little access to the water of Mumbai's dams. Then, during the monsoon, in what is a cruel irony, the residents of Shahpur's villages have to contend with flash floods when the floodgates of the overflowing dams are opened so as to protect the integrity of the structures. As Rao told me when we spoke of the monsoon months:

In the rainy season there is a major operation. It is necessary to . . . to use appropriate power while operating the gates. [No one will argue with me] if I say it is necessary to open all the gates. But ultimately there would be some mishap on the downstream side of the area. . . . So it is necessary to use a bit of your head while operating the gates . . . so that you can maintain the [river and reservoir] levels. Don't create panic. That is the job of the engineer who is working on the site.

Hydraulic engineers like Rao see themselves as mobilizing the passage of water through the management of gravity and other geophysical variables like pressure and flow (Coelho 2006). They also use these terms to describe how and why certain citizens have water and others do not. At the dams, they constantly make "technical" decisions. Yet these decisions are to secure the interests of the city over the rural areas they work in. Engineers like Rao manage the overflow gates with caution and do try to avoid flooding downstream towns and villages. Yet, following the prolific deluge of the monsoon, they are conflicted between protecting the dam on the one hand, and preventing flooding in the area on the other. At these times, they have to make what are fundamentally political decisions, arbitrating between the interests of the city and those of the downstream fields and villages. They calibrate the effect of dangerous surges should they open the gates against their responsibilities of maintaining the dam infrastructures. These decisions are always saturated with values and political demands that privilege the city over those living nearby.[36]

Situated one hundred kilometers from the city, the city's dams, pipes, and purification systems are a material reminder of how it depends upon and draws resources from far beyond its borders. Posted in these distant locations, the engineers are aware of the significant inequalities they are called upon to mediate and reproduce, during not just the monsoon, but also the dry season, during which time residents are hard pressed find enough water to hydrate their fields and families.

Living in the towns and villages of Shahpur, where they work, Rao and his junior engineers were aware of the water problems in the area. "They don't even have enough water for drinking," one of his juniors told me when I asked about the viability of farms and agriculture in the area. Nevertheless, when I asked why this was so, Rao suggested that Shahpur's agricultural problems had to do with its *elevation*. "It's too high for us to provide water," Rao had told me. All the storages, except Bhatsa, are too *far away*, he reported.

In terms of geographic distance, Tansa and Bhatsa are not far from Shahpur. They are both approximately ten kilometers from the town and even closer to some agricultural areas which do not get the water they hold. Water from these dams travels much farther in pipes and tunnels to Mumbai. In stating that the Tansa and Vaitarna Dams were "far away" from Shahpur, Rao was not referring to the physical distance between the dams and Shahpur. Rao's comment indexed the *legal* and *political* distance between the city's dams and the needs of nearby rural residents. Through legal agreements with the state, the city owns the Tansa and Vaitarna Dams. While nearby residents are free to protest the appropriation of their water, city engineers are generally not required to recognize the petitions and pleas of rural residents who are not subjects of their government.[37]

Built in 1981 with World Bank funding, the Bhatsa Dam is different. It is managed by the Water Resources Department of the state government. A multipurpose dam, Bhatsa was partly constructed to make agriculture more viable in the district. Particularly because they are citizens of the state, Shahpur's residents can make claims on the Bhatsa Dam's waters for their agricultural and other needs. But while the legal form and the political intention for building the Bhatsa Dam *should* make it easier for Shahpur's residents to claim its water for irrigation and their households, the *practice* of allocating Bhatsa's water shows how, even here, the city is privileged over the agrarian needs of proximate villages.

I talked about the Bhatsa Dam with Mr. Gawde, an engineer at the state's water resources department in Mumbai, to learn how the Bhatsa's waters were allocated. To manage Bhatsa, he told me, he was in daily communication with Mumbai's control room regarding its water needs. When I asked Gawde about how much water the city drew from the dam on a daily basis, he replied: "There is no hard and fast rule. It depends on the requirement." Tellingly, the requirement he spoke of was not that of the villages but of the city. The needs of rural residents were less articulated and second on Gawde's list of priorities. "Whatever water *is left in balance* goes for irrigation purposes, as per demand," he told me. Gawde did not see this as a problem. He noted that there was not much demand for agricultural water. People prefer to work in Mumbai, and are not as *interested* in agriculture. "Agriculture is not in good progress," he explained.

For Gawde, agricultural and rural needs were less of a priority not because of the power and influence of the city but because people were not interested in agriculture these days. This narrative contradicted my fieldwork in Shahpur. The lack of interest Gawde identified could not explain why people

FIGURE 4. Drylands. Residents living very near the Tansa Dam depend on tube wells to hydrate their homes. Note the line of pots to the right of the well.

had difficulty accessing even *drinking* water. As I traveled around Shahpur, I heard, time and again, of the semiarid area's water problems. They were exacerbated by large quantities of water being dispatched daily to Mumbai on one hand, and use restrictions that governed the water stored at the dam on the other.

Further, the canal construction project required village and district councils to fund the irrigation ditches and canals from the dam to their farms. With little access to capital, the area's Village and District Councils (Gram Panchayats and Zila Parishads) have been unable to invest in drawing water from Bhatsa. I asked the state's engineers whether it could be possible that people are going to Mumbai *because* of the dry conditions, and not the other way around. Indeed, a research paper by Madhav Chitale (who also served as the head of Mumbai's water supply commission) argues that the "stability of employment in agriculture is largely dependent on the assured availability of water all the year round for agricultural purposes" (1997, 1). Wouldn't agriculture be more viable if the irrigation canals that were planned for the Bhatsa project were actually completed? If the canals had been built, people could grow two crops a year instead of one, making agriculture a far more interesting (and viable) occupation.

Gawde, however, expressed helplessness, saying his agency was unable to do the work of canal construction. He spoke of the environmental approvals that were necessary before canal construction could begin. Because the rivers were located in a forest area, the canal construction required federal clearance. Without permissions, the Bhatsa's canals could not be built. Yet this could only explain part of the difficulty. Federal environmental approvals necessary for the construction of the new Middle Vaitarna Dam (also to serve Mumbai) were filed more recently and were granted by the Ministry of Environment in 2008.

The city's privilege over its adjoining areas is further cemented in the state's water policy. In 2005 the state of Maharashtra revised its water policy to prioritize water allocations to urban and industrial areas *over* those of agriculture. According to the Maharashtra Water Resources Regulatory Authority Act (2005), the state is to allocate its water resources *first* for drinking purposes, next for industrial purposes, and finally to agriculture. The city claims preferential allocations of water from the state government under the sign of "drinking" water. It *claims* that most of its water is for "drinking purposes," even though much of this water is used for different purposes (washing, flushing, commerce, and industry), and is thereby prioritized in the allocation of state water.

Thus, the power of the city is cemented by policy, pipes, and everyday practices of both the city and the state's hydraulic engineers.[38] Mumbai deploys the state government's power to allocate to it the water of entire rivers, finance the construction of dams, and secure necessary clearances from federal government ministries.

A study of the distribution figures for the 930 million cubic meters of water from the Bhatsa Dam materially describes this power in volumetric terms. The Bhatsa Dam was designed as a multipurpose dam. Project planning documents drawn up at the time indicated that while part of the dam's accumulations were intended for the city's water needs, a majority of its allocations were intended for agricultural purposes. Yet twenty years after the dam was first commissioned, only 22 percent of Bhatsa's water is formally allocated for irrigation.[39] In practice, the state actually draws even less water for irrigation (nearly 17 percent). In 2008, over 80 percent of this water was sent to hydrate the cities of Mumbai and Thane.

Such imbalances are exacerbated in times of scarce rainfall. For instance, the scanty rain of 2009 affected both Mumbai and the Thane district. Confronted with this drought, the state government undertook to make an even larger allocation of water from the Bhatsa Dam to the city at the expense of agrarian populations. In an interview following the crisis of 2009, the state's minister for water resources justified diverting this water from rural areas to the city. A newspaper story reported this imbalance:

> "We know we are taking a risk but we are doing this as Mumbai is financial capital and we don't want the economic hub of the country to be disturbed due to the impending water cuts," Pawar said. . . .
>
> The state government's move however is fraught with risks. If the rains play truant this year too, then the state would have a tough job of explaining this move to the farmers as the state is diverting water meant for farming purposes. (Ganesh 2010)

Thus, by directing water away from fields and into the city, the state unmakes farmers and their livelihoods. In making water Mumbai's, and making Mumbai livable, the state government disembeds farmers and agricultural workers, who, like the water of their rivers, are directed to the city in search of life (cf. Polanyi 2001).

Outsiders

Like those displaced by Mumbai's thirst for water, others who are internally displaced in India are moved by similar projects to consolidate and centralize resources. Land, food, water, minerals, and construction materials are collected in rural areas and directed to satiate the thirst of those living in cities. In her book *For the Greater Common Good*, Arundhati Roy (2001) has calculated the number of those internally displaced by resource projects in India over the last fifty years to exceed fifty million people, of which forty million have been displaced by dam projects alone. Nevertheless, even as the displaced are compelled to move to the city in search of resources with which they may remake their livelihoods, their bodies are seen as problems to those living and governing in the city. A news article touches on this matter:

> The Shiv Sena has blamed migrants for Mumbai's water crisis and reiterated its demand for a permit system. . . . "The wrong policies of the Maharashtra and Central governments . . . are responsible (for water scarcity). . . . Mumbai's population has increased excessively, but water sources and water schemes have not. . . . Mumbai's water supply scheme is designed to cater to a population of 50 lakh [5 million]. This

has gone up to 1.50 crore [15 million] and 90 per cent of them are migrants," it said.... "Stop the migration to Mumbai-Thane," it said, reiterating the demand for a permit system. "If this influx is stopped and migrants sent out, Mumbaikars will get not 24 but 48 hours' water supply. But to stop influx is the job of the government." ("Sena Insistent, Blames Water Crisis on Migrants," *Indian Express*, December 8, 2009)

As evident in the newspaper article quoted above, the nativist right-wing party, the Shiv Sena and its affiliates, have periodically deployed Mumbai's limited water resources as a prime reason to demand a permit system to restrict and prevent outsiders from settling in the city.[40] Drawing on Malthusian discourses of water scarcity on the one hand, and new regimes of security and risk on the other, those who have already established themselves in Mumbai—its engineers, upper-class residents, and even many of those living in settlements—see outsiders who have come after them as a danger to the city, primarily because of the ways in which they threaten its water system.

Amid a ridiculous calculus (because it is not possible to supply forty-eight hours of water per day), the news story from Mumbai draws attention to the way political parties deploy Mumbai's limited water resources as grounds to send migrants out of the city. Yet this nativist environmental politics is not peculiar to parochial political parties. Amid the politics of the left, right, and center, arguments against migration are often validated by raising concerns about limited ecological resources. Nowhere is this truer than in Mumbai. Produced, channeled, and delivered to the city by documents, policies, and structures that discursively produce Mumbai's water scarcity, Mumbai's water is inseparable from the attendant anxieties that produce it. Therefore, while scarcity talk first enabled the city to plan and control the water resources of proximate rural areas, it also has a troubling afterlife in its politics. Concerns around water scarcity provide the grounds to mark migrant bodies as dangerous outsiders, who, by drawing on the city's resources, are seen as a threat to urban life. As xenophobia begins to crystallize in the city's water, it builds on other anxieties that leaders and administrators have about unknown, mobile outsiders.

For example, when I asked Mr. Patkar, the senior hydraulic engineer, a question about the challenges to the city's water supply, he replied, with a deadpan expression: "The biggest challenge is the explosion of population immigrating from our neighboring countries. There are people from Bangladesh, from Sri Lanka.... You must be knowing... Pakistanis... we don't even know how many." I will focus more on the ways in which the city administration creates and treats "outsiders" in chapter 6. At this point it is sufficient to note that to mitigate the threats to the ordered city (and by extension to its public), the city government has perpetuated policies that make it difficult for settlers to live in it. It has followed state directives to clamp down on migration by making it extremely difficult for settlers who do not have the correct documents to establish legitimate water connections.[41]

Even among the cities in India, these directives are particular to Mumbai. Only in Mumbai do settlers require a panoply of documents to get a water connection, including a food ration card, as well as proof of habitation over the last twenty years determined by the appearance of their name on the city's electoral rolls. They must also present a certificate of good character from their local councilor. These requirements have been designed to make public water supply difficult for Indian citizens, who come "from anywhere" to live in Mumbai's settlements.

Thus, while water is first made the city's through a series of slippages that involve practices of forgetting and silencing, citizens living in settlements are made *not of the city* by a series of parallel slippages. By conflating those that do not have property papers with those from outside the state—and outsiders with terrorists, immigrants, or other dangerous classes—many of those who have settled in the city, often for an entire generation, are denied access to the city's water supply simply because they have not successfully mobilized the relevant documents to establish their urban citizenship. As a result, many remain outsiders to the city and its hydraulic system. In Mumbai, the system does not provide water as a right to the citizens of India. It provides water as a municipal entitlement to those who can belong to the city by having a state-sanctioned urban residence while continuing to pay the relevant taxes and bills.

Conclusion

Mobilizing discourses of scarcity and shortage, Mumbai's public water department has, since 1860, consistently appropriated more water from ever more distant watersheds, and made these Mumbai's. In order to do so, the department has not only generated discourses of impending scarcity but has also proliferated silences about the multiple sources of water available within the city and about the effects of this material appropriation on the farms and villages on the city's margins.

To make its case for securing water from increasingly distant sources, the water department "black-boxes" the city's demand and supply into simple, singular numbers demonstrating the city's dramatic water deficit (Latour 1987). By portraying the city in this way, engineers are able to align different actors to demand and constitute a significant and singular demand for more water. City residents across class clamor for more water amid discourses of water scarcity and experiences of daily water rations, industries that use large allocations, state government officials committed to making the city world class, and a large number of engineering firms that continue to encourage engineers to propose even bigger hydraulic projects and award bigger contracts for their construction. Nevertheless, the city also requires the cooperation of human and nonhuman others for this water to materialize. To reproduce the system, they depend on the reliability of the monsoons, silence-able populations in the nearby villages, as well as advantageously situated rivers to enable their designs.

Confronted with the specter of Mumbai's unquenchable thirst that they discursively produce, state agencies divert prodigious quantities of water to the city, while doing far less for more proximate populations, such as those in Shahpur subdistrict. They assume that Mumbai's water consumption—delivered at the rate of 250 liters per person per day—is entirely "for drinking" and needs to be delivered before the requirements of smaller, more proximate rural communities. Unable to compel the state for water the way that Mumbai's residents do, many residents of Shahpur now follow water to the city in search of work.

Finally, even as water is drawn from beyond the city's borders, it is mobilized to deny hydraulic citizenship to urban populations deemed to be "from outside." Powerful nativist political parties in the city have consistently pointed to Mumbai's limited resources (especially water) to make a case for excluding "outsiders" from the city. The outsiders underserved here, as Waikar points out at the beginning of the chapter, aren't new IT professionals, or international investors that are often based in Mumbai. The outsiders here are poorer migrant populations that are seen to disrupt the order and infrastructure of the city. Therefore, the Malthusian discourse of scarcity that is essential to producing new water sources for the city also has a troubling political afterlife. Animated and constituted by scarcity, Mumbai's hydraulic planning activities preclude the realization of water as a citizenship right to all who live in the city. Instead, through laws and policies, water is constituted as an entitlement that is "granted" by the city administration only when a person "belongs" to the city. Restricted only to those who can demonstrate their urban citizenship, this water system produces an anxious municipal public—one whose members need to establish they belong to the city so that they can claim its water. Such chauvinisms, enforced through both law and quotidian practices, produce a public that sits between the nation and the home. Against the national citizen, Mumbai's water creates a municipal public. Articulated through the politics of the city, this public constitutes a powerful formation through which water and other natural and human resources are made to flow.

Interlude. Fieldwork

"Why do you have to go so far away to do your fieldwork?" my father asked. "You should come with me on my walk in the mornings. You will see people lining up for water just downstairs." My father was asking about my decision to learn how settlers access water in Jogeshwari, a northern suburb of Mumbai. He knew of my interest in studying how water systems were administered and claimed in the city. Yet he was puzzled by my decision to do ethnography "so far away." His was a good question, and one that anthropology has long struggled to answer (Gupta and Ferguson 1997). I did not tell him that most anthropologists traveled far beyond the places where they grew up, and that a fifteen-mile journey in these terms was not far away. Nevertheless, my journey to "the field" across the city did involve a bit of a commute. I would get there by entreating a taxi driver to take me to the nearby train station, then boarding a standing-room-only compartment of the local train, and finally taking a shared auto-rickshaw to my field site. Like many, I would try my best to make this journey bearable by completing random tasks or sleeping along the way. Nevertheless, it would take an hour and a half in each direction. Why was I going so "far"? What was I going so far from? As a "native" and urban ethnographer, I asked myself what was at stake as I spatially marked my boundaries of home and the field.

There were several reasons to have picked the field site I did. The municipal government had identified the neighborhood as a pilot site for its first water privatization project. Coincidentally, based on my previous work in a human rights organization many years before, the neighborhood was also home to friends of mine who lived in the settlements that I wished to study. I could therefore "arrive" at my field site as a friend of friends, rather than as an employer of domestic workers (as would be the case in the settlements near my home), or as an NGO-affiliated researcher.[1] But working away from home was also easier because the very same journey to the field afforded me a comfort that working in the settlements close to home would not allow. By going to Jogeshwari, I could overlook the very personal relations of privilege and servitude—between myself and others who work in our home—that constitute my place as native and outsider in the cities of Mumbai. The journey also allowed me to get away from the various compulsions, duties, and responsibilities of home.

Layered and textured in an unpredictable manner, Mumbai's cities confront you as soon as you step outside the affective safety of home. Its contrasts and contradictions do excellent work in disorienting its residents and their cognitive categories. Focusing on several urban locations—state offices, friends' houses, squatter settlements, and NGO offices—I found myself emotionally drained as I tacked between Mumbai's different places. When I moved to live in the settlements midway through fieldwork, the strain did not become easier to manage. I continued to cross the city to maintain relations that being a good friend, family member, and fieldworker required. At times, my activities were marked by stark contrasts—with some school friends, I would spend my monthly rent (in the settlements) over a single meal in a nice restaurant.

Crossing class boundaries quickly and repeatedly is likely a condition common to many large cities, particularly in the Global South where class structures visibly manifest in the proximate and dense accretion of shanties and luxury buildings that constitute the city. In comparison to wealthy residents who try and fail to insulate themselves from these contrasts, Mumbai's serving class is compelled to make these crossings daily for their livelihood— to work in the city's affluent homes and businesses, its shopping malls, luxury hotels, and restaurants. As my habit, language, and dress changed through these crossings, I wondered about what kinds of sensory and somatic rupture were required for this daily passage between home and work to be bearable. One settler told me of his work in the five-star Taj Mahal hotel as part of its housekeeping staff. "Sometimes, I get sent to turn off a tap in a guest's bathroom that they forgot to turn off before leaving the room," he told me, in a matter-of-fact voice, tinged with only the slightest trace of irony, as we waited by his tap for the water to come. What holds cities of inequality together? How is the cognitive dissonance of the journey across class in space inhabited? The city fragments its subjects, forcing them to suspend their comparisons and claims in the haste of just getting on and getting by.

As I developed friendships with my informants in the settlements, I found that they often approached these questions pragmatically, like my father. As we shared chai and our urban places (mine—art galleries, clubs, and restaurants; theirs—parks, street corners, beaches, and movie theaters), they were eager to make the most of our relationship across difference. Through our unequal and limited engagement, we satiated some of our curiosities about the other—where we lived, what we ate, how we ate. Our mutually constituted stories had different meanings for us. I called mine research. They called theirs friendship. Truth be told, for all of us, it was a bit of both.

That the boundaries between research, friendship, and politics were blurry became apparent toward the end of the year, when both fieldwork and friendship were drawn into projects with political effects. Over time, Mr. Pandit, a senior state bureaucrat and family friend, was eager to help alleviate some of my informants' difficulties. With the insights he gained from a "field trip" I took him on, he summoned municipal administrators and ordered they get things done in the settlements I was living and working in. Almost immediately, and just on the basis of this oral instruction, the machineries of the state temporarily moved to help provide some settlers with services they had been long entitled to but had only partly received.

The consequent visits of various state officers to the settlements to get things done elevated my social status in the field from friend to more powerful friend. I was soon inundated by requests—a food ration card had been unjustly denied, an application for a community center renovation lay gathering dust in the municipal ward office. Could I do something to solve the problem? A friend who worked in the city water department asked if I could instruct the department to give the settlement he lived in more water. As I made the field my home, its familiar obligations began to absorb much of my time.

Fieldwork has been frequently and justly criticized for the unequal relationship between the ethnographer and her all-too-often marginalized subjects. Nevertheless, such critiques overlook how research subjects often engage ethnographers in similar ways—as potentially useful friends. As ethnographers increasingly work across state and welfare organizations, both with powerful and subjugated groups, they mobilize both ethnographic authority and the social relations effected by fieldwork with powerful groups to help politically marginalized research subjects through personal and situated interventions. These messy, awkward collaborations are not necessarily the stuff of revolutionary theory, but they may be nonetheless significant.

Such practices of politics—of helping friends through personal, provisional, and improvisational introductions to "key" people—are a critical way in which people access state services in Mumbai today. The city is made through such unequal relationships between those who "help" others known to them—friends, employees, clients, siblings, and fictive kin. Such practices may not reduce the inequality that structures the city, but they do somehow manage to accommodate its extraordinarily diverse population against impossible odds. I had to "go" to the field to find that what made it home were its diverse and intensely personal–political obligations. They are the conditions of possibility for fieldwork, for social belonging, and also for urban citizenship.

2. SETTLEMENT

Two Cities?

We are in fact human earthmovers and tractors. We leveled the land first. We have contributed to the city. We carry your shit out of the city. I don't see citizens' groups dredging sewers and digging roads. This city is not for the rich only. We need each other. I don't beg, I wash your clothes. Women can go to work because we are there to look after their children. The staff in Mantralaya [the state government], the collectorate, the BMC, even the police live in slums. Because we are there, women can walk safely at night. . . . It's my dream that one day, all slum-dwellers will refuse to go to work. Will Mumbai survive that day? Who will build your grand projects and work in your malls? You want us to be your coolies, you want all our services, but you don't want us to live here. It's the whole serving class that has made Mumbai a world-class city, not the middle class. —JOCKIN ARPUTHAM, president of the National Slum Dwellers Federation, interviewed by Jyoti Punwani (*Times of India*, January 18, 2005)

In the winter of 2004, the state government orchestrated the destruction of over sixty-seven thousand homes in Mumbai without so much as even the promise of rehabilitating the quarter of a million people who were evicted.[1] Jockin Arputham, president of the National Slum Dwellers Federation, was outraged and made an impassioned plea to recognize settlers (whom he calls slum dwellers) as legitimate citizens of the city. Mr. Arputham suggests that settlers should be recognized as legitimate citizens, not just because of humanitarian considerations. He insists that urban life depends on their labor. Mr. Arputham argues that rather than impede the development of the city, the urban poor—what he calls the "serving class"—have long played an important part in constructing, maintaining, and managing urban life (see also K. Sharma 2000).

For much of the twentieth century, modernist planners had the hope, hubris, and imagination to expect that social and political inequalities in the city could be eliminated through rational ordered planning processes (Kalia 1999; Scott 1998). Yet in the time since, experiences around the world have shown that attempts to revitalize urban neighborhoods through modernist planning projects have often rendered the lives of marginalized residents even more precarious. Scholars working in cities as diverse as Brasília, Cairo, New York, Paris, and Delhi have demonstrated how these projects were insufficiently resourced *and* far too rigid to accommodate the diverse lifeworlds of their subjects.[2] Instead, efforts to "clean up" the city have been built on a logic of erasure, through which city planners have seen settlements and the people that live in them as urban dirt to be *swept out* of the metropolis.[3] It was precisely this treatment of slum dwellers—as dirt to be cleaned up from the city—that Mr. Arputham protested most forcefully during the demolitions of 2004–5. He made an impassioned plea for slum dwellers to be considered and recognized as performing essential services for the city.

It is surprising that just five years after the BMC conducted these most violent demolitions, it published its first *Mumbai Human Development Report* that insisted on the very recognition that Mr. Arputham desired. The opening chapter of the report's chapter on slums insists that both the "haves and have-nots" need each other in the city.

> Mumbai, allegorically speaking, is actually two cities: A city of the "haves," and a city of the "have-nots." The "haves and have-nots" are within the same geographical territory but occupy entirely different economic, physical, and social spaces. Among these two, one is better laid out and the other has developed in a haphazard manner which seems orderless. Both depend on each other despite their economic and social asymmetry . . . Thus, they are two distinct but inter-dependent cities within one. (Municipal Corporation of Greater Mumbai 2010, 55)

In insisting the city of haves is dependent on the city of have-nots, the *Mumbai Human Development Report* follows a turn in urban planning through which planners try to accommodate the inequality and poverty that orders the city (Anand and Rademacher 2011). Planners and architects in the city now argue that the informal city does not threaten the formal city. Instead, the informal city creates the conditions *necessary* for the formal city to survive (see Dwivedi and Mehrotra 1995).[4] In this work, the two cities are not spatially contiguous but instead are coincident—often occupying different realms in the same geographic space. The first city is described to be one of order, formal infrastructure, rules, and laws. The second city—poorer and more perilous—exists alongside, but separate from, the first. This second city, as the report describes, is characterized by precarious forms of labor and housing, of informality and politics, of dynamism and illegality.

Yet even as it creates discursive and political space for settlers and other informalized residents in the city, the move to see Mumbai as "two cities" also articulates with a long-standing tradition of seeing urban polities of the Global South (and indeed national polities of the postcolony) as structured by an irrevocable inequality between rulers and the "haves" on the one hand, and the "have-nots" on the other.[5] This work takes inequality to be always already rigidly present in the spatial practices of the city. It describes an inequality (of access to materials, spaces, and social practices) that is structured and structuring of polities in the city.

For instance, in recent years, Partha Chatterjee has drawn attention to the ways in which residents of these two cities in Kolkata practice different kinds of politics. Arguing that "most of the inhabitants of India are only tenuously, and even then ambiguously and contextually, rights-bearing citizens in the sense imagined by the constitution" (Chatterjee 2005, 83), he explains that the domain of *civil society*—composed of those who can deploy civil and institutional forms to access resources they need to live—is limited and circumscribed in postcolonial cities. Chatterjee asserts that those who are beyond this domain are denied the rights and entailments of substantive citizenship, such as housing, electricity, water, or health. They make their claims to state resources through "political society," which has to pick its way through uncertain legal terrain "by making a large array of connections outside the group—with other groups in similar situations, privileged and influential groups, with government functionaries, with political parties and leaders, and so on" (85).

By expanding the political field beyond the space of formal associations—bureaucracies, planning departments, or social movements for justice and inclusion—and toward a range of "informal" relations whose sovereignties lie alongside those of the nation-state, this work has been tremendously generative to scholars seeking to account for how marginalized subjects are able to live in the city (see, e.g., Anjaria 2016; Zeiderman 2016). It makes visible the practices through which settlers and other populations make claims because of their special status—as exceptions to the rules and policies that otherwise exclude them. It *returns* our attention to the vital role played by big men (*dadas*), friends, families, and followers to get services like water, housing, and electricity in democratic societies.[6] As a category of analysis, "political society" enables sociologists and anthropologists to theorize and recognize the ubiquity of political practices beyond those that are seen by liberal political theory.[7]

Yet, in identifying the practices of political society as separate from those of civil society, Chatterjee sets up a rigid categorical distinction that appears difficult to transcend (either theoretically or socially). Further, this distinction appears isomorphic with others in urban planning, for instance between formality and informality, or of static and kinetic cities (Ananya Roy and AlSayyad 2004; Dwivedi and Mehrotra 1995). In fact, a reading of the literatures together suggests that the kinetic, informal city is the city of political society, whereas the static, formal, planned city is the one inhabited by civil society.

Here I suggest we need to move past the trope of two cities and two polities. I urge this not because things are more complex on the ground. Nor do I suggest that the inequalities that structure the city are not a trenchant problem. In fact, Chatterjee's account, like the work of Sharada Dwivedi and Rahul Mehrotra, compels us to recognize the ways in which informal residents of the city are not without power but instead are constantly working to secure their homes, bodies, and lives through active and critical political actions. Instead, I suggest we move beyond dualist accounts in order to better attend to the more dynamic and heterogeneous social and political processes through which cities and citizens are made.

A dualist treatment of urban politics is unable to account for the fluidity of urban life or describe how marginalized subjects in particular deploy formal *and* informal political institutions to make possible their life and politics in the city, despite the rules, exclusions, and violence of states and markets. To secure their lives in the city, urban subjects simultaneously occupy and navigate diverse political, social, and material domains (such as those of civil/political society and in/formal cities), as a means of securing their lives in the city.[8] Residents in Mumbai (both rich and poor) are multiply constituted subjects, simultaneously composed of the relations of both civil society and political society.

Second, as Ananya Roy has pointed out, urban informality (or, by extension, the politics of political society) is not an exceptional practice but "a mode of urbanization," "a system of norms that governs the process of urban transformation itself" (2005, 148; see also Anjaria 2016). This is the recognition Mr. Arputham (quoted in the opening of the chapter) dwells on when he insists that members of the "serving class" have made, and make the city. As residents (both powerful and marginalized) simultaneously combine diverse kinds of social, material, and political subjectivities, they make and inhabit cities that challenge liberal accounts and expectations of urban politics and urban life.

Liberal Cities

In his marvelous work that explores the emergence of liberalism and the modern city in nineteenth-century Britain, historian Patrick Joyce demonstrates how the urban environment was restructured to make cities that were conducive of liberal modes of government and subject formation. Joyce argues that infrastructures became a central concern of liberal rule because of the ways in which liberal thinkers privileged the free flow of things, persons, and information (Joyce 2003, 86). Combining work in science studies with a "historical sociology of material culture" (Joyce 2003, 6), Joyce explores how liberal modes of government were brought into being through the production and management of a series of urban infrastructures including indoor markets, water and sewer lines, and roads.

Infrastructures do more than just carry things or people from one place to the other (Larkin 2013). They are also key sites for working through modes of liberal reasoning (Collier 2011). By working through and with their restive materials, liberal theorists worked to redraw the boundaries of important social and political domains such as those of the public and the private, the technical and the political, and the political and the material.[9] They permitted the enlargement and expansion of a technical and administrative field of governmental regulation, which was identified as discrete from the fields and practices of politics (Joyce 2003). Political questions—such as those of water supply distribution—became matters of technical administration through the management of infrastructure. They could be administered from a realm beyond politics and serve to regulate populations at a distance.

The creation of a discrete technical administration went hand in hand with a reorganization of political life. Joyce demonstrates how, prior to the emergence of urban infrastructures, residents of nineteenth-century Manchester were governed by a patchwork of political institutions—corporations, manorial institutions, parishes, voluntary societies, and Improvement Acts. These jurisdictions had discrete sources of authority that "splintered" the political subject and made him accountable to a variety of sovereign institutions.

Liberal reforms of the mid-nineteenth century served to centralize diverse authorities in the body of the municipal corporation. They promised to administer the goods of infrastructure to a community of ratepayers with transparency and equality.[10] The centralization of power took place through both changes to the law and a privileging of different practices of government. For instance, municipal government was celebrated as being more open and transparent. Practices like audits, information relayed through open meetings, were aesthetic forms of rule that had a political purpose (see Ghertner 2015). They marked feudal practices as static, corrupt, and backward, and valorized liberal modes of rule. In showing the modern, transparent promise of liberal modes of government, municipal reforms sought to construct a singular, consolidated institution through which the power to live and die could be technically and rationally administered.

While scholars have, following Foucault, shown how the liberal subject emerged in Europe through reforms in the late nineteenth century, Ann Laura Stoler (1995) and Peter Redfield (2005) have demonstrated how such modes of liberal reasoning and rule were also dialectically formed in and through experiments with colonial rule in Africa and Asia. As colonialism expanded most prolifically "when the principles of modern liberalism were being established" (Kaviraj 2003, 153), liberal reforms were tried and tested in colonial cities like Mumbai at more or less the same time as in British cities. Indeed, the British colonial government in Bombay (alternately administered by the East India Company and the British crown) also began to consolidate power in civil institutions (from a variety of different political and juridical authorities) in Indian cities during this period (Dossal 2010). Hydraulic imaginaries, sanitary models, tenurial regimes, and even engineers and public health officials (such as Chadwick and Conybeare, for instance) traveled between the metropole and the colonial city. Modes of municipal government were tried and tested as much in Bombay as they were in Manchester.[11]

Nevertheless, despite these reforms, the liberal public subject has never been "free" of other kinds of political commitments and attachments (with social workers, religious leaders, politicians, and friends) in Mumbai.[12] Liberalism has always been always a partial and compromised project in colonial and postcolonial India; while liberal governmental institutions do exist, they are not the sole locus of sovereign authority in the city (Hansen and Verkaaik 2009). Today, as Chatterjee suggests, many residents of the postcolonial city continue to depend on patrons, friends, and a variety of different kinds of relations to obtain *some* urban services in the city—housing, water, electricity. These various relations beyond liberalism, frequently bundled under the category of "patronage," continue to matter to residents in the city.[13]

Accordingly, in this ambiguous and partly formed terrain of liberal rule, the political and administrative spheres are not discrete spheres of life in the postcolonial city. Neither is the political subject singular and accountable just to the state through the provision of municipal services. As residents simultaneously engage (and thereby reproduce) a variety of different kinds of relations (friends, social workers, helpers, kin, political representatives, and city administrators) to establish access to the "goods" of urban life, these diverse relations and the exchanges that make them are productive of societies and polities that continue to trouble the formation of liberal subjects. As such, the political subject is seldom an individual citizen—one whose political subjectivity is singular and described by relations with "the state." Instead, the political subject is plural. She is composed of a multiplicity of social, personal, and political relations that make her life possible in the city.[14]

Challenging the deeply seated "Western conceptions of the unitary self that presumes a one to one relation between property and thing," anthropologist Marilyn Strathern (1988, 157) has pointed to the multiplicity that is the person to suggest we rethink the normativity of the individual in political life. Drawing on her fieldwork in Papua New Guinea, Strathern suggests that while many social theorists have drawn on Western notions of personhood in proposing that exchanges between individuals produce society, her work in Melanesia demonstrates that exchanges in society constitute persons (Strathern 1991, 587). Transactions in gifts, commodities, and rights constitute *dividuated* forms of personhood. Accordingly, she suggests we might better consider individuals as "dividuals"—"fractal persons" who have several worlds of relationships that are constitutive of the social and political worlds they inhabit (Strathern 1991, 584).

Drawing on Strathern's work, here I suggest that Mumbai's residents may be better understood as *dividuals*—differentially and simultaneously constituted through the discrete exchange of gifts, commodities, and rights, enabled through infrastructure services in the city (see also Haraway 1991). As residents come to access housing, water services, work, electricity, or education through different kinds of social and political institutions, they are constituted through and by different forms of political subjectivity. As state services partially and incompletely extend to the city's different publics, residents in Mumbai might be recognized by the state simultaneously as citizens (e.g., for voting in elections, or for food rations), as illegal occupants (squatting on public land), and as customers (of the privatized electricity utility).

Recognizing that they *simultaneously* occupy different political locations at the same time, Mumbai's residents carefully and creatively manage and maneuver between different political subjectivities to make more durable forms of settlement possible in the city. They draw on their heterogeneous personal, social, and political identities to make powerful claims to life and living in the city. To demonstrate this, let me turn to the histories of settlement and tenancy in the neighborhood of Jogeshwari.

The establishment of tenancy has long been critical for the establishment of substantive citizenship not just in Mumbai but in many parts of the world.[15] In Mumbai, tenancy recognized by the state is critical not just to claim access to shelter but also to gain formal access to water. As per the city's water rules, residents need to demonstrate that their housing has been recognized (both legally and politically) by the city administration before a water connection can be sanctioned. Thus, to be recognized as formal residents, settlers mobilize not only personal relationships with city administrators, big men, and social workers but also the forms and norms of citizenship—voting, rallying, and protesting. Through these diverse forms of political practice, settlers constantly work to be seen as deserving subjects by the city-state—to be counted and mapped on the forms and papers of the state so that they may claim access to the things that they need to live, such as water, energy, and work (see Corbridge et al. 2005; Scott 1998).

By drawing attention to this process, I demonstrate how material and political settlement is enabled by acting not just with but also beyond the registers of civil society. Taken together, the politics of friendship, political society, *and* those of citizenship remain vital in urban housing and hydraulic politics in Mumbai. While these kinds of political practices have been transformed with the expansion of liberal procedures and political representation in the last four decades, the practices of political society have not abated with the (temporary, precarious, and partial) achievements of liberal citizenship. Instead, they are transformed and given new life. As such, it might be productive to consider these "other" social relations of patronage and friendship as a nonconstitutive outside to the formation of liberal citizenship—an outside that is not necessarily diminished or absorbed by the expansion of liberal citizenship in the city. They continue to matter to both the formation and the proscription of substantive urban citizenship.

Difficult Areas

Situated between the proliferating information technology centers of Andheri and the more established middle-class residential conclave of Goregaon, Jogeshwari is sometimes difficult to find and has been made easy to miss. While I was conducting fieldwork between 2007 and 2008, residents told me that new residential developments in Jogeshwari usually advertised themselves as being located in Andheri. In part, this is because Jogeshwari has intermittently appeared as a dangerous place in Mumbai's newspapers. Growing up in south central Mumbai, I had known Jogeshwari to be a troubled northern suburb, beyond the closeted margins of the city I knew. The first time I recall hearing about the neighborhood in the city's news was when I was seventeen. The city was on edge after the shameful demolition of the sixteenth-century mosque Babri Masjid in 1992. Riots had broken out all over the city. Jogeshwari was one area that appeared in newspaper reports, time and again. They said it was where the violence all began. A governmental inquiry instituted after the violence ended implicated leaders of the Shiv Sena in the attacks (Hansen 1998; Srikrishna Commission 1998). During the period of calm that followed, the lines between Hindu and Muslim settlers in Jogeshwari's settlements hardened, as each relocated to the areas in which they were the numerical majority.[16] Premnagar became an even denser Muslim "pocket" and is now surrounded by Hindu *bastis* (settlements), whose residents are supporters of the Shiv Sena—the political party that has run the city's government for the last two decades.[17]

Fifteen years later, during fieldwork I was surprised to learn that Jogeshwari continued to be remembered for the riots. Friends told me that Jogeshwari is "famous" as a "black area"—one known for its history of riots, violence, and precariousness. "No hi-fi people want to live in Jogeshwari," Kamlesh, a resident of Jogeshwari, told me. "It is a 'black area.' Banks won't give you a loan if you live here." It was also hard to obtain state documents such as driver's licenses or passports as a result of living in Jogeshwari. Indeed, Jogeshwari does not even appear on the popular street map of Mumbai sold by its vendors. Nevertheless, the neighborhood's in-between location between country and city and legality and illegality, as well as its situation between the city's national park, urban river, international airport, and industrial zone, also tells the story of how the postcolonial city of Mumbai has been made by people living on its margins.

Ramesh, a good friend and a water rights activist who worked for one of the city's more prominent NGOs, had lived in Jogeshwari for most of his

life. One afternoon, he came over to my home and we spoke about what Jogeshwari was like when he was in school. He spoke of an almost rural, forested landscape that lay beyond the gaze of urban government. Narrating his
memory of his neighborhood, Ramesh recounted, "Jogeshwari was a place
that people would come to on weekends. . . . Even when I was small, there
were a number of trails [*payvaad*] here. . . . I have walked on paths lined with
jungle on both sides." As he told me of his memories of Jogeshwari, Ramesh,
and indeed many others, described a landscape untamed by the powers of
the state or the interests of property developers. He spoke of Jogeshwari
as being on the margins of the city, where things were somewhat wild and
untrammeled.

Jogeshwari is just south of Sanjay Gandhi National Park (also known as
Borivali National Park), a 104 square kilometer protected zone that hosts
over a thousand species of plants, 40 species of mammals (including leop-
ards), and 250 species of birds in what is now the heart of the city (see Government of Maharashtra 2015). The park also holds two of the cities' dams
(Tulsi and Vihar), the two-thousand-year-old Kanheri caves, as well as
several settlements of indigenous peoples.[18] In 1944 the British granted the
land just south of the forested areas of Borivali (and beyond the northern
boundary of the city) to a loyal and wealthy Parsi merchant, Jeejeebhoy Byramjee (Kothari and Contractor 1996). Jogeshwari was incorporated into
the Municipal Corporation of Bombay (BMC) in 1945, just prior to Indian
independence.

Jogeshwari's location—as situated between the country and the city—has
been key to its formation as a neighborhood. In 1949, then Prime Minister
Jawaharlal Nehru inaugurated the Aarey Milk Colony, a large, state-run milk
distribution plant in the southern margins of the park just north of Jogeshwari. To take advantage of this new development, migrants from North India
built their own dairy farms in Jogeshwari—either by buying land directly
from the Jeejeebhoy Byramjee Parsee Charitable Trust or by squatting on it.
For decades after, the area was known as "Mumbai's dairy." Making use of its
liminal location between the country and the city, *tabela* owners reared cattle
by buying grasses and feed from villages in the north, and delivering milk to
the large urban markets in Mumbai city in the south (Kandviker 1978).

Shortly after independence, the state government acquired a portion of
Jeejeebhoy's land and designated it a "squatters colony"—a place to settle
those evicted by state-run demolitions in the central and southern parts of
the city between 1948 and 1980. The area (now known locally as Premnagar)

continues to bear traces of the displaced settlers' pasts. The names of its various neighborhoods—Colaba Plot, Bandra Plot, and Andheri Plot—refer to the locations from which the original settlers were evicted.

Early residents of Premnagar remember it as an inhospitable and wild place—full of jungles, animals, and thugs. Yet because Premnagar was a formal "site and services" resettlement colony, its residents benefited from the early extension of water and electricity infrastructure. Accordingly, the colony soon drew other settlers to its margins. Residents began to build and subsequently rent homes in adjoining areas. As unrecognized settlements, these homes were not legally eligible for water, but they were near several potential sources. Residents gathered their water from Premnagar's shared standposts or bought it (by the *handa*) from its residents. They supplemented their supplies with other waters, drawn from a number of wells, tanks, and springs in the neighborhood. Critically, these aquifers held water all year round, enabling the lives even of those not connected by city water mains.

As the city began to move its residents outside the crowded center, either through processes of slum demolitions or mill closures, the area grew quickly. Small houses and pieces of land sold here had many takers, especially among former millworkers who, having worked in the city's central mills for much of the mid-twentieth century, found themselves out of work during the textile strikes in the late 1970s and early 1980s (M. Menon and Adarkar 2004). Ramesh's family was part of this northward migration from the center of the city to its margin. Sensing a demand for housing, dairy farm owners made small rooms on the lands they occupied. According to Ramesh:

> This is the story of the city. . . . One person from the Konkan would come to [work in] the mills. . . . They would come, live, and call others to live in the same room. Soon those people need[ed] houses . . . so they looked [for housing] together. Take me, for example. My father has five brothers. Three of them went to work in the mills. All of them lived in [one room in] Chinchpokli. Then, when one moved, all moved to Jogeshwari. They found houses for cheap in these parts in '74, '75.

In the absence of large public housing initiatives, these single-room houses were built all over the city and served as warehouses for the city's large workforce. They proliferated in Jogeshwari despite their illegality, in large part because of their geographic marginality, affordability, and ability to accommodate working people and their families, many of whom shared kinship, village, and regional ties.

The settlements of Mumbai have thus produced a particular form of cosmopolitanism in India's most diverse city, where different ethnic and social groups live not among, but alongside, one another (N. Rao 2013). In a sense, both resettled evictees of Premnagar and their tenants—mostly former millworkers—moved to Jogeshwari through processes of displacement. The former were displaced by the state when it bulldozed their houses and resettled them in Premnagar. The latter moved to the area when the textile strikes pushed them out of the formal labor market in central Mumbai. The stories of residents in Jogeshwari, therefore, are stories of the city of the displaced and the displaced city, where those marginalized by the state and the market have come over the past four decades to establish new homes and begin new lives.[19]

The State of Informality

Close to sixty years of age, Yusuf bhai has an extraordinary amount of confidence, which he called forth in his retelling of the area's history.[20] Residents of the area were extremely deferent to his authority and knowledge. In his telling, this was because he played a variety of leadership roles in the area, especially in times past. He began as one of the area's early settlers, and with political "protection" built informal and illegal settlements on public and private land. When I met him in 2008, he was negotiating with one of the city's largest builders to construct a slum rehabilitation building for the residents of his chawls.

One evening, as we sat in a teashop sheltered from the rain, I asked Yusuf bhai if he would look back through the area's history to tell me how settlements in the area were built. He began by telling me that people were shifted to the resettlement colony in the 1950s and 1960s. As evictees, a few people were allotted land in "squatters colony." Over time, they built more houses in the open space, which they then sold or rented for income. Nearby—in Meghwadi, Shyamnagar, and other neighborhoods—dairy farm owners, noting the demand for housing, also got in on the act, sometimes converting their cowsheds into houses and sometimes building new ones.

Intrigued by his pioneering account of settlement, I asked Yusuf bhai about the authorities under which houses were built and rented. "*Jiski lathi uski bhens*," he replied. "He who has the stick has the buffalo." Of course, he was speaking here not just of the administration of cattle in an area once known as Mumbai's dairy but also of people (see Pandian 2008). His phrase pointed to the diffuse nature of the law and authority in the settlement's early days. Self-styled leaders and big men in Jogeshwari were made by their ability to (sometimes violently) flout the laws of the state, often with the help of state officials.[21] Once an "area" was "captured" (Yusuf used the Hindi word *kabza*) by construction, the bhai would quickly pay the relevant administrators of the municipal government for their inaction and subsequently rent space to families who were looking for a home. Sharing a common cause against state evictions with their tenants, it was the responsibility of the bhai to ensure that the city's demolition crews overlooked their settlements when doing the rounds. Sometimes they did this with money and sometimes with favors for municipal officials. At other times they mobilized the courts, obtaining stay orders on the demolition of homes *even before these were built* (Awachat 1975).

During our conversation, Yusuf bhai demonstrated an acute awareness of both the powers of state officials and also the fungibility of favors and petitions in his line of work. While Jogeshwari was on the margins of the city, this was not an area where the state was absent. He could not make houses without the informal permission of the authorities, he told me. In fact, in his stories, it was junior municipal officers who were responsible for commissioning his first construction projects. He told me that a junior BMC officer gave him his first break by awarding him a three-thousand-rupee contract to build a room. He built and returned two rooms to the officer for that price. The officer was very pleased when able to realize a 100 percent profit from the sale. So the next time around, the officer gave him a contract for eight houses. After these were turned over successfully, Yusuf bhai was given the proceeds from the sale of one of the rooms for his efforts. So he started out on his own, and began to build and turn over rooms in the *pagdi* system, calling upon the official's "name" whenever necessary.[22] Yusuf spoke of this municipal officer fondly and with deference. He told me that they still meet with each other, even when there is no business to transact.

Yusuf bhai also had good relations with police officers, even if these relations were sometimes made in adverse circumstances. For instance, in the violence following the demolition of the Babri Masjid, an additional commissioner of police threatened to put Yusuf bhai behind bars under a notoriously abused law, the Terrorist and Disruptive Activities Act (TADA).[23] Yusuf bhai protested, saying that there was no charge and no reason to do so. Yusuf bhai suggested that the police officer's threat was not unrelated to his private business interests. He told me that the police officer asked Yusuf bhai to sell an unauthorized shop to his son in exchange for deferring his arrest. Threatened with arrest, Yusuf bhai sold the shop at a discount. But this financial loss translated into a relational gain. Yusuf bhai explained, "Now, when I go to him, I won't need to give him a bribe, or any money. He will do my work for free . . . for our friendship. That is how things work here."

Of course, I wasn't able to verify with the former police officer if this story was true. Regardless, the account revealed a certain moral economy that Yusuf bhai followed while living in the city. His stories reminded me of several others with which I was familiar—those of my own friends and family, upper-class residents who are able to work in Mumbai through the careful cultivation of personal–professional relations. Relations make influence, and those more influential can draw on such "relations" to get their work done at minimal cost (see Boissevain 1974).

In much of the development literature about India, these relations are known through the tropes of coercion, corruption, cronyism, and nepotism (J. Davis 2003; Witsoe 2011). For Yusuf bhai, these words had less meaning or import in his everyday life.[24] Using the English word, he reported a value-neutral "*relation*," and described his relations frequently in terms of affection and care. Having little access to housing or land under existing laws, lower-level state officials and settlers invested their social and financial resources in *helping* each other out. Unlike market exchanges or state-based rights and responsibilities, the practices of friendship and helping are ambiguous and marked by excess—an excess that carries the relation forward into the future.[25]

"Helping" systems of collaboration work across and within regimes of difference and inequality (Tsing 2005). In Jogeshwari, Yusuf bhai became powerful by working for the personal gain of lower-level state functionaries. By building homes and shops for state officials, he was able to forge social relations that exceeded the transaction for which he was commissioned. These relations were not always relations of choice, nor were they always amicable. For example, Yusuf bhai was *compelled* to sell one of his shops to evade arrest. But by doing so, he cemented a social relation for the future that made him more powerful. He drew little distinction between helping the officer and helping the anthropologist. Addressing me directly, he said, "See, you are here today. We have met a few times and I am helping you with your work. . . . If we meet ten times, maybe after sharing dinner, we will know each other well. Maybe you will remember me in ten or fifteen years when I come to you for help." Noncommensurable, unsettled friendships are powerful stuff (Bourdieu 1977).[26] They can live alongside different regimes—of both rights and patronage—and make life manageable through their various exclusions.

Of course, Yusuf bhai was not the only person in the area who would offer such services. Many others "lent" their name, or patronage, to build chawls and rent them to people seeking housing. These included people in political parties, state offices, crime syndicates, and others who had established their local importance (Auyero 2000; Schmidt 1977). As an attention to Yusuf bhai's narrative makes clear, though the state has been formally absent at one level, its officials were intimately involved in the production and governance of Jogeshwari's early settlements. Their rule was based on state authority being present in its formal absence; that is to say, in the absence of substantive state programs to provide affordable housing, *dadas* or other "big men" have been critical figures to securing housing in the city—not only because they provided places to live but also because they offered protection from the periodic and punctuated appearances of state bulldozers, officers, and their disciplinary actions (see Weinstein 2014).

The Security of Friendship

Patronage relations with bhais did not exclusively mediate the relationship between people and their homes. Some groups of settlers made arrangements with others. For instance, Anku tai and her group came from Hyderabad. As members of a traditionally nomadic tribe (one with no established village), they had few contacts in the city. She told me at length about how they came to settle in Jogeshwari.

For some time, the men of her group would be traveling through different parts of Jogeshwari, selling combs and hair clips for a living. One day, they chanced upon an empty piece of land, just north of a cemetery. They made friends with its security guard, shared several drinks with him, and learned more about its conditions. Recognizing his sympathies were mobilized by their friendship, one day the men in Anku tai's group "sweetly, and with affection" expressed that they—as twenty to thirty households—needed a place to stay. The guard cautiously advised them to build their homes near the cemetery with the disclaimer that they be discreet both in the process of constructing their homes and with the details of their arrangement with him. With his tacit permission, Anku tai built houses right where he had suggested.

Soon after, they were repeatedly threatened by the landowners. At first, the owners dispatched their private security guards to demolish the homes with police protection. Anku tai told me that the landlord sent men who came and threatened them with swords. At other times, the landlord would complain to the BMC and pressure it to evict the squatters. The BMC would sometimes come and demolish their homes.

Faced with little choice, they would gather their belongings and build in the same place again. Anku tai explained:

> The BMC would come to demolish homes. They came four or five times. They would break and we would build. They would break and we would build. Where could we go? Two or three times we went to the police station. . . . We didn't get scared there also. We told them, "You have a place, a job. Where can we poor people go? Is the city for rich people only?" There was a good inspector there. He listened to our complaints and also filed a case against the [landlords] that were threatening us.

The celebrated "resilience" of settlers and marginal residents in the city is borne out of their fundamental and basic need to survive. With nowhere else to turn, Anku tai and her neighbors would appeal to the conscience of state officials to halt, or at least slow, the performance of their disciplinary apparatus. At the police station, they identified sympathetic officers and made claims to their consciences, even when they were taken there for property violations. Anku tai describes a commonplace way that those living in settlements work against their displacement—by mobilizing a "politics of conscience" at a variety of state offices (Appadurai 2002). These claims might sometimes be assisted with the promise of money. Despite the cash transfers, Anku tai saw those helping her family as mobilized by their humanitarian sensibilities.

For instance, she told me how "good people" in the offices of subsidized food rations and water supply would understand the plight of poor people and "help" them. Anku tai told me that she obtained food ration cards from someone who was associated with the Food and Civil Supplies office in Andheri. The state employee, she said, took one hundred rupees per application and made forty to fifty cards for the group. Going above and beyond the requirements of a public official, he also went so far as to drop them off at their homes. "He was such a good man," Anku tai reminisced. "He didn't sit in a chair [was not an officer]. He made our papers outside the office. Only for one hundred rupees in those days." While the amount of money was significant, Anku tai did not seem to begrudge paying it. Faced with a state that was otherwise impossible to access and that refused to recognize settlers, she was appreciative of state workers who understood their needs and responded to them, even if it was for a fee.

In speaking of interactions with state employees at the police station or the food office, Anku tai did not speak the language of rights and entitlements, which settlers such as herself did not have initially, neither formally nor in practice. Lacking the power to change the laws that governed their exclusion, Anku tai and other settlers frequently worked with state officials whose job it was to implement state law and policy. By mobilizing their sympathies, and coaxing them with small amounts of money, these arrangements— which drew on both the sympathies of humanitarianism *and* the interests of money—made very exclusive rules and laws more accommodating and made life in the city possible (see Scott 1969). Yet these enduring relations of clientship were not ahistorical forms of connection. As James Scott and others argued four decades ago, they are constantly inflected through and by practices of citizenship, here in the postcolonial city (see Lamarchand 1977; Schmidt 1977; Scott 1969, 1977; Wade 1982).

Representing People

Prior to 1970, settlers who squatted on public or private property had few, if any, rights recognized by the city. Throughout the first half of the twentieth century, the strategies of slum clearance and eradication typified the way in which slums were governed in Indian cities (Anand and Rademacher 2011; Ghertner 2015). For instance, in 1912 prominent Scottish town planner Patrick Geddes recommended the clearance of settlements in several Indian cities to ensure public health and order (Kalia 2004). The approach did not vary considerably in the postcolonial government's first slum policy. Following national norms, the state government issued its first Slum Clearance Plan in 1956. It aggressively sought to bulldoze, evict, and subsequently police squatted government lands. In the decades following, however, the demands for democratic inclusion began to proliferate in newly postcolonial Mumbai through a variety of political routes. Increasingly empowered city councilors, social movements, and even the World Bank began to pressure the administration to recognize those living in settlements as populations deserving of urban services.

In our conversations around the histories of Jogeshwari, veteran activist Mrinal Gore highlighted the dynamic political terrain that was emergent in the 1960s and 1970s as social movements and city councilors representing settlers increasingly began to protest the living conditions to which they were subjected through liberal democratic means. In the time since, Gore had come to be known as the *paniwali bai* (water woman), particularly because she led large and very successful protest marches for water during this period. When I interviewed her in the summer of 2009, she described the political process through which the area was incrementally settled by focusing on the dramatic urban politics of the time:

> We [organized] big *morchas* [protest marches]. I remember when our morcha first went, the women who came with us had never seen the Fort area. They would ask, "Tai, what is this?" Rajabai tower. "What is that?" [The] university. Who would take these poor people? So these were the two interests for the women who came. If their demands were fulfilled it was such a big deal [*badi baat*]. You can get work [in Mumbai] and make houses. If you can [also] get water and toilets, then what else do you need?

As Gore spoke to me about these marches, she highlighted how they accomplished different things for their participants. At their most explicit level, the marches were for substantive urban rights: to change urban policy from one of slum *erasure* to slum *improvement* and to call upon government to deliver better water services. These marches petitioned the government to abandon bulldozers in favor of infrastructure that would make settlements more dignified places to live. Nevertheless, for many settlers sequestered in the city's suburbs, the protests were also a way to experience life in the center of the city. They were able to walk through the city's formerly colonial and now business enclave and participate in its pleasures. They enjoyed experiencing its grand buildings and tall towers. In addition to being a protest march, this was also a sort of powerful flânerie—both pleasurable and political. Gore believed that the marches were successful precisely because they were effective at multiple levels. By marching on the streets of the city center, residents were not only claiming their right to urban space; they were also enjoying themselves. They were demonstrating their durability and the ultimate futility of the state if it were to continue on its path of slum evictions.

For both participants and their intended audience—the city government—the marches were a visual spectacle. Whereas the protests enabled settlers to see the city in a new way, the city administration was made nervous as they witnessed a large number of protestors assembling on the grounds outside their headquarters. The marches emboldened the elected city council, which began to assert the needs of its constituents against appointed technocrats. Gore, who by then was also a city councilor, explained the impact of these marches:

> We asked [the BMC administrators]: "Do you think people living in slums want to live there, and not in buildings?" . . . If you cannot give

everyone a house, then let's talk about improving the slums at least. Take care of the three responsibilities—water, sanitation, and roads. Slums are bad because they lack these facilities. People will do the rest . . . but water and toilets are the biggest issues. Don't do slum eradication, do the work of slum fixing/solving [Slum eradication *nahi*, *slum sudharane ka kaam karo*].

Through the slogans and demands voiced during the protests, settlers learned the ways in which they could frame and present their entitlements, the ways to talk as citizens of the city. Instead of acknowledging the power of the state, they pointed to its inefficacy at producing a satisfactory housing infrastructure for the poor and also at demolitions and slum clearances. In so doing, Gore and her fellow activists sought to effect a transition in how administrators saw slums. She asked them not to look at slums as a problem of the poor. Sounding a lot like the World Bank officials who also began frequenting the city, she said that slums were instead the result of the state's *inability* to provide housing for all. If the state could not afford to build public housing, she argued, then must it not at least provide basic services to its residents? Gore described how she raised the protestors' demands within council meetings. The protests outside the BMC building gave her both legitimacy and authority to speak as a councilor. Her words, as well as those of other councilors with a mass base, held a moral authority because of the protestors chanting outside.

From its earliest days under colonial rule, Bombay has been governed by municipal commissioners—appointed state government bureaucrats—who implement various urban development and regulation programs while keeping the city's population, and its restive legislators, in check.[27] Until the early 1960s, councilors had been under the command of city administrators who governed the city by administrative fiat. But as the city's limits were shifting (suburbs like Jogeshwari and Goregaon sent their first representatives to the city council in 1962), so were the demands of its councilors, who began increasingly to intervene in the city's administration. In our interview, Gore described how city councilors began making demands in the council in the 1960s and 1970s. Elected largely by settlers, councilors began to review contracts of government projects, worked to stymie municipal eviction drives for their particular constituencies, and drew on personal relations with the city administrators to bring discretionary development projects to their wards—schools, hospitals, and roads.[28]

The Recognitions of Law

The campaigns of social activists and the practices of accommodation engaged by city councilors for improving the homes of settlers also articulated with those of development specialists at the World Bank, who, by the 1970s, were involved in urban development projects in Mumbai. During this time, they funded new water augmentation programs at the Hydraulic Engineering Department, and in so doing began to attach conditions to their loans. Like the socialist activist Gore, World Bank officials were looking at neoliberal techniques through which living conditions in the "slums" could be improved as an alternative to (more expensive) public housing projects. In an uneasy confluence of different agendas, they, like Gore, argued that problems in the settlements were due not so much to their existence per se as to the absence of critical infrastructure, including water and sanitation.

Therefore, following pressure from both activists in the city and transnational policy experts, approaches to governing slums in the 1970s shifted to recognize, at least incrementally, the services that the city government needed to provide. Housing rights activist Sundar Burra explains: "During the 1970s, for a variety of reasons relating to both equity and practical considerations, slums began to be viewed as 'housing solutions.' Legislation and policy were developed to provide civic amenities in slums, and it began to be recognized that when slums were to be demolished, some form of resettlement was needed" (Burra 2005, 70). The variety of reasons Burra points to include the funding prerogatives of international agencies and the rise of different political initiatives in the council and beyond to make life better for residents living in settlements.

Accordingly, a proliferation of governmental acts and policies emerged that sought to "upgrade" the living conditions of settlements in Mumbai. For instance, in 1971 the state passed the Maharashtra Slum Areas (Improvement, Clearance and Redevelopment) Act. While the state had previously passed a slum act, the 1971 act, for the first time, identified a procedure for the declaration of slums and also made provisions for resettlement in the event of slum demolitions (Bardhan et al. 2015). At the same time, the act also continued to give legal cover to the periodic demolitions of slum areas that had characterized the approach of the city government toward "managing" slums for the past century. The very first line of the Slum Areas Act displays the differentiated and ambivalent approach through which Mumbai's government is called upon to manage "slum areas": it is "an Act to make better provision for the improvement and clearance of slum areas in the State and their redevelopment (and for the protection of occupiers from eviction and distress warrants)." The language of improvement, when read together with the parenthetical text about protection of slum occupants, provides a legal basis for the city to extend services to particular slum areas, even as it continues to make provisions for the clearance of slums in the state.

All at once then, the Slum Areas Act urges improvement and clearance.[29] Nevertheless, in providing means and procedures through which settlers can claim both the protection of the state (from the state) and also biopolitical services (such as health care, water, and electricity), the act is significant. There are provisions in the act that lay out a process for unauthorized structures to be protected from demolition without compensation. Relatedly, there are also different provisions in the act through which residents living in "slum areas" can come to receive municipal services (such as water or garbage pickup) in their settlements. These two processes are discrete, and yet they provide a critical opening through which settlers can establish and ameliorate their lives in the city.

Today, residents who can prove that they have inhabited the same dwelling since the cutoff date of 2000 can receive a "photo-pass" establishing their residence in the unauthorized structure.[30] The photo-pass is a document that has legal effects. It protects the dwelling from demolition, establishes a tenancy in the eyes of the state, and entitles its residents to compensation in the event that the land is required for the "larger public interest" or is to be redeveloped under subsequent slum rehabilitation housing schemes.

Yet, while the photo-pass establishes the relationship between resident, their dwellings, and their settlements, this does not make them eligible for water services. Ordinary water connections are only extended to applicants who go through the permitting process prior to the building construction. Of course, because settlers do not live in housing authorized by the city prior to its construction, they are not extended water connections or other urban infrastructure in this way. Accordingly, for residents in these settlements to receive water services, the state government first has to declare the settlement a "slum area"—deemed to have substandard housing, overcrowding, and insufficient urban infrastructure. Under the act, the city government may "declare" certain areas to be slum areas because of the *quality* (and not the legality) of the housing in question. The city is then permitted to improve these areas, identified by this declaration as a danger to public health, regardless of their legal standing.

Accordingly, for settlers, the declaration of their neighborhood as a slum area is an ambiguous yet potentially promising event, particularly because once declared, there is a procedure in the 1972 act through which slum areas can be "improved" by the municipal administration. The act specifies that if the expenses of improvement are reasonable, the city can notify landowners (either public or private) of its intention to extend urban services (sewage, toilets, water, street paving) to those occupying and residing on the owner's property.[31] Both the "declaration" of slums and their "regularization" by the state are discretionary events. These events are contingent on the micropolitics of each settlement—the willfulness of the landowner (to prevent notification), the political power of squatters (to demand it), and the various regulations to which the property (public or private) is subject. Public land may be easier to squat on, but it is sometimes harder to regularize. The city government is reluctant to declare slums (and therefore functionally appropriate) land owned by other state agencies. Settlements that are the preferred constituencies of city or state legislators, meanwhile, are often declared "slum areas" before those living in adjacent, sometimes older settlements. For example, in their study of Jogeshwari, Miloon Kothari and Nasreen Contractor (1996) point to how the Shiv Sena managed to get the Hindu settlement of Sundarnagar "declared" much before the nearby Muslim settlement of Aminanagar.

Authorized, tolerated and regularized, declared and undeclared. The vocabulary of the state in regard to slums and their structures categorizes and indexes residents' formal claims to state services and their entitlements to compensation in the event of eviction. I was very confused for much of my fieldwork as I attempted to sort through the terms of government and of the possibilities for settlers under each of these terms. Mr. Patankar, a municipal engineer, helped me understand how the water department sees different structures and their inhabitants. The department extends water connections to three different kinds of built structures. He began by telling me about "authorized" structures. These are structures that have been approved and sanctioned by the Building Proposal Department of the BMC prior to their construction—typically apartment buildings and businesses. Next, there are structures that are "tolerated." These include structures built prior to 1964 in urban villages (gaothans) and fishing villages that lie alongside, but not in violation of city plans. Finally, there are "protected structures." These are the homes (in settlements) that the state government has periodically "recognized" and "declared" via cutoff dates and legal notifications. Residents living in "declared" slums are both protected from the state's bulldozers and eligible for urban services. Residents in the first two settlement categories get individual water connections. Those living in the third category get group water connections.[32] Those living in undeclared slums are not eligible to apply for water connections; they are only eligible for garbage collection services.

In this fluid landscape, the legal status of each settlement is in dynamic motion. The difficulty for state agencies, of course, is in distinguishing and ordering settlements as per these categories, particularly because the cutoff date—currently 2000—has consistently been brought nearer (but never quite at) the ever-advancing present.[33] Through political and social processes, settlers attempt to have their areas "declared" slum areas so that they may claim and receive urban services. As settlements and structures become recognized over time, their residents can trust that their homes will not be demolished without rehabilitation. Yet many respond to this security not only by making steady and substantive investments in their housing infrastructure. They also sometimes let out portions of their homes to new renters to provide themselves with an additional source of income. As a result, Mumbai's settlements, even those that are recognized, simultaneously contain many diverse times and spaces of legality that are difficult to map or know. Together, they produce a dynamic urban landscape that state administrators have long found difficult to know and to govern in the city.[34]

Proof of Life

While the gains effected by the politics of state recognition are substantial, they should not be read as teleological, or leading steadily toward the substantive and permanent recognition of larger numbers of Mumbai's residents as legal citizens. Even as liberal governmental technologies have proliferated through the nineteenth and twentieth centuries, these have not taken the place of other forms of rule (including the police) (see Bröckling et al. 2011). The Slum Areas Act contains diverse modes of government and different technologies of power. Through the act, these are differentially and discontinuously applied in Mumbai, both within and between settlements.

The extent to which certain dwellings are marked for clearance and others are marked for improvement depends, in no small measure, on the documents that their inhabitants produce to establish their tenure in a particular dwelling. As settlers navigate the precarious zone between being too invisible and too visible to state agencies, they continue gathering documents they would require to make claims at an anticipated but unknown moment of the future—receipts, fines, voter identity cards, photo-passes, bank account statements, ration cards, driver's licenses, electricity bills, water bills, and photographs—so as to be able to document their continued presence in their homes.[35] These pieces of paper, occasionally marked with indigo stamps and red covers and often stored in sealed plastic bags, bear critical marks of urban citizenship. Settlers collect papers even if these indicate they moved into their dwellings after 2000 and are not protected by the law. Anticipating that the cutoff date will move forward to accommodate them before they are displaced by the law, they collect "proofs," as they are called, to establish—either in the present or at some point in the future—their continued presence in the city.

Interestingly, the type of state document collected is not always of import in establishing residency. What matters is that as papers of the state, they join the person to the place that they are occupying at a particular time. For example, a housing activist told me how she had successfully used a previously issued (but unexecuted) eviction order as a proof of tenancy to prevent evictions when the bulldozers came around several years later. The court accepted the document as proof of address and occupation and stayed the demolition. In another settlement, one resident showed me two electricity connections he had in his house. He used the illegal connection because it provided free electricity. He used the legal connection only because he wished to collect the electricity bills it generated to present to the state as proof of occupation in case he received an eviction notice.

In a world where paper is a critical force for claims making, legal water connections deliver a lot more than water in Mumbai. They also deliver vital water bills. Bills serve as powerful documents proving that certain homes were known to the state at a particular moment in history. Aware of the ways in which settlers use these bills, the city water administration tries to ensure that it does not extend water services to any settlers who cannot prove the habitation of their dwellings prior to 2000.

The reason for this rule is not so much that the city has insufficient water, nor is it to exclude the homes of unauthorized residents from the water supply. Engineers are aware that these homes have other means of obtaining water. The city and state government try hard not to issue bills to recent settlers because they are aware that these documents may be used to make tenure claims at some point in the future.

A retired senior engineer who has a long history in the department, Mr. Patel, explained to me: "See, if you have a [legal] connection, your existence is known to the BMC. The court would take a sympathetic view. So I [as the water department] must not provide documentation that will allow you to claim your existence for so long here." Patel reminds us that papers (here, bills)—even when they do not accompany water supply—are powerful. They connect populations to particular places, and can be called upon by the courts to prove that settlers have lived in the structure with the knowledge of the state. So while settlers try to be counted and documented by state agencies through various forms of documentation, including water bills, state agencies in the city go to extraordinary lengths to ensure that they do *not* issue settlers documents that could later be used as claims of residence, belonging, and citizenship.[36]

The curious lives of documents in the city—where state bureaucracies seek to avoid issuing them and settlers are in constant pursuit of them—pose a stark reminder to scholars of governmentality who critique state projects to count, map, measure, and know populations through documents and identity cards. This work often assumes the power of these technologies to regulate rights-bearing citizens through liberal languages of care and responsibility. In Mumbai, the state works hard *not to count* and works hard *not to know* certain populations as liberal citizens. It works hard *not to provide* water bills and other documents through which they can be seen and known by state institutions.

Conversely, residents in the settlement, correctly recognizing that their claims might be recognized if they have the right documents, do extraordinary social and political work to gain access to these documents. They work hard to be seen by the state through not just water bills but a range of different documents issued by the state.[37] With their lives managed by diverse state programs, settlers acquire voter ID cards, food ration cards, photopasses, school leaving certificates, water bills, electricity bills, and political party membership cards to be counted as eligible citizens for different state agencies.

In order to verify the eligibility, residents wishing to apply for state services frequently need to provide documentation issued by other agencies that demonstrate their legitimacy. When conducting research in 2008, settlers wishing to receive a shared water connection had to furnish a range of documents, including:

a. An application form for a new connection.
b. A resolution/memorandum declaring a new (water) society, with a secretary in charge of collecting and paying dues.
c. A list of "members" of the society with their food ration cards numbers in one column and the electoral roll ID number in another.[38]
d. Supporting documentation that includes copies of every member's (food) ration card, and a copy of the 1995 electoral roll, with each

of their names highlighted. Each page needed to be certified as a true copy by the junior engineer.
   e. A list of members "verified" as per the junior engineer.
   f. A receipt that two hundred rupees have been paid to the BMC for "scrutinizing" the application.
   g. A certification nominating a licensed plumber to do the pipe laying works.

The application form and the supporting documents tie the eligibility for city water services to the legal status of the applicant's home. The ration card serves as "address proof" and the applicant's name on the 1995 voter list indicates their presence as a voting citizen prior to that date. Taken together, the ration card and the name on the voter list are intended to unequivocally indicate to department engineers that residents are living in recognized structures and entitled to the city's water.

Of course, those who are excluded by the city's water rules respond with their own designs, most frequently by engaging the plumbers that the application form itself requires. These arrangements vary tremendously, both across and within settlements, but their effectiveness is manifest in the continued presence of settlers in the city. Again, Patel, the retired engineer, was aware of these arrangements: "I will tell you how it is done. I know how they manipulate documentation. They provide someone else's ration card and signature, not the person who will get the water. Then for the [copy] of the voter list, they make a bogus list. Antisocial and political fellows are helping them do this. . . . We just accept their application and give the connection."

With a detailed knowledge of Mumbai's informal water system, Patel guided me through the ways in which otherwise unqualified residents navigate its exclusive rules. He told me that while supplying water to unauthorized settlements is against government rules, the previous city commissioner had urged the water department "not to go into depth" (that is, to verify the authenticity) of every application.

Patel argued that approving ineligible applicants for water connections surreptitiously was necessary because the state/high court had forbidden them to give water to unqualified residents. Yet he recognized both the social and material effects of such a denial. People might protest, or damage city pipes in an attempt to get water on their own. This would cause difficulty for officials in the water department. In the current arrangement, he pointed out, engineers could feign ignorance if people began questioning the legitimacy of these connections (see chapter 5).

Patel's comments demonstrate the heterogeneity of the state and its officials (Gupta 1995). Its formidable rules, made by ministers and judges, allow its engineers to open up profitable and yet deeply sympathetic regimes of access for the urban poor. I found it interesting how Patel argued that those excluded by the rules were "anyway getting water." As per his reasoning, they were accommodated not by making the laws more inclusive but by *not implementing* exclusive laws. Looking the other way when settlers do not follow the rules enables them to access water and to live in the city. Yet making rules settlers cannot follow is also a way of managing their demands. When settlers get water connections using fake documents they cannot complain about these for fear that their subterfuge might be found out and their connections disconnected.

The rules were also generative of the power of state officials. In a subsequent interview, Patel did acknowledge that the water rules rendered the application process rather exploitative. Through bribes and gifts, it enriched state officials at the expense of the poor. He recognized that the city water network's formal procedures continue to require the discretionary power of politicians and other "anti/social workers." He was aware that the city's water infrastructure provides one more platform for the performance and legitimation of patronage relations in the settlements.

Such relations are not only necessary for unrecognized settlers to get water. Residents living in recognized settlements with legal entitlements also engage councilors and politicians to help them. This help is a necessary component of the system's *unwritten* rules. Applications for water connections are generally approved if they are accompanied by a letter of support from the politician "requesting" the engineer's help. These letters are not required by the city's formal procedures. Yet they are necessary to the water system. Talking in his public sector office, a former Shiv Sena leader, Mr. Surve, explained the system to me. I had asked why plumbers did not go to the water authority directly. Why did they first stop by the party office for a letter of support? He replied:

> The BMC can sanction water connections without the councilor or the Shakha Pramukh [the Shiv Sena's branch office head]. But if it does so, then they [the councilors] won't get any *maal* [stuff, colloq. for money] in the middle. So they have created a "system" [English usage]. The system is that you tell the councilor or political party member that you want a water connection. That way, the local councilor is respected, he will get *maal*.... So the system—of ration cards, forms,

etcetera—these are all *procedures*, so [that] people say it's better to go to the councilor [first]. Some people say it's about the money. There is the money, but that is not the only thing going on.

As per city water rules, settlement residents of recognized and declared settlements should be able to connect to the water system without councilors calling in favors. But, as Surve argues, that is not how the system has been made. It requires procedures that depend on personal networks of legitimation and endorsement in order to work.[39] Therefore, even once urban residents achieve state recognition after years of delicate political and social maneuvering, their illiberal relations with councilors or political parties continue to play a significant role. Patronage politics run right through the state's water system. They explain not only why very senior engineers are required to approve water connections but also why the councilor is required to sanction water connections in the settlement. The in/formal permissions that are required from both parties entangle politicians in webs of political obligations with municipal engineers.

As Surve points out (and Yusuf described earlier), these relations exceed the financial considerations that accompany them. They also trouble any attempt to characterize them as belonging to kinetic cities (Dwivedi and Mehrotra 1995) or political society (see chapter 4). As councilors and other politicians insert themselves as gatekeepers, they secure the complicity of not only engineers but also the resident populations that they serve. It is a discretionary system, established through the supply of water. Its various unspoken requirements—of councilor or social worker recommendation letters, for example—appear important to access water legally, and to get the bills, documents, and papers that settlers need to formally establish their rights. Therefore, to make themselves durable homes in the city, those living in Mumbai's settlements need to engage in a series of practices that transgress the boundaries of legitimacy on the one hand and liberal government on the other.

Multiplicities

The cities of Mumbai have been made by traversing across the boundaries of il/legality and il/liberalism. In the short history of Jogeshwari in this chapter, it is clear that settlers, like other residents of the city, have engaged in practices beyond those authorized by the law at certain times and claimed laws at others. In tracing the dynamic histories of these processes, attention is given to the diverse roles that the illiberal politics of patrons, dadas, and other big men continue to play in accommodating and housing Mumbai's residents, *together* with discourses and movements for housing rights. While the state has not, as yet, produced large public housing projects, its officials, motivated at once by sympathy and money, have frequently assisted in discrete yet significant projects to hydrate the city's more marginal residents.

The exigencies of adult suffrage on the one hand and those of multilateral aid on the other have articulated with the everyday practices of settlement to compel the postcolonial state to recognize millions of settlers and deliver them municipal services. They have also compelled the state to desist from demolishing settled communities without providing rehabilitation. As a closer study of Jogeshwari indicates, these interventions have improved the quality of life for many living in its settlements. Nevertheless, the dramatic expansion of liberal regimes of politics has not necessarily entailed the diminishment of diverse political subjectivities or the role of social and political relations beyond those sanctioned by the state. Instead, the continued vitality of these relations has been invigorated by the discrete promises and infrastructures of citizenship. As residents are called upon by the forms and norms of the state to connect to its infrastructures, they do so in ways that also revitalize the powers of various other authorities—particularly big men in settlements.

As such, the relations of patronage and political society as they appear here are not constitutive of outside or other liberal polities necessarily diminished by the expansion of liberal rule. The bodies that constitute political society are not discrete from those of civil society, nor are their practices as distinct. Instead, as settlers mobilize their different and dividuated subjectivities to establish lives, forms, documents, and water connections in the city, their practices reveal how the illiberal relations of patronage, clientship, and friendship are not antecedents of liberal rule that are either outside or encompassed by the processes of democracy and citizenship. These diverse relations are often reproduced with liberal rule in the city. They make room for diversity, difference, and inequality in and among the urban polity. They alternately enable or foreclose the formation of liberal citizens.

To recognize the multiply enacted and yet partial, dividuated histories of political and civic engagement in the settlements of Mumbai is more than a simple scholarly endeavor. It forces us to acknowledge the uncomfortable procedures through which some settlers have claimed and now seek to transcend their right to homes in the city by demanding that they be counted as subjects of the state's care.

City water department engineers are nervous about what these recognitions do, both to the structures of property ownership in the city and also to the ways in which the department is called upon to serve an ever-growing population. They work hard to maintain the line between political society, governed by humanitarian exception, and civil society, governed by the rules and norms the water department employs to deny settlers documented water connections. Living between bulldozers, state service entitlements, and incentives, settlers, like most of Mumbai's residents, live at once in multiple regimes of sovereignty and rationality. Their work produces cities that accommodate inequality and difference in ways that trouble the deeply cultural, liberal imaginary of urban life. As they blur the boundaries of civic and political life through diverse relational and documentary practices, their work not only produces the effect of state, as Akhil Gupta (1995) has suggested. It also produces the appearance of the citizen—a particular kind of governmental subject who, through papers, petitions, and politics, makes moral and legal claims to membership in the postcolonial city.

Interlude. Renewing Water

There are deep histories of habitation in and around Jogeshwari. The area is named after the Jogeshwari caves built in the fifth century. Archaeologist Anita Rane-Kothare (2012) explains that many of the caves found in the northern suburbs of Mumbai were part of a network of rest areas, built for Buddhist pilgrims traveling between different monasteries en route to Bassein (now called Vasai). Today, settlers continue to use the caves for worship, particularly around the Mahashivratri festival. A couple of kilometers from the Jogeshwari caves, the Kanheri caves are today hidden deep in Borivali National Park, Over the last three decades, the Kanheri and Jogeshwari caves have been increasingly surrounded by the city and its inhabitants (Zérah and Landy 2013). The Kanheri caves were once an important Buddhist site, and were occupied continuously between the first and seventh centuries A D. Over four thousand monks lived in the caves through the year. Constructed on and out of solid basalt rock, the Kanheri caves, like the Jogeshwari caves, are located on ground that is particularly good for storing and drawing water. As the city water department finds itself at its limits in provisioning water to the city, activists within and outside the government have been pointing to the "indigenous systems" of water harvesting in the Kanheri caves to propose older paradigms of water infrastructure anew (see Morrison 2015):

> The Kanheri cave has 109 cells cut into the flank of the hill. Each cell has a plinth that served as a bed for monks. Outside each cell, there are reservoirs and several lines of channels fed rainwater into these channels and several tanks—each can retain from 15,000 to 50,000 litres of water—carved into the rock inside the cave. Kubal explained . . . that in ancient times, water was an integral part of the lifestyle of people and rainwater was not wasted. "But with urbanization, the practice of storing water came to an end. We have lost track of maintaining the water system. And the traditional knowledge of rainwater harvesting is missing today," he said. ("2000-Year-Old-Model May Be Answer to City's Water Woes," *Economic Times*, September 8, 2007)

As manifest in the news article, activists are alarmed by the precarious condition of water resources in cities and in the country, and have been insisting on recuperating the viability and ubiquity of premodern infrastructures. In their pioneering book *Dying Wisdom*, the Center for Science and Environment based in Delhi has suggested that traditional water harvesting systems are efficient and less risky modes of provisioning water in areas where the management of these infrastructures is more decentralized (Agarwal and Narain 1997). There is much to be said for these approaches. Even so, they make city water engineers very nervous. Engineers working in the hydraulic engineering department are unsure of how they might govern and control water that emerges from a more decentralized production system. They worry this water would be harder to regulate, treat, purify, and manage. Indeed, Mumbai's forgotten wells are sometimes forgotten because the city can neither keep track of them, nor is it as easy for engineers to manage them.

3. TIME PÉ (ON TIME)

Urban living is ceaselessly rhythmed by its excesses and scarcities; its dispersals and immobilisations; its homogeneity and heterogeneity; its total boundlessness and the totalitarian nature of its endless restrictions; its frequent moments of violent efferves-cence and the boredom of endless waiting. —FILIP DE BOECK 2015

Residents of Mumbai have long been governed by the time of water. As a child growing up in the city, my mornings would often begin at 7:00 a.m. with a wake-up call to bathe. "The water has come!" my mother would shout, by way of telling us to begin our day. Because the water arrived only half an hour before the school bus, she was understandably concerned that one of her three children might miss the bus if we did not shower immediately. Her announcement was the second one to rouse us. Minutes before her words, our bathroom walls and pipes would make the announcement themselves. The mixtures of air and water would gush into the empty toilet cistern, noisily clanking and creaking pipes along the way. Taps we sometimes left open and dry the night before poured water with a force that headily announced that it was a new day, that it was past 6:45 in the morning, that it was "time to get up!" For us, and for many others, water supply marked time. We, like others who lived in the city, collected our daily rations from the state at water time. Our ability to do so made it possible to live in the city, to drink, cook, bathe, and wash—all acts necessary to rejuvenate and reproduce our lives for another day.

For much of its history, Mumbai's water has been delivered to residents on a water supply schedule. Divided into different water supply zones, each neighborhood receives water for a fixed period of time. Conditioned by scarcity, the city water department actively manages supply, regulating how much and when water is delivered to each neighborhood. To the extent that neighborhoods in Mumbai are varied (high-rise buildings and settlements frequently adjoin each other), diverse classes of residents are together subject to the peculiar temporality of the intermittent water supply produced by the BMC.

Since my childhood, water's daily arrival in my parents' home has lost some of its magic. Over time, my parents, like those inhabiting many other households in the city, have installed hardware that enables us to ignore the city's water schedule. Today, overhead storage tanks, non-return valves, and auto-switch pumps in each bathroom draw water automatically from the apartment building's underground sumps, suction pumps, and tanks.[1] Now, when the water "comes," this assemblage of pumps, tanks, and pipes serially and (mostly) silently collects and stores as much water as possible, and directs it to the various bathrooms, faucets, and the kitchen throughout the day.

Like those who live in buildings, settlers share water connections with their neighbors and collectively pay the city their water dues. However, because settlers are connected to the city by a different and differentiating regime of pipes and policies, they often cannot draw on the same techno-political arrangements as those living in buildings. They are not permitted (neither legally nor logistically) the construction of large underground sumps or overhead storage tanks. Their shared connections are often much smaller, making the volume of water that arrives every day significantly more contested. Settlers are formally not allowed to extend water connections from the shared line into their homes. Even those who go ahead and do so often find that their individual lines do not have the pressure necessary to fill the vessels in more than one home at once. At water time, therefore, they are sometimes compelled to order themselves in a series, collecting water for twenty or so minutes each. Therefore, it continues to be especially critical for settlers to be present to collect water at the right time. When the water "comes," members of each household collect and store their daily supplies separately in a dense agglomeration of water containers—drums, tubs, buckets, and vessels.

In this chapter, I attend to the ways in which Mumbai's water infrastructure produces and scales time in the city.[2] The intermittent water supply— its schedules and varying pressures—produces a particular arrangement of time and tempo in the city, and particularly in the settlements. For settlers, water time is an active social event, requiring negotiation with the city's engineers and councilors (to extend, expand, or shift water time), neighbors (to distribute water fairly between them), and family members (to decide whose responsibility it is to collect water). The peculiar and very temporary daily appearance of water is often a cause of stress for those (most often women) who are responsible for obtaining the household's water. The viability of the household depends on not only the way in which they can arrange and clear their daily schedule of competing demands but also their ability to manage amiable relations with the neighbors with whom they share connections. These social negotiations for and over time—with family members, neighbors, and city workers—are a central feature of living in the city that are produced through water's emergent temporality.

In her detailed and careful analysis of socialist Romania, anthropologist Katherine Verdery (1996) has drawn attention to the way in which time was made, controlled, and governed by the state. In Romania, officials sought to efficiently regulate the distribution of basic needs and consumption of vital resources. Verdery describes how the Romanian state did so by controlling the time of its populations. It compelled citizens to line up for essential provisions. These forms of regulation produced the effects they sought to control. As bodies were immobilized, waiting to gather allocations of essential provisions, the state's seizures of time, Verdery points out, "produced incapacity, and therefore enhanced the state's power" (1996, 46). By drawing attention to the "etatization of time" and the ways in which state time was inhabited, formed, and contested by its subjects, Verdery provides a compelling account of the temporal connections between the techniques of government and those of the self.

Verdery's account of time and waiting in Romania is especially instructive in the case of Mumbai, as state officials control and govern the city's water supply and its population by governing time. An attention to water time helps describe how experts, urban water, and urban residents are made and managed. Further, as the city water utility has begun projects to provide not intermittent but continuous (or 24/7) water supply, changing the time of water is also a critical project of reform. The project to make water available not on time but all the time is a project to produce not only a new kind of state but also a new kind of urban subject—a citizen–consumer "liberated" from the exigencies of water time. I delve into the technopolitics of the new proposal, and particularly the contentions among engineers, later in the book. Here, I extend Verdery's work by describing how infrastructure's times effect gendered subjectivities in the settlement. I explore the consequences of how and why settlers in Mumbai do not demand water all the time. Configured by daily experiences and political imaginaries of waste, excess, and cost, they do not object to the state's management of water time. Instead, they demand modest quantities of water "on time." Accordingly, water time is a time of normalization, a temporal regime through which gendered and classed forms of personhood are produced and reinscribed.

Making Water Time

To manage water scarcity, engineers at Mumbai's water department distribute fixed allocations of water (quotas) to the city's residents on a supply schedule. By managing water schedules, engineers are able to control the volumes and quantities of water distributed to different urban populations. As such, the water schedule creates a distribution regime through which differentiated citizens and cities are produced in Mumbai.

While the schedule is sought to be drawn up and implemented from the planning cell of the water department (Bjorkman 2015), in practice this schedule is put together by assistant engineers in each of the city's twenty-four wards, together with senior engineers in the zonal offices of the city's water department. Based on the existing network and on the location of pipes and valves, engineers subdivide each ward into several zones. They try to calculate each zone's water demand as a complex function of population, housing type, and commercial/industrial demand. In performing these calculations and producing the water schedule, engineers exercise and establish their authority as public officials—experts who allocate water by recognizing different kinds of residents and providing them with different quantities of water at different times of the day. By materializing the schedule, by moving water to various parts of the system, city engineers and key workers are a powerful location in which class and cultural difference are recognized and produced.

For example, engineers do not provide for all citizens equally. For the purposes of their calculations, those living in buildings are allocated 120 liters per person per day (LPCD). Those living in settlements, meanwhile, are allocated 90 LPCD.[3] Furthermore, engineers do not (and refuse to) count all residents in the settlements. Domestic help, construction workers, illegitimate renters, or other "floating populations" are often not included in the state's various calculations. By not counting "floating populations" (see chapter 1), engineers produce a lower water demand figure[4]—a more convenient figure that allows them slightly more flexibility and possibility in creating and managing a water schedule.

Having (under)estimated demand, engineers then focus on the existing infrastructure of the water network—its pipe diameters, pressure, and elevation—to determine how much time is necessary to deliver each zone's share of water. The higher the pressure (or the larger the pipe diameter), the less time is necessary to fulfill the calculated demand of a particular zone. The duration required to meet each zone's demand then has to be balanced with not only the demands of other zones but also the material demands of the water network. That is to say that in directing water to different neighborhoods at different times of the day, the city water utility needs to ensure that water is not drawn out of the reservoirs or from proximate service mains too quickly. Either situation would cause a debilitating loss of pressure in the system.[5]

Therefore, to ensure that residents in settlements are able to open their taps and receive water with sufficient pressure, engineers stagger distribution between zones, delivering water to each zone at a different time of the day. For example, they deploy the same service main to deliver water to adjacent settlements in Sunder Nagar (see figure 5). By operating valves, the higher levels get water in the early morning, and lower levels in the late morning. The differentiated water times allow engineers to maintain the pressure necessary to deliver water to different parts of the network. Engineers, therefore, must decide not only how much water people will receive but also when they will receive it and for how long. Places deemed to be of commercial or industrial importance are frequently privileged in the schedule. For instance, in the schedule shown in figure 3.1, the Maharashtra Industrial Development Corporation (MIDC) and Mumbai's Chhatrapati Shivaji International Airport are each mandated to receive water for twenty-four hours a day. Most other zones receive water between three and four hours a day, while some settlements get water for just under three hours (see Jogeshwari East). The difference in water time and supply duration is a powerful illustration of how structural inequality is produced through daily activity in the city.

The timetable shown in figure 5 divides K-East ward into seventeen water supply zones. The four columns of the schedule list the water supply zone, the normal and actual times of supply, and the reservoir from which the water is sourced (e.g., V-I denotes Veravali One reservoir). Each water supply zone is made into a discrete hydraulic entity through the installation of valves at the boundaries of each zone.

The water schedule is realized through the work of municipal employees, called chaviwallas (key people), whose primary job is to turn the valves on the water pipes as per the schedule drawn up by engineers. Forty-five valves need to be turned at least twice every day in K-East ward alone to distribute water to each zone at its assigned time. Beginning at 7:00 in the morning, the

WARD	WATER SUPPLY ZONE	NORMAL TIME	PRESENT TIME	REMARKS Sou...
1	Jogeshwari (East),	4.45 to 8.45	4.45 to 7.30	VI ~ Andheri (E.)
2.	Sahar Village	5.00 to 9.00	5.00 to 8.30	Tansa West
3.	Bhavani Nagar Marol	10.00 to 17.00	11.00 to 2.00	VIII ~ Andheri M.I.D.C.
4.	Mahakali Road	5.00 to 9.00	5.00 to 8.30	VII ~ Parla
5.	Vile Parle (East)	16.00 to 20.00	16.00 to 19.30	VII ~ Parla
6.	Andheri Sahar Road	19.00 to 23.00		Tansa West
7.	Gunravali (High Level)	16.00 to 20.00	16.00 to 19.30	VI ~ Andheri (E.)
8.	Parsi Panchayat Road & A.K. Road	20.00 to 24.00	19.30 to 23.15	VI ~ Andheri (E.)
9.	Marol Pipe Line & Marol Maroshi Road Military Road, Vijay Nagar, J.B. Nag r, Charatsingh Colony	19.00 to 23.00	19.00 to 23.00	Tansa West
10.	Lok group, Hill View	19.00 to 23.00	19.00 to 23.00	Go Chord
11.	M.I.D.C.	24 Hours	12 Hours	VIII ~ Andheri M.I.D.C.
12.	Airport Authority	24 Hours	24 Hours	V III ~ Bandra
13.	Sunder Nagar (Higher & Lower Level)	7.00 to 10.00	6.00 to 8.00 & 8.00 to 10.00	VHL ~ Mahakali
14.	Kajupada, A.G. Link Road, Chakala	16.30 to 20.30	16.00 to 20.00	VII ~ Parla
15.	Pump Supply Shiv Tekdi (Pratap Nagar)	5.00 to 9.00	8.30 to 10.30	VI ~ Jogeshwari (W)
	Samarth Nagar	5.00 to 9.00	4.45 to 7.30	VI ~ Andheri (E.)
16.	Jogeshwari Link Road, Agarwal Nagar, Pratap Nagar (Part)	19.00 to 23.00	19.00 to 22.30	VI ~ Jogeshwari (W)
17.	Bandrekar Wadi		4.45 to 7.30	VI ~ Jogeshwari (W)

FIGURE 5. The water schedule of K-East ward.

chaviwallas work in three eight-hour shifts, traveling across the ward through-out the day to turn valves off and on at scheduled times. The combination of these ninety turns, accomplished over a twenty-four-hour day, divert and materialize water times and hydraulic zones in the ward. The everyday imple-mentation of these water plans establishes not only the city's urban water system but also its residents' peculiar experiences of time in the city.

I acquired a better sense of the critical (and rather unsung) work of chavi-wallas when I accompanied them on their rounds in September 2007. Fol-lowing my repeated requests, the ward engineer, Mr. Patankar, had agreed to arrange a ride-along with the chaviwallas as they worked. On the day of our field trip, I arrived at Patankar's office a few minutes after eight, in time to join the workers for their first shift.[6] While no other workers were there yet, I was pleasantly surprised to find Patankar already present, alert, and actively working. Dressed in the trademark blues I had come to associate with the Municipal Corporation's midlevel engineers (light blue shirt, dark blue trousers), Patankar was comparing the readings entered on the green-colored cards used by meter readers to record consumption with the readings of water consumption that appeared on bills generated by the city's new computer billing system. While I was busy wondering about the kinds of discrepancies and disjunctures that made it necessary for Patankar, an engineer, to audit computer-generated bills, the chaviwallas called to tell us that they were waiting for us at the Marol Pipeline. Patankar replied that we would be there in a few minutes. He very quickly wrapped up his work, sat me on his bike, and rode us to where the large, gray municipal truck was parked. Seven men were waiting for us, having tea. Patankar parked his bike near the truck and we quickly got into the front seat. The workers looked confused. "Where shall we go, sir?" the driver asked Patankar. "Go on your rounds like you always do," he told the driver. "He is a student; he wants to see what you do." The confusion revealed the unusualness of both the request and also of Patankar's presence in the truck. The driver started the truck and drove to the first valve, at Sahar village.

Sahar village sits between the cargo and passenger terminals of the airport (or more accurately, the cargo and passenger terminals of the international airport were built on Sahar village). We made our first stop right by a little bridge. The city's water mains run under the bridge. Some of these pipes have been cemented over by settlers, who live directly on top of them. Though they lived on top of high-pressure water mains, their access to water was regulated by a valve that released water to them between 5:30 and 8:30 in the morning.

It was 8:30 a.m., and the workers had arrived to turn off the valve. We got out of the truck and walked to the side of the bridge. Hidden in plain sight, the valves of the municipal water network were located just beneath the surface of the city's streets. The workers inserted a large "key" and crank through the metal plate on the road. Working together, two of them begin to turn the crank. Two others later joined them. I marveled at this mundane operation. Using their own physical labor, workers turned the valve shut. As they did so, water, the enabler of urban life, was moved, swirled, shifted, and diverted right under our feet. These hidden flows structure the everyday life of the city. As water changed course, new zones of hydraulic pressure were enabled, and almost unseen (but for the chaviwallas that stood over the pipes), different parts of the city were thereby made to live.

The daily manual labor of chaviwallas gives pause to contemporary accounts that frequently situate government "at a distance"—embedded in laws, policies, procedures, and plans—especially under the sign of neoliberalism

FIGURE 6. Two pairs of chaviwallas turn the valves of underground city water pipes while the mukadam (foreman) looks on.

(see Khan 2006). Through technologies like the survey, the plan, and the development program, scholars have drawn on work by Foucault to show how the art of liberal government is performed through these technologies, which merge the "techniques of domination" with "techniques of the self" (Burchell 1996, 20), where governmental dispositions are enacted and regulated by the subjects of this government.

Nevertheless, as they proceed to turn subterranean valves on and off daily in the city's various neighborhoods, the appearance of chaviwallas makes a critical site of state regulation both proximate and visible to populations. Their daily labor reveals how biopolitical government in Mumbai takes place not just at a distance or through self-governing individuals but also through intimate material and physical forms of labor conducted by hundreds of employees of the city's water department.

The chaviwallas returned to the truck, and we moved on toward our next stop. By now more comfortable with their supervisor present, the workers took the opportunity to show the engineer some problem spots in the system. We came to the second stop. Here the pipes were *above* ground, running parallel to a road and flanked by buildings. One of the chaviwallas made his way to the pipes with a wrench in his hand. As he turned the valve, I asked Patankar whether the valves were ever turned without his authority. What stopped anyone from turning valves off and on themselves? Patankar agreed. He told me that it happens sometimes. When I looked puzzled, he continued, cynically: "This is in India, no, people won't be punished!" He went on to explain that if they found valves are open or closed not per the schedule, they would catch the person doing it and send them to the police. Patankar confessed that the perpetrator would likely pay a bribe to release them from the police station, but yet, "even paying the bribe is a punishment."

Patankar was not afraid to point out the helplessness of the water department in monitoring and prosecuting unauthorized manipulations of the water system. The government was not the only one who controlled its valves, and it was possible for residents to turn valves and control the network without the department's knowledge. Provoked by social workers and city politicians, intransigent populations were difficult to discipline. The police were corrupt, he told me. Nevertheless, this is not to say they were not effective. Patankar pointed out that even though it was not official, the bribe that the policemen would demand dissuaded residents from tampering with the valves. Even as police officers put this money in their pockets, their private collections asserted the punitive power of the state.

As we proceeded on our tour of the chaviwallas' work, we spoke of the special negotiations that being a chaviwalla entails. Their work required not only a certain *metis*, a field knowledge and sense of how to turn a valve (too much force damages it), as well as an understanding of how to most effectively get to places on time, but also sufficient social engagement (Scott 1998). It was difficult to deliver water on time every day. The everyday life of the city and the materiality of the street presented many challenges (see Barak 2009). Often, traffic made it difficult to reach the valves on time. One day, the chaviwallas could not turn a valve because a car had parked over it, and many people did not receive water that day. When the chaviwallas returned the next day to turn the valve, an angry group gathered around them, threatening to beat them up for their transgression. The residents had been waiting all day for the water to come.

This was an exceptional incident, a story told largely to convince me of the extraordinary work that goes into making the system function. I was receptive to the message. In the eighteen continuous months that I conducted fieldwork, I seldom heard of the system totally shutting down.[7] This was remarkable. Eight hundred valves are operated at least twice daily in the city (once in each direction). Taken together, a valve is turned somewhere in the city between one and two times every minute, all day, every day. Yet most of the time the infrastructure works. Residents expect and receive water daily.

Like all infrastructures, this is a vibrant, vital, heaving system—one that seems to have a life of its own, a life that is nevertheless brought into being and (not quite completely) managed by humans (see Bennett 2010). It is enabled by human labor, gravity, and machines. Yet, it is not a stable system of fixed and continuous flows. As valves turn, water is channeled in different directions, constantly diverted and rearranged. Its rapidly changing movements send the bulk meters, installed on the distribution mains, into a tizzy.[8] Pipes open and close. Leaks appear when valves are turned one way, and then disappear when they are turned off. Engineers, consultants, and experts are unable to map and measure water amid these constantly changing flows (see chapter 5).

Because water is vital to urban life, the infrastructure and all of its human and mechanical parts need to keep working all year. It needs to work through the heat of the city's summer and the floods of its monsoon. When there is a fire in the city, chaviwallas are deployed to turn valves, so that the fire department's nearby hydrants will have sufficently pressured water. When gunmen attacked the Taj Mahal and Oberoi hotels in 2008, setting off fires and explosions, it was not just the police and fire department that were pressed into action. Water engineers rushed through the city, trying to work a combination of valves that would produce enough pressure for the water from the city's fire hydrants to reach the upper floors of the burning hotels. Likewise, during the unprecedented floods of 2005, when most of the city was underwater, chaviwallas still had to do their rounds, driving through an inundated city and inserting their keys through a few feet of water on the flooded road so that water could flow out of city taps. Despite all of these uncertainties, people in the city most often receive their water in a timely fashion. That water generally arrives on time speaks not only to the power of the system but also to the reliability of state employees.

Changing Times

Chaviwallas are a critical locus of state labor and produce the city's intermittent water supply system with commendable regularity. Through the work of materializing the water schedule, the chaviwallas govermentalize time in the city. As they make water available to households by turning valves, they not only bring the state to bear on intimate regimes of domestic provisioning—

when clothes are washed or whether people bathe or drink. They also render public the everyday ways in which water is used by marginalized settlers in the city.

To governmentalize time, state officials draw up and deliver water on a schedule. While scheduled water times are regular, they are also always shifting. Note on the water schedule (see figure 5) that the shorter "present times" of supply are *typed* into the schedule and are distinct and different from "normal times." This suggests that the "present time" is not a temporary stopgap measure. It has a past and also a future. That the "present time" is different from the "normal time" also demonstrates that the water schedule ironically needs to be in a constant state of flux to keep working.

There are many reasons for the constant recalibration of the water schedule. First, the quantities of bulk water delivered to the city are reviewed and revised every day by the water department's Planning and Control cell. Maintenance works or leakages on the water mains, for instance, constantly constrain how much water can flow. Furthermore, with the city dependent entirely on the monsoons for replenishing and recharging the dams (see chapter 1), engineers in charge of planning the city's water supply are always calibrating how much water can safely be released in the summer months before the monsoon, without compromising future supply. Counting the city's water reserves in "days of supply," the department rations the quantity of water released from the dams so that the city may have enough water until the estimated arrival of the monsoon rains.

Of course, the monsoon is notoriously hard to predict. As the lake levels diminish, engineers become increasingly concerned over whether the reserves will be sufficient. What if the rains are late? Will the city need to be evacuated? Therefore, *every year*, as the monsoon approaches (and lakes reach critical levels), engineers in Planning and Control institute water cuts. As less water enters the city's service reservoirs, engineers in city wards are compelled to react to upstream water cuts by enacting cuts of their own. They do this by reducing the duration of water supply to each zone. In these zones, the water "goes away" earlier, causing considerable concern, most particularly among settlers.

Through the rationing produced by the water schedule, the state produces "a redistributive system that delivers power into the hands of those persons or bureaucratic segments that dispose of large pools of resources to allocate" (Verdery 1996, 45). The water schedule first requires people to wait for water and then to hurriedly mobilize around its collection and storage. When settlers do not receive sufficient water, they often make their claims on the water department by making claims on time—by asking that the department extend, change, or alter the allotted water time.

Patankar said as much when I asked about the difficulties of managing the water schedule. He tries to optimize the schedule in such a way that people stop shouting (or shout less). Pressured by both residents on the one hand and engineers in the planning department on the other, the schedule is always changing. As a result, even though the schedule is intended to produce regularity (an expectation of when water will "come"), it also produces uncertainty. Will water come for long enough? Who will not get water if it doesn't? Uncertain about the time and duration of its appearance, settlers, like their neighbors living in buildings, collect all the water they can (and sometimes more water than they need) during supply hours. Who knows when it will come again?

Thus, water time not only governs social life in the city but also produces water use practices that contribute to the very same water scarcity that schedules were enacted to resolve. Taken together, the practices of city residents and engineers make time an intensely contested political terrain.

Social Time

There are two times of the day. There are the four hours of water supply, when all of us, very good friends even, are each other's enemies. And then there are the other twenty hours, when we are the best of friends, when we would do anything to help each other. —RAFIQ BHAI, September 2009

When water comes out of the tap, these relations of ours . . . change. —SHARIF, 2008

By turning valves with their keys, chaviwallas create water time—a time when residents of settlements and high-rises alike collect their daily supplies of water.[9] Water time is an especially stressful time for many settlers in the areas where I conducted fieldwork. Called on by city policies and infrastructural arrangements to collect water themselves from shared water lines, water time simultaneously enables settlers to live in the city while requiring them to mobilize social relations (with neighbors and friends) to negotiate access to water. Anxiety over whether water will be sufficient to meet their household's needs—whether it will come for a sufficient amount of time and with sufficient pressure—often makes these relations strained and contentious. As settlers from each household try to collect enough water to meet their daily needs, they risk fracturing the durable and extensive network of social relations that they depend on to survive.

The state water schedule calibrates and composes a "social time"—a shared sense of experience and time in the settlement. As a time shared by a group, water time "orients individuals' sense of time" (Greenhouse 1996, 27) and compels collective social activity—a tense collaborative endeavor of collecting, and storing water in different households. When water flows out of taps in settlements at water time, it reproduces and reconfigures existing social relations in the settlement. Here, I illustrate how the negotiations that water time requires "call out" particular and differentiated experiences of personhood (Althusser 1971; Bergson 1921). To demonstrate the extraordinarily diverse set of experiences it produces, I describe the water work of three women as they live through and with water time.

EASY TIME

Kamla tai had lived in Jogeshwari for much of her life. She had grown up in the area, married, and had two children. When I visited her house for the first time in 2008, I noted that it was rather small and filled with all the things that typically characterize one- and two-room houses in the settlements: roll-up beds, posters on the walls, cooking vessels, a stove, a washing place, a bureau that doubled as a bed, a small loft to accommodate a sleeping body, some clothes, and schoolbooks. Yet Kamla tai's chief problem was not space. It was water. Her water line did not deliver water with sufficient pressure, causing her "tension" every day. The problem had gotten so severe that Kamla tai had resigned from her position as a women's rights activist at a city NGO so that she could take care of her household—oversee the education of her two young children and also collect water. In our conversations we found it quite ironic that her work outside the home—on matters of gender inequality, no less—were proscribed by domestic duties in the home.

Kamla tai's family subsequently responded to their water difficulties by moving into a new home, also on rent, just a few doors down from her old place. Here, she seemed happy. The house was larger. It had a little alley on both sides and a small, open space right in front of it. There was more natural light. More importantly, however, the water line was much better. She told me with great relief that the water arrived at around 3:30 p.m. every day, and remained until 11:00 at night. Moreover, the municipal tap was located just outside her home and was shared with a group that included only six others. Because of the extraordinarily fortunate duration of water supply and also the size of the group, Kamla tai spoke of how little trouble they had encountered over water. They did not even need electric pumps.

FIGURE 7. Storing water. Residents repurpose commercial three-hundred-liter chemi-cal drums to store their daily water supplies outside their homes. Ubiquitous in most settlements, the drums are purchased from the second-hand market, where they have been collected and cleaned following their first life as containers for oils and other petrochemicals.

When it was her turn to collect water (generally at around 5:00 in the evening), Kamla tai would unroll her PVC pipe and attach one end to the common tap. As water flowed through the other end, she would sequentially fill her various storage vessels. First, she would fill the smaller *handis*, buck-ets and bottles, used most often in the kitchen for drinking, cooking, and washing. Then she filled the large, three-hundred-liter blue drum that (unlike other households) she stored inside her house. In about twenty minutes, her work was done. Together, the different containers stored five hundred liters of water, most of which she used before water time the next day.

Kamla tai used most of her water in the morning. Mornings were when families in the settlement used water not only for bodily activities—for the toilet and to bathe—but also for cooking and dish washing. "*Jévan, nashta, angol, bhandi*," she told me of her morning chores, all involving water. "Lunch, breakfast, bathing, dishes." She would make lunch in the morning (so that her husband could take it to work), together with breakfast, all while rushing

FIGURE 8. Washing clothes outside on a rainy day. Photo by Govindi Gudilu.

to get the children ready for school. Soon after they left, she would begin to
wash their clothes and to sweep and wash the floors.

Kamla tai was not alone in her preferences to do most of her water chores
in the morning. By 10:00 a.m., the alleys of the settlement would shimmer
with water and were soaked in the talk and rhythm of women doing laundry
on their stoops and stairs. After meals, pots and pans would also be washed
outside the home. Washing was a social time—a time that women used to
exchange stories of local events and festivals, the temples they visited, and
concerns about their children in school.

Surprised by the time and location of water work, particularly when
they had washing places inside their homes, I asked Kamla tai why women
washed *outside* in the *morning*. It was cool and fresh in the morning, she told
me. Washing outside was more pleasant. There was more space and ventila-
tion, and it prevented the fragile drains in their homes from getting clogged.
Given the size of their homes, washing outside was also a way for women
to extend their homes beyond their four walls, Kamla tai told me. In doing
so, they blurred the boundaries between home and public space, effectively
claiming the area outside their doors as their own.[10]

As she continued to speak, it became clear that washing outside was also
a public performance of good comportment. Washing clothes (and dishes)
outside allowed people to keep separate the spaces of washing (outside) and

bathing (inside). For bathing, bathrooms afforded privacy. Washing outside, meanwhile, was a demonstration, not of dirty laundry but of good moral character. It stretched the boundaries of the home and created acceptable (and even expected) ways for women to be seen outside. She explained: "Women who do not wash their clothes in the morning get noticed. . . . Other women gossip about how she is not doing her job as caretaker of the house very well. This is especially hard for working women because they only wash clothes after they get home at the end of the day." When Kamla tai describes the ways in which washing is necessary to produce social membership, she is describing what Bourdieu would identify as habitus—a structuring structure that is produced by "respecting the collective rhythm" of the group (Bourdieu 1977, 162). Women were required to wash their clothes in the morning to perform their social belonging. This not only made them proper neighbors but also demonstrated that they were good wives.

This, in and of itself, is not peculiar to Mumbai. Kamla tai's story was not dissimilar to one I had heard from a friend's grandmother in Germany a few years before. Living in a small village near Frankfurt, she spoke of how important it was to be seen hanging washed clothes outside in the mornings. People would gossip if a woman did not hang clothes at the right time of day. Only lazy women did not do so, she had said.

Back in Mumbai, Kamla tai seemed slightly uncomfortable telling me about this. I wondered if it was because other women had been gossiping about her in this way. Having been employed by an NGO previously, she would not often have been at home to wash clothes during the day. Moreover, while she had recently stopped going to work, she had also acquired a washing machine, making her work of washing clothes much easier. Now, all she had to do was manually fill the washing machine with water prior to the start of the cycle. Her new machine not only made it easier for her to wash clothes at any time but also brought this performance inside the home. In so doing, it had made her a less social person among her neighbors.

Nevertheless, Kamla tai was happy with her new water situation. Its more adaptable schedule allowed her a degree of flexibility in her day. She also spoke of how water availability had effected a change in her practices. Sometimes, she put her clothes through two cycles, just to make sure that they were clean. "When we have more time, and have more water, we use more water," she said thoughtfully. She spoke to me of how her neighbor scrubbed her pots many times a day. Others washed their floors daily. Indeed, while conducting fieldwork, I often noticed how sparkling clean and well arranged the floors in settlers' homes were. They were far cleaner than many of the homes with which I was familiar in other middle- or upper-class locations. Kamla tai wondered alound if this had to do with her neighbors wanting to compensate for the image that comes with living in a slum. To elicit respect when guests visited, settlers might want to keep the insides of their homes very clean.

Therefore, the easy availability of water enabled settlers not only to produce clean, sparkling houses and bodies but also to establish their social reputations. Sufficient water allowed them to transcend the stigma of living in a settlement. By using water in the right place at the right time, the women sought to exceed the expectations of their social locations. In so doing, they reproduced gendered forms of personhood. Their production as good women depended not only on their work in the home but also on the time at which this work was carried out (see Bryson 2007). Good women were those who used water at the right times of the day and in the right place.

DIFFICULT TIMES

Kamla tai told me that she was happy with her new water situation. She was lucky. Several other homes near her had puzzling water pressure problems. For instance, in the adjacent settlement of Inquilab Nagar, Smita and her neighbors had encountered an altogether different set of issues. Her daughter, Amisha, who was a member of the youth group at Asha, the community center, invited me to Smita's home in June 2009. In our interactions at Asha, Amisha had always been a little quiet and shy. Now, at home with her mother, she appeared more calm and confident.

A TV was playing a Marathi film over the bed. The kitchen was on the other side of a partition wall, chock full of pots, pans, and dishes. There was also an adjacent bathroom, lined with pink and green buckets. They offered me a seat on the bed and, at first, stood around me. Smita was distracted by the necessary chore of collecting water and frequently left the conversation. While she was busy ensuring that the pipe was, in fact, filling her drum, Amisha explained that she worked at a data processing center, entering pharmaceutical research into a database for an American company. She worked the evening shift—from 3:00 p.m. to 11:00 p.m. That way, she could go to college in the mornings and to work in the afternoons. Her friends also worked the evening shift, and they would all return home together—an arrangement that pleased her parents, who worried about her safety.

When Smita finally returned, she sat on a chair and began speaking immediately, confusing me at first with another researcher who had come to talk with her about slum redevelopment. Later, she recollected that I was more interested in water, but the fragility of our association reminded me of how the neighborhood had hosted many researchers in times past. In the current moment, the "slum" and particularly the emergent possibilities of real estate development occupied the concerns not just of researchers but also residents (see Anand and Rademacher 2011; Weinstein 2014).

I asked Smita to tell me about what the settlement was like when she first came to this area. I learned that she did not live at her current location right away. At first, she and her husband's family had stayed in an adjacent house, but they moved into her current home in 1992 when her husband's family left it for a state housing project. At first, things were very precarious. "There were no *facilities*," she said, using the English word. "Our houses were made from bamboo [*chatai*] and plastic." She described, in great detail, the waves of demolition her family and others had to suffer because they had illegally built homes on land that (though marked for public housing) had been lying vacant for decades. "Then we used our heads, and decided to file a case together. The lawyer cost thirty-two thousand [rupees] in 1991 [approximately US$1,000]. . . . After many years, we won the case. The judgment said that until MHADA [the public housing authority] makes permanent houses for us, that we shouldn't be moved." Following their victory in the courts, Smita and her neighbors gained some degree of surety that their homes would not be demolished. Rather than waiting for the public housing authority to do its job, they began to make material improvements. They received water connections in 1996 and electricity connections in 1997 by paying "agents" large sums of money to get their connections approved. Recalling this history, Smita reminisced about the changing times. In so doing, she too talked about the changing patterns of consumption in the settlement:

Then [in 1996] the electricity bill was 150 rupees or so. Now it's 300 or so. . . . We now have four points [sockets]—TV, fan, light, and [a couple of others for] different kitchen appliances. First we had a light, a fan, and a mixer. We had no iron then. Now we sometimes iron, too. . . . Water came in June 1996. First, when we got the connection, we had lines outside—four taps in all. It would come between 3:00 p.m. [and] 7:00 p.m. The water we would get in Jogeshwari, then, came with a pressure that you wouldn't find in all of Bombay! In ten to fifteen minutes— at most in twenty-five—the water would be filled. Now, things have changed. We use more water. Its fashion has increased.

For Smita, her water and electricity connections were directly linked to processes of state recognition. Her account illustrates the powerful ways in which water and electricity infrastructures have been critical grounds for the contestation and formation of settlements. Indexing her transformed relationship to these infrastructures, Smita used the English words *fashion* and *facility* to speak about the changing consumption practices in her home. Over time, her household has come to use water and electricity, even as it remains highly sensitive to the accompanying costs. Smita and her neighbors have since been facing water shortages. Water's "fashion" has increased, not just in the settlements but also among the middle and upper classes (like my family's neighborhood). At the same time, the lines have corroded and the schedule has been shortened, making the city's water time more precarious.

As we continued to speak, I learned that the problem for Smita has been exacerbated in Jogeshwari since new settlers moved into the area, creating an additional demand. Smita told me that a few years back, some of her neighbors responded to a state resettlement proposal and were rehoused in a public housing building constructed right next to the settlement. The homes of those resettled were to be demolished by the city authorities following their resettlement. Instead, those who were resettled promptly found new renters to move into their previous homes, turning them into sources of income. As a result, the same water network was facing additional demand—not only because of the increased consumption of those living in the area (both in the settlement *and* the nearby building) but also the additional consumption of those who had recently moved there.

Smita had a very clear sense that those resettled were doing something wrong by renting out their former homes. They were unfairly exploiting (*galat phayda*) the system. Briefly forgetting her own history of settlement, her daughter Amisha told me that the rented homes were illegal. "The BMC is supposed to [demolish] their houses after they move into the building," she said. Rather than articulating the subaltern consciousness that scholars and activists frequently attribute to "slum dwellers,"[11] Smita and Amisha expressed their difficulties with the legality of new residents—a poignant reminder of how settlements are also places of inequality and difference.

Having made some critical improvements to their lives through a combination of legal cases, surreptitious infrastructural arrangements, and various modes and means of consumption, Smita's household is no longer as unstable. She now views her other, more precarious neighbors with a measure of disdain. The social anxieties she experienced with her neighbors were produced and articulated through the social life of water. Thus, the water system not only harmonized and brought different settlers together as a community and committee that shared a water connection. It also divided them as they struggled with each other to provision enough water for their individual homes.

Seeing the newer renters as the cause of their water problems, Smita, together with some of her neighbors (who were not resettled), recently applied for a new water line. Deliberately excluding both those who had moved into the neighboring building and their renters, Smita reported that her group has collectively spent close to ninety thousand rupees (US$2,000), for the new plumbing works—taps in every home, new pipes, and so on. However, their work was suspended because city engineers refused to approve their connection to the city's water network. Smita suspects her former neighbors might have something to do with their problems at the department. "They are upset because we haven't included their tenants in the proposal," she said, "so they have gone and told the engineer that our complaints are false, that we are getting enough water and just [creating] drama to get more."

As a result, the proposal for a new connection has not been approved. Clearly upset at what she perceived to be the intransigence of city water department officials, Smita said, "The engineers should understand that our problems are real . . . that we wouldn't apply for a new connection and spend all this money if we were getting water!" The city department's unwillingness to sanction the connection, effected at least partly by a social conflict in the settlement, was a source of great difficulty for her and other residents in the area.

By the end of 2008, the forty households in Inquilab Nagar all shared a single, 1.5-inch water line. During water time, residents collect their water in sequence, by "number." If someone was second in line today, they would be third tomorrow. The last person in line would be first the next day, and the cycle would continue. But regardless of their position no one gets their full requirement of water, Smita complained. "And there's no pressure in the taps, either. We need to pull it from the pipes [using a pump]. And everyone is so stressed about it that everyone takes care of only themselves. Everyone is busy doing their own work [*Apna apna kaam mein busy hai*]. No one saves two to three *handis* for each other." Instead, owing to their water stresses, fights often break out between neighbors if they perceive each other to be taking more than their share. Smita was rather upset at how the water situation produced neighbors who did not look out or care for each other in these difficult times. They only cared to fulfill their own needs.

Right on cue, a woman whom Smita recognized came to her front door. She went to greet her. They spoke in hushed whispers, and then Smita ac-

FIGURE 9. Shared water lines, Mumbai. Water lines run just above the surface of Jogeshwari's alleys.

companied her outside. She returned after ten minutes or so to tell me of a strange coincidence. The woman, a friend of hers, lived on the other side of the new building and did not get water that day. She had come to Smita's home to request a couple of handis of water. Smita hesitatingly obliged, saying that she could have some water today, but not every time. She explained: "The water meter is shared by everybody. [The neighbors] will complain if I always give others water. One or two times is OK, but not every time. This is how things are. I can't say no and I can't say yes. She's a friend, but my neighbors will shout—that I give everybody water. If it was my own meter [as with electricity] it wouldn't be a problem. But now when forty of us share one meter then we can't just give water to anyone." Smita explained that her connection is first on the line so her water pressure is better than most. She believed it was good to share water with others. Yet her ability to do so was compromised by the fact that it was not her water to share. The water meter brought a social group into being. This group was responsible for collectively paying the water bill. Accordingly, Smita felt ambivalent about sharing water with friends that were not part of the group.

Smita's difficulties point to important ways in which the water network produces and mediates social life in the settlement (see Furlong 2011). As it moves from the municipal network and into the pipes of authorized users, water passes through a variety of states that confound easy distinctions between the public and the private, bringing many other mediating social and infrastructural collectives into being. The connection from which Smita draws water belongs to a group of which she is a part. This group—enumerated on the water department application forms as authorized and eligible—is constituted by the procedures required by the Municipal Corporation.[12] Bound by their investments, application documents, and bills, those inside the group share the water connection with one another, settle bills, and maintain pipes. Those "outside," even friends, are not easily able to obtain water from this connection.

Thus, both Kamla tai and Smita tai experienced water problems that affected their social aspirations, and the structure of their days: Kamla tai could not operate her washing machine in her old home, nor could she go to work. Smita tai had difficulty giving water to her friend and also using it in the new upwardly mobile "fashions" as befitting her household. Their difficulties show how water regimes are not entirely synchronous with social mobility. In very quotidian and yet effective ways, their water problems figure them as "slum dwellers." Both Kamla tai and Smita tai have sought to transcend these difficulties by using some combination of geographic knowledge (which pipes/homes have water), social knowledge (what to do if they stop working), and money (to pay for materials, plumbers, and engineers). Kamla tai moved to a house with better water. Smita tai was in the process of wresting a new connection from the Municipal Corporation despite the objections of her neighbors.[13]

NO TIME

Many settlers, however, do not have the means to afford new and repeated repairs to water connections. Living a few hundred yards from Smita's house in a different settlement, Anku *mausi* was no longer able to afford a regular water connection.[14] As I walked to her home with my research assistant one day, I noticed that many households in the settlement had a more precarious water system. A few dozen women were in the process of rushing to or walking from a gushing water pipe situated at the settlement's edges. Others were waiting at the pipe for their turn. As empty handis were brought to the tap, filled, and carted back to the house several times, I wondered how many trips each woman had to make back and forth every day.[15]

When I first arrived at Anku mausi's home, I learned that she, too, was down at the pipe collecting water with her children. We were told to wait and that she would be back shortly. A small mat was set down for us, and we sat in a corner of the house. I took in the surroundings. There was no window, which was not unusual, but the house was quite dark. The walls were made of a mix of tin sheets and plaster. In the dark loft over our heads, kids were doing their homework. Several other children, between the ages of three and five years old, came to the house and peered at me. I put my glasses on one of them and we played a little.

Anku mausi was a vendor who traversed various neighborhoods every day, selling combs, *bindis*, and other beauty products. As she was in her fifties, she had developed health problems and had taken the day off work. This of course did not preclude her from having to collect and carry water to her house. Shortly after 4:00 p.m. she arrived home carrying a large handi. Beads of sweat trickled down the sides of her face. Seeing us, she sat down and, wiping the sweat from her brow with her sari, began to speak with us. She seemed to be in a hurry to return to her water collection tasks, and I felt quite certain that we had arrived at an inconvenient time. But then, after noticing that her children were doing a good job of transporting large vessels of water on their heads, she began to relax.

Anku mausi had been in the area for a long time. She could not recall the exact year she had moved there but said that she had done so before having children—now, she has a big family. She had arrived with four other families. "It was all jungle," she said, adding that they would come home from work before sunset because they didn't want to walk in the dark. I asked her whether she was more scared of animals or people.[16] She said she was not scared at the time. Back then she was more naïve. Before the arrival of city water pipes, Anku mausi told me, the settlers would collect water from a nearby spring. Sometimes, when it went dry, they would dig into the mud and lay a cloth down in the hole. Clean water would percolate through the cloth, and they scooped this water into buckets for use. There were also two wells that they used, but these were situated far away from the house.[17]

Things became easier when they were finally allowed to install a tap outside. But then the tap went dry, and the bills kept coming. So they stopped paying and they stopped receiving tap water. Anku mausi had neither the money nor the patience to install a new line. "Who has three to four thousand rupees to spend for a new connection?" she asked. Neither was she convinced that spending money would solve the problem. People nearby had connections, she pointed out. "Even [for] those that do [have connections] the pressure is low." As a result, Anku mausi obtains water from a ruptured line quite a distance from her home. This line was meant to take water further up into the settlement to a different group. When the pressure dropped

FIGURE 10. Lining up for water.

and that group no longer received water in their homes, they cut their pipes at a lower elevation at some distance from their homes, and began collecting water at the base of their settlement. Now, many people line up near the un-metered, broken line to get water. Anku mausi filled in the details: "Some people had paid money for this connection, but even so, many others line up for water. You should see how long the line is. But we need this water for drinking. [At] first, the time was good. It would be between 3:30 and 10:30 p.m. Even when people came at 10:00 p.m. they would get water. Now, there is no time. It comes anytime between 3:00 and 4:30 p.m. Everyone rushes to [get] water at this time." While Anku mausi was aging and unwell, she did not complain about having to carry water back and forth. Neither did she complain about the line of women that she had to wait with and jostle through. This was part of her routine.

What she did complain about, however, was when the supply times were arbitrarily changed and shortened. Now, with as many people rushing to collect water during this condensed time, many are not able to sufficiently provide for their homes. For Anku mausi, this is even more difficult because the revised time is not one that fits easily with her work schedule. As a result, if she returns from work late or is too tired, she does not get water. On those days, she goes to her friends' houses and asks for a little water: one or two handis for the day. "They give [me] two handis. They don't say no. But how many days can this go on for?" she asked, echoing Smita's concern.

Gender and the Time of Times

The main thing in Bombay is this—water. If we don't get to eat for two days, *chalega* [It's OK/we'll keep going]. If we don't get work for eight days, that's also OK. But if we don't get water for one day, then the house won't run. . . . Everything depends on water. . . . [A twenty-four-hour water supply] will be good for people who go to work. Now if they go to work at 7:00 a.m., and the water comes at 4:00 p.m., . . . they have to return from work running, before the water [goes] away. . . . There's traffic. You don't get rickshaws. Everybody's so stressed about it. If it [water supply] becomes twenty-four hours, it will be good, very good. —SMITA TAI, June 2009

When conducting fieldwork, I had asked Smita tai about a proposal by the water department to deliver water "continuously" for twenty-four hours a day. In telling me why she supported the idea, she spoke of the way in which the current scheduled water supply demanded and produced a particular experience of time for women in the settlements, particularly for those who had paying jobs to sustain. Smita tai spoke of the ways in which settlers are constantly struggling to manage the different and demanding schedules of their workdays, their housework, and water time.

In his article on time, E. P. Thompson points to the way in which the expansion and extension of industrial clock time and the working week were predicated on the existence and subsistence of a different temporality in the home.

Such hours were endurable only because one part of the work, with the children and in the home, disclosed itself as necessary and inevitable, rather than as an external imposition. This remains true to this day, and, despite school times and television times, the rhythms of women's work in the home are not wholly attuned to the measurement of the clock. . . . The mother of young children has an imperfect sense of time and attends to other human tides. She has not yet altogether moved out of the conventions of "pre-industrial" society. (Thompson 1967, 79)

In an argument that precedes Claude Meillassoux's (1981) attention to the reproductive base of wage labor, Thompson argues that capitalism, and with it, clock time, is rendered possible due to the differentially constituted rhythm of "women's work in the home," a rhythm that is outside of clock time (see also Barak 2013). In so doing, Thompson points to the resilience of different (gendered) temporalities that continue to persist in industrial life, and upon which the performance of modern time depends.

Nevertheless, in and around settlements in Mumbai, women have to negotiate several imperfect yet significant times, *all of which* are clock times—caring for children, preparing for festivals and their attendant social obligations, work, going to the market, washing, cleaning homes, cooking, and earning wages. These times lie not necessarily outside, but alongside, those of modern capitalism in the city. Thus while Thompson is astute in pointing to the dependencies of capitalism on other temporalities of personhood, Mumbai's water infrastructure reveals how time is both clocked and "tidal" in the city. Precisely because it is scheduled by the city's water department, as water advances and retreats in city pipes, the cyclical rhythm of supply cannot be understood as a "pre-industrial time." It is a time produced by a modern, engineered water supply—a clock time that is an "external imposition" inserted deep into the diverse times that householders need to consider, negotiate, and resolve. It represents one more "dimension" of sociocultural time that settlers have to negotiate and incorporate as they compose their lives (Munn 1992).

In recent years, Mumbai's water department has been compelled to explore projects to deliver water not at scheduled times but for twenty-four hours per day (see chapter 5). Proponents of "anytime" water seek to release water from the regulations of time, nature, and the state. Proposed by the World Bank and the Asian Development Bank and heralded as a world-class water supply standard, continuous water supply is a modern fantasy of capitalist development—a hydraulic regime that seeks to make water available anytime to anyone who can pay for it. And in fact, when I asked her to speak about 24/7 water, Smita tai became excited. "No one will say no," she said. Like other women, she too welcomed the fantasy of not worrying about water's temporary daily appearance. She said that she would be relieved at not having to be subject to the unstable and dyssynchronous times of water in the city.

Yet it was striking that during my fieldwork, while the proposal for 24/7 water was under consideration, no one aside from the management consultants were *demanding* 24/7 water. Instead, women in the settlements (including Smita tai) were very concerned about the spiraling cost of water and electricity, particularly given contemporary "fashions" of consumption. In order to reduce their water bills, they would sometimes collectively restrict water supply, even when it was available for a long time.

For example, in a nearby settlement, one group received water for a long time—approximately eight hours a day. The group kept the common tap locked for about half that period! Due to the wastage and high bills that resulted from a longer water supply, residents told me that they had mutually agreed to restrain their consumption by restricting water time. Perhaps it was because of monetary concerns—of realizing that anytime water was a domain of privilege they could not afford—that several residents in Jogeshwari, recognizing their class positions, advocated for water to appear not all the time but at the *right* time, and with the right pressure.

The arrival of water on a daily schedule does make it easier for settlers to plan and allocate time for water supply in accordance with the other things they need to do to reproduce their lives. Yet the right time for some might be the wrong time for others (see Simone and Fauzan 2013). For Anku mausi, it was all right when the schedule allowed her to come home and collect water after her work. That schedule and tempo of water time was consistent with the other rhythms of her daily life. However, when the water time changed, it compelled her to make a difficult decision. It required her to choose between two times and two kinds of subjectivity that had been made inconsistent: between the times she could be earning wages and the time she needed to collect water. This is not a viable choice. Both water and work are vital for sustaining life in the city.

In urging us to think beyond heterogeneous time, Louis Althusser points to the importance of tempo and articulation in the resolution of different times: "It is not enough, therefore, to say, as modern historians do, that *there are* different periodizations for different times, that each time has its own rhythms, some short, some long; we must also think these differences in rhythm and punctuation in their foundation, in the type of articulation, displacement and torsion which harmonizes these different times with one another" (Althusser 1970, 99–101). Beginning with the experience of multiple, heterogeneous times, Althusser draws our attention to think of the ways in which they may (or may not) work together (see also Barak 2013). Pointing to their different rhythms, tempos, and articulations, Althusser suggests that we attend to not only times that are consciously counted, measured, and apprehended but also others that matter. For instance, lying behind the time of the scheduled water supply are several other times, including those of the monsoons and those of scheduled pipeline maintenance works. These times also matter to the visible, materialized time of water supply. Similarly, elections (when more water is released), school exams, and festivals also punctuate and influence both the water schedule as well as social life in the settlements. Water time depends on the different rhythms and appearances of these other times (Fabian 1983).

For settlers then, the viability and possibility of their urban lives is contingent on the manner in which they temporarily anticipate and negotiate the diverse times, tempos, and demands of urban life (Simone and Fauzan 2013). As settlers are not permitted (either by law or by the state of their water connections) access to machines (sumps, tanks, and pumps) that apartment residents use to collect water for themselves at any time of the day, they work to amalgamate different times and tempos of water time into their daily life (De Boeck 2015). In so doing, they are called on to limit, constrain, and commit to certain possibilities of life and living in the city.

Thus, if water is scheduled in the morning hours, its rhythms might be consistent for women who are based at home—Kamla could run her washing machine and others (like Smita) might be able to collect water while washing clothes or the floors with their neighbors outside the house. Yet as Smita and Kamla both point out, water in the morning presents difficulties for those women who have no members of the household present to collect water (parents, children, extended family) at water time and who also have to work outside the home. A morning supply is difficult because it forces women (or their children) to choose between paid work and water collection. Kamla tai had made that choice. She told me that water collection, at least initially, was a big reason why she had to stop working at the NGO. Instead, she began tutoring preschool children at home so that she could be there when the water came. The water schedule therefore effects and articulates the difficulties and contradictions between different kinds of agency (Greenhouse 1996). The way that these are resolved produces not only different compositions of personhood (Bergson 1921) but also different kinds (and experiences) of time and of the city.

Conclusion

Water time draws on and reproduces the gendered division of labor. It is based on the assumption that someone will be at home and available to collect water when the water comes. It draws on the assumption that this person will be a woman whose routines and rituals include provisioning food and water for the household. As women leave other kinds of work to rush and collect all the water they can during the finicky water time, their concerns about not getting enough water and their desire for more water are seen to be formative to their identity.

"Women are those who are always fighting over water," a man told me outside Smita tai's house one day. "No matter how much we get they are always wanting more." Gendering women by not only their concern around water but also their desire for "more," the neighbor's comment obscures the way in which the temporary and limited time of water produces this anxiety. That water shortage is understood as a matter for "women's concern" points to the way in which intermittent water supply constitutes and structures their agency in the settlement. As they work to join a city water supply regime to the provisioning of sufficient water in the household, women are hailed and engendered by the politics of water time.

The fact that the stress of water shortage falls unfairly on women was explicated in a conversation I had with the women in the savings group Disha. They were only too clear about the differentiated agency and subjectivity that water problems produce:

> The men would say that water is women's work; it would be better if we handled it. We have had to pick up, carry water, two to three handis at a time and bring it home. We know what we had to do to get this water. And the men, they would just come behind us [benefit from our labor]. And now this water they drink, they drink the water the women worked to get! Even now, if any good work has been done on water, [you will see] women have done it.

It is women's groups that are called upon most frequently to address the difficulties produced by a finicky water supply (see chapter 4).[18] Working with social workers, politicians, and engineers, women's groups work to extend water supply timings as well as address pressure problems and insufficient supply. In doing so, they also structure their agency around the provisioning of water.

Yet, conditioned by the experiences of class and city expertise, women's groups in Jogeshwari's settlements did not demand a twenty-four-hour water supply. They instead demand that water arrive in the settlements *"time pé* [on time]." This is a more modest demand, one that recognizes that for people of their class position, a scheduled water supply might be cheaper than one regulated by market tariffs. When realized, this political demand—for water on time—ensures that the work of water collection can be completed quickly and seamlessly along with the other demands that structure their days. Joining together the different times—of work and social work, of seasons and festivals, of school and house cleaning, of collecting water and washing the dishes—the ways that women in the settlements resolve the competing demands of different times figures the vitality of their household and the settlements in which they live.

Yet as I have shown, demanding (or receiving) water "on time" does not necessarily resolve the problem that scheduled water supply presents in the settlements. Without machinery that can do the work in their absence, scheduled water supply requires women to be home during supply hours. While some times are more convenient than others, there is no single "right time" for *all* women living in the settlements. The "right time" is a socially and materially mediated desire and depends on the way in which women's lives are arranged in several other spheres of living as well (at work and at home, among their families, friends, and neighbors) (see Strathern 1988). As a social demand, the demand that water come "on time," therefore, is a demand that normalizes a particular form of social life in the settlement, one that makes water, and the concern over water, women's work. As residents living in the settlements demand water "on time," they not only seek to ameliorate the difficulties produced by a water supply regime but also reinforce the very same regime that genders water work, personhood, and agency in the city.

Interlude. Flood

Built from the sea, Mumbai has never been able to rid itself of unwanted waters entirely. Between late June and August every year, the southwest monsoon winds bring winds and lumbering, bloated dark clouds from the Arabian Sea. Ocean waves break over the sea walls, reminding us that we, in fact, inhabit a city that is as liquid as it is solid. And as the monsoon rains arrive from the Indian Ocean, residents return to wondering when, how often, and for how long the city will flood. The rains, therefore, are greeted with excitement and ambivalence. On the one hand, the cool winds and waters bring welcome relief from the scorching sun. The radio plays songs that wax poetic about the sound and the feeling of rain in the city.[1] With their eyes on rising reservoir levels, engineers and residents also greet the rain with a sigh of relief.

Yet the rains are also a source of complaint and anxiety as they flood the city with waters that often refuse to leave. When the city is reclaimed by water, it slows the city's commerce, schools, and government, and sometimes raises taxi fares. Residents arrive for meetings even later, or do not show up to work. Rains slow trading in the city's markets and stock exchanges. Transport infrastructures clog with water and human bodies. People and the press ritually and routinely ridicule the government for failing to make adequate arrangements for flood waters.

The likelihood that any part of the city will flood depends on a complex figuration of historic assemblies of nature, culture, and infrastructure.[2] The former wetlands of the city—intermittently claimed by residents and real estate developers for more terrestrial and profitable pleasures—are often the first to be returned to their aqueous state during the monsoons. These neighborhoods—Kurla, Sion, Matunga, Parel, Lower Parel, and Tardeo—are also vital corridors of the city, hosting the city's surface commuter train network that carries more than four million residents a day. The extent of flooding in these areas depends not just on whether it rains, but also how and when it rains—the intensity and duration of rainfall, whether this rain falls during the high tide, and the degree to which the city's municipal administration has succeeded in unclogging its sewers and drains. In Mumbai, the rising waters of flood are dependent on the situated and temporal relations between the city's geography, its waste-water assemblages, and the rains and tides (Jensen 2016; Ranganathan 2015).[3]

But even for the city's more seasoned residents accustomed to the rain-flood rituals of Mumbai living, the rains of July 26, 2005, were different. In their intensity and duration, that day's rains were unprecedented. While the residents of the city were long accustomed to its periodic flooding, they did not expect what followed the extraordinary rains of that day.

That afternoon, I was meeting with a group of urban researchers at Pukar's offices in South Mumbai, where we discussed our diverse research programs of thinking about and studying the city. As the day ended but the rains continued, many of us began receiving phone calls from our families asking after our whereabouts. The trains had stopped running, we were told. In and of itself, this was not unprecedented. The trains regularly stopped running during intense rain showers. We began discussing other ways we might return colleagues and friends to different neighborhoods in the suburbs.[4] Upon hearing that the roads too were flooded and traffic was at a standstill, some of my colleagues decided to stay the night with friends in South Mumbai before endeavoring a return home to the northern suburbs the following day. I drove to my home in central Mumbai, inconvenienced by a terrible traffic jam but not much more. It was nothing out of the ordinary when the city routinely floods. It was more intense but not qualitatively different.

I did not experience the floods in the same way as my friends in Jogeshwari did. Take, for instance, the stories that filmmakers Pooja Sawant and Tapasvi Kaulkar told about that day in their neighborhood in their film titled 26/7.

> In a house in Meghwadi, when it rained a lot, water did not enter inside because the door was closed. Water had entered the houses of all the neighbors. But this was one house in which water did not enter. [Worried], the neighbors knocked on the door and asked the people inside to open it [to see if they were OK]. When the woman opened the door, the water went in with such force that a little girl who was standing by the wall ... was dashed against the wall with great force. And such was the force that she died right there. ... When she was taken to the doctor, the doctor said on the spot that she had died. (Sawant and Kaulkar 2008)

The storm of July 26 tripped powerlines, flooded homes, and caused land-slides and deaths, primarily of the lower and middle class in areas north of central Mumbai. When the deluge was done, somewhere between one and five thousand people were killed in the region on account of the floods (NDTV 2015). Whereas the state was all but invisible and citizens were outraged, much of the crisis was ameliorated by the city's residents who opened their homes, cars, and kitchens to strangers that evening (Anjaria 2006).

In explaining their lack of preparedness for the event, city and state officials pointed out that the rainfall in the suburbs—ninety-four centimeters (or three feet) in a twenty-four-hour period—was unprecedented in the city's history (Government of Maharashtra 2006). Together with an untimely, unusually high tide, the rainfall made the city's storm water drains all but nonfunctional. The governmental enquiry and the flood fact finding report that ensued drew attention to the disaster: hundreds of human deaths, 24,000 animal carcasses (15,000 sheep and goats, 1,600 cattle) were disposed of, 3,700 people were rescued, and 25,000 were provided shelter. Anxious about an outbreak of cholera, or malaria, the city's health department swung into action.

The flood made visible the precarious nature-cultures that form the city and are subject to the workings of its different infrastructures. While the state actively pointed to the scale of the rainfall event that overwhelmed its apparatus, it also more quietly acknowledged that the flood also had much to do with the ways in which the city has neither managed nor maintained its natural and technological storm water infrastructures over the last six decades.[5] Instead, its transportation and commercial development projects continue to come in the way of water draining to the sea.

While the city incorporated its suburbs into the Municipal Corporation after independence (see chapter 1), these areas still lack significant sewerage and storm water drainage networks. As a result, most unwanted waters in these parts are carried to the sea through streams and rivers (often serving as open drains). Yet, as the suburbs have grown prolifically in the time since, these natural infrastructures have come under severe stress. On the one hand, more sewage and runoff is made to flow into these channels, particularly during the monsoons. On the other hand, the banks and deltas of these channels have been narrowed and made more rigid and more prone to flooding, by both public and private infrastructure projects that impede the flow of water to the sea. For example, the largest of these "drains," the Mithi River, has been constricted by the extension of the airport runway over its banks, the construction of the Bandra Kurla Complex (a high-tech industrial park) in its estuary, and the narrowing of its mouth by the Bandra-Worli Sea Link (a highway project).

Therefore, when the city flooded in 2005, it was not just because it rained as much as it did or because these rains happened to fall at high tide. The city's suburbs also flooded because this prolific deluge of water that landed in the city had nowhere to go. The floodwaters swirled through the city's suburbs for days, causing a significant loss of life and property. In the scale of damage that resulted, the floods of July 26 would parallel another man-made hydraulic disaster that unfolded a month later halfway around the world: Hurricane Katrina.

4. SOCIAL WORK

I did not know that it was International Women's Day until I walked through
the basti and into the offices of Asha, one of the two community centers
that I frequented during my fieldwork. Vishnu, a social worker and Asha's
president, was in animated conversation with two women from a *mahila gath*
(Women's Group), Sandhya and Lata, working through the logistical details
of the event they had organized to commemorate the occasion. The event
was a cooking contest, planned only two days prior with an officer from the
Women's Development Center, an NGO based in Mumbai. As I wondered
about the symbolism of women cooking to celebrate Women's Day, Sandhya
and Lata busied themselves looking for judges. They settled on a couple of senior inspectors from the local police station, and the visiting anthropologist.
Eager to eat, the policemen were there in half an hour. By then, other members
of the women's group had arrived and laid out the food, neatly labeled, on the
table—*kharvas, ghavna,* beets, *gajar halwa, jalebi,* samosas. All of us milled
about, excited by the preparations. Then, once the inspection was complete,
the women, seated on the floor, brought small plates of food samples to the
judges, who were sitting on chairs. Kebabs were among the more familiar
foods, but all of them were truly delicious. The police asked questions of each
contestant, their interrogation skills somewhat tempered by their ignorance
of culinary techniques. Shortly after, they selected the winner, accepted honorific words and flowers, and returned to their offices, satiated.

 Not all of Asha's community activities were as sumptuous or as secular.
But the small community's calendar was remarkably full of "programs."
These programs made Asha's work possible in at least two ways. First, they
enabled Asha to work with NGOs on various campaigns—against sexual

FIGURE 11. Asha members participate in an event where they fly kites with messages against domestic violence.

harassment or in pursuit of ration cards, for example. Such programs not only drew different settlers to the center but also made Asha an important location in what its leaders called the "social field." It was an important site for the circulation and cultivation of new (and often liberal) political subjectivities. Asha was a critical location at which different kinds of social and political imperatives were translated, received, and transfigured (Gaonkar and Povinelli 2003). On the day I visited, for instance, Women's Day came to be celebrated by a group of women cooking for a jury of male police officers. On a different day, they organized a kite flying festival to protest sexual harassment and domestic violence, inviting city administrators and ward officials (see figure 11).

Second, these programs provided the space for Asha to invite, honor, and reproduce relations with officials in the city government (such as the police or city politicians). Honored by invitations to participate in its social life, politicians, administrators, and police were especially responsive to Asha's requests throughout the year and came to know it as an organization that did "good work." Through these programs and the relations they produced, Asha became a critical location enabling city saviors both within and outside government to join with settlers and others who sought to access their services.

Asha is only one of several different community organizations in the settlements of Jogeshwari. Its success, like that of other groups, is contingent on the ways in which it can sustain and support the various cultural, political, and social needs of its constituents by drawing on relations with political actors, including administrators, politicians, and NGOs. Through this work, Asha's workers and volunteers serve to delicately marshal, mediate, and manage the production of political subjectivities among the settlement's residents. Asha's workers would call this social work, or work that was of the "social field." To do this work, they carefully deployed diverse languages of helping, friendship, patronage, and rights. In so doing, Asha not only became a key site for the making of personhood in the settlements. It was also a site where the contradictions of liberal citizenship, patronage, and friendship often collided and needed to be carefully resolved.

Between 2007 and 2009, I followed Asha's leaders as they tacked between different kinds of "social work" in the settlement. I observed the innovative and precarious ways in which Asha's workers not only facilitated access to near-term necessities in the settlements (such as water connections, schools, or hospital admissions) but also joined larger campaigns for structural change by claiming durable rights for many of the city's settlers (such as disability rights and the right to water and food rations). Asha's workers act as brokers, connecting the life needs of their friends, neighbors, and families to the biopolitical programs of the state.[1] In this chapter I draw attention to these practices not only to demonstrate how brokers like those in Asha connect people to vital resources. Together with plumbers, Asha's workers, in fact, are also called on to perform delicate acts of political arbitrage in Mumbai.[2] They bring about important compromises that ensure the stability of structures of power and government, while also allowing settlers to make crucial, durable settlements in the city. The hydraulic public that settlers come to constitute through these infrastructural relations are not anonymous and undifferentiated. Instead, the hydraulic public that is brought into being here emerges through known relations of difference, kinship, and friendship.[3]

As discussed in chapter 2, residents in Mumbai mobilize a variety of social relations beyond those of liberal subjectivity—friendship, patronage, and citizenship—to get things done in the city. Subjects need to carefully manage the incommensurabilities between their *dividuated* relations that are cultivated through these exchanges (Strathern 1991). In this chapter, I attend to the struggles over conflicting forms of political subjectivity as they emerged at a public consultation for water reforms. When Asha's leaders and others mobilized the languages of rights and protest at the meeting, they did so against city councilors whose loyalties they had carefully cultivated over the years. Their transgression produced a "moment of danger" (W. Benjamin 1969), which revealed how the hydraulic regime is not stable but one in which diverse forms of personhood and political subjectivity are in active tension and always in the making.

Founding Asha

As we sat in his small community center one day, Vishnu, Asha's president, told me of Asha's origins. He was in the tenth standard, he told me, when riots and communal violence ravaged his neighborhood in 1992–93 (see Hansen 2001). Along with some friends, he was inspired to do something good for the area. As they sat on street corners eating *vada pav*, his friends expressed a desire to "do something big" but had little idea of what this could be. Vishnu and his friends' ambitions found a home at an NGO, Vikas, that was very involved in training youth in the settlements to claim their citizenship rights in the 1990s. While attending workshops, leadership camps, and other meetings that Vikas organized, Vishnu learned about the kinds of work they could do, particularly in connecting residents in the settlement to their state entitlements. Vikas' workers also taught Vishnu about the different institutional avenues open to settlers (Mandals, Sansthas) and the ways in which these "community based organizations" (CBOs) could legally be constituted.[4] With the help and support of Vikas' lead activist, Ramesh, Vishnu and his friends created Asha and registered it as a welfare organization with the state government's charity commissioner.

Asha's beginnings, like the beginnings of dozens of other social service groups in the settlement, were small. Working at first without an office, Asha's three founders initially worked to mobilize resources for those in need. If someone needed schoolbooks, a blood donation, or a water connection, Vishnu would try to find *someone*—at an NGO or trust, or another more powerful social worker—who could help. Over time, Asha became known as an organization that did this kind of work. By networking and staying in touch with other social workers in the area, Vishnu and his colleagues developed a keen understanding of individual settlers' difficulties and struggles.

Soon NGOs and trusts would come *to* Vishnu with various development programs and resources. When a company wanted to donate a few sewing machines, its representative called Vishnu to see if he would be interested.

Asha rented an "office space" in which it could offer tailoring classes to women as a means of generating livelihood. On the days that classes were not scheduled, the space was used for "leadership camps," just like the ones that were instrumental in Asha's creation. Asha's volunteers invited "resource persons" from various city organizations and unions to speak at meetings, and they also invited their brothers, sisters, and friends, so that they too could learn about their rights, and the procedures and protocols through which they could formally access government programs—water, food rations, and livelihood assistance. This continued for many years.

Vishnu told me that Asha became "famous" after the floods of July 2005. Jogeshwari had been badly affected. As waters rose in the low-lying settlements, many abandoned their homes and retreated to those of friends and family. When they returned days later, many found their homes and belongings covered with sludge (*keechad*). Others needed help with food and water supplies, as the floodwaters had swept their provisions away. Vishnu said that he worked day and night with his friends, helping people clean out their homes. He spoke of how this work made him especially well known among women who were relegated the responsibility of recomposing households while their husbands went to work. The social networks his relief work produced were a condition of possibility for his setting up of women's savings groups a few years later. By the end of 2008, Asha organized and maintained more than thirty active women's savings groups in the area.

By doing this kind of social work—leading training workshops *and* helping people in need—Asha gained the attention of various politicians in the area, most notably the powerful city councilor. Faced with diverse kinds of requests, Vishnu and other Asha workers would frequently approach the councilor with their needs. By sympathizing and supporting the residents' requests, not only did Asha and the councilor both gain the petitioner's appreciation but Asha also became known as a center through which such things could be accomplished. To cultivate Asha's loyalty and to house the aura of its good works closer to his offices, in 2006 the councilor built Asha its very own office. Since then, the councilor has worked closely with Asha, often honoring its requests with due consideration and support.

In building his and Asha's reputation in this way, Vishnu has, over the years, become a specialist in the settlement, offering to fix people's various problems by connecting them to the administrative, nongovernmental, or political patrons who can help them (Hansen and Verkaaik 2009). His ability to conduct this social work, all without any substantive funding from NGOs or development institutions, has been enabled by his familiarity with state officials—a closeness developed through social work. It has also provided him with a basic livelihood. Following the steady decentralization of municipal garbage services in the settlements, Vishnu mobilized these relations to receive a garbage collection contract from the city. Vishnu does not go door-to-door himself. He has hired a few workers to do so and keeps a cut of the city contract to manage the employees and their work.

Thus, Vishnu and Asha's workers mobilize diverse forms of the state's development apparatus to make life possible in the settlement by working with both civil and political associations. They practice an art of mediating, managing, and arbitrating the city's social services. Their art as urban specialists requires a particular kind of knowledge. Thomas Blom Hansen and Oskar Verkaaik call this kind of charismatic, caring, and somewhat invisible authority "infrapower" (see also Foucault 1995). For Hansen and Verkaaik, infrapower is "a web of connections and structures of solidarity, fear, desire and affect that traverse communities and neighborhoods. These are connections that are neither fully visible to an outside gaze, nor officially codified, but also neither concealed nor secret. . . . Infrapower is a rhizomatic connectivity that spirals in and out of formal organizations, formal economies, formal politics and bureaucratic structures of government and policing" (2009, 20). As Vishnu builds Asha into a credible, brick-and-mortar community center, what sustains the organization is its situated knowledge of the locality,[5] its ability to facilitate connections between residents of the settlement, the various "programs" of government and nongovernmental organizations, and the friends, relatives, and associates they employ. As "people in the know," Asha's workers are vital links for settlers—a social infrastructure of relations that runs through the market and the state and enables their life in the city (Elyachar 2010).

While social workers and lower-level party officials provide critical urban services to settlers, the proliferation of different banners in every settlement makes it abundantly clear that there are many potential helpers in the community, many of whom are associated with political parties. For many living in settlements, affiliation with political parties has not only increased their access to development projects, water lines, or lucrative city contracts. As one rickshaw driver explained to me while proudly displaying his party identity card, such affiliations also increased their social standing in a city that marks settlers as dirty, marginal bodies undeserving of citizenship or respect. In such a world, to belong to a political party is to command a form of respect or authority that settlers otherwise have difficulty claiming.[6] For many denied access to the privileges of class, accessing political parties is often a critical way to gain dignity, social goods and biopolitical services in the settlement and in the city. Political parties provide a network of support, in terms of not only social standing but also economic inducements, dispositions, and favors that come with being part of a powerful political formation.

In exchange for this patronage, party workers are expected to mobilize the bodies of their friends, associates, and others whom they "helped" to support the party in different social and political programs (see also Bedi 2016). A leader of the Shiv Sena women's group, for instance, told me that she was obliged to bring between twenty and fifty people to its political rallies whenever party officials asked her.[7] Similarly, it was her group's responsibility to identify ten students in the area who could receive Shiv Sena "scholarships"—textbooks and notebooks at the start of each academic year. As grassroots political workers, such leaders gained importance by brokering party patronage of these events and endowments with the loyalty of their friends and neighbors in the settlement (Hansen 2001; Scott 1969).

Name Recognition

To honor and further make visible its respect for and connection to various politicians, Asha, like other groups, often erected large billboards honoring party leaders on its outer walls. In a topography of political authority, the boards frequently displayed a headshot of the leader at the top, followed by midlevel officers, with junior leaders and social workers pictured below. A ubiquitous feature of the urban landscape in Mumbai, such "banners" were ostensibly put up during certain key festivals (Diwali, Dassera, Id, etc.) to communicate the best wishes of the party leader to the public. But as evidenced by their form, these banners were also intended to identify and honor the various workers and saviors whom the public could approach for help if necessary. The billboards' intended audience was not just the public but also the party leaders themselves—they served as political symbols that represented the good wishes and loyalties of the leaders' subordinates. Banners were a source of continuous anxiety and tension among the social workers I encountered during my fieldwork. Who should be on the banner and who should not were questions constantly debated and worked through at meetings. The result (see figure 12) would be a visible map of the social networks that workers such as Vishnu depended upon to obtain resources for the city's settlers.

Even though being associated with political parties allows social workers to draw on and claim their extensive resources, most especially when they

FIGURE 12. A political party banner displaying the topography of social work and political authority of the party in an urban neighborhood.

have state power, not all social workers in the settlement like to work "full time" for political parties. At Asha, Vishnu was widely seen as being "close" to the Sena, and was seen by many to be dependent on the patronage of Sena's councilors (who built him the community center). Many of the women in Asha's savings groups were also loyal to the Sena. But Vishnu did not like the reputation of corruption and cronyism that came with party membership. When I spoke with him, he constantly reminded me that Asha was an autonomous institution that would work with a wide range of neighborhood groups and political parties.

There were many reasons Vishnu may have insisted on this. Social organizations not affiliated with political parties were more respected by residents because of their independence from party machines. They could also approach a wider network of potential donors and supporters in NGOs and trusts. Further, it was not convenient to be in a party that was not in state office. Not affiliating with the Sena allowed Vishnu to work with leaders in other political parties should the government change. Therefore, as a sort of compromise—of both belonging and remaining unaffiliated—Vishnu would participate in events organized by a range of leaders across the political spectrum. By performing his loyalty for a variety of different groups, he would seek to maintain his connection with many of the settlement's saviors. This would enable him to maintain a "full house" of potential strategies to meet the center's diverse needs and those of its affiliated women's groups (Ferguson 1999).

Vishnu was conscious that he needed to maintain Asha's identity, and hosted politicians from various parties as chief guests at a wide range of "cultural programs"—health camps and devotional prayer meetings, as well as song and dance performances. Following the events, Asha's members would excitedly share their thoughts about why certain leaders had come, while others did not. They would take pictures with the leaders who attended— shaking hands, and exchanging roses and other gifts that marked their relationship. These acts demonstrated that the leaders of various political parties supported Asha's work. They also produced Vishnu's own status in the area as a big/good man.

Not all of Asha's programs had material benefits or were linked to political parties. Asha also maintained ties and relations with several NGOs and groups beyond the settlement. For instance, Asha worked with Maitri—a prominent city NGO focusing on gender rights. During the time that I conducted fieldwork, Maitri's dynamic outreach worker (who lived near Vishnu) collaborated with Asha to organize a health camp (cosponsored by the city health department), a collective protest against domestic violence and sexual harassment, two trainings for women's livelihood programs, and a scholarship program for twelve promising female students who were to attend college. Finally, Asha maintained good relations with officers in the social service wing of the municipal administration. Because of these relations, Asha has successfully obtained benefits from different government programs—small business loans, grants, and other endowments—for the forty-two women's savings groups that are now associated with the organization.

Interpenetrated by the relations of civil and political society and joined by NGOs, political patrons, and social movements, Asha's work challenged any easy distinction between state and society on the one hand, and political and civil formations on the other (Gupta 1995). Its success lay in being able to combine the various contradictory elements of diverse political agendas to forward its work of connecting settlers with critical urban services. Yet the precariousness and limits of infrapower were particularly evident when settlers tried to negotiate their citizenship rights with city councilors.

Organizing Publics

When I arrived in Mumbai in 2007 to do fieldwork, the "social field"—
comprised of NGOs such as Vikas, and community groups (community based
organizations, or CBOs) such as Asha—was busy organizing itself into a credible opposition to the Municipal Corporation's Water Development Improvement Project (WDIP).[8] Two years earlier, the water department had
commissioned a World Bank–financed study on ways to "improve" water
supply in K-East ward.[9] As the city's largest ward, K-East ward housed a
population of over one million residents, most of whom lived in settlements.
Recognizing the "improvement program" to be a thinly veiled attempt to
privatize water distribution in the city, NGOs and CBOs organized a wide-
spanning opposition to the reforms under the banner of the Water Rights
Campaign. Through participation in the campaign, Asha, along with its
mahila gaths and youth groups, had worked hard to alert settlers about the
reforms being undertaken at the Municipal Corporation. They performed
street plays on the issue, and went door-to-door, explaining the privatization
initiative and relating it to the privatization of electricity distribution.[10] This
struck a chord among many in the settlements. They were only too familiar
with the problems of escalating rates that accompanied the privatization of
electricity and were concerned about the same thing happening with water.

In addition to discussions with community residents, youth and women's
groups were also delegated the responsibility of meeting with councilors to
communicate their opposition to the reforms. Yet they had difficulty engaging with councilors on matters of the city's water policy. These difficulties,
and the NGO rights trainings and workshops that preceded and followed
them in Mumbai, require us to reconsider how NGOs engage with political
parties and political questions in the city.[11]

I attended my first Water Rights Campaign meeting during the monsoon
of 2007. The meeting, which took place at a small community center next
to Asha's, was attended by both NGOs and CBOs. The NGO workers, like
me, were the only ones who arrived early by arriving on time. An hour later,
close to 8:00 in the evening, the meeting began. The room was filled with
about thirty people from different NGOs and local settler organizations. The
meeting began with NGO workers updating the group about their discussions with city engineers and labor unions regarding the current state of the
reforms. They reported that following strident opposition from state employees, World Bank consultants had been, in their words, "put on the back
foot." The consultants were no longer proposing a management contract for

a private operator and were instead proposing that the city water department manage smaller contracts. Ramesh, Vikas' senior activist (who was also Vishnu's mentor), told the group that these milder recommendations from the consultant were due to be presented at the third consultation in a few months. It was important for the CBOs to not only organize people to come to the meeting, he said, but also to put pressure on their city councilors to oppose the reforms. Saying this, he circulated some written materials to the group. In so doing, Ramesh and the other NGO workers sought to bring information to community groups in keeping with the idea that in a democracy, the informed electorate would have a say in the laws that govern them by making their opinions known to city legislators.

But while the settlers' groups were comfortable with the language of water rights at the NGO meeting and also in our conversations, they knew that their councilors did not necessarily see or hear them as the rights-bearing subjects imagined by proponents of liberal democracy. "They don't want to talk," a leader of one youth group complained. They insisted that an NGO worker accompany them to the meeting and articulate their demands—someone like Ramesh, who was both comfortable with the language of rights and not as subject to the councilor's discretionary power. "How can we say what's wrong?" one of the women affiliated with Asha complained. "The councilor is one of those people who answers our questions with another question. He doesn't talk properly. . . . That is why we want you to come with us."

In articulating their discomfort with addressing their councilor as a rights bearing constituent, settlers revealed the ways in which they are sometimes seen and read by politicians in the city. Councilors, like other elected political representatives, seldom consulted with their constituents on matters of policy.[12] This is not to say they did not engage with their constituents. They were in close touch about provisioning for different necessities—water, food, schools—or arbitrating local disputes such as marriages, property matters, or employment. They were simply not accustomed to listening to them on matters of making laws or policies. For this, the city's councilors were used to hearing from the city's NGOs and (more senior) state politicians in the city.

While NGOs are often staffed by middle and upper class residents, this is not always the case. Ramesh's biography demonstrates how he was not always an NGO worker and he was not only an NGO worker. In 1984, when he was thirteen, Ramesh came to Jogeshwari from a village in Satara to live with his uncle. At the time, Jogeshwari was at the city's frontier and was well known for its milk dairies. His uncle started a milk dealership, and Ramesh helped his uncle with this work. He would distribute milk between 5:00

and 7:00 in the morning before going to school. He worked in the business all the way through college. In the meantime, his uncle made it big—he bought property and cars. At this point, Ramesh left home to start out on his own because he had "fulfilled his debt" to his uncle for providing for him.

Ramesh stayed with a friend for a number of years. They worked together on starting a youth group in the settlements. A mutual friend's sickness was what brought them together. "We had a friend . . . [who] is now a big BJP [Bharatiya Janata Party] leader. . . . He was sick. . . . He had surgery, so we got together to help him. We made a small group, gave it a name and began to help each other," he told me one afternoon. Soon after, they began talking of other ways to provide assistance in the settlements. As they came from the same school, they immediately thought of giving back to their alma mater by setting up a library for its students. "Then the headmistress, who was working with us—she began to question our proposals . . . so we thought why make it for one school, we'll do it with other schools." In 1998, as they were building another library, the young men came into contact with political groups. Leftist and Dalit leaders began providing them with a political education—teaching them about political ideology and urging them toward broader social engagement. "In 1998 we were introduced to Sambhaji Bhagat. He told us what communism is, what politics is, what the youth of today should do, what globalization is," Ramesh told me, speaking of his political awakening.

Ramesh was involved as a full-time activist with the youth group between 1994 and 2000. During this time, they worked on citywide campaigns for housing rights, gender justice, and a range of other social issues. They worked on campaigns to fight the demolitions in Borivali National Park, a few miles from their homes (see Zérah and Landy 2013). On occasion, they were beaten by the police. At other times, they were threatened by politicians who were complicit in the city's reterritorialization under the sign of capital. Ramesh told me that he did all of this work without a paid job. He depended on his friends for three to four years to put him up and feed him. Realizing that this could not be a long-term strategy, he joined the NGO Vikas in 1998, first on an activist fellowship (between 1998 and 2000) and finally as staff in 2000. Now, Ramesh is a full-time worker in Vikas' urban development program, working on a series of community development and mobilization projects. The Water Rights Campaign was one of his projects.

As a settler-turned-rights-activist, Ramesh's biography points to the powerful ways in which settlers have learned the language of rights in the city: through communist organizations looking for new members and NGOs deploying the framework of rights to make demands for housing. In some ways, his work and that of other NGO workers cultivated from the settlements destabilizes assumptions that NGOs and "civil society" are populated only by the middle and upper classes. It also troubles contemporary theorizations of politics that frequently identify in NGOs the cause of the withering away of the state and of political citizenship. Ramesh's biography reveals the way in which ideas of rights, justice, and entitlements engaged by demands for a public system are not discourses that come from "outside" but are threads of an ongoing conversation between NGO activists, state officials, and residents in Mumbai's settlements.

Nevertheless, the settlers' reluctance to articulate policy demands directly to their councilors was troubling. It drew on histories of activist campaigns in India, where the "head work" (the work of policy, and debating the intricacies of privatization) was the domain of middle-class NGOs, while the "body work" (the work of assembling large numbers of people to oppose privatization) was left to politically marginalized groups (living in the settlements).[13] Over the course of the campaign against water privatization, this led to many fractures and debates among those involved.

Yet, in this instance, Ramesh eagerly wanted Asha's members to do the head work of speaking to the councilor, and it was Asha's members who were reluctant. For them, the problem was not necessarily that NGOs led from the front in discussions with technocrats and engineers but that unless NGOs attended meetings with councilors and other representatives, their concerns would not be treated with any seriousness. Councilors would see them as "local" women from the settlement, they said—women who could not know about "bigger" things. Articulating gendered divisions of political labor, Rajni tai, a long-time Asha member, pleaded to Ramesh: "Only people like you will do. We don't have the language [*bhasha*] to engage this." At the meeting, Ramesh looked a little embarrassed by the way Asha's members recognized their own marginality. They were highlighting the fact that despite the many rights trainings that he had organized for them, there was still much work to do for settlers to see and claim their rights to the city.

Making Connections

Affiliated with Asha through their savings group, Sunita tai and Rajni tai also attended the campaign meeting. Working together over the years, they knew both Ramesh and Vishnu well. Through the meeting, Sunita and Rajni registered their disapproval for the reforms and offered whatever help they could to mobilize people to protest water privatization. While Sunita and Rajni came to the meeting to learn and oppose privatization, they also had a specific grievance they came to address: their settlement was not receiving water from the public utility that they were explicitly defending. After the meeting, they stayed behind to speak to Vishnu and Ramesh about how this might be remedied. I was amazed by the efficacy and familiarity with which each knew what they had to do. They wrote out a letter on Asha's letterhead and called one of the councilor's assistants to set up a meeting. This was the first step, I learned later, in the process to get a new water connection.

This was not the first time that Sunita and Rajni's settlement had water problems. In Mumbai, water services for settlers are in a state of constant flux. Years earlier, when they had first moved to the city, they had obtained a water line after facing significant difficulties. At that time, Vishnu had helped them get a water connection. Since then, that line too had gone dry. This was not an uncommon situation for many living in the city's settlements. For a range of political and material reasons, their infrastructure is increasingly prone to blockage and leakage. Annual hydrological cycles, population increases, main line leakages, shifting demography, and unanticipated cluster developments constantly compelled city engineers to tinker with and alter the water system. They were always rearranging the pipes, pressures, and water timings to cope with changing and growing demand.[14] "Slum connections" are thinner and frequently run above the ground. They are more prone to breakage and leakage and are especially vulnerable to changes in pressure. With constant rearrangements, residents in connected settlements such as Sundarnagar frequently find that their connections—struggled for and negotiated years before—slowly go dry. As a result, when lines stop working every five or so years, settlers need to find ways to make re-newed connections to the public system.

I gained an appreciation for this cyclical and historical process when, upon their invitation, I visited Sunita tai and Rajni tai's savings group meeting one day. While we waited for other members to arrive, Sunita told me about how the group was formed. They too owed their existence to Vikas. This was the same NGO Ramesh worked for and the one that trained Vishnu. They spoke of how Vikas helped form the group and taught them how to save money. They were trained by NGO activists to make applications, learn of their rights and the responsibilities of officials in various state departments (water, sanitation, roads, garbage), and also to understand the repertoires they needed to get officials to respond to their requests.

Sunita pointed out that years before, when they were formally denied water services by the rules of the city government and the councilor expressed an inability to help, it was a worker who took them in a big group to the water department's headquarters to get their application passed. Following up on previous conversations, I asked Sunita and Rajni whether their most recent water request—for a new line—had been approved. I was pleased to learn that though it took some time, the councilor had eventually put a new line in the settlement. Armed with Vishnu's letter, they had met the city councilor to seek his help in solving their water difficulties. In recounting the meeting to me, Rajni tai said: "We told him, we don't want money. Our vote is worth one lakh rupees [approximately US$2,000 in 2008]. We only want to use that amount now. Because we don't have money. So he put the pipe [in], and took advantage of it. In four to five places he put [in] a 'T' connection [to divert water elsewhere]."

I was slightly surprised by the ways in which Rajni spoke of her meeting with the councilor. Rajni did not consider the meeting as a place to demand water as a right. But neither did she speak of the meeting with the councilor as though she were a supplicant. Whether she was as explicit at the meeting as she was with me in our interview, I cannot be sure. But throughout our conversation, she argued that the councilor was *obliged* to give them a new line because they gave him their votes. He owed his position to their votes. It was now his obligation to hold up his end of the exchange, by helping them with their water connection. Not only did Rajni and others in the mahila gath want his permission to lay the water line, but they also expected him to fund its procurement. Rajni demanded that he step up to his responsibility to help them. She articulated a very justified and a very transactional understanding of citizenship, framed around the exchange of a water pipe. Rajni was unambiguous, warning the councilor that his votes (and voters) were on the line. In the weeks that followed, the councilor did respond. He laid the line, but not before diverting some of the resulting water to other constituents.

As Mukulika Banerjee (2008) reminds us, settlers and other relatively subaltern populations are only too aware that the funds politicians access for development projects are being misappropriated by their elected representatives. Yet this does not preclude settlers from claiming a fair (if also unequal) entitlement to these funds. Rajni clearly saw her vote as entitling her to a share of the councilor's funds. She did not want to be paid directly, but she did claim that the money be put in service of their settlement. Rajni saw her vote as entitling her group to the finances and favors of the councilor. This transaction, enabled by certain democratic rights (namely universal suffrage), does not produce, in and of itself, a citizenship right to water. Instead it produces a moral and political relation through which the councilor is obliged to help settlers—a relation that is partially effected both by the vote and also by relations of patronage.

Representing Democracy

Councilors also recognize their obligation to work on water services. Several councilors and their party workers identified water services, together with drainage and small roads, to be their primary area of responsibility. "Water, gutter, passage," councilors would tell me when I asked them of their responsibilities. During elections, expanded water services are a ubiquitous campaign promise.[15] Politicians frequently point to reliable water services in the settlements they rule as evidence of their efficacy. Indeed, while walking through settlements, settlers would frequently show me water lines, identifying them with particular city and state politicians. "This is Waikar's line," I would hear, or "This is Shetty's line." Named after the politician who sponsored the connection, the lines connect critical service infrastructures with the *person* (and sometimes the political party) who brought the line to the settlement. Signage on water tanks, toilets, and other water infrastructures frequently advertised the politician who commissioned the works. In Mumbai, therefore, water connections represent a very personal development, one that is produced by charismatic authority as much as it is pressured by votes.

Each of Mumbai's over two hundred city councilors represents an electorate of approximately sixty thousand people. With most of their voters coming from settlements, councilors find themselves responsible for large numbers of residents, many of whom form a perpetual line outside their offices to address a range of concerns, including urban services (road repair), family disputes (abusive husbands), as well as construction projects (such as home expansion). To conduct their work more effectively, councilors themselves rely on a series of intermediaries to advise them which people have "genuine" problems. They depend on independent social workers such as Vishnu or their own party workers to screen and recommend cases that require their most expedient attentions.

I learned more about the importance of party volunteers in a conversation with Ismail, a city councilor. In one conversation, Ismail began by speaking of the importance of good relations with city engineers and the importance of talking to them properly. *"Relation ke upar depend hai,"* he told me, speaking of how councilors can work with the city administration. "It depends on the relation."

Yet getting things done not only depended on the degree to which his projects were supported by the city administration. Ismail also spoke of the importance of having a good support network within his political party: "For any man to work, he must have a circle. My eyes and ears are the Youth Brigade [the party's youth wing]. It is through them that work gets done [*Inke madhyam se kaam banta hai*]. Because of this work, they build their name/ respect [*izzat*] in the basti. If they are our people, the work gets done quickly [*phata-phat*]. Anyway, anyhow, the work must get done." Therefore, while Ismail mediated access between the administration and the community, his volunteers were critical in helping him accomplish this. In the fissures between making work and doing work, Ismail drew on the help of junior party workers (his "circle") in the settlement. This not only gave his workers respect—*izzat*—in the settlement but also produced them as future leaders. Doing good work spread the "good name" of the party, Ismail told me. A good name was critical to the party's success in city elections as well as those at the state and federal levels.[16]

In the interview, Ismail had suggested that the work of the youth brigade was not only necessary to actually oversee the implementation of the works projects. The youth were also his "ears." As such, they were tuned in to the local talk of the area, and could assess whether the people who were to be helped were loyal and deserving subjects. Alluding to their political loyalties, he said, that work is done quicker if they were people loyal to his party. If not, would he be able to secure their loyalties if he did the work? The unspoken assumption, of course, was that if not, the work might take longer (or never get done at all).

In Mumbai, politicians eagerly compete for the political loyalties of their subjects through direct, known, and personal interventions. Councilors play close attention and respond to the political loyalties of their subject populations in choosing which of their petitioners will be extended the councilor's considerable local area discretionary development funds.[17] Conversations I had with lower-level party workers confirmed this. "If we have twenty-five proposals, we will only take up the five that are important to us and for which there is no dispute with other residents or political parties," a councilor's deputy told me one day. He spoke of the difficulty in mediating such proposals and, more importantly, in getting credit for development works, particularly when the settlement has many potential saviors, each clamoring for attention. "Many times, people from different parties want to work on and try and get credit for the same projects. Fights often break out between people on different sides." The party worker is often reluctant to take up works projects that are claimed by other leaders and volunteers. If it seems like doing something would be a lot of headache (*jhanjhat*), then he will stay clear of those projects. Skipping over projects whose political outcomes are uncertain or contentious, party workers prefer to focus on projects that will provide them with "respect" and loyalty without too much trouble, either with rival political interests or with the law.

Back in Sundarnagar, Rajni and Sunita had done their work well. They had succeeded in convincing the politician of their loyalty, and the councilor installed a line at his own cost. This had spared Sunita and Rajni's group the difficulty of raising the money for the pipeline on its own. But the work was still not complete. The councilor had laid a new line in the settlement, but the pipe would not be of very much use until it was actually connected to the city's water system. To do this, the group had to approach the engineers in their water department. Unfortunately, the junior engineer did not immediately fulfill their request. Sunita explains:

> We had such problems. Twenty to twenty-five women would go in the morning, to the Andheri office, to ask the engineer to make the connection. The engineer would ask, "Why are you coming here in a morcha? If one or two of you would come your work would be done." But no. We went with twenty to twenty-five women every time, that's why our work got done. . . . We said we are a mahila mandal with water problems, do our work! [The engineers] began nit-picking, saying, "Not today, tomorrow!" That way many days passed. [Finally], we asked them, "Are you going to do the work or not, tell us straight!" . . . We said, "Just as every day matters for you, it matters for us. Why are you sitting in this chair [position]? Because you are sitting in this chair you have to do our work." That way we answered his answers [talked back].

In their years of working in the mahila gath, Sunita and Rajni tai had learned the rituals of claiming hydraulic citizenship. Knowing that engineers frequently ignored the requests of individual settlers unless they went and made noise in a large group, they took many women with them every time. Doing so, they knew, might make it easier for the engineer to respond to their demand than to ignore them. Pressured by their numbers, the engineer had tried to remind the women that he had "bigger" concerns to look after—that his responsibility was not to their small, particularistic problem. Yet Sunita did not make a claim as a supplicant or a shouting member of political society. She responded by equating her difficulties with the engineers. Trained well through Vikas' rights trainings and workshops, she spoke the language of an entitled, rights-bearing citizen—one whom the city engineer was employed to serve. Unlike the intimidation they expressed in meeting with councilors (who asked questions of their questions), here Sunita answered the engineer's answers.[18]

Effectively required to request new water connections periodically, Sunita and Rajni were both familiar with the processes and procedures necessary to obtain such connections when we met. For them, the rituals of hydraulic citizenship needed to be reiterated every few years. It was not a onetime event (as the languages of housing recognition and regularization would suggest). Instead, hydraulic citizenship emerges as a set of entitlements that needed to be constantly reclaimed and maintained by navigating the rituals of rights and entitlements that established their belonging to the city.[19] Crystallized in the discretions of the councilor and the demands of the engineer, this was citizenship that was habitual and always in the making. "We have learned how to talk in the city," a settler told me one day as we spoke of the ways she accessed urban services. To get water, she needed to constantly make herself known to city authorities, to claim belonging and entitlements through the language of rights and of supportive, voting clients.

The hydraulic public, therefore, is not an anonymous population of undifferentiated, rights-bearing citizens but a set of intimately known and negotiated relations between settlers, social workers, and councilors. Here lies the importance of Asha's work, and the work of several community organizations based in the settlement. Letters, documents, and "activities," such as the cooking contest at Asha on Women's Day or the antiprivatization meeting, provide the grounds not only for social-political connections to be made and maintained between settlers and community organizations, and between community organizations and NGOs, but also for the continual learning, testing, and performance of new languages of entitlement. When performed correctly, social connections and new discursive formations are critical to accessing water and other urban services. Nevertheless, these languages are not always mutually compatible, and they may fail as often as they succeed.

The Trouble with Rights

On November 13, 2007, the Municipal Corporation organized the third public consultation for reviewing its proposed water reforms. In part, the consultation was a ritual of participation required by World Bank projects. It was a liberal ritual of urban governance, one that called upon "civil society" to take part in governmental processes by providing input (Rahnema

1992). The third consultation for water reforms was scheduled only months earlier. It was made necessary by proceedings at the second consultation, where activists of the Water Rights Campaign demanded that the water department give them time to review the reforms being proposed at that meeting. Invested in the processes of participation, the consultant and commissioner had acceded to the request and promised to hold a third consultation where NGOs and civil society organizations could provide their input a few months later.

Yet even before the third meeting could take place, the Assistant Commissioner of the city had already announced the launch of a new program—Sujal Mumbai [Good Water Mumbai]—which drew on many of the reforms recommended by the study to restructure the water department's operations. This upset the activists a great deal and they resolved to protest these decisions at the third meeting. When the date of the third consultation was announced, therefore, NGOs and CBOs worked through the Diwali break to ensure that people showed their concern by attending the meeting.

I was impressed when I arrived at the auditorium on the day of the meeting. There were at least two hundred residents from the settlements in attendance. Kicking things off with a protest outside the gate, they moved into the auditorium soon after the meeting began. Engineers, academics, and consultants I had been working with occupied the first five rows of the auditorium. My friends and colleagues from the settlements I had also been working with occupied the back of the hall. Conscious of my visibility and positionality, I took care to sit in the middle of the auditorium, right next to professors, it turned out, from the Indian Institute of Technology.

The consultation was long and tedious. It began with the consultant, speaking in English and serially translated into Marathi, making the case for water reforms. His introduction was followed by a PowerPoint presentation by the chief hydraulic engineer. The engineer's presentation was far less fluent. Stammering through his talk, he looked to the PowerPoint presentation to guide him as to what he should say next. I could not help noticing that many of the slides were lifted and pasted directly from the consultant's report I had seen earlier. It seemed almost as if the chief engineer was learning of the reforms through the act of reading the PowerPoint slides. As he halted and hesitated, not quite confident about the reforms being proposed, the assistant commissioner—a smartly dressed, confident bureaucrat who was posted as a powerful projects commissioner in the BMC—sought to rescue the talk by filling in program details where the chief hydraulic engineer omitted them.

The Assistant Commissioner spoke the World Bank's language of water regulation comfortably, highlighting words and meanings that the engineer had overlooked on each slide. His familiarity with the slides, and his conviction about the need for reforms, made it abundantly clear that the water reforms were his initiative. Nevertheless, after about an hour and a half of hearing officials present the reforms, someone from the audience shouted out from the audience, asking when they might be allowed to speak in this "consultation." Many murmured in support. The engineer droned on.

The audience's discontent broke into a full-scale disruption when the bureaucrat announced that contracts were going to be given to private contractors for the maintenance and upkeep of the system. *"Paani aamchya hakkacha, nahi kuna cha bapaacha."* Shouting over the voice of the Assistant Commissioner, the protestors chanted, "Water is our right, it's not anybody's father's [property]." The assistant commissioner pleaded to be allowed to continue. Disregarding him, many began to walk toward the stage in protest. For the media and the police, who had long appeared bored and forlorn, things had suddenly become interesting.

Shouting at city employees is a relatively common way to articulate discontent with public services in postcolonial cities (Chakrabarty 2007). Recognizing that they were losing control of the meeting, the administrator and engineer invited the city councilors ("your representatives," they assured the audience) to the stage. Recognizing the power and authority of the councilors, and their special (and historical) ability to manage and discipline their populations,[20] the engineers had guessed correctly that settlers would not be quite so vocal with the councilors. Awed by the presence of their councilors and the city mayor, many in the audience quickly quieted down. The mayor, now on stage, asked the protestors to allow for the presentation's completion. The protestors quickly agreed.

The chief hydraulic engineer resumed his presentation. Unfortunately for him, however, he was imprisoned by the sequence of his PowerPoint presentation. The very next slide led him straight to a very contentious proposal for prepaid water meters for unregularized slums. The audience roared in protest at both the engineers and the councilors, who by this time were sitting mute, quite literally on the same side as engineers and administrators proposing the reforms. This proved to be too much for the youth groups. As a mass of bodies rolled down the aisles shouting slogans, it was apparent that the rest of the "consultation" was going to be far less scripted.

With chants and demands, the protesters walked right through a frazzled yet helpless police force to take control of the stage and its microphones.

Standing now at the same level as city councilors and administrators, they challenged their authority, proceeding to rail against the initiative. They berated the Municipal Corporation for overseeing a takeover of the utility by private, foreign companies. By now, things had reached such a pitch that even the mayor and the city councilors could not keep things under control. The youth groups refused to cede the stage to the councilors and shouted them down whenever they tried to speak. Flustered, the mayor left the meeting. It was only when the Assistant Commissioner took a microphone and offered to answer questions that, somewhat miraculously, a large number of protestors quieted down and began filing behind the microphone to ask questions. The rituals of democracy were rescued and resumed from what, moments before, had seemed an impossible situation.

Realizing that they now needed to have substantive questions, many in the group near the stage began looking for Ramesh, the Vikas activist who was the spirited force behind the Water Rights Campaign. He took the stage and, with expertise and authority, began asking difficult questions of the water department. I quote his engagement at length, not only because I admire it as an articulate, rights-based critique of the reform project coming from a representative of the city's NGOs *and* its settlements but also because it points to the contradictions between the apparent motivations for the reforms and their potential effects:

> I would like to say that the World Bank has created this farce [of consultation, privatization] not only here today, but everywhere in the world. . . . I want to make two more points clear. I am a person living in the slums. . . . Yes, I agree that there is inequitable distribution. But you have found a medicine that is worse than the disease! The disease is that people don't get water and the solution [you propose] is that you will fix prepaid meters! Prepaid meters have not only been experienced in Asia but are largely responsible for what is happening in Africa. In South Africa. Many have died in the cholera epidemic. Even in the most developed nations whose principles we would like to emulate, even in those countries prepaid meters were banned in the '90s. In such a scenario, when we know that the road ahead is full of pitfalls, why are we going in that direction? We are in a quandary over this matter and we would like you to clarify.

By introducing himself not only as an NGO worker but also as someone who lived in the settlements, Ramesh foregrounded his own experience in accessing water. He raised a conventional and powerful right versus commodity dichotomy, very prevalent in debates over water distribution and frequently articulated in community meetings in the settlements, and presented a powerful case for why water should remain a public good.[21] Nevertheless, Ramesh acknowledged the difficulty and inequality that he faces when accessing the public system. He asked how the BMC could transition to a 24/7 system when it cannot even provide him with a few hours of water each day. The issue of prepaid water meters was even more contentious. Preferring the status quo to "a medicine that might be worse," he asked that the current system be expanded to all settlers, not just to those who can mobilize the correct documents of belonging.

The audience roared in support of his suggestion, making it difficult for the commissioner to respond to his queries. By now, the audience was not prepared to listen to the experts anymore. Chanting against the reforms, they occupied the stage, not only protesting the World Bank and the BMC engineers but also berating the work of city councilors. As the melee continued, one young protestor got hold of a microphone and, looking directly at the city councilors, accused them of being *dalals* (agents) of private companies. Revealing the public secret—that councilors frequently act as agents of private companies—was a transgression that electrified everybody at the consultation (Taussig 1999). The children were shouting that the councilor rajas (kings) had no clothes.[22]

With their authority being so explicitly questioned and mocked, the Shiv Sena councilors lost face. They were already upset by the ways in which their normally deferential subjects were disregarding and disrespecting their power and authority. Unable to sit still while they were being insulted, they got off their chairs and rushed to assault the questioner. As councilors sought to restore order by resorting to physical violence, their reaction revealed another public secret—that their authority was based as much on their threats of physical violence and intimidation in the settlements as on their position as elected representatives (Hansen 2005).

No sooner did the councilors and their supporters begin to assault the protestor that others from the audience came to his rescue. Surrounding him for protection, they turned to the councilors and shouted in English, "Shame shame shame shame!" The councilors, worried at this turn of the crowds against them, took themselves offstage to safety. They called their offices, apprising them of the situation, and asked that their party followers come to the meeting venue for support. Soon after, the councilors decided to leave the building. As they got into a car, the youth groups assembled to block its movement. They refused to let the car leave the meeting before the councilors

FIGURE 13. News coverage of the water consultation and the ensuing protest.

apologized. They began shouting slogans that compared the councilors' violence to Hitler's fascism. Soon after, the councilors' boys arrived from Jogeshwari to rescue them. Living in the same neighborhood, the protestors and councilors' supporters recognized one another. Though many of them were friends at home, some began fighting each other until (finally) the police broke the two groups apart and ordered them to go home.[23]

Damaged Relations

A couple of days later, activists and protestors gathered quietly at a community center to watch a video of the meeting and to review what had happened. Some of the younger protestors were excited to have put the councilors in their place by inverting the political relations in the settlement, even if it was just for a brief moment. They liked having an opportunity to point to the vacillations and corruptions of councilors in public and spoke excitedly about how they shook the councilors' authority and confidence. Others, however, were more circumspect. The disruptions, while quite powerful, had closed all lines of communication and negotiation with both councilors in the settlement and engineers at the city water department without achieving any tangible results. The more senior activists and social workers would have preferred that the unequal theater of stakeholder consultations nevertheless remain open. At least that way their voices could have some traction, they reasoned. Instead, activists and CBO groups had damaged their relations— not only with the city's water department but also with local city councilors.

The primary consequence of these damaged relations for NGO activists was that they now had to file Right to Information appeals to get any details from the water department about the reforms. The engineers no longer willingly gave this information to them. Yet for those living and working in the settlements, the consequences of breaking relations were more severe. Because they were known and familiar, Asha's leaders, along with other CBOs in the settlement, were threatened by the councilor's "circle" of party workers. Even though Vishnu had recognized the danger and slipped out of the meeting without engaging in a confrontation, the councilor's deputy had taken note of his presence among the protestors and had informed the councilor of his loyalties. Expressing disappointment with Vishnu, the councilor suspended his plan to expand the community center and was not as responsive to his requests. The councilor's workers threatened to beat Vishnu up.

The youth groups that took a more active part in the protest were in even more trouble. Dependent on the cleaning and sweeping contracts that the councilor arranged to ensure their financial viability, they were informed that their contracts were cancelled. A woman from a mahila gath, who was identified at the consultation, was told that she no longer had a job when she went to work the next day. As news of the protest reverberated through the settlement, several of its participants began to fear what the councilor's workers might do to them if they were caught in the wrong place at the wrong time. Far from a celebration of their success at disrupting the meeting, settlers were more circumspect and quiet about the effects of their protests on their everyday lives.

The events that transpired at and after the consultation were a very visible manifestation of the intimate nature of the public sphere in Mumbai. Even though it is one of the largest cities in the world, its people are not invisible in public. To access the many resources they need to live in the settlements, settlers were often known and identifiable to both social workers and party workers. Their visibility compromised both social workers and residents in different ways as they returned to the settlement and sought to live and work in a vitiated political environment. Knowing how to talk, therefore, was not just about knowing and mobilizing the languages of rights and relations. It was also about learning and knowing the appropriate fora and manner in which these claims could be engaged so as to expand access to urban resources. Transgressing these repertoires produced a moment of danger—a situation that not only revealed the councilors' vulnerability but also provided the grounds for the reinscription of their power.

Conclusion

Asha's workers work in Jogeshwari with diverse political languages and subjectivities. On the one hand, Asha's workers join settlers desiring the care of the state to the diverse bureaucracies of government through highly visible and known relations. Yet social workers in organizations like Asha do not only engage in acts of "brokerage." They also work with NGOs to produce liberal political subjectivities. Settlers learn (or are reminded of the importance) of their formal rights and entitlements through the different programs that it hosts. As savings groups, NGOs, and community organizations try out different and new languages of rights, they provide settlers with new ground for interventions in the politics of the city—politics that, marked by relations of inequality, are nevertheless also saturated with ideas of justice, entitlement, and political membership.

Settlers in Mumbai are connected to those in power not just through situated, everyday acts of patronage but also through training programs that cultivate languages and entitlements of democracy and representation. They often demand and expect that their political representatives act as good patrons. As rights and duties entail each other, these produce a powerful set of expectations around the responsibilities of state politicians and city engineers (Banerjee 2008). Thus, it is not only subjects who are responsibilized through the language of rights and justice (Foucault 1991; Rose 1999). Rights talk also responsibilizes the leaders, dadas, and engineers of the city's public system. Willing to overlook the corruptions of councilors and engineers, settlers evaluate the morality of city government by the ways in which they help "ordinary people" accomplish ordinary things. Despite being in very unequal relationships with councilors, they expect them to provide basic services (including water) to all, *especially* those who cannot afford it.

Attending to these quotidian practices in the settlements complicates contemporary theorizations of urban politics, which for some time now have centered on rather static and dualistic distinctions between civil society and political society and between patronage and citizenship. Indeed, the cyclical and constant concern that Sunita and Rajni's group faces around matters of water supply is an unstable arrangement that constantly calls upon them to negotiate their water connection with their patrons through intermediaries such those working at Asha. At the same time, the analytic of political society seems a little too fixed, in this instance, to describe their changing relationship to the city's politicians, and the confidence and fluency with which they are now able to obtain water connections. Their fluency is effected in part by their learning of the languages of urban belonging—the practiced and familiar ways in which they make claims to matters of life in the city (see McFarlane 2011).

For instance, when Rajni questions the legitimacy of the city engineer or recognizes that the councilor is not just a raja of the settlement but one who also depends on them for his election to the position, her practices elucidate a far more dynamic and multiply constituted form of personhood that cannot be explained by relegating her politics to that of political society or civil society.[24] Yet, precisely because the subjects here are a known gathering of social relations, there are consequences for settlers who do not "talk properly" or who do not mobilize the correct repertoires of claiming access to the city's resources. The public consultation spiraled out of control when settlers sought to hold their city councilors to account. The bitter standoff that ensued between residents and councilors revealed how settlers and social workers are not always seen and treated as liberal, rights-bearing citizens. As settlers mobilized powerful rights claims and protested the councilors' willingness to "sell" their water supply, they were not allowed to forget that they continue to be subject to the discretionary and profane force of the city's municipal system—a system that continues to be based on violence and inequality.

Interlude. River/Sewer

The floods of 2005 drew unprecedented attention to the flows and future of the Mithi River. Originating in Borivali National Park, the Mithi River releases its waters into Mahim Bay.[1] But this has not always been the case. In their history of the city's estuarine landscape designers, Anuradha Mathur and Dilip da Cunha (2009) detail how a seasonal surface flow was consolidated as a river through practices of cartographic representation on the one hand, and infrastructure projects (such as railways and dams) on the other (see map 1). This river, the Mithi River, is, in the absence of sewerage works, the primary drainage system for many of the area's industries and homes. Over the last few decades, there have been several conversations in urban government to "clean up" the Mithi.

However, in 2008 state officials saw in the toxic mixes of the Mithi not a problem of waste and contamination but an opportunity. Rather than build new sewage infrastructure, the state government has argued that the Mithi is not just a river but also a drain, and as such deserving of federal urban infrastructure funding. The application for funding confused the Union (Federal) Finance Ministry, which began to ask questions of the state government. The *Hindustan Times* carried the story:

A call from the Union Finance Ministry on Saturday left officials in the state secretariat puzzled. The ministry wanted to know whether the Mithi, blamed for much of the 26/7 [flood] damage, was a river or a drain. . . .

"Finance Ministry officials said that if the Mithi was a river, then it could not be funded as an urban renewal project and the state may have to look for funding under some other scheme," said a [state] official on condition of anonymity.

State officials then had to convince the Finance Ministry that the Mithi was a 14.7-km river, but one which carried both sewage and storm water discharge to the sea. Hence, they argued, it could be classified as an urban renewal project. ("Is Mithi a River or a Drain, Asks Centre," *Hindustan Times*, September 3, 2007)

Their claim, however, was not convincing to the central government, which argued that environmental improvement was not in the mandate of the urban renewal mission. It argued that the Mithi was not urban "infrastructure" but "environment," and as such, urban renewal funds could not be used to improve it.

The incident demonstrates how the words we use to name water or any other resource matter. The different names we have for water do, or do not, make it amenable certain kinds of human interventions. "By turning names into things," Eric Wolf reminds us, "we create models of reality, targets for development and war" (1982, 6). The controversy demonstrates how the question of whether the Mithi was called a river or drain was of tremendous consequence for the agency that could be called on to be responsible for its management. By calling the Mithi a drain, the state government sought to call for a set of interventions that would make the Mithi a sewer.

The controversy also begets the question: what is a river? The answer is far from clear (see Mathur and Da Cunha 2001). The only thing we do know is that Mithi's existence as a river cannot be extricated from the people who make and remake Bombay a city. Over the last four hundred years, the form of the Mithi has been materially, spatially, and symbolically intertwined with the form of the city.

5. LEAKS

"Water supply is difficult for a normal person to understand," Haresh, a charismatic water engineer based in Mumbai, told me in late 2007 as I spoke with him about the city's water system and its ongoing privatization initiative. He suggested that attempts to measure the quantities of water flowing through city pipes were always already compromised. "When you are dealing with water, you are dealing with an approximation," he explained. "Because management consultants don't understand this most basic fact about water, all their projects fail. Management consultants focus on the financial aspects and lose perspective of the technical constraints of water. That's why the K-East project failed. . . . If you look at privatization . . . anywhere that management consultants have gone, these projects have failed. . . . The government is the other devil. It's not in its interest for water supply to succeed."

In his categorical dismissal of the work of both public and private water managers, I was surprised to hear Haresh speak of water as an approximation. As a rather basic element with little variation, I (like policy makers) had imagined water to be especially amenable to calculation and hydraulic modeling as H_2O—conducive to being governed as a relatively homogenous, known material from a distance.[1] In fact, in learning about Mumbai's water system, I was overwhelmed by the calculations necessary for its production—from figures for daily demand to more mundane numbers of pipe widths, water levels, and pressure needed to make the water flow to diverse residents. Haresh, however, was telling me that it was critical to see water's variously generated numbers as representing not verifiable quantities but approximations. As approximations, the numbers concealed both the city's prolific water leaks and the beneficiaries of these leaks (residents, state officials, and its different wells) in the city.

Haresh had intimate knowledge of water's peculiar ways. On the one hand, he experienced its fickle appearances in his taps as one of Mumbai's residents. On the other hand, he had recently concluded a study as a consultant for the World Bank–sponsored Water Distribution Improvement Project (WDIP) in K-East ward. As part of his study, Haresh found substantive leakages in the city's water network. He and his colleagues provided figures to suggest that over a third of the city's water was "leaking" both into the ground and to residents drawing water through unauthorized connections. Yet the numbers he had provided were tremendously contentious. Embarrassed by the figures of extensive leakage that his study produced, Mumbai's water department engineers dismissed the figures and, by extension, the World Bank project as a fraudulent, thinly veiled attempt to privatize the city's water supply.[2] When we met amid the controversy, Haresh acknowledged that this could be one unanticipated effect of his efforts to audit the ward's water flows. While wishing to distance himself from the political controversies generated by his measurements, he nonetheless continued to emphatically stand by them.

In his work, David Nugent has urged an attention to the moments when political rule stumbles: "Much can be learned about state formation by examining moments in which political rule falters or fails, for it is then that the lineaments of power and control, that otherwise remain masked, become visible" (2010, 681). In this chapter, I investigate how and why engineers have stumbled through efforts to measure and manage leakages. Engineers know about water leakages and yet are unable to either measure or prevent them. As they rush around the city attempting to fix leaks that they are only occasionally able to find, identify, and repair, their difficulties point to the powers of social and material relations that constitute the city's water infrastructure.

The qualities and quantities of leakage slide quickly and perniciously between various types of ignorance—the not-as-yet known, the forgotten, and the unknowable. As such, they become very difficult to map, count, know, and contain through the audit technologies of state officials (Strathern 2000). Leakages are seldom easily brought into control, nor do they always serve as a site for the exercise of state power. Instead, as they also often compromise and interrupt the work and form of the knowing state, leakages trouble the form and formation of government. As unstable, uncontrollable flows of water, leakages interrupt the performances of the authoritative, knowing state with a powerful reminder of the obduracy of water and the infrastructures that form, channel, and deliver it to the city.

In recent years, scholars in science studies and geography have drawn attention to the politics of infrastructural systems we live "with," and have also urged we consider nonhumans as actants in our political cultures.[3] For instance, Jane Bennett has urged an attention to not just the social but also the material actants that form infrastructure. She shows how electricity grids are "living, throbbing confederations" of human and nonhuman relations "that are able to function despite the persistent presence of energies that confound them from within" (Bennett 2010, 24). In this chapter, I draw attention to the way that urban water infrastructures are composed of not only the political regimes of humans in the present, but also the politics accreted in the materials and histories of the city's water infrastructure (Bennett 2010, 29). Yet water and its infrastructures do not act and perform beyond the regimes of human responsibility. Indeed, the very appearance and disappearance of leaking water in the city demonstrates how its form cannot be disaggregated from the humans who manage it in everyday life.

24/7 Mumbai

Over the last one and a half centuries, Mumbai's water system has been extended and managed amid heightened concerns over water scarcity (see chapter 1). Engineers frequently rearrange the city's water network and schedules so as to ensure that water continues to reach its residents. When engineers spoke of severe, citywide water shortages, they described how these schedules were frequently rearranged to ensure some kind of equity. They took these schedules very seriously—combining their intuition and experience to determine how a particularly bewildering combination of valves, pipes, and timings would work for their districts (see chapter 3). Faced with the state of this leaky infrastructure, municipal administrators, state government politicians, and central bureaucrats have recently initiated dramatic urban development programs to "fix" the system and make water available continuously.

The project to ensure continuous water supply is not merely an attempt to make water available for more hours in a day. Thus, for Srinivas Chary, director of the Centre for Energy, Environment, Urban Governance and Infrastructure Development (and one of India's most prominent proponents for 24/7 water supply), 24/7 is not an outcome whereby more water becomes available to residents anytime. Instead, it is a result of a series of steps, including hydraulic and technical modeling, leakage reduction transformations in customer attitudes, and financial restructuring, that are essential to modern water supply systems.

As such, 24/7 water systems entail new relations among engineers, consultants, and residents. They call for new relations between the state, the consumer, the citizen, and the market (see von Schnitlzer 2008). For Chary, and indeed many of the project's advocates, a 24/7 water system is just not about providing unlimited water to residents. It is a water system that also promises to shift the locus of regulation from city water engineers (who regulate water supplies by regulating water time in Mumbai) to the city's residents (who as consumers, would regulate their consumption by trying to reduce their water bills). Thus, the proposal to create a 24/7 water system is also a proposal to create a new kind of political subject in the city—the careful consumer who is aware of and moderates his or her consumption based on water's price.[4]

Despite Chary's enthusiasm, the "series of steps" required to make water supply "continuous" have been deeply contested not only by urban citizens unwilling to pay higher prices for water (see chapter 3) and by state officials in urban administrations. The 24/7 water projects have also been challenged by the significant degree of water leakages in the city. Left unchecked, leaky pipes lose significantly more water in a 24/7 system than in an intermittent system (where leaky pipes are turned off for most of the day), and quickly make the regime unviable.[5] Accordingly, Chary and many other experts agree that leakage reduction is a necessary first step for making a 24/7 water network.

Nevertheless, in Mumbai and indeed in many other cities around the world, it has been very difficult to even measure leakage (let alone reduce it).[6] Confronted with intransigent water officials, difficult water flows, and a public that is ambivalent about the effects of 24/7 water supply, one official at the Ministry of Urban Development in Delhi confessed that the situation was "hopeless" and that he has urged his colleagues to "forget about 24/7 supply."

Why are hydraulic engineers, who spend their professional lives operating and maintaining urban water infrastructures, opposed to 24/7 water or to leakage reduction? Why are those pushing for urban "reforms" so invested in 24/7 supply? And finally, what might leaking pipes tell us about the constitution and contestation of political responsibility in the city? To explore these questions, and what they mean for our understanding of urban government, it is important to investigate the ways in which infrastructure and leakage are managed and maintained in everyday life.

Knowing Leakage

Engineers have repeatedly cited inadequate sources and the "scarcity problem" to explain why 24/7 projects cannot work. Yet, through preliminary calculations based on government documents I have reviewed, it appears that there is enough water entering Mumbai for *all* residents of the city. Consistent with the diagnosis provided by Haresh (quoted at the beginning of this chapter), the "water shortage" problems can be largely attributed to "leakages"—flows of water in city pipes that are not fully authorized, controlled, and known by city authorities.

Formally, the BMC has reported leakage figures of approximately 25 percent. Yet, with over half the city's water meters out of service, it is unclear how this figure has been calculated. I heard the figure in several interviews with city engineers, and saw it cited in city papers. Yet during more than a year of fieldwork, I never learned how the water department calculated leakage when the tools and meters of measurement were silent and unreliable.

I gained some insight as to how this figure was determined when I visited Mr. Karmarkar's office at the municipal headquarters one day. Karmarkar was a deputy hydraulic engineer in Mumbai, second only to the city's chief hydraulic engineer. His office was responsible for calculating and projecting the large numbers that moved Mumbai's water system. Though he was quite senior, Karmarkar's office was small, and since we last met he had rearranged his furniture. His desk was turned ninety degrees and no longer faced the door. When I entered, Karmarkar was going over some figures with his junior engineer. Trying to make conversation, I asked about the new office arrangement. Without looking up from his papers, Karmarkar pointed to the place above where his desk once sat. The column had a deep structural crack, and above it, the ceiling was beginning to give way. Pieces of plaster had fallen off, revealing the rusty iron *salias* (rebar) that lay below them. "Why take a chance?" he said wryly. Noticing the precarious state of his workspace, where the roof could, quite literally, fall on his head, I wondered aloud whether remaining in the office was taking a chance. Yet the state of his office did not seem to bother Karmarkar *too* much. Like many engineers who had worked for decades in city offices, he did not make a fuss about his working conditions. He managed.

Karmarkar was busy with an engineer from the billing and metering office, going over the city's water distribution figures. The city had recently begun charging metered users "telescopic" water rates, according to which consumers with higher volumes of consumption paid more per unit of water used. He then went on to calculate leakage, writing out figures on a piece of paper.

i.	Water supplied through metered connections	2079 MLD
ii.	Water supplied through unmetered connections	500 MLD
iii.	Therefore total supply	2579 MLD
iv.	Total water delivered to Mumbai	3280 MLD
v.	Unaccounted for water	700 MLD
		=20 percent of total supply

This very basic calculation of water leakage was frequently iterated in newspaper stories about the city's water. The leakage figure was a sum of the water quantities from a series of different connection types (metered/unmetered), measured against the water delivered to the city. What these figures pretended to know are the quantities of water that are distributed throughout the city. However, these measures are dependent on reliable technologies of counting, which, simply put, are not at work in Mumbai.

For instance, most of the meters on the city's water connections (60 percent by one estimate) are not working. Without access to a reliable measure of how much water has been consumed by customers on these connections, water department officials frequently estimate these quantities for the purposes of billing. As a result, many residents get water through metered connections by paying what is effectively a flat (estimated) rate. Second, water meters have been installed only on newer water connections (i in Karmarkar's list above). For connections that were approved and granted prior to the implementation of water meters, customers pay fixed water rates (based on the ratable value of their property, ii). While these water connections frequently deliver significant revenues to the government, the water quantity they disperse is not measured by volume and is frequently estimated. As I watched Karmarkar tentatively pencil in a value in the row for unmetered connections, I wondered whether this neat, round number—500 million liters per day (MLD)—was inscribed by estimating what would eventually ensure a comfortable and respectable figure for the city's "total water supply" (iii) and, by extension, its unaccounted-for water (v).

Numerical fictions such as these are powerful, not least because they produce the city water department as a well-performing water utility. International norms, including those that are used by the World Bank as well as those used by the Centre for Energy, Environment, Urban Governance and Infrastructure Development in Hyderabad, indicate that unaccounted-for water should be around 20–25 percent and not significantly higher. In fact, this is likely why the city's water leakage figure is said to be 20 percent. By producing a figure in this range, the city water department is able to demonstrate its efficacy as a utility that does not need any external intervention from the federal Ministry of Urban Development or the World Bank.

Not accidentally, the fiction began to unravel when Haresh and the World Bank consultants began to conduct water audits as part of the reform initiative. By measuring water flows in non-supply hours in a single ward, the consultants calculated that approximately 35 percent of K-East ward's water was leaking. Yet, in the absence of universal, working water meters, the consultants, like the city engineers, were also compelled to derive the quantities of water consumption (and thereby also water leakage), using speculative modes of reasoning. Thus, even in the audits conducted by the consultants, water was more frequently estimated than measured.[7] In this respect, the consultants' extrapolations of leakage appear rather similar to engineer Karmarkar's derivations of water loss noted at the beginning of this chapter. They were brought into being by the assumptions embedded in their protocols (see Anand 2015).

Particularly given their political potency, the consultants' leakage figures were relentlessly scrutinized by the engineers of the water department. Engineers questioned the assumptions embedded in the consultants' leakage measurement protocols, the methods used to calculate leakage, and tools to measure water flow. City engineers questioned the objectivity of the numbers. They wondered aloud whether the significant measure of leakage derived by the consultants had anything to do with their desire for a water distribution contract. In the press conferences that followed the release of the study, engineers announced that the consultants were not able to successfully measure water leakages in the city. When newspapers featured the story in the following days, they announced to the city's public that Castalia Strategic Advisors, the consultancy firm, "has been unable to calculate the amount of water the ward [lost] to leakages" (S. Rao 2007).

The measurement of leakage, therefore, was not independent of the social-political context in which it was sought to be established. For the consultants, measurement promised a point of entry for a much larger intervention on the water distribution system (Bowker 1994). City engineers, meanwhile, insisted on the veracity of their measuring practices, in part that they could continue to claim an effective management of the city's water distribution infrastructure. In this controversy, both engineers and consultants found it difficult to stabilize quantitative facts about the city's water (Harvey and Knox 2015).

Thus the difficulty of measuring water was not an effect of technical incompetence. Neither were the fuzzy numbers generated to measure leakage solely the result of a politically motivated ignorance and knowledge.[8] As I watched both the consultants and engineers work hard and fail to stabilize the measure of water leakage in the city, it seemed apparent that their difficulties also brought into view the difficulties of measuring water embedded in the subterranean pipes of the city's water infrastructure (Muehlmann 2012). Measuring water in pipes is difficult for a variety of reasons—reasons that also constantly compromise the power engineers have to govern water by measure.

Measuring Responsibility

In her work with the epistemology of physicist Niels Bohr, Karen Barad has insisted that measurement practices are not as clear and distinct as Newtonian approaches would suggest. Barad challenges classical assumptions that objects and observers occupy distinct physical and epistemological locations and that matter, as such, is available for measurement by humans wielding tools, meters, or microscopes. She suggests that the technologies of measurement are not independent of but part of the phenomena they seek to apprehend. Water, meters, engineers, and pipes, for Barad, are but parts of a single-acting phenomenon, where "the objects of knowledge are participants in the production of knowledge" (Barad 1996, 163). For concepts such as leakage to appear evident, stable, and objective, a Cartesian cut that defines fixed subject, object, and context needs to be able to be performed consistently and reliably enough that the conditions necessary for measure appear fixed, constant, and taken-as-given (see Latour 2005; Poovey 1998).

Barad's insights on the labor and conditions necessary for measurement are helpful to understanding the difficulty of measuring water leakages in Mumbai. Leakage emerges as such in a particular, historical effort to govern the flow of water. Without engineered pipes that are designed to be water tight, there is no such "thing" as leakage (Schrader 2010).[9] Water wells, for instance, do not leak; that water seeps through earth is a condition of their possibility. Leakage is brought into existence through certain technological imaginary of controlling water flows. Further, even in engineered systems, the concept of leakage is not ahistorical or natural but emerges as a "matter of concern" in Mumbai at a particular historical moment (Latour 1996). The interest in measuring and governing water leakage in Mumbai (and indeed in the world) proliferated amid projects to make things countable by neo-liberal technologies (see also Bjorkman 2015).[10] For water leakages to be made visible and measured by water meters, however, the proponents of leakage reduction need to assume that water flows are discrete and knowable through independent, verifiable measurement practices. They need to assume that the tools of measurement—water meters—are reliable, objective, uncontroversial devices that can apprehend and deliver reliable results through their operation.

Mumbai's water infrastructure is anything but a stable, knowable form that enables uncontroversial flows. Instead, as water is made to flow through the system in pulses of intermittent supply, changing direction every few minutes and leaking to unauthorized human and nonhuman others, the political situation of the city's water infrastructure regularly muddies the distinction between objects, subjects, and context. Water only flows in certain pipes at certain times, and water pressure at any given location spikes and tapers throughout the day, making it difficult to measure volumes using flow calculations.

Water also appears and disappears in ways that are difficult to map. Because over a million settlers are denied water through city water rules, residents work with engineers, plumbers, and city politicians to ensure they quietly receive water through special and discreet favors, the measure of which engineers, politicians, and plumbers alike are actively involved in concealing. Even water meters are not stable and neutral arbiters of measure. They are known to be unreliable across the world.[11] In the water audit, the fickleness of the meter became visible when engineers and consultants argued about which *kind* of meter was more reliable and appropriate to use in the measurement exercise. Finally, the engineers disagreed with consultants about the boundaries of the system they proposed to study when the network of city water mains did not neatly map onto the political boundaries of the municipal ward. The water the meters measured was not just consumed in the political boundaries of the ward but also traveled from one ward to the next. This resulted in a bitter dispute about how much water was being consumed by residents of K-East ward, how much leaked, and how much water "moved on" to be consumed by residents in other wards.

Taken together, engineers and consultants found it difficult agree on the techniques of measurement, the assumptions of their measurement models, and the choice of meters that were used. Amid an unstable set of enabling conditions and technologies of measurement, both the engineers and the consultants could only generate figures that were too provisional, and too interested, to be considered reliable.[12] Not wanting to be embarrassed by the degree of water leakages in the city that the consultants were finding, engineers relentlessly questioned the assumptions and context of the measurement models the consultants used. Given the unstable situation of their measurements, the consultants did not always have the answers. While they were unable to stabilize leakage figures in the city, the controversy over the leakage figures did succeed in straining relations between the engineers and the World Bank consultants.

Yet if the controversy over water leakages revealed the precarity of measure, it also called for a different accounting of responsibility for water leakages in the city—one in which we may consider the role of nonhuman actors.[13] In his examination of engineering and expertise in Egypt in the early twentieth century, political theorist Timothy Mitchell has critiqued the tendency in the social sciences to privilege the role of humans in our accounting of historical events. "One always knows in advance who the protagonists are," he protests, as he peruses histories of dam making in Egypt during this period. "Human beings are the agents around whose actions and intentions the story is written" (Mitchell 2002, 29). Yet, as Mitchell attends more closely to the histories of hydraulic engineering, he demonstrates how expertise was subject to the "ambivalent relations" between mosquitoes, wars, epidemics, famines, and fertilizers. The expertise of dam building was produced on-site, as engineers confronted and sought to mediate different human and nonhuman forces.[14]

By suggesting that chemicals, mosquitos, and crops were historical actors, Mitchell follows scholars in STS who have urged that we disassemble constitutive distinctions between humans and nonhumans, nature and culture, subject and object in theorizing social and political life.[15] As was evident in the water audit, the distinctions between subjects and objects are historically situated, interested ways of ordering the world. They give special status and form to human agency. The failure of the water audit made evident how human bodies, water, pipes, and water meters are not already constituted subjects or objects. As water is made to flow in pipes to hydrate human lives that produce the technologies of distributing and measuring water, an attention to the iterative process reveals how infrastructures, natures, and humans are actively co-constituted through emergent relations *with* each other.

Following a series of large infrastructural breakdowns, new materialist scholarship has suggested we think more modestly about the powers that humans have in controlling and managing the worlds that we make. Indeed, even as humans play a vital role in structuring infrastructures, infrastructures are processes that are constantly productive of relations that exceed human control. As such, they challenge humanist framings of agency and compel us to think more humbly about the power of human agency to manage the tremendous force of the infrastructures we create.[16]

For example, in her account of the massive electricity blackout on the east coast of the United States in 2003, Bennett refuses to hold any single law, corporation, or regulatory authority responsible for the event. Instead, she suggests that the kind of agency that her theorization of the blackout makes visible "is not the strong kind of agency traditionally attributed exclusively to humans. . . . The contention, rather, is that if one looks closely enough, the productive power behind effects is always a collectivity" (Bennett 2005, 463). For Bennett, the blackout that affected more than fifty million people did not just occur because of the corporate modes of running electricity infrastructures at near capacity, the special interested laws of the state, or even just a software glitch. It occurred also because reactive power, a kind of electricity, was also made "to travel too far" by an emergent political regime whose human protagonists working in energy companies were overly preoccupied with cost and capacity efficiencies (Bennett 2005, 454). To understand the blackout, Bennett suggests, we also have to acknowledge the agency not of individuals, but of assemblages; an agency that emerges from human- non-human relations.

In drawing attention to the ways that electricity acts despite and with human designs for its control, Bennett's work demonstrates how we inhabit a world that, while already terraformed by humans (Masco 2014), is not one that is easily controlled by modern political institutions. While urban planners, government officials, and engineers have long designed infrastructures to be centrally controlled by bureaucratic institutions (Scott 1998), Bennett's work suggests that modern technopolitical forms are nevertheless compromised by the intransigence of their accreted material politics, and the excesses that form them (see also Collier 2011).

As new materialists have drawn attention to the vital powers of nonhumans in the production of catastrophic events, their work has been criticized by postcolonial scholars who worry that questions of political and social difference might be overlooked as we identify nonhumans as political actors.[17]

Critical humanists worry that assigning agency to electrons, water, or pipes risks eviscerating the "special responsibility" that humans have in governing resources and arbitrating over critical questions of distribution in everyday life (Appadurai 2015).[18] Thus if "a materialist analysis of politics is one which must attend to the resistance of matter to political control" (Barry 2001, 26), critical humanists are concerned that these attentions deflect from an attention to political practices of social differentiation at best, or explain away social difference as caused by nonhuman matter at worst.

An attention the power of Mumbai's hydraulic infrastructures does not entail a form of material determinism that critical theorists are rightfully cautious of. In focusing on the actions of the city's leaking water pipes, I do not suggest that their materialities are the cause of social difference (or leakage) in the city, nor do I ascribe "naturalness" to their political form. Instead, I wish to understand why engineers are unable to account for leaks, and how in the absence of this measure they act and authorize water flows in the city.

In Mumbai, engineers seek to manage and control the city's water infrastructure and to make water known and flow in predictable ways. Nevertheless, they are unable to constitute and measure water as a stable object that flows through the city's water infrastructure. Its surreptitious and unnoticed flows—into the earth or the bodies of differentiated residents—make it difficult to control through audit technologies. I do not wish to suggest that engineers are unaccountable for the city's water infrastructure, or that they are able to escape the political consequences of the inequitable distribution regime they manage. They design the city's water infrastructure to deliver less water to residents of the settlements (chapter 1). These residents of the city would frequently hold its urban administration and its political apparatus responsible for the difficulties they had accessing water in everyday life. As Kregg Hetherington points out, "responsibility is less a characteristic of people than a form of description that one offers of the relationships between different actors in an event whose causal sequences are not merely mechanical" (2013, 71). Engineers consider themselves, and are considered by publics, to be responsible for water distribution issues in the city.

What is less clear is how engineers are able to act and manage a leaking system that is always on the verge of being beyond their control. Recognizing that their power, measure, and knowledge are compromised in this vibrant system, Bennett's theorization of distributive agency helps us understand why engineers—the measurers of all things—do not spend much time measuring water consumption or leakage in the city. Instead, they govern leakage by crafting heterogeneous and improvised sociotechnical practices.[19] Their work acknowledges the vitality and vibrancy of human and nonhuman actors and the difficulties they have in managing them. Their work also demonstrates how material technologies are neither autonomous of human-centric notions of agency nor encompassed by it.[20] Engineers do not rule *over* the city's water system. In their quotidian efforts to control leakages, engineers "manage" water leakages as compromised and compromising experts. They manage leakages much as Karmarkar did his roof—by moving out of the way, or by making discrete and situated compromises with water's fickle flows.

Managing Leakage

As they work to address the thousands of leaks that fill their schedules every day, engineers in the city's ward offices are only too aware that governing water is difficult precisely because of the deeply ambivalent, unknown, and fungible relations between what is apparent and what is real, between what is physical and what is social. As a result, they are not too concerned about measuring leakage. Instead, they are very busy fixing leaks to keep the water system working.

Take, for instance, K-East ward, one of twenty-four wards in Mumbai. The ward has a population of more than 800,000 residents and is twenty-eight square kilometers in area. In the process of studying the ward for their privatization initiative, Castalia, the management consultants, collated the number of leakages that people *complained* about. Nearly three thousand leakages were reported throughout the ward in one year alone; more than six hundred were classified as "major joint leaks and bursts." This is to say that more than eight leakages were reported every day in K-East ward alone. This figure did not include leaks from customer service lines that also resulted in complaints. Because city engineers respond to these leakages less urgently than bursts on larger and more significant trunk mains, smaller connection leakages actually cause a greater loss of water from the system than bigger bursts (Kingdom, Liemberger, and Marin 2006).

Confronted with thousands of leaks per year, engineers speak of their department as functioning by "fire-fighting" and attending only to the problems that—for social, political, and material reasons—are impossible to ignore. Nevertheless, they are challenged in their effort to do so. Engineers frequently report that their work of leakage reduction is compromised by a lack of qualified engineers in the department. The city administration's hiring freeze—a consequence of state policy intended to shrink the size of the

TABLE 1. Complaints received, attended, and completed
in K-East ward, 2004–2005

Month	Connection leakage	Major joint leaks and bursts	Contamination	Short supply
April	253	48	16	123
May	260	54	10	132
June	235	69	9	121
July	243	62	10	141
August	247	47	12	124
September	248	62	12	127
October	288	44	9	123
November	277	56	9	131
December	271	58	9	117
January	283	61	14	137
February	295	63	19	123
March	283	57	15	142

Source: Leak burst data, K-East WDIP, Municipal Corporation of Greater Mumbai.

public sector—has meant that several engineers' posts have remained vacant for years (*Mumbai Mirror*, October 5, 2007; Bjorkman 2015). In K-East ward alone, with a population of over eight hundred thousand residents, only six engineers are available to manage the entire ward's water supply, including fixing its three thousand leakages. Engineers, therefore, can only attend to the major problems. The rest of the water just leaks away.

With their hands already occupied with known leakages, engineers do not spend much time looking for unknown leakages, not least because of the material and technological barriers to finding leaks. As pipes rust, break, or rupture underground, many leakages go unnoticed and unreported. Because the city is largely built on wetlands, much water leaking from the underground mains flows away without giving notice. Sometimes, these leaks produce spectacular effects. Left unattended for years, they eat away at the earth and eventually cause random and chaotic sinkholes in the city, a phenomenon that only too vividly reminds the city's residents that the firmness of the city's ground is contingent on the subterranean flows of water within and beyond the pipes of the city. Take, for instance, this news article from 2008, which describes the way that a sinkhole swallowed cars in the city:

The Saat Rasta crater incident that has served as an eye-opener for the civic authorities—and a nightmare for citizens—may be just the beginning of problems in store for Mumbaikars. That's because the entire island city rests on a hollow surface due to multiple pipeline leakages underneath which are steadily causing soil erosion. This is paving the way for more horror holes, which if not plugged in immediately, will give room for similar incidents to reoccur.

Madhukar Kamble, BMC hydraulic engineer, said, "We adopt a technique to detect the leakages underground. But due to the cluster of utilities, magnetic waves often fail to identify the exact leakage spots." He also revealed that failure of magnetic detection is also largely due to the noise levels in the city. For effective implementation, one requires silence to capture the sound waves. In Mumbai, this is possible only at night. However, at night due to the absence of water flowing through the lines, it becomes next to impossible to find faults in them. (Mhaske 2008)

"Horror holes" are caused by the large leakages in their city's underground water mains. The news article also points to the difficulty in detecting leaks given the material situation of the city's water infrastructure. For instance, a common method for detecting leaks involves using sonic equipment, which, placed over pipes or valves, can isolate and register the peculiar sound made by a leaky pipe. But here, too, engineers dismissed their efficacy in the peculiar "context" of Mumbai. Sonar (and magnetic) technologies only work when there is little background noise, when no one is using the road. Yet water largely flows in Mumbai's network during the day, at which time the streets are filled with the sounds of cars and traffic, of commuters and the city. Engineers complain that the city produces too much noise, rendering sonar technologies ineffective. Sonic technologies are harder to use at night because water does not flow through the pipes at night.[21] Other cities detect leakages using pressure monitors, by monitoring for sudden drops in pressure. However, pressure monitors are compromised by the intermittent system, because the water pressure in the pipes is always changing. As valves are constantly opening and closing, the changing pressures stress the instruments and cause them to break down. Even when instruments work, engineers complain that they are unable to tell whether the drop in pressure is due to leakage or because of valves turning upstream or downstream of the monitors in the varying, dynamic system.

Subterranean Hydraulics

Haresh, the engineer, had spoken of the technical constraints of water. When you are dealing with water, he had said, you are dealing with an approximation. Indeed, as I came to learn more and more about the water service system in Mumbai, I realized that the city's water infrastructure delivers and produces not known quantities of water but approximations. In Mumbai, the materiality of water and its infrastructures entailed these approximations. Because water infrastructure needed to be used and maintained at the same time, fixing the hydraulic system takes extraordinary work that can be quite disruptive to those dependent on its daily operation. This is not just true of postcolonial cities like Mumbai. Take a recent article about leakage repair works in New York:

> All tunnels leak, but this one is a sieve. For most of the last two decades, the Rondout-West Branch tunnel—45 miles long, 13.5 feet wide, up to 1,200 feet below ground and responsible for ferrying half of New York City's water supply from reservoirs in the Catskill Mountains— has been leaking some 20 million gallons a day. [To fix the tunnel,] the city has enlisted six deep-sea divers who are living for more than a month in a sealed 24-foot tubular pressurized tank complete with showers, a television and a Nerf basketball hoop, breathing air that is 97.5 percent helium and 2.5 percent oxygen, so their high-pitched squeals are all but unintelligible. They leave the tank only to transfer to a diving bell that is lowered 70 stories into the earth, where they work 12-hour shifts, with each man taking a four-hour turn hacking away at concrete to expose the valve. (Belson 2008)

In this spectacular story of workers who live in a submarine inside New York City's water tunnels, note the ambiguous and extreme conditions in which their work of leakage repair is situated. First, estimates of water leakage from this single tunnel are significant (around twenty million gallons daily). These are only approximations, entailed by the way in which unknowns are constitutive of the urban water system. Second, the article shows how leakage detection is extremely difficult work, not only because the pipes are deep underground but also because the city's residents continue to require their use even as they are being maintained. Workers needed to work in the tunnel even as water was flowing. New York, therefore, decided to fix leakages by placing divers in submarines in their water tunnel.

In some ways it is easier to fix water mains in a submarine, breathing helium, than it is to fix three thousand small, leaking service lines. Such work is not only time-consuming but also requires engineers to know the network intimately well—to understand where leakages are, employing little if any technology. As such, regardless of their seniority, Mumbai's engineers have only a partial, experiential knowledge of the distribution system and rely on field engineers to reveal its local state. I talked about the water system one day with Mr. Surve, one of the department's most senior engineers, referred to by his juniors as one of the five rajas of the city's water supply. However, when we met, I learned that even this king seemed to have only a partial grasp of the distribution system.

Always genial and friendly on the phone, it was only after months of persistence that Surve could make time to meet with me. When I arrived at his office, he was reviewing some works proposals and requested a few minutes to finish up. I utilized my time by taking in Surve's surroundings. As one of the city's rajas, he had a large office. I recognized, by now, the government-supplied, glass-topped desk (reserved for senior officers) at which he sat. The glass encased a long phone list with the cell phone numbers of all others in the department—a list essential to engineers, who delegated their responsibilities through phone calls. On the table behind him, a bundle of papers was wrapped in government-issued red cloth paper. The wall to my left displayed a large, electric model of the water network.

Working between the phone list, government documents, and a network map, Surve started by telling me Mumbai's water story. This story, which I had by now heard several times before, began with the catchment of Mumbai's water several miles away. To help me understand, he tellingly did not refer to the map on the wall but drew me one of his very own—enlarging and extending it as the story went on. The map, which he drew with some ease, was filled with pipe diameters and place names, pumps and filtration plants (see figure 14). People, even the engineers, were almost entirely absent from the account. This was a story of careful management and effective control—of directing water from dammed rivers to the water treatment plant, a massive feat of technopolitical achievement by any standard.

The map, however, became considerably more complex and hard to quantify when he began to extend it into the secondary network, in which water subsequently flowed from the treatment plant to twenty-seven service reservoirs. Up until that point, water is generally counted, and metered. By the time Surve began speaking of the tertiary network that draws water from

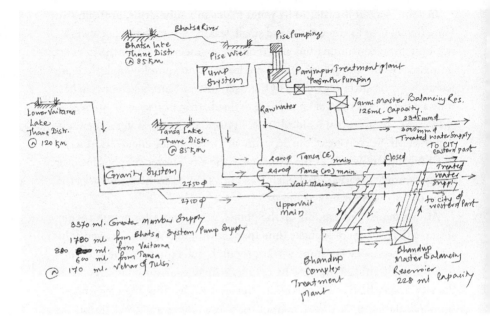

FIGURE 14. Surve's diagram of the water network.

reservoirs to the service mains, his map-making skills and knowledge of the system had reached their limit. It is these unmapped networks that are the subject of both leakage work and reform efforts.

Proponents of twenty-four-hour supply argue that tertiary networks should be continuously charged with water. But this proposition is the source of much anxiety for engineers like Surve who realize how little is known about leakages in the tertiary network. A system of 24/7 water supply would require a state of knowledge, a level of control, that he simply could not access. "We just don't know the alignment of lines in the city," he said. I asked if they had maps.

> Yes, but how far and how deep from the road [the pipes are], no one knows. There is no exact GIS to tell us this. Then, we have been searching for equipment to tell us where the leaks are. There is no equipment anywhere in the world that can tell us this. Mumbai sits on reclaimed land.... Therefore, the [leaking] water just goes away, it does not come to the surface.... There are pressure monitors.... But for these questions the person in the field is the best judge.

With most of the tertiary network underground, engineers have trouble lo-
cating exactly where its many parts are, much less what condition they are
in. The maps they had were clearly not up to the task, and are sparingly used.
The maps they do have do not contain elevation information—a critical detail necessary for water supply.

As a result, engineers draw on the experience and knowledge of their colleagues in the field for any major or minor works. Ward engineers are in a
constant search to locate pipes and their leaks beneath the structures of the
city. They need to know where the pipes can be found—how far from the
sidewalk, how deep in the ground, whether water will climb hills and how
it can do so. As Surve suggests, they are the city's pressure monitors and geographic information systems. In a city of consistent breakdowns and hydraulic
difficulties, engineers must consistently gauge and judge individual problems
and fashion solutions to each of them. Sometimes, retired engineers have
been summoned back to work just so that they can point to where the pipes
lie beneath the ground (see also Coelho 2006).

Repair

Fixing leaks is hard, necessary, time-consuming work. With most of the city's
network underground, water leaking from a pipe presents both material and
social challenges. Engineers use their management skills not so much as authoritarian rulers but as compromised experts, subjectified by the situations
of the politics, labor, and materials of the city's water infrastructure. To ensure that the system continues to function, they need to negotiate with not
only the city's pipes but also its water, residents, municipal employees, and
a range of social actors that are connected to the city's pipes in a variety of
ways. Thus, far from being a mechanical process, leakage repair makes visible
the sociological and technical work that engineers are required to perform as
they deploy their ingenuity and improvisational skill to manage the problem
(Latour 1996, 33).

Like the political anthropologist, the engineer is only too aware of the
ways in which his efforts to maintain the city's infrastructure is deeply situated in ambivalent social-technical environments of uncertainty, ignorance,
and improvisation. For instance, one afternoon I accompanied Patankar—a
water engineer who worked in a different city ward—on his "field" visits.
Identified by his colleagues, seniors, and subjects as a diligent public servant,
Patankar oversaw the maintenance of mains and service connections in the

ward. Trained at an engineering college in a nearby city, Patankar had lived and worked in the same ward for the past twenty years. As such, he was familiar with its diverse neighborhoods and their hydraulic politics. He exercised extraordinary energy in managing and mediating knowledge of the ward's water network and took a great deal of care in deciding which leakages to attend to and which others to ignore.

As I rode on the back of his motorcycle through city traffic from the site of one water problem to another, I was struck by the way in which Patankar approached each problem with experience, an eye for improvisation, and a social intuition that he could have only learned on the job. We rode across the ward to investigate a leaky main. I had been to the line previously, just a couple of weeks prior, when city workers were patching it up. A few nights before, the pipe had burst again, and residents of the neighboring ward had not received water for two days. Patankar told me that he had been working long hours just to locate the origin of the leak. The city's infrastructure was not cooperating with his efforts. The pipe lay nearly ten meters under the surface of the street, and Patankar had told me that whenever his team tried to uncover the pipe, the sodden, marshy soil would collapse over it again. As we disembarked from the bike and walked toward the troublesome pipe, we crossed over a bridge. I noticed a different pipe running alongside the bridge, with many smaller connections protruding from it. One small connection was leaking with high pressure into the *nalla* (canal/drain) below. Patankar did not even give this pipe a second glance. With his time and expertise already stretched, he walked toward the twenty-four-inch water main, where the bigger problem lay.

We arrived at the site to find water department employees and heavy machinery already at work. A shop had once stood where the maintenance team was now unearthing the large pipe. As we paused for a moment to observe their efforts, a couple of people came up to talk to us. "Will you cut our water again?" one of them asked, referring to a two-day cut that had occurred when the pipe was previously repaired. Not suggesting that water would be cut, nor telling them it would not, Patankar assured the residents that they would be notified if this was to be the case. A second person was not as pleased. He objected to the works project and aggressively complained about how a shop had stood there for two years before it was demolished due to maintenance works. Patankar smiled and responded by asking of the absent shopkeeper: "Who told him to build a shop on a water line? Did the pipe come first or the shop?" The petitioner, somewhat silenced by the question, observed: "The pipe, of course."

As we spoke, the maintenance team was trying to find a valve that could shut off the water to the burst pipe so that they could better inspect it. Patankar walked across another bridge and, noting a thick metal sheet that lay by the side of the road, asked his four men to move it to one side. As they grunted and heaved the sheet aside, they found an opening in the ground. There, about ten feet deep, lay a layer of water, below which a manhole cover might have been visible. Patankar asked whether it might be possible for the maintenance crew to go into the manhole, and find the valve. The crew members, each of whom had firm opinions about the matter, were understandably not enthusiastic. They suggested lowering a camera to find the valve. Patankar agreed, and wondered whether this could be accomplished during supply hours, when water was flowing through the line. The junior staff disagreed. Instead, they concluded that they would come back with a camera the next day. Realizing that the issue would require another day to be resolved, Patankar said a few words to the supervisor before we left the site to attend to another problem.

This everyday work of fixing water connections drew my attention to the contingency, improvisation, and social/material mediation Patankar and other engineers frequently employed to maintain the water network in working condition. To govern water pipes effectively required not only a (very contested) *metis* for repair and recovery (Latour 1996; Scott 1998) but also an understanding of how to handle the uncertainties and difficulties affiliated with the city's water infrastructure. As Patankar and his workers struggled to locate the leak, they were required to deal with both restive political subjects and the challenges presented by the water network—the opacity of water and earth, as well as the pipe network's corrosions, containments, and concealments.

In the absence of flexible protocols that could apprehend and direct how this leak could be known and plugged, state authority was not just improvised but was also diffuse and actively negotiated between the experts, laborers, and objects of Mumbai's water infrastructure. It was not just Patankar, the senior engineer, who was an expert of the system but also his less formally trained workers. Fixing the unknown leak on the pipe, therefore, required not only the cooperation of the earth not to collapse onto the pipe every time it was revealed. It also required the cooperation of city workers who, while charged with maintenance works, had their own ideas about how this maintenance could be done. In order to maintain and govern the city's water network effectively, Patankar needed to know certain key facts about the line (where the leak was, how it might be found and patched) as well as how this infrastructure was situated in regimes of labor, nature, materiality, and the law. To fix the pipe, Patankar required an acute sociotechnical knowledge that was attentive to contingency, obduracy, and the ignorances of people and things.

Discreet States

Leakages not only emerge from the corroding materialities of the city's infrastructure. Facing demands for water from residents that they are either legally or structurally unable to serve because of exclusive city water rules, engineers and other city authorities also participate in the production of leakage (euphemistically called *social leakage*) when they permit otherwise ineligible residents to connect to the water system. As engineers tacitly sanction different kinds of connections for these groups, these leakages are not documented, nor are they visible to their superiors in the head office.

By enabling water connections while keeping the higher-ups in the city administration ignorant of these informal connections, ward engineers allow for otherwise ineligible residents to receive state services, even as they reproduce their authority as experts of Mumbai's water system. Let me illustrate this point with an example. One day, I arrived at the field engineer's office to find the city councilor there with a party worker. Patankar (the engineer) was courteous and receptive, as always. As I tried to gather what was going on, I slowly realized it was a negotiation over an illegal connection. Months before, certain tenements had been in the news for threatening the sanctity of a site of cultural importance, and the court had ordered that the tenements' water connections be cut. Patankar was compelled to follow the court's order and cut their water supply. Now, a party functionary who worked in the area had come to him for permission to reconnect the lines. Patankar responded by neither approving nor refusing his request. "What did I tell you then?" he said. "I said I have to cut the connection. After I cut it, you can do what you want."

With this single directive, Patankar fulfilled his duty as a public officer twice over. He carried out the court's order, cutting the connection, while allowing its contradiction, water supply, to continue via other means. His instruction relinquished some of his knowledge and control over the ward's water pipes to the realm of ignorance and to the party workers, plumbers, and residents responsible. This was not an exceptional incident. Engineers like Patankar were often guiding councilors and plumbers through and around its rules, marshaling the powers of ignorance and ignoring the rules when they proved too exclusive. Such practices of ignorance—"do what you want (don't tell me)"—relieved the pressure on city engineers to deliver water and pointed to important ways in which ignorance, indifference, and enforcement were arbitrarily mobilized to produce state authority in the city.[22] By allowing councilors, their party workers, and plumbers to make connections without the written approval of the water department, these practices of ignorance allowed settlers to access public services while maintaining the political authority of the city councilors whose support the engineers required.

I was not able to follow up with this party worker to learn whether he ever made the connection, and I am not sure that Patankar followed up, either. If the party worker did reconnect the water line, the water supply would return to his voting clients' homes as "leakage." This leakage and the ignorance about this leakage, produce gaps in the control of the public system—gaps that both allow people to live in the city (despite the law) and yet place them beyond the accounting regimes of the state. Unauthorized connections are often buried underground, beneath the gaze of the state, and are undocumented and uncounted by the state's knowledge regimes (bills, meters, etc.). They are difficult to expose by those who do not know about them. They are as difficult to detect and fix as discreet physical leaks in the city. As area engineers of the water department participate in the production of leakage, both engineers in the head offices of the water department and the World Bank consultants are unable to parse out how much water is leaking to unauthorized groups or even where these connections exist. Through their everyday work, area engineers in Mumbai make the city's distribution system flow by mobilizing relations of knowledge and ignorance, and leakage and repair. As they improvise solutions to keep water flowing to differentiated groups, their compromised activities make them vitally necessary to the everyday work of water supply.

In the course of doing fieldwork, I was struck by the influence councilors had over engineers and workers in the water supply department. In a telling arrangement, field engineers are not arranged in the ward by the geography of water infrastructure zones. Instead, each engineer is deputed to attend to the needs of specific city councilors. As such, they are often called upon to exercise discretionary power to attend to their requests. When councilors came into their offices, engineers would quickly smile, get up from their seat, and offer them tea and biscuits. They would listen attentively and agree to solve many problems. Almost daily, councilors had requests of the engineers—to send more water to their ward, waive unpaid bills, or arrange new connections for those who were or were not otherwise eligible for water services.

Such quotidian interactions reveal critical shifts in the relationship between the technocratic and democratic state. In Mumbai, particularly as it pertains to water supply, municipal councilors also rule its water system.[23]

As artisans of Mumbai's water system, city engineers are not very happy with its popularized state. They are rueful experts, frequently grumbling about "interference" by councilors, and are nostalgic for times when their power was not as compromised. City engineers like Gupte resent the constant and consistent intervention of councilors who always have special and specific requests for identified constituencies (see also Coelho 2006). "People use water to do politics," Gupte said. "To win in elections, they use the department as an instrument. . . . Without water they cannot win." Gupte described water as "an extremely sensitive issue" and, as such, politicians continuously insisted and demanded their constituency get more water. "But the politicians have no foresight," he said. "They don't want to understand the system, its problems. . . . They only want more water for their ward."

Engineers complain when water—a technical issue for them—becomes encompassed by the world of politics. Nevertheless, because they are dependent on councilors to approve their works contracts and careers and also because councilors can quickly mobilize protesting publics that can embarrass engineers, engineers work to satisfy councilors' requests, marshaling the powers of procedure, technics, and ignorance to do so.

Some of the connections that engineers provide on the behalf of councilors are metered, documented, and counted. Some are simply documented but not metered, while others do not even exist on paper. Finally, there are connections that are unknown even to the engineers. Sequestered and buried under the surface of the city, these surreptitious connections—like those that leak into the ground—exceed the engineers' capacities and technologies of detection. Moreover, their detection is also not always in the engineer's interest.

Plumbing the System

To be included in the public system requires some combination of cultural competency, social connections, and varying amounts of cash (see chapter 2). An attention to these arrangements requires a more nuanced understanding of how the public system works in Mumbai. The multiple locations of power and authority in the public system produce many locations at which residents can make claims (or leaks). The success of otherwise unqualified settlers in joining the system depends on their ability to mobilize their relations in the BMC to make water connections, their access to political leaders, and, finally, their ability to grease the engines and palms, with money, of the state. It is a complicated state of affairs that requires plumbers to assist in its navigation.

Maqbool, a plumber by profession, had a delicate sense of the system and how it functioned. As we sat at a roadside chai shop one day, amid traffic and in the setting sun, he explained how many settlers obtained water from the system: "It all depends on the councilor," he said. "Because Shinde [the councilor] fights [with the engineers], the people here get water," Maqbool explained. "He has been a councilor for fifteen years. The engineers fear him and do his work. Nearby, Khan is a new councilor. It's not even been five years. She has no chance [to wield that kind of influence]." Maqbool foregrounds the importance of councilors in his account of how settlers obtain water. Describing the process of making connections, he points to how engineers pay close attention to which councilor's letter of support (an implicit requirement) was attached to applications for new connections to be approved.[24] Chances were further improved if you engaged the services of certain plumbers. Each councilor had his plumbers who put applications to the Municipal Corporation, he told me. These plumbers knew how, where, and to whom money had to be passed, under the gaze (and blessings) of the city councilor.

As Maqbool told me: "They [the plumbers and the councilors] have an understanding, and [the engineers] make sure that with Shinde's blessings, connections are granted. Residents are free to choose another plumber. But they would have to deposit fees in the office for Shinde. Councilors pressure the BMC to ensure they do not give water to anyone without a letter." From the conversation, it was clear that Maqbool was not one of the councilor's preferred plumbers. His description of the public system reveals its very personal nature, one that is tied to, but not determined by, money. In a world of connections, the involvement of the councilor and the necessity of his consent produces an intimate relation between the governing and the governed.

The extremely personal and political negotiations between engineers, residents, and councilors fostering this leakage trouble the normative assumptions of public and private systems. In Mumbai, the poor are seldom just customers, nor are they citizens. They are also "helped'" through relations that sit alongside the practices of citizenship, markets, and the law. In much of the development literature, specifically about India, such "helping" practices are known through the discourses of corruption (J. Davis 2004; Witsoe 2011). Indeed settlers also often talk about these practices as corruption (Gupta 1995). While there is much we need to consider around such practices,[25] here, I want to take Maqbool's provocation seriously—that there is the money, but that it is not the only thing that is going on. In fact, those in more powerful settlements (or more powerful corporations) sometimes do not need to spend their money.[26] In Mumbai, such relations (that at times accompanies the exchange of cash) are a critical way through which settlers overcome structural denials (either by laws or everyday practices) to access the most basic entitlement of life—water. It is these corruptions—these leakages—that make it possible to live.[27]

For those living in settlements, the public system is made through personal-political relations—between residents and councilors, councilors and engineers, and the plumbers who connect them. It is a public system of favors, and one marked with relations of patronage, voting, and money. While settlers are often quite successful in mobilizing water from the public system to their homes, their inclusion in this system reproduces its inequalities and reinscribes the power of its authorities. Recognizing the state of this infrastructure, settlers in Mumbai are constantly trying to find its legitimate patrons, cracks, and fissures so as to survive. With friends and relatives, they petition city councilors and volunteers to write letters on their behalf (see chapter 2). With money, they approach plumbers for new connections to pipes that have more water. With plumbers, they arrive at the water office with a long list of documents, letters, and copies of bills and ration cards. With these relations and contacts, they know the technical geography of the network, frequently drawing pen diagrams for engineers on the backs of envelopes to argue their case. Engineers listen and consider the political geography of the proposed connection on those very same maps. Who is presenting the proposal? Who is around? Who will get less water as a result? In Mumbai, you need to create pressure to make water flow. If residents apply the right kind of pressure—through an eclectic mix of protest marches, phone calls, and petitions in the correct languages of belonging, if they sometimes introduce financial considerations—they get water, often through leaks in the public system.

Conclusion

One afternoon, I took Patankar to lunch so that we could talk a little bit more about the water system and the various causes of leakage. In the quiet, shaded, and air-conditioned environs of the restaurant, Patankar reviewed his methodology. People get angry when they do not get water, he told me.

"It's our job to find and fix the problem." He wondered aloud if the engineers of a private company might be able to do the job more effectively, given their expectations of revenue and the watertight management regimes with which they were more preoccupied. The pursuit of revenue water (or the reduction of nonrevenue water) meant that they were less willing to compromise with the materiality and politics of the system. "Even the chief engineer of the water department, a few years ago, said that he doesn't understand how the system works," Patankar said. "How will these private fellows manage?"

As Patankar described the difficulty that even the most senior and qualified engineers have in comprehending the system, I recalled Haresh's cautions about the difficulties that engineers encounter when measuring water's quantities. Despite efforts to contain, control, and manage water through large infrastructure projects, the differentiated social, material, and political histories that form these infrastructures make it difficult for state officials to know enough about and contain leakages. Engineers were constantly challenged by the relations between errant employees, nonworking meters, corroded pipes, and exclusive water laws. As they negotiated, ignored, or fixed leakages, their improvised practices revealed how the sociotechnical assemblages of water distribution lay just beyond their domains, control, and expertise.

Therefore, when Patankar managed the city's water infrastructure, he did so not by working *on* it but by working *through* it, making discrete improvisations and accommodations so that it could deliver water reliably, while remaining ignorant of the chaos of the system so that he could do his work (Scott 1998). In doing so, he revealed how the expertise of the engineer does not emerge out of his ability to operate and control Mumbai's water infrastructures as objects, tools, or technologies from a distance. Instead, this expertise emerges from very proximate, compromised relations with the materials, persons, and politics of the city's leaky infrastructure—relations that Patankar did not know everything about. The ward's water infrastructure exceeded his control. As attempts to fix leaks are often contested not just by city residents but also by the intransigence of his workers and the muddy, murky subterranean situation of earth, water, and steel, Patankar and other engineers are unable to prevent leakage in the city. They repair leakages just enough so as to maintain sufficient water pressure in the network.

In so doing, Patankar and other engineers reproduce a particular leaky form of the state. As they patch up holes on water lines or disconnect illegal connections, their work is productive of state authority. Nevertheless, as leakages persist, they also diffuse the state's authority. Pipes—as assemblages of valves, steel, laws, persons, and objects—"act" despite and beyond state power. As leakages exceed both the semiotics and politics of subjects and experts in the city, leaking pipes at times enable state formation. At others, they interrupt and lie beside state control, dispersing power and water as they do so.

Indeed, when Haresh reminds us that water has "technical constraints," he is urging us to recognize the ways in which its corporality and its relations to the city's infrastructure reveal not the limits of water but instead the limits of reform efforts in the city. City engineers recognize that their control of Mumbai's water is compromised by the fungibility of materiality and politics. They have more modest demands of its flows. One of Mumbai's most senior engineers described water supply as an "event-driven process." With their control both constituted and compromised by the leaky materialities of the city's water infrastructure, and the exigencies of democratic politics, engineers in Mumbai only try to contain the most egregious (political and material) leakages. They have expressed an inability to make the city's water infrastructure more watertight. Their inability points not only to the limits of human expertise over sociotechnical systems but also the compromised yet significant effects of democratic politics in Mumbai, particularly as they produce and encourage leaky technologies of rule. In this technopolitical environment, leakages are not an exception but a condition of Mumbai's water system; they are often easier to leave alone than to repair, seal, and foreclose.

Nevertheless, even as leakages exceed human efforts to control water flows, they do not have an existence that is independent of human technologies. Like engineers who act through water infrastructures, water only acts through relations with infrastructures as well, including engineers and "mediating technologies" they install on the network—meters, valves, pipes, and so on (see Furlong 2011). As Andrew Barry reminds us, things become political through relations (Barry 2011). Politics, therefore, always emerges as plural, through diverse relations between humans and relations with and between nonhumans. While the properties of water do matter to the events of leakage, these are not independent of human relations and human responsibility.

As such, leaks are more-than-human flows of water in that they are formed with but exceed human intentionality and action (Braun 2005; Braun and Whatmore 2011). This is not to say that leaks are impossible to diagnose and fix with existing technologies. Nor is it to say that settlers who are denied formal water connections celebrate the socially and politically mediated leakages that hydrate their lives. Instead, accreted histories of law, technology, and politics—the intermittent supply, aging pipes, laws proscribing access, fickle meters, engineers allocating water—challenge city engineers to control, count, know, and govern leakage. While leaks establish a particular form of state power, they also render that power "porous" and unstable (S. Benjamin 2005; Fuller and Harriss 2001). They make the state vulnerable not only to calls and demands for neoliberal reform and to the demands of residents denied water. As pipes quietly leak underground for years, they also corrode the very grounds upon which the state and its governmental projects stand.

Interlude. Jharna (Spring)

The settlements of Jogeshwari are filled with many sources and stories of water. While I was conducting fieldwork, residents told me of the various ways in which they obtained water prior to state recognition. Many spoke of purchasing it from considerate neighbors. Others would point to wells or describe how they got water from the ground by digging shallow pits. But perhaps most remarkable was the story of a spring located at the heart of a settlement. To this day, the spring continues to push water out of the earth, all day, every day.

Neighbors are uncertain about the source of this water. Is it from a leaky water main? Or is it rainwater runoff? No one really knows. But the water is saturated with memories—memories of how it made settlement possible. Here, I present Durga Gudilu's memories of the spring told through her film *Yaadé*, made in the series *Ek Dozen Paani*.

> There is a spring. This spring is older than when the Sanjay Nagar basti first came up here. The water of this spring keeps flowing like this for twenty-four hours. In the beginning Sanjay Nagar's residents used to fill water from this spring. And [we used to] go there to wash clothes, utensils. . . . When I was twelve, thirteen [years old], I would go with my sister to the spring to fill water. My sister used to carry a big handi [vessel] to fill water. I had polio as a child . . . so I could not carry a heavy handi. My mother, too, would not allow me to take along a big handi. I used to feel very bad that my sister and everyone [else] would come with such big handis and I would be given only a small handi to carry! (D. Gudilu 2008)

The work of collecting water from the spring was in some ways not unlike the labor necessary in other households at water time. It is a social activity that is generative of relations, meanings, and subjectivities. Through her story, Durga describes how her disability was revealed in her childhood because

FIGURE 15. A mysterious spring. Water emerges from the rocks on this Jogeshwari hillside. The spring continues to hydrate Jogeshwari's settlements even as no one is certain of its source.

of her inability to labor for water as her siblings and friends did. Her being afflicted with polio meant she could not fully participate in water's social life.

Now, Durga's household receives water at 7:00 in the morning through a tap outside her home. The water comes at the same time every day, with good pressure. Accordingly, Durga's family does not go to collect water from the spring anymore. Yet it continues to flow, promising to make other lives possible. These days, Durga tells me "Bihari people" use it to collect water, to bathe, to wash their clothes. As newer migrants, they have difficulty obtaining proper connections from the city water department. So, they use this water for their daily needs. They visit the spring more often in the morning than the evening, Durga said. There is a correct time to use this water, even as the spring continues to flow all day every day.

6. DISCONNECTION

For fifteen years I have heard the MP-MLA say, "It's coming—the line is coming." What can I say? They don't want to develop this area. They only [want to] see how can the votes be gathered. To gather goodwill, they say, "We aren't in power in the BMC, so we will construct a tank." This way, ten to twelve bore wells have been dug. Some of them are good and some are not, and there are people who rule them [*logon ka raaj hai*]. But the bore well water is not potable. Some of the bore wells are next to the toilets. Gutter water seeps into them. Is this development, or what? —ASIF IN SHAIKH 2008

I was speaking with Asif bhai, a longtime resident of Premnagar, a settlement in Mumbai's northern suburbs. Seeing us interview Salim, another informant, in a neighborhood teashop, Asif had eagerly joined our conversation about water problems. Visibly upset, he said that Premnagar's residents have grown tired of waiting for the Municipal Corporation to improve, maintain, and extend its water network into the settlement. State and federal legislators (MLAs and MPs) had expressed their helplessness at drawing water from the municipal system, he said, and instead sponsored the construction of bore wells in the area. On the one hand, these wells have given settlers some relief, providing them with much-needed water, albeit for a price. Households pay setup costs of approximately US$100 each to connect to the well system and also a monthly fee for bore well water. Yet Asif and many others do not desire bore well water as much as treated municipal water. They see their water supply as "backward," "like water you get in the villages and farms." Asif considered well water dirty and impure, water that reflected the city water department's neglect and abjection of the settlement's residents. Despite such perceptions, however, many in Premnagar have little choice. Over time, municipal pipes, installed more than forty years ago, have been allowed to rust, leak, and slowly go dry.

As Asif and other Muslim settlers discuss how they are no longer able to claim the modern, purified, treated, municipal water to which they once had access, I draw on theorizations of abjection to point to ways in which Muslim settlers are being quite literally disconnected from its municipal water system. As James Ferguson points out, to be disconnected is different from being unconnected (Ferguson 1999, 239). It is an active process through which subjects are "thrown down," or cast out of the social and political systems that they were once able to access and claim.[1] In this chapter I focus on the iterative process between state officials, populations, and their intermediaries (municipal plumbers) through which both certain settlers and groundwater are rendered abject through the everyday work of maintaining and managing water infrastructure.

Recent work on urban citizenship has pointed to the ways in which city and state laws and policies produce precarious, informal, and abject populations.[2] For example, in their work in cities as diverse as Kolkata, Delhi, and São Paulo, Ananya Roy (2004), Asher Ghertner (2015), and James Holston (2008) show how housing regulations and aesthetic legal regimes have long marginalized settlers by marking their housing in the city as unsafe and dangerous. In chapter 2, I drew on this work to show how settlers are marginalized by city water rules that allocate them smaller pipes and water quotas.

The water shortages experienced by Muslim settlers, however, do not exist because they are "unrecognized" or marginalized by the differentiated categories of citizenship (Holston 2008). Nor are their water difficulties a consequence of being unconnected to Mumbai's water system. As a basti resettled by the city government since the early 1970s, Premnagar previously had access to good, treated water. When I was conducting fieldwork, the complaints of Premnagar's residents centered around the lack of maintenance—water lines serving the settlement had been allowed to remain leaky and go dry, even as more recent, neighboring settlers were able to access reliable water from city pipes.

The abjection that Premnagar's settlers experience, as indexed by their water supply, demonstrates the precariousness and reversibility of citizenship gains. Having neither the substantive rights of civil society nor the "strategic leverage of electoral mobilization" (Chatterjee 2008, 61), residents of Premnagar need to access other kinds of water to maintain their lives. To live in the city, they need to pay plumbers very high prices—either to connect them illegally to the municipal system or to connect them to the incipient well water network, creating, in Michelle Murphy's terms, "a densely populated elsewhere within the here" (2006, 157).

City engineers point to the effects of abjection—the lack of cleanliness and illegal connections—as the cause of their area's water problems. Yet the lack of infrastructure maintenance in the area by the Municipal Corporation also participates in the production of abjection in the settlement. Drawing on Akhil Gupta and Aradhana Sharma's (2006) provocation to focus on the narratives and practices of state officials, I show how city engineers, as political subjects and experts who inhabit the city, view and make Muslims as dangerous outsiders through infrastructural practices. The pumps, pipes, and valves they arrange and maintain play a critical role in elucidating not only the political and social relations that constitute the city but also the religious identities of its settlers.[3] Pointing to the ways in which Muslim settlers connect to the water system, city hydraulic engineers view them as "not good" and undeserving of hydraulic citizenship—as dirty, troublesome, and threatening to the city's water system and, by extension, the viability of the city itself.

These everyday discriminations are neither incidental nor exceptional. The abjection Mumbai's water system produces does not require ignorance or a forgetting of history, nor is it a result of being governed at a distance. Neither can the living conditions experienced by Premnagar's population be explained as an effect of differentiating legal regimes. Settlers who reside on more precarious legal ground adjacent to Premnagar have better access to water. Rather, abjection is enabled by the cultural politics of city engineers. As city engineers work with and around Premnagar's population, abjection is a dialectical process produced out of deeply situated discursive relationships and material practices, where histories of difference are emergent and reproduced through the production, management, and maintenance of urban infrastructure.

Shadow Lines

As discussed in earlier chapters, the residents of Jogeshwari's bastis, particularly those who support the Shiv Sena, have made significant qualitative improvements to their material infrastructures by claiming state services through their elected patron politicians. For instance, Reshma tai and Alka tai have been able to work with political parties and community organizations like Asha to claim water as hydraulic citizens (see introduction, chapter 3). The extent to which they have been able to do so has been enabled by the democratic practices of voting and protesting, which together have established a degree of precarious yet substantive citizenship.[4] One settlement in which this has *not* happened, however, is Premnagar, where the water network has been slowly crumbling over time. As engineers of the city water department neglect their leaky pipes, residents in Premnagar have been unable able to access water without the use of pumps and surreptitious pipes at supply times that are a source of tremendous inconvenience.

The difficulties of Premnagar's residents in their daily labors of water collection were very evident when I visited them in the early mornings during water time. One morning, I visited my friend Salim, to "hang out" with him while he collected his daily supplies. When I arrived just before 5:00 a.m., the sun was not up yet. Shadowy figures stumbled back and forth, still very much asleep. I heard motors whirring quietly. Salim was awake and getting ready for the day. Still sleepy, I asked why he did not collect water later in the morning. Perhaps at 7:00 or so, just before it went away? Salim told me that it was hard to get water after 5:30 in the morning because people at lower elevations would start collecting water at that time from the same line. Once they opened their taps, the pressure would drop in Salim's tap, making it difficult for him to provision enough water for the day.

Even at this early hour, however, Salim had to share his water line with others. As we waited our turn, Salim pointed to the man who would give him a temporary connection for fifteen minutes. He was a young, thin man, perhaps in his twenties, dressed in jeans and a vest, moving back and forth faster than anyone else in the area. He looked quite busy, constantly connecting and disconnecting plastic pipes that led into different homes, effectively doing the regulatory work of the chaviwalla within the neighborhood. "Salim bhai, I will give you the pipe in ten to fifteen minutes, OK?" he promised.

The pump–pipe arrangement that provided Salim with water originated at the side of the road, some thirty meters from his home. We followed the plastic pipes downhill to their source—a surreptitious connection to the mains that lay on one side of the road. It joined the main water line beneath the pavement. Water seldom climbed up any higher than this point, Salim told me. So, Salim and his neighbors had collectively tapped the main line here, and pumped water up to their homes at their own cost. As the morning progressed, other people woke up, and they too unwound their plastic pipes, sticking one end in a pump and another into a storage drum. They would then connect another pipe from the pump to their own secretly tapped water main down the hill. I was amazed to see how these taps were both hidden from sight and accessible enough to be joined and disconnected every day.

The assemblage of secrete, private lines linked to public water pipes that only delivered water at lower elevations revealed the manner in which public water services had retreated (or at least did not travel as far) for certain populations. As residents worked to retrieve this water with their own "private" technologies—pumps and pipes—they described how this work was necessary not just because of their topographically disadvantaged location but also because of the ways in which the leaky line had not been upgraded in years.

When it was his turn, Salim was given a pipe with which he could fill his indoor storage tank. Just after he had finished collecting his daily water requirement, he began to wake his half-dozen workers who lived in his workshop. By around 9:00 a.m., they would begin to start making the intricate *zari* for dresses that would eventually find their way to shopping malls as far away as Delhi and Dubai.

Social Engineering

While engineers were aware that Premnagar's residents had water problems, they did not do many works projects in the area. This is not to say that they overlooked all the city's settlements. In fact, their lists—jotted down in cell phones and small notebooks—were always very long and full of projects in other settlements. They were always busy and often working hard. They simply were not as busy in Premnagar. For example, in chapter 5, I described how Patankar, one of three sub-engineers in the ward office, had to negotiate an impossible range of demands on his workday. All at once, every day, he had to address leakages on large service lines as well as councilor complaints of water quality, attend administrative meetings at the Municipal Corporation's head office, and review applications for new connections brought to him by a never-ending line of plumbers and politicians at the ward office. I often wondered how Patankar, one of the most conscientious municipal engineers I met, managed such impossible demands. When there was more work than time in the day, which complaints did he attend to first?

Patankar was a hard-working officer without any obvious biases against Muslims. Nevertheless, when I asked him why Premnagar had water problems, he would often insist that what plagued the residents of Premnagar was not short supply. It was that they were not good customers. "They are getting enough water," he told me. The problem, he suggested, was with their disposition. *"Vaha sar uthake nahi jeete hai,"* he said. "They do not live honorably [literally 'with their heads held high']." He went on to describe how

Premnagar's residents do not play by the city's water rules. They were "stealing" it from the city's pipes. Accordingly, he was limited in his ability to respond to their problems. Rhetorically, he asked me to investigate whether the residents who spoke of their water difficulties had taken the appropriate steps to redress their grievances at the water office: "Check with them—ask for copies of their complaints; check the BMC acknowledgment stamp, and date. No one will have this. They do not complain. They do not complain because they are not paying bills! When they are not paying bills, they can shout, but they cannot complain." Patankar here makes a distinction between "shouting" for water and "complaining."[5] For Patankar shouting was not an appropriate mode of resolving water problems.

Time and again, over our many conversations, Patankar told me that he preferred to help settlers who were "educated" and behaved as good *customers*. Those who lived honorably paid for water. Like many engineers, he saw water as the "movable property" of the water department, and as property, it had to be properly paid for when exchanged.[6] Challenging the rights/commodity distinctions that many activists made when it came to public and private management of water, good citizens, for Patankar, were those who *paid* for water and followed the appropriate bureaucratic procedures to make complaints in the event that water services were erratic.

That Patankar required residents to furnish copies of paid bills prior to complaining about water connections suggests that he saw residents of the city more as customers than citizens. His approach troubles contemporary debates about privatization that overlook ways in which the workers in public utilities also legitimate their work through the language of private service provision (Baviskar 2003b). The problem with Premnagar's residents, he suggested, was that they did not behave as appropriate "consumers" of government services. They did not pay their bills. In the absence of payment, he explained, residents would not be permitted to document their concerns in the ward's complaint register. They would not be seen by their complaint.

Residents, however, protested that the BMC regularly billed them for water they never received. "Whether or not the water comes, the bills always come," the members of a women's savings group told me one day. Formally, the water is to be billed based on the quantity consumed over two months. Yet, because over half the city's water meters are not working, and also because state meter readers are often reticent to spend their days reading meters, in practice many residents are billed based on "estimated consumption" by meter readers who seldom leave their offices. Therefore, even in the event that connections did not provide water, the bills and arrears would continue to mount for Premnagar's residents.

Rather than complain about bills, residents found it easier to let the bills be and to let the arrears mount. They did not go to the office to complain and instead started making their own arrangements. Engineers, too, were willing to leave the situation alone, acting on the unpaid arrears only if a customer complained about water problems. They acted by *refusing* to fix the problem until the bills were paid. For engineers such as Patankar, "nonpayment" was thus a technique of management—a way of excluding those who did not pay their bills from the attentions of the state.

Yet the problems experienced by Premnagar's residents cannot be attributed to unpaid arrears alone. Because the settlement is at a slightly higher elevation, water supply has been difficult even for those residents who pay their water bills. To get water to Premnagar, engineers must ensure that the water level in the service reservoir is high enough to push water into the settlement with sufficient pressure. Yet because the water system is so leaky, and also because engineers are always trying to satiate the demands of other areas, they have a difficult time pressurizing the system so that it is able to deliver water up into Premnagar. Thus, residents such as Salim are compelled to draw water using their own booster pumps and pipe networks, at significant costs to their households (see figure 16).

Water systems depend on pressure to work. By placing a discreet demand on city pipes, one not accounted for by engineers, booster pumps trouble engineers' meticulous pipe and pressure calculations, making it difficult for the water system to perform as they intend (see Barnes 2014). Patankar described how booster pumps compromised his water network designs, preferentially diverting water to those who used them and away from those who did not. Engineers therefore saw the use of booster pumps as a social vice—a morally questionable technology that, while effective for the owner, also evacuated water pressure from the system for all others. The prolific use of booster pumps in Premnagar emerged as yet another reason why the neighborhood was "not a good area."

Yet, because water has difficulty climbing hills, pumps *were* necessary in Jogeshwari's higher regions, whether or not they were incorporated into official designs. There simply was not enough pressure in the system, given the demands placed on the reservoir network. When I asked engineers why they did not install city pumps in these locations, they replied that the costs of pumping water were prohibitive and would disturb the cost effectiveness of the entire urban water system. But topography, techniques, and elevation

FIGURE 16. Water lines serving Premnagar. Some of these lines are legal; others are illegal. It is difficult for engineers (or anyone else) to tell them apart.

only matter for some. The state's willingness to bear the cost of pumping depends on who lives at higher elevations. For instance, throughout its history, the department has not hesitated to pump water up to Malabar Hill—home to the city's economic and politically powerful. In Mumbai, as in other cities, the costs of public service tend to matter more if the residents are poor than if they are wealthy.[7]

Such class-based interpretations that account for the production of difference in cities can only be part of the explanation, however. I learned midway through my fieldwork that some other settlements have managed to get the city to install pumps on their behalf. For instance, residents of Bandrekar Wadi, a settlement very close to Premnagar, have managed to pressure engineers to install pumps to send water up to their homes. Their success reveals how the city administration does, at times, treat settlers as it does wealthier citizens.

That Bandrekar Wadi benefits from pumps on its water lines is also surprising because it is a more recent slum area whose legal status relative to Premnagar was more tenuous on account of its location near a national park. How did Bandrekar Wadi come to municipal pumping? I asked Kerkar, another city engineer why Bandrekar Wadi had water pumps and Premnagar did not. "There, they have a strong local leader, who works with the BMC," he explained. "That makes the difference." Indeed, the city councilor repre-senting Bandrekar Wadi belongs to the Shiv Sena—the majority party in power in the Municipal Corporation. Engineers suggested it was his political "strength" (and not either topography or law) that mattered to the ability of the settlers of Bandrekar Wadi to receive municipal water.

Kerkar went on to suggest that it was not only the strong leader who made the difference. The difference between Premnagar and Bandrekar Wadi also emerged from his understandings of what these residents were "like" in dif-ferent areas.

> *Our* people [those in Bandrekar Wadi] are from the village. They get jobs in the city, work, and are very particular about keeping the area clean. Meanwhile, *their* people are from outside. They come and want to stay in Premnagar only. They don't go outside. They will live in dirty conditions, no problem. When we do work in Bandrekar Wadi, people see us doing something good for the area, and they are helping [us do the work]. They are taking care of the area. In Premnagar, people see us doing something and start to fight. If we do [public] works, it's more of a problem. It's better to do nothing at all.

Kerkar's presentations of slums inhabited by "our" people and "their" people reveals how city water engineers form their dispositions and affections with and through the city's xenophobic political frames. With the rise of the Shiv Sena and majoritarian politics in Mumbai (and indeed in India more gener-ally), city engineers articulate ideas of the self and other, of us and them, here by deploying extant categories of region, religion, and belonging to identify Marathi residents as "our people" and Premnagar's Muslim residents as the other, as "they/them."

Yet it was not just a case of Kerkar drawing on parochial renditions of urban identity and difference. His dispositions emerged from his experiences of urban subjects as he went about his day fixing different infrastructural problems in the settlements of the city. The dirty conditions in Premnagar dissuaded Kerkar from doing works projects in the settlement. For Kerkar, "dirty areas" were difficult places to work not only because they were aestheti-cally disturbing or filled with othered bodies. Infrastructural improvements also seemed fleeting and thus futile in these areas of the city: "If we go work in dirty areas, then it doesn't even seem like we did anything there. And our work is such a thing that it doesn't even remain [effective]," Kerkar told me. As evidence for this, he spoke of a new road he had built in Janata colony just seven months prior. Despite his efforts, it did not last long. "Now it is already dug up, and coming apart at the edges." On the other hand, in "posh localities, there are fewer users," he said. "So the works last much longer, leaving both us and the people more satisfied." Rather than get involved in the "headache" of works projects in dirty and congested areas—especially those as "congested" as Premnagar—Kerkar suggested it was better just to leave them alone.[8]

Kerkar felt disinclined to work in Premnagar, othered and congested through histories of marginalization and difference. To him, the area was abject—associated with dirty, "defiled, dangerous outsiders" (S. Moore 2008). He found it to be a particularly contentious settlement in which to work as a public official. "They don't even give our laborers a glass of water to drink when we are working," another engineer told me. "They," in Premnagar, were not only from "outside" the state's boundaries but also Muslim, unwilling to leave their dirty ghettos or allow engineers to improve them. "They will live in dirty conditions, no problem."

Engineers saw Muslims' hydraulic practices—marked by the pervasiveness of private infrastructure such as pumps and pipes—as evidence of their lack of a public sensibility, evidence that they "steal" water from the public system. Like Kerkar, Gupte was a city water engineer who was committed to the idea of a public system. And like Kerkar, he did not see "slum dwellers," or "the poor," as an undifferentiated category. Instead, he considered Premnagar's settlers to be less deserving of public service than others. In December 2008 he elucidated his dispositions during an informal conversation we had at his office.

Gupte was fed up with his previous position as a field engineer, he told me, speaking of the phone calls he constantly had to take from different people (especially politicians). His current job—as a water planner, overseeing the technical and physical state of the water mains—suited him more. Fewer people bothered him now that he was no longer responsible for distribution. I told him of some of my work in Premnagar. He paused for a moment. "Premnagar is not a good area," he said. "On the other side, in Bandrekar Wadi, people are good," he continued, his sentence trailing. I asked what he meant by "not a good area." Those people in Premnagar are "not loyal to Bombay," he said. "In Bandrekar Wadi there are Marathi people. Not in Premnagar. There, they are stealing the water—Muslim people—they are tampering with and damaging the mains." But it was not just illegal tapping that caused the problem in Premnagar; it also had to do with where its residents came from. In Premnagar, people are generally from Uttar Pradesh, he told me. "There [in Uttar

Pradesh], they have the Ganga Yamuna. . . . They need ample water. So they find where water is good and settle in those areas of Mumbai."

Gupte's words turned uncomfortably in my head. They found me at the same time that I was wrestling with the xenophobic violence invoked by the city's new right-wing party, founded by Raj Thackeray.[9] As Gupte began to list Mumbai's various "communities"—Jain, Parsi, Muslim, Gujarati—by their hydraulic practices, I learned how cultural-political understandings of "native place," religion, and loyalty are at work placing the undifferentiated public for the city's technocrats (Gupta and Ferguson 1992). Gupte sees certain hydraulic practices as constitutive of particular communities. As Gupte's words suggest, city engineers differentiate settlers into good and bad, insiders and outsiders based on not only the settlements in which they live but also their hydraulic practices.

Gupte made clear that tampering with the mains is not something all poor people do—it is something Muslim people do. Like Kerkar, Gupte did not rely on hearsay or rumor to justify his position. He quickly listed specific reasons to argue that his impressions were not prejudiced as much as they were based on situated experiences in the settlement, particularly around illegal connections. "All over the city, the Muslim bastis are always the problem," Gupte complained. In Dharavi, where he previously worked, the plumbers would guarantee reconnection up to three times if the line was taken away, he told me. At the time, Gupte and his team would set out every Thursday to disconnect unauthorized lines. "The truck taking the illegal lines away looked like a sugarcane truck!" Gupte said, speaking of the volume of illegal pipes unearthed and confiscated by his department. Yet, by the following week, "they came back," he said. While Gupte was the hydraulic engineer in charge of the settlement, he certainly was not the only one in control of its pipes.

Gupte's difficulties demonstrate the very tenuous control of water that city engineers have in many of the city's settlements. In Premnagar, for instance, they are able to control its service mains, but in many ways, it is plumbers who govern the water system within the settlement. As Salim's water arrangements show, even abject populations need, and are capable of obtaining, water. Their connections are not administered by the municipal government even if they are eventually connected to its pipes. They are managed through other technopolitical arrangements uneasily connected to the municipal system. In Premnagar and other Muslim areas, the abjection produced by the municipal hydraulic system both draws on and has effected the power of plumbers, who mediate, connect, and sometimes flagrantly challenge engineers' authority in an attempt to control the locality's hydraulic system.

Plumber Raj

In Premnagar, as in other parts of the city, plumbers are required, by the city's formal rules *and* informal practices, to help people get water connections. Like city councilors, they are urban specialists (Hansen and Verkaaik 2009)—middlemen who connect settlers to the services of the city. Made as necessary by city water rules (which require private plumbers to make water connections) as by informal practices (to navigate settlers through a differentiating regime of accessing water), plumbers are critical to Mumbai's water system and, more particularly, to Premnagar. Working between the settler and the city engineer, plumbers have intimate knowledge of the city system and how it works, of how to access water in the city.

Not only were plumbers able to quickly and blatantly connect their customers to the water network without the engineers' authorization. Engineers also claim that plumbers are able to prevent residents from approaching engineers directly for water connections. Gupte, for example, expressed frustration that plumbers do not permit residents to approach him directly. "Plumbers won't let people come to us," he said. Patankar agrees: "They sit outside my office, and when someone from Premnagar comes to the office, they don't let them come inside to talk to me!" he complained. "What can I do?" Engineers said that there was little they could do to rein in plumbers. Made necessary by municipal rules and procedures that require their work to connect settlers to the municipal system, plumbers also knew how to violate municipal authority, should their work with it be made too difficult.

I met Rafiq bhai, a plumber by profession, in Patankar's office, when he came to apply for a water connection on behalf of one of his clients. Patankar had told me that Rafiq bhai was one of the good plumbers of Premnagar, and suggested I talk with him about the area. Later in the week, I called him on the phone and set a time to meet with him. Not knowing that I was familiar with the settlement, he came to the "border" road on a motorcycle, to pick me up.[10] As we walked through the settlement, I saw that Rafiq bhai was well known to many there, exchanging hellos every few minutes till we reached the back room of a small teashop. While we waited for the tea to arrive, we began talking about the water system and particularly about the difficulties in Premnagar, the settlement where he was born some forty years prior. "You must have noticed the difference between here and Meghwadi," Rafiq bhai began. I said that I had—there were fewer finished roads, more dust and gar-bage, and less order relative to the nearby settlement of Meghwadi.

But Rafiq bhai was not just talking about infrastructure. He was thinking more of the difference in the social life between the two settlements. He told me how, in Premnagar, there were mainly contractors and renters, entrepre-neurs working in small businesses. "Here, people don't want to be employ-ees; people have bad habits. They live largely on rents they receive in the settlement. They sleep late and wake late living on these rents. . . . People are not educated," he told me. I found it strange that Rafiq bhai's character-izations of the settlement resembled not only those of its Hindu neighbors but also those of city engineers. Indeed, many of Premnagar's residents also told me that people in Premnagar, generally self-employed, did not leave the neighborhood very often.

Rafiq bhai had been a plumber for the past ten years. I learned it was a family tradition—all of the men in his family were plumbers, and though many of them did this work, he was the only one making legal connections. All the rest lived just outside the system, setting up illicit connections for whomever paid them. I asked Rafiq bhai how he came to work as a plumber, and as one who made legal connections. He responded that his life was trans-formed by a relationship he had with Atré, a city engineer. "He taught me how to dress, how to walk, how to speak[,] . . . that I should wear shoes," Rafiq bhai explained. But Atré's training was not in Rafiq bhai's socialization alone. He also helped him find work. Based on Atré's recommendation, Rafiq bhai received a contract to do the plumbing works in a nearby slum rehabilitation project. Rafiq bhai was moved by his influence. Rafiq bhai told me that when he tried to give Atré a cash gift as a token of his gratitude, Atré took it and put it in a fixed deposit, one that he returned *with interest* to Rafiq bhai when it matured.

As I heard Rafiq bhai's story, I recalled how Yusuf bhai had also told me of how his mentorship with a municipal official had transformed his life (see chapter 2). Indeed, many engineers had deep and sympathetic relations with people living in the settlements—friendships that cut across ethnic, religious, and social lines. Rafiq bhai's friendship with Atré (or, for that matter, Yusuf bhai's friendship with police and municipal officials) challenges any neat and easy explanations of social, economic, or religious divisions in the city. In-deed, while discrete (and arbitrary) personal relationships between state officials and othered residents are constitutive of state violence (see Gupta 2012), these sympathetic relations have also transformed life, work, and futures for so many in Jogeshwari. "I was the dada of the area," Rafiq told me.

"No one in my family earns an honest living. I would only be a boy of the area if not for him," he said of Atré, his voice growing soft. He had a tremendous respect for the engineer, who had changed his life. They still spoke regularly, even though Atré had retired. Their relation continued even in the absence of work to join them.[11]

Rafiq bhai pointed out that for many youth in the settlement, plumbing is an attractive profession largely because you do not need to invest your own capital. "It's a business that depends on trust [*bharosa ka dhandha hai*]," he said, referring to how he would initially ask his customers to pay him 50 percent prior to passing the application, 20 percent upon its passing, and the final 30 percent on completion of the works. Rafiq bhai told me that he needed money in advance mainly because of the bribes he needed to pay the engineers to keep the papers moving. Every application had to be moved from the junior engineer to the sub-engineer to the assistant engineer to the executive engineer and the deputy hydraulic engineer. He also had to pay the meter supervisor (to approve the installation of the meter), the roads department (for their "No Objection" certificate to dig the road), and finally the junior engineer (who was responsible for actually making the connection to the service main).

I learned from Rafiq bhai that the water problem in Premnagar had been there for some time. He pointed to the overworked and unrepaired water lines as the primary problem. The network had not been upgraded for years, despite the area's growing population. Premnagar's unrepaired and smaller lines stand in sharp contrast to the larger, newer lines now serving Megh-wadi, a neighboring settlement that backs (and is backed by) the Shiv Sena. In these wards, councilors and engineers have worked toward installing large lines, between 300 and 450 mm, that deliver six to eight times more water than the 150 mm lines that service Premnagar (see map 3). These renewed, maintained lines have made water services more reliable for residents in Meghwadi. In contrast, Premnagar has largely been bypassed for such pipe upgradation works projects. "The Ramgadh line [which brought water into the settlement] is overworked," Rafiq told me. It leaks, and its fickle lines have a smaller capacity than the lines serving adjacent settlements. They had been neither maintained nor upgraded for years.

Infrastructures are fragile and tenuous assemblages of materials, humans, laws, and practices that are always falling apart. To cohere and perform, they need constant maintenance work. Here, the difference between life in Meghwadi and life in Premnagar does not emerge from their legal history. The difference here emerges from the ways in which the infrastructure has

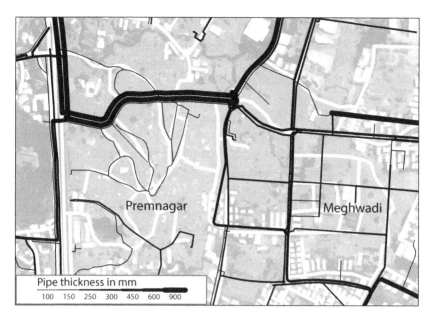

MAP 3. Water network map for Premnagar and Meghwadi. The width of the water lines on the map has been scaled to correspond to the width of the pipelines serving the neighborhood. Based on "Water Network Map," K-East WDIP, Municipal Corporation of Greater Mumbai.

been maintained and upgraded in each settlement. Taken further, one might argue that these contiguous settlements are made different through and by the ways in which the city's government treats maintenance and upgradation projects in each area.

To get water, residents of Premnagar would apply for water connections to be made from the newer water lines passing through Meghwadi. If these connections are approved, the residents must spend their own money for pipes to bring water from Meghwadi some distance to their homes. For residents of Premnagar, these costs are significant and depend largely on whether larger pipelines are already in place. Rafiq bhai told me he had recently spent one lakh rupees (US$2,000) making a water connection for a Premnagar resident by joining him to the water main at Meghwadi. Even Rafiq—a plumber—was subject to these costs. He told me of how he had spent close to that amount for connections to his own home in Premnagar.

As we left the teashop and began to walk around the settlement, I asked Rafiq bhai why the service network had not been upgraded in years. Rafiq bhai suggested that the city's neglect of maintenance works in Premnagar was an effect of majoritarian electoral politics. For many years, Premnagar was in the same municipal electoral constituency as Marathi settlements such as Meghwadi. For several election cycles, their councilor had been a Shiv Sena party member who had little interest in cultivating them as a constituency. "They were not interested in the Muslim vote. They never came into the settlement to see the problem," he said. Things had changed recently, however, with the redistricting of constituencies. Premnagar is its own constituency now. Its residents had, for the first time, been able to elect a councilor from the Congress party. Rafiq bhai expressed anticipation and hope for the new representative's ability to effect change.

As we walked through the settlement, Rafiq bhai asked me if I was alarmed by the crowds of men milling around. He was surprised to hear that I was familiar with the area. Many city engineers he brought here found it frightening, he told me. They were scared to walk around Premnagar, because it was a "danger area." Rafiq bhai's concern revealed the difficulty that engineers had with working in Premnagar. They saw Premnagar as dangerous and asked to be escorted through its alleys whenever they visited. Fortunately for the engineers, with the Sena controlling the city administration since 1985, they had not been compelled to work in Premnagar. Unlike other Marathi wards that had been the focus of much municipal activity, Premnagar has largely been bypassed by the municipal administration's works projects.[12] With little political pressure to connect Premnagar to the water system or upgrade its infrastructure, city engineers have no need to visit Premnagar. Instead, they provide water connections at its margins, boundaries, and borders, leaving it to plumbers like Rafiq bhai to extend and maintain connections from these locations to the uncounted homes within the settlement.

As we neared the end of our interview, Rafiq bhai asked if my study could help alleviate the area's water problems. I told him that it might, but that I did not think the problems in Premnagar were those borne of insufficient knowledge. Engineers, in fact, knew quite a lot about Premnagar. They knew who the plumbers were, which ones stole water, the state of the main lines, and that it was difficult to obtain water without the use of booster pumps. They also knew the extent of the network, and that it was insufficient for the number of people actually residing in Premnagar.[13] They simply left the area, and its problems, alone, often buried in histories of disconnection, leakage, and exclusion. Rafiq bhai paused for a second and agreed that the problems in Premnagar did not arise because engineers were not aware of its problems. "It's about discrimination [bhed bhav]," he said, and told me of his frustrating day at the water office.

Earlier that day, Rafiq bhai had had gone to the office to get approval for a water application. It was the day before the Diwali break, and not many others were at the office. The assistant engineer told him that plumbers should not be working that day and that the office would attend to matters after Diwali. As a plumber, Rafiq bhai saw this to be an allusion to or attack on his religious identity. Was he a bad plumber (or a bad person) because he was working the day before Diwali? Because he was not Hindu? Rafiq bhai told me why he was upset: "On every issue they make things difficult. . . . The assistant engineer asked me, 'Why should I help you?' I got so upset. He has known me for so long, and yet he asks me this question? So I [said], 'If it's about money, how much are we talking about? Five hundred? One thousand? Two thousand? Tell me!' Patankar is not like that. If you pay money or don't pay, he follows the rules and does the work. Not everyone is like that."

While very upset about this incident, Rafiq bhai took care to distinguish the good engineers from the bad ones. Taking bribes did not qualify them as bad engineers if they did the work. In fact, Rafiq bhai had nothing but praise for Patankar—not because he did not take money but because he was committed to doing the work. Patankar was "good" because his relationship with the plumber was not determined by money. In contrast, Rafiq bhai was annoyed with the assistant engineer because he refused to acknowledge the relationship that they shared prior to his appearing at his office the day before Diwali. In so doing, the engineer demonstrated that the relationship was worth little more than money.

By upholding their difference and not the social relation that Rafiq bhai had forged with him previously, the assistant engineer had made the exchange profane—about money and nothing more. They may as well have been strangers. This upset Rafiq bhai, who believed that a Marathi plumber would not be treated the same way. The religious holiday had become a way for the engineer to discriminate against Rafiq bhai. It made Rafiq bhai's experience at the office rather unpleasant, and one that he would have rather done without.

In Mumbai, engineers, activists, and residents of Muslim bastis agree that bastis that are predominantly Muslim have severe water problems and draw water extensively through unauthorized connections. In Premnagar, residents and engineers dispute whether unauthorized water connections are a response to the difficulties of obtaining water or the cause of water problems in the area. Either way, to the extent that residents of Premnagar get water from municipal pipes, they do so largely through unauthorized, illegal connections made by plumbers without permission from the municipal office.

Plumbers and settlers in Premnagar prefer unauthorized connections for a number of reasons. First, they do away with the trouble of the long list of documents and "ID proofs" required for a formal water application. Few settlers in Premnagar have these documents. Of those who do, many have documents with spelling mistakes and other inconsistencies that trouble their recognition. Second, plumbers do not need the formal consent of municipal engineers to make unauthorized connections. They are thus exempt from the "hassles" and the time required to get engineers to do their work. As Rafiq bhai points out, many (but not all) engineers are interested in making things more difficult—officers can make money by stalling the approval of (legal) connections. Third, these connections cost as much as, if not less (in raw materials and labor) than, legal connections. With the municipal system not providing any subsidies or assistance for settlers to connect legally to the water system, settlers often *save* on the bribes and payments that they would have to pay to connect. Finally, they are saved the hassle of getting billed for water they do or do not receive.

Plumbers told me that all illegal connections need is a competent plumber who has knowledge of which parts of the area's crumbling network still have water, the "daring" to make the connection themselves, and a series of small payments to "manage" the police and other authorities. The process is poignantly captured in a meditative documentary, *Pyasa Premnagar*, made by Shaali Shaikh. He explains:

> If 10 percent are legal and 90 percent are illegal, what is the reason for that? We got to know that when it was legal, for some years water would come. . . . But slowly the water became less in both the lines; the water became less in the line[s] of those who paid the bill and it became less even in the line[s] of those who did not pay the bill. Because it became less, people went to plumbers. There is one thing—nobody from the basti went directly to the BMC. They went to the plumbers. (Shaikh 2008)

In contrast to legal connections that take time to process, plumbers make illegal connections quickly. They draw on the legal network to locate and tap its ever-changing flows of water for a substantial fee. As they add new connections upstream of their older customers' lines, the connections soon go dry, requiring residents to make new connections with the same plumbers every few years. Therefore, not only do Premnagar's settlers pay rather large setup costs, but they also do so repeatedly. "*Premnagar plumber ka khazana hai,*" a plumber told me one day. "Premnagar is a treasury of plumbers." Indeed, not only does Premnagar have a wealth of plumbers, but amid all the financial opportunities, it is a goldmine for plumbers as well.

Legal or not, most of Premnagar's residents have unauthorized water connections, depending on plumbers to link them discreetly to the system. As they mediate connections to the city's piped network, plumbers have been able to exert a significant degree of control over the area and its residents. City officials have varying degrees of knowledge about their activities but say they are powerless to stop them. With a registered voting population of more than forty thousand adults—and likely as many children and unregistered citizens—dependent on this network, officials express a helplessness in both awarding legal connections and, in the absence of a reliable system, cutting illegal ones.

The precarity of the situation was instantiated in late 2007, when the engineers attempted to enforce the law while expanding the network in neighboring Meghwadi. The Shiv Sena councilor of Meghwadi had managed to get a larger pipeline sanctioned for his constituency. During the upgradation works, the councilor insisted that hundreds of illegal connections serving Premnagar's residents that were formerly made on "his" line be cut. As the water department prepared to cut these connections, Premnagar's plumbers physically prevented them from doing so. Ahmed, a septuagenarian plumber from the area, explained the standoff: "Recently, the [Shiv Sena] councilor of the nearby ward cut all the connections on this line, saying that these were illegal connections. He said he was doing something good. The plumbers of this area said, 'OK, if you cut this line, then we won't let you fix the new eighteen-inch line.' So the road stayed dug open for some time while this was happening."

The negotiations took approximately three weeks. During this time, the road remained dug up—quite literally exposing the contentious state of the city's infrastructure. When the "compromise" was reached, many more connections were remade. Some of these were legal. As other plumbers told me later, many other (illegal) lines were also joined after being fitted with stolen and nonfunctioning water meters so as to *look* legal. Before these connections could be questioned, they were quickly buried under two feet of cement and concrete, safe from the gaze of municipal engineers.

These days, while engineers have a limited amount of control over the water entering the settlement, they have almost no authority over the system within Premnagar's boundaries. City engineers cite the regressive social and environmental conditions produced out of their inaction as challenges to their effectiveness. They can justify not working to rehabilitate, repair, and expand the capacity and pressures of Premnagar's lines by pointing to the damage inflicted on the network by illegal connections. Hacking into existing lines and making them even more porous to the claims of their clients, plumbers are able to make the "not good" area habitable. But in doing so, they also make the area "not good" for city engineers to work in. Their illegal connections serve to justify the engineers' disdain for the area and its people and continually reproduce Premnagar as an abject area undeserving of their substantive attentions.

Subterranean Water

Owing to their significant difficulties, not all of Premnagar's water needs are met through the appropriation of water from the municipal water network. Having confronted water difficulties and a leaky system for some time now, residents have also begun returning to draw water from wells that were heavily used before the arrival of city water supplies in the early 1970s. Following the extension of tap water supplies, many of these wells had fallen into disuse and disrepair. But as municipal connections in the settlement become increasingly leaky and unreliable, many have returned to these wells and their subterranean water.

> The well has been here for fifty years and people would use the water from the well . . . but when the BMC water started coming, people paid little attention to the well. . . . Because of this, the well water slowly became bad, and because the BMC's water was available, people eventually closed the well. . . . In the beginning, the [BMC] supply was good . . . then slowly the pressure dropped and people started to get less water. . . . So people became helpless, if they did not get water, what could they do? [So] they must have talked to the MLA [state legislator]. . . . The MLA saw that there is no BMC water supply and what did he do . . . ? He said let's take water out of the ground, and to give people this facility he made a bore well right next to [the old well]. (Shaikh 2008)

By drawing attention to the renewed relevance of wells in Premnagar, I make two points. First, Premnagar's residents recognize the diffuse, plastic multiplicity and plurality of "the state." Like "the public," the state, too, is differentiated, and is represented by an array of administrators and legislators not only in the municipal government but also in the state and the central government. Denied improvements by the municipal state, residents approached a state legislator for help. Though he was unable to pressurize the city's water pipes, the legislator mobilized the state-controlled housing agency to build bore wells to serve Premnagar's residents. Thus, at the time of my fieldwork, Premnagar hosted close to a dozen bore wells in active use. These wells often lay adjacent to wells that existed prior to the extension of municipal services in the area decades before. Some of these bore wells were built with the legislator's discretionary development fund. They were used to construct a water network parallel to that of the city administration and its plumbers.

With their own patrons, bore wells have their own management regimes, and produce their own political and social networks that run through and parallel to municipal systems of legitimation and patronage. Wells therefore produce different forms of political authority and regimes of belonging in the city (L. Mehta 2005; see also Giglioli and Swyngedouw 2008).

Second, contrary to the language of "recognition," which foregrounds citizenship as a historical event that is achieved by possessing papers and demonstrating continuous occupation in the city for over a decade, such recognition is not a one-off, linear event. As manifest in the work necessary to continue to ensure water supply, substantive citizenship is a *process* that requires continuous renewal work, maintenance, and revalidation by political authorities (see Chu 2014; Subramanian 2009). Residents are compelled to act in ways that show they continue to be deserving of the state's resources, the care of its experts, and its maintenance projects.

Nevertheless, here I return to Asif, who asked whether the provision of well water, contaminated with sewage, could be called development. Asif was angry about the way in which "gutter water" and untreated municipal supply was being made available to Premnagar's residents. Like Asif, many in the city, including its municipal officers, see bore well water as dirty and undesirable. Drawn from the ground, contaminated by unknown mixtures of the chemicals and sewage of urban life, and not subject to the procedures and purifications of technoscience, water from urban wells is unfit for drinking and a danger to health, according to engineers. I do not question the purity of their claims here (see introduction; Kooy and Bakker 2008). What matters is that Asif and other residents of Premnagar find it deeply offensive to be subjected to well water—water that is believed to be contaminated with all the dirt that a modern water supply was a response to. Linear narratives of progress, development, and modernity are undone as Premnagar's residents are returned to the same water sources they had abandoned as backward and impure three decades before.

For Premnagar's residents, this water is itself abject—lying below the surface of modern citizenship. Associating wells with village life, Asif expressed outrage at being made to drink it in the city. To drink well water, Asif suggests, is to literally imbibe a toxic and dangerous form of hydraulic subjectification, one that marks their own bodies dirty, dangerous, and abject—a material practice that instantiates how their bodies are not clean enough to be considered and treated as citizens of the city.

Persistent Water

In one of anthropology's classic texts, *The Gift*, Marcel Mauss (1925) famously argued that all forms of exchange draw upon and produce particular kinds of moral communities. Contemporary debates around the privatization of water tend to focus predominantly on two forms of its exchange—as a commodity in capital markets and as a right of citizens in states—and tend to view the transition from public to private through modernist teleologies. A brief review of the anthropological and sociological literature suggests, however, that we need to pay attention to other practices of drawing and distributing water that are reproduced alongside these regimes. As Amita Baviskar points out, the "political economy of a natural resource is meaningful only through the wider networks of cultural politics in which it is embedded" (2003b, 5051). An attention to these cultural politics might give us a better sense of the ways in which resources not only are situated in wider structures of meaning but also articulate the processes of identity formation through which subjects can claim or are denied resources.

In Mumbai, as in other places, the ways in which people provision and are able to access water describe and produce the layered social, cultural, and political infrastructures they inhabit. In drawing attention to the iterative process through which settlers and engineers constitute Premnagar's water supply, I connect studies of urban infrastructure with those of citizenship and the state to understand how abjection is effected in the postcolonial city.[14]

Though they formally qualify as citizens in every respect, Premnagar's residents are excluded from the city's public water system. The way in which they are "pushed down" from the city's water supply has sobering implications for urban citizenship. Though urban citizenship is sometimes seen as a form of membership that can bypass national exclusions (Holston 2008), it can be even more restrictive, elusive, prejudiced, and precarious. With the discourses of belonging in/to Mumbai being rendered in religious and regionalist colors, large numbers of residents are being made "outsiders" and are denied urban membership despite their deep histories of belonging to the city. This arena of political exclusion is neither spatially outside the city's jurisdiction nor temporally prior to it. In the heart of the growing city and peopled for more than forty years through state and market displacements, Premnagar had access to good water at one point in time, and newer settlements adjacent to Premnagar now enjoy far better services. This research suggests that abjection is not an effect of ignorance, nor does it require a degree of spatial distance. Abjection here is a dialectical process produced out of deeply situated relationships, where difference is constantly reproduced, enacted, and foregrounded between people who have deep, overlapping social and relational histories. The city engineers know Premnagar, its plumbers, and its water problems very well. The zone of abjection has been produced with chauvinistic cultural politics of the city, a politics in which each group intimately knows, lives with, and is marked by histories and ongoing projects of making a difference.

Subsequently, "it is not the lack of cleanliness or health that causes abjection, but that which disturbs identity, system and order" (Kristeva 1982). While representatives and employees of Mumbai's municipal government see Premnagar as a place inhabited by dirty outsiders, or migrant labor from Uttar Pradesh and Bangladesh, they overlook how Premnagar has been made desperate and dirty through their (lack of) actions in the settlement. Doubly identified as Muslim and migrant, Premnagar's residents are deemed to be dangerous to the city's systems and infrastructures by the municipal government. These everyday discriminations are neither incidental nor exceptional. They constitute Mumbai's public water system, one in which the claims and needs of its Muslim residents are seen as pathological to the city.

As Nugent points out, "the ability to engage in everyday bureaucratic practice is itself an expression and result of power relations" (2006, 301). Engineers point to the water usage practices of Premnagar's settlers to illustrate why they are undeserving urban residents. While representatives and employees of Mumbai's municipal government see Premnagar as a place beyond their control, they overlook how they have produced their absence by not maintaining and upgrading infrastructure in the settlement. The abjection that their inaction produces is also a condition of its possibility. As exclusion provokes the symptoms of abjection—the lack of cleanliness and health—it also produces practices that reaffirm and reproduce the ways in which engineers see Premnagar and its residents. This is not to say that abjection is a resilient and durable process. As manifest in the precarious negotiations in which engineers are compelled to engage with Premnagar's residents and plumbers, abjection is an incomplete and reversible form of social control, one that while iterative is also full of its own instabilities, leaks, and slippages of authority (Murphy 2006).

Alienated by and from city politics, Premnagar's residents draw on diverse sociopolitical networks to obtain water. To this day, access to the municipal system is mediated and governed by plumbers who have an ambiguous and difficult relationship with the water department's engineers. Willing to avoid the problems of obtaining legal connections through the water department, Premnagar's plumbers now manage and authorize access to the settlement's pipes, grant connections, and negotiate with water department engineers. Engineers complain that plumbers determine who meets them at their office and the illegal connections that will be allowed on their pipes. Claiming they cannot control Premnagar's water network, they prefer to leave it be.

Those who do not obtain water from the illegal network get it from the many bore wells that now proliferate in Premnagar. To be clear, bore wells and illegal connections do not appear as "alternatives" for Premnagar's residents as they are effects of disenfranchisement.[15] Like water engineers, Premnagar's residents see groundwater in Mumbai to be of poorer quality and not potable. Nevertheless, these wells are important markers of how Premnagar's residents are able to make life viable in the city. Because water is not fully controlled by the municipal water department, they are able to create new structures of authority through the production of these networks. Though not beyond political party patronage, bore wells produce a ghettoized public; a public that is underserved because it is seen to be undeserving of urban services. This abject public draws on both ground and piped water to survive.

As such, bawdis (wells), jharnas (springs), and bore wells do not disappear with state projects to pipe and control water. Even in India's largest capitalist city, such unexpected water and its specific moralities of access continue to matter. To focus on different kinds of water, therefore, is also to recognize the varied possibilities of politics and personhood that are enabled by this strange, liquid material. An attention to water's multiplicities allows us to better situate public and private flows within diverse moralities of exchange.

Finally, this chapter urges a consideration toward thinking of ways in which the materiality of water challenges the most brazen attempts at its control. As some have argued, scholars of political ecology and governmentality have too often assumed that the social and natural are simply canvases, incidental to and effectively controlled by the determinations of politics.[16] As it is made to surreptitiously leak through steel pipes, or reappear from subterranean depths, water's physical properties challenge us to explore and understand a certain indeterminacy that is fundamental to not only political projects but also intellectual ones. Thus, the biophysical properties of water—situated in a matrix of social and ecological relations—also affect the regimes and projects that seek to regulate its movement.

Owing to water's continued availability outside political economic systems, and because of the ways in which it interrupts projects to control it, studies of water have provided a fertile field to push beyond the determinacy of political economy. The multiple appearances of water direct our attention to overlapping processes through which political structures, entitlements, and cultures of belonging are produced and articulated. The multiple forms of water introduce a degree of uncertainty that compels modifications even to the most powerful and totalizing of systems. In Premnagar, for instance, rampant leakage and pilferage of municipal water, and the availability of well water, are the primary reasons why the water department is considering offering an amnesty scheme for those who wish to reconnect to the system legally. They promise to waive all unpaid bills (for water not always delivered) if residents apply for and connect legally to the city's system again. Such schemes of forgiveness and accommodation promise to reconnect, reabsorb, and refigure difference in the city through renewed infrastructures of connection and citizenship.

Interlude. Miracles

Faithfuls flocked by the dozens to the Mahim creek on Friday to sip "sweet" water. Only nobody stopped to think twice before cupping his hands to drink the unfiltered water. As police tried to control the crowd thronging the beach ... reason seemed to take a backseat.

The believers wouldn't have cared to listen at that moment of mass hysteria that the salty taste of the seawater across India's coastline naturally drops during the monsoon due to an inflow of freshwater from the Mithi River, especially at low tide. But who can blame the common folk when Mayor Datta Dalvi himself exulted "Chamatkar ho gaya (It's a miracle)." "Mahim creek is not fit to even bathe in," Rakesh Kumar, head, National Environmental and Engineering Research Institute (NEERI) zonal office, told HT. "It's always Mumbai's most polluted creek in our regular test results." ...

The believers—Muslim, Hindu and Christian—would have none of it. They drank the scum-laced water, praised the lord—and carried on the strangest beach party that Mumbai's ever seen. Crowds grew through the night, leading to late-night traffic jams and police reinforcement. The enterprising among the crowds even bottled and sold the murky water. "This is like Ganga *jal*. We will store it at home and purify the house with it," said Santacruz resident Mahadev Gujar. By Saturday morning, the water was even "curing" the sick. Asim, a teenager from Rabali in Thane, claimed he got immediate relief from his back pain after drinking a mouthful of water. —"Faithfuls Gulp Mahim's Mithi Water," *Hindustan Times*, August 19, 2006

One year after the most dreadful floods in the city's history, Mumbai's water was again in its news. The summer prior, in July 2005, city residents had tried for days to get out of the flooding Mithi River, and to get the flooding river out of their homes. Hundreds died in the effort. A year later, as this article in the *Hindustan Times* illustrates, people were trying to get *in* to the river at Mahim Creek. They headed toward Mahim's beaches in droves to partake of water's magical qualities. "Faithfuls," the police, journalists, friends, political leaders, and scientists each created their own story with these waters. Some flocked to the Mithi and, drinking its water, insisted their afflictions were cured. Scientists rushed to the Mithi to try and explain why it suddenly turned sweet. The police rushed to the Mithi to maintain public order, prevent drownings, and, in all likelihood, behold the spectacle of believers on the beach. Together, on the banks of where the river-creek-sewer meets the sea, the scientists, police, and publics experienced a liquid material that was simultaneously sewage, sea, a miracle, a health risk, a health cure, a business opportunity, evening entertainment, and a law and order problem.

As it nourishes both the imagination and the body, water is a strange, political, poetic material that is fundamental not only to the formation of human bodies but also to the ways in which we make meaning in the world (Strang 2004). Constituting over two-thirds of the earth's surface, half of our body weight, and 70 percent of our brain, it is perhaps not surprising that water is saturated with layers of meaning and vitality. Indeed, the world over, water is a special material through which we can study the relations between politics, ecology, and social life. On that balmy night in August, water provided a surface for incommensurable regimes of value to condense in the same place and time, to contest and compete in cosmological battles of knowledge and belief, power and meaning, health and vitality.

Despite focusing on a certain kind of water—the kind that comes through city pipes—my research for this book was constantly interrupted by the effects and affects of different kinds of water in the city: rainstorms and floods canceled city trains and with them, my interviews; monsoons reclaimed the city's coastline; perennial springs disrupted carefully crafted narratives of scarcity in the settlements; and displacements of and by the river Mithi claimed both life and governmental attentions.

As residents encounter water in different times and places, they know water in multiple and incommensurable ways. They recognize that water simultaneously bears different qualities—not only in terms of its microbiology and total dissolved solids but also in its relation to religious ritual, its processes of production and circulation, and the kinds of modernity, purity, and citizenship it symbolizes and (often) materializes.

Despite the extraordinary efforts of city bureaucracies to make water predictable, legible, and boring, water remains enchanted. Its stories proliferate beyond the repertoires of states and their scientists. Water is never just H_2O. While scientists like Rakesh Kumar often have stories and facts about the water (e.g., its properties and purity), these explanations often are not the primary ways in which people know, see and understand water. Water carries meanings and symbols far in excess of its material substance. In its periodic cycles of abundance and scarcity—of floods and drought (in whose productions humans participate)—water delivers life and death, dirt and purity, toxicity and vitality. Its potential to both nourish and poison bodies makes it a peculiar substance that is not only vital to persons but also a fickle arbiter of miracles, of memory, of myth, and of life.

CONCLUSION

Gov. Rick Snyder of Michigan declared a state of emergency for the Flint area on Tuesday as concerns grew about the health effects of lead-tainted water there. . . . Flint, which had long received water from Lake Huron provided by Detroit's water utility, began drawing its water from the Flint River in 2014 in an effort to save money while a new pipeline was built. Residents soon complained about rashes and strange odors from the river water, but city and state officials mostly insisted that it was safe to drink. Last year, elevated levels of lead were found in children's blood, and in October, Flint switched back to Detroit's water system. —M. SMITH, *New York Times*, March 25, 2015

In April 2014, the city of Flint, Michigan, of the United States switched water sources from Detroit's water system to its own local source, the Flint River. The water of the Flint River is not unlike that of the Mithi River. It has long been contaminated by the effluents of industry. Nevertheless, the governor-appointed managers of the city made the decision primarily on cost considerations. The move would save the city of Flint five million dollars a year.

By January 2015, residents of Flint began to complain of rashes, hair loss, and sickness in public meetings with their city councilors (*Detroit Free Press*, January 14, 2015). On television and in national newspapers, they reported on the color and smell of the water, complaining that it was contaminated with fecal coliform bacteria (M. Smith 2015). City officials insisted that the water, while smelly and colored, was safe. They used questionable protocols to establish that it met city standards. At the same time, they also agreed to take precautionary measures. The city administration doused the water with elevated doses of chlorine and continued to distribute the toxic water to city residents. This process succeeded in leaching lead from city pipes into the city's water supply.

By the time a pediatric study documented elevated lead levels in children in September 2015, residents had been subject to water from the river for over a year. In the controversy that ensued, the city switched back to Detroit's water system. Nevertheless, by that time, much damage was done. The toxic water has precipitated an outbreak of Legionnaire's disease, killing over eighty residents and infecting hundreds more. More than five thousand children are now known to be poisoned by lead from the city's water pipes. Even as the city has switched back to Detroit's water system, the disaster has not ended. The city's service lines continue to leach lead into the water. Stories of death and disease continue to proliferate. These stories now join others about how the city and state governments deliberately suppressed their knowledge of the contamination of the water they supplied.

The news reporting around Flint has provoked outrage across the United States. For many, it demonstrates the raced and classed geographies of abjection, made yet again through the administration and management of infrastructures.[1] Indeed, that the city and state ignored and blocked regulators' warnings about water's toxicity while continuing to distribute water for nearly a year after the first complaints surfaced is shocking. Critics correctly point out how the provision of safe water would not be subject to the stringent control of cost had Flint been wealthier and white.[2]

Yet much of the indignation in Flint and beyond has a lot to do with the particular matter at hand—water. There is a long history of raced and classed others receiving inadequate and attenuated public services in the United States through governmental neglect and inattention.[3] The events in Flint, in some ways, follow this history. Yet these events did not produce outrage in the same way and at the same scale as the controversy around water poisoning in Flint.

In Flint, city and state administrators knowingly acted to continue distributing toxic water even after concerns about its quality and safety were raised. That this latest abuse took place through the governmental *action* of distribution (as opposed to the perceived "inaction" of other forms structural violence), and that it took place with *water—a matter of life*—are not incidental to violation that is expressed in the controversy.[4] Residents of Flint and beyond protest how the state knew and actively concealed the knowledge that the water they were distributing to make people live was in fact secretly distributing illness and death instead. They complain that the social (and material) contract between citizens and the state—to make people live—has been, quite literally, poisoned. The city's more eminent voices have demanded criminal proceedings against the city and state's politicians so that the public's faith in city and state institutions can be restored. While criminal charges have now been filed against three government employees, less clear is how residents can continue to live in Flint (or for that matter, many other American cities) with pipes that continue to leach lead into the water supply.

In this book, I have focused on water that flows from dammed rivers through city pipes because it is this kind of water that generally nourishes and reproduces human life in cities around the world. In the United States, as in India, water services are a vital, materially instantiated form of the social contract between the state and the citizen. Urban residents in Mumbai, Flint, and most places in between are made to live through and by the provision of water services. It is the piped municipal water supply that is imbued with the practices and politics of urban citizenship, and residents in cities in different parts of the world recognize that a safe, reliable piped water infrastructure is critical for making and establishing life in the liberal city.[5]

The poisoned water pipes in Flint, or the water shutoffs that preceded them by a few months in Detroit, demonstrate how the technical and political controversies I describe in this book are not the province of cities in the Global South alone.[6] Mumbai's leaky infrastructures, bursting as they are at the seams in environments of disrepair, are not metonymic of cities in the Global South. Such an approach to seeing infrastructure as leaking and "dysfunctional" *because* it is in the South is not just empirically inaccurate, as the crisis in Flint or the leakages in New York's tunnels demonstrate (see chapter 5). This approach is also politically problematic. In marking cities of the South as places that are typified by dysfunctional and differentiated infrastructure, we risk overlooking the ways in which such infrastructures also divide and differentiate publics in the Global North. Further, by placing dysfunction, scarcity, and lack in the South, neocolonial environmental and urban discourses further marginalize the precarious residents in cities of the South (see chapter 1). Accordingly, I write about Mumbai's very ordinary, prolific, profitable, and porous infrastructures to urge an attention to how these creaky, historical, technopolitical forms mediate, extend, and differentiate human life not just in Mumbai but also in many parts of the world, including those formerly considered "developed."

There are other good reasons to think more generally about the promises and compromised workings of infrastructure at this political and theoretical moment. In recent years, environmental scientists anxiously announce that we are in the midst of a new geologic period—the Anthropocene, one in which the earth's climate approaches a "tipping point" owing to the ways in which humans have been releasing carbon into the atmosphere (Waters et al. 2016). In these times of climate change, scientists and social scientists are announcing apocalyptic futures for humanity and the earth, and have urged that we need to imagine new paradigms with which "we," as the human *species*, need to apprehend, imagine, and narrate our place on and relations with the planet.[7]

While I am sympathetic to this project, I am simultaneously concerned about who is served and what also becomes possible in the name of a common, planetary humanity. As Anna Tsing (2015) has cautioned, some of those insisting on the singularity of a global humanity also recuperate ethnocentric, masculinist fantasies of modernity. For instance, some geoengineers have responded to the crisis of climate change by proposing a series of new technocratic, planetary infrastructures to moderate its effects (Calderia et al. 2013; Masco 2016). They suggest that new planetary infrastructures can avert some of the catastrophes that await us in times of climate change.

This study of an ordinary and urban water infrastructure makes three contributions to these wider conversations around infrastructure, environment, and the future of humanity as we try to make sense of, and create new ways of living in, our anthropogenic environment.

First, a caution about what infrastructures—even infrastructures that are designated as public—do. If geoengineers begin to imagine new infrastructures at a planetary scale to mitigate the effects of climate change, this book demonstrates how infrastructures are always productive of social and political difference. In Mumbai, modernist infrastructures make human life possible, but they do not produce reliable flows of water for an undifferentiated public in the city. They never have. Indeed, for some residents living in the city, the city's water infrastructure does produce reliable measures of water with which they live. Yet for many others, it takes a significant amount of labor to ensure they are able to procure the water they need. Public infrastructures are productive of abandonment, abjection, and exclusion in everyday life. How would planetary infrastructures imagine, produce, and differentiate a planetary public? As I show in this book, infrastructures rescale geographies, frequently privileging more powerful populations over others, both in their design and in their everyday administration.

Second, while infrastructures elicit demanding environments, this ethnography of infrastructure demonstrates that there is nothing inevitable in infrastructural forms. Infrastructures are always being remade in the present to make futures anew. As new ideologies of management are always being grafted onto older ones, our energy, transportation, hydraulic, and media infrastructures are more contingent than we imagine. As infrastructures, they are processes that are always in formation, constantly transforming to do something else. As such, existing infrastructures—of energy, water and transportation—are potentially revolutionary sites with which to engage and posit a different set of relations between people and the environment (Boyer 2016).

Finally, as our existing fossil fuel driven energy infrastructures are driving climate change to portend a future planetary apocalypse—one of uncertain and tenuous access to vital life supports—this research demonstrates that the apocalypse is already a mundane part of everyday life for millions of people around the world (Braun 2014). Millions are already living in its aftermath (Jackson 2014). Disruption and breakdown are constant, "patchy," and ordinary features of life in the hydraulic city.[8] This is a sobering recognition, and also one of circumscribed possibility. As settlers in Mumbai reassemble their social and material relations in the city following everyday infrastructural breakdowns, they reveal how the infrastructures of life are being made and remade in challenging social and political environments. Their practices continue to pluralize universalist accounts of politics and environment in the city.

Accordingly, this account of Mumbai's water infrastructures is not just about Mumbai, or water, or infrastructure. It describes how people live with improvised technologies and emergent political-ecological relations in uncertain times. As scholars from environmental anthropology, urban geography, and postcolonial science and technology studies draw attention to the vital infrastructures of living on a climate-altered planet, I conclude with four contributions to these literatures. These are: (i) the unequal distributions of life, (ii) the political ecology of infrastructure, (iii) the novelty of maintenance, and (iv) the difficulties of neoliberal reform in these sodden and uncertain times.

The Distributions of Life

Infrastructures distribute things. In cities, the infrastructures of water distribution are a vital site at which the matter of human life is most frequently nourished, formed, and rendered unequal.[9] Yet the process of water distribution is not smooth and fluid but full of interruptions, contestations, and claims. The social, material, and political frictions produced in the delivery and distribution of water compromise projects to consolidate political authority and govern resources "at a distance" in everyday life, especially under the sign of neo/liberalism.[10]

Through technologies including the survey, the plan, and the development program, scholars have drawn on work by Foucault (1991) to show how the art of liberal government is performed through governmentality, where governmental dispositions are enacted and regulated by the subjects of government. Indeed, Mumbai's hydraulic infrastructure actively constitutes experts and publics that are made and managed through water services. The daily practices of chaviwallas, engineers, and councilors seek to enact these rationalities in everyday life. State employees and various intermediaries materialize connections between the laws, policies, and plans of the polis and the intimate regimes of provisioning in the household—when water arrives, how long it arrives for, and who needs to collect it. Through their work, populations are made to live.

Nevertheless, these connections remain sites of constant social and technical claims, particularly for marginalized residents. Here, the infrastructures of government do not disappear into the background, permitting an appearance of invisibility or distance. They remain visible and proximate sites of power and contestation. Controversies around the operation of pipes or different kinds of water meters demonstrate how states and citizens are formed not only through the management and regulation of populations (a process Foucault [2008] calls biopolitics), nor just through the governmentalization of the self, but also through cyclical and dynamic claims to the politics and materials of water infrastructures. In Mumbai, water is actively claimed and accessed through a contested "politics of life"; a politics in which residents are aware that the inequality of state distribution is generative of unequal material outcomes for bodies living in the city (Fassin 2011).[11] As the city's water infrastructures distribute differentiated allocations of water to different kinds of residents, some residents do not need to worry about choosing between washing dishes and bathing, or between working inside or outside the home (see chapter 3). For others this is a difficult choice that in turn structures their everyday life. Material inequalities of water have a bearing on the very possibility of life, its duration, and the degree to which social aspirations can be realized within it.

In Mumbai (and indeed more generally), residents are very aware of unequal distributions of life in the city made through water connections. They constantly speak of groups that get (and waste) more water in moral and political terms. They also know how to pressure the city administration to deliver more water to their households. As residents protest on and around water infrastructures, they demonstrate how the infrastructures of inequality and exclusion are contested not just by discursive claims to belonging and rights or by debates in the public sphere (cf. Warner 2002), but also by claims on the very materials, pipes, and valves of the water system that form them.

James Ferguson (2015) has recently argued that while distribution has long been central to the reproduction of life, it continues to be treated as secondary in our social analyses. Amid threats of climate change, drought, and increasing environmental uncertainty, Ferguson's approach is timely. While governments, policy makers, and academics anxiously point to the uncertain futures of our food and water supplies (especially with growing populations), what is often overlooked is that hunger and thirst persist despite sufficient production of food and water. As Amartya Sen (1981) famously demonstrated in his landmark study of famine in Bengal and Jessica Barnes (2014) has recently shown in her study of river irrigation in Egypt, the famines and water scarcities *that already structure our present* are effects of distributive practices and not production (or supply). Similarly, if residents of Mumbai experience water shortages, this is not because of insufficient water. There is enough water entering the city for all of Mumbai's residents. The city has enough technological and financial power to extend its services to underserved neighborhoods. That it does not do so suggests that problems of water supply have more to do with the practices of distribution and leakage that structure the city's water system.

Recognizing that uncertainty and scarcity are political effects of their marginalization, settlers often directly negotiate their distributions with city councilors, plumbers, and social workers. They work together with city employees, elected representatives, plumbers, residents, and social workers to claim access to the city's water (chapter 2). To do this, they simultaneously employ not only the practices and claims of rights but also a variety of other relational practices—as friends, neighbors, political leaders, and clients. These social claims are not anterior to rights claims of liberal polities, nor do they exclude them (chapter 4). As marginal subjects actively make claims of rights, friendship, clientship, and other social claims, their multiple political practices are vital to the possibility and politics of hydrating their lives.

As such, the diverse relations made through urban water infrastructures make a particular kind of water infrastructure and particular kinds of political subjects in the city—subjects who have built their lives, homes, and aspirations around the periodic appearance of water (see chapter 3). Thus, it is not just persons, their desires, and their political institutions that form water infrastructures. As materialized relations, infrastructures also form persons, giving shape to their vitalities, imaginations, desires, and politics. Indeed, the very ordinary, bureaucratic administration of Mumbai's modern water system does not efface social identities but in fact produces regional, classed, gendered, and religious persons in the postcolonial city. It produces Muslims and "outsiders" who experience the abjection of municipal government (see chapter 6), women who are gendered by the responsibilities for water provision (see chapter 3), and classed bodies who are conscious of the water they receive and waste (see chapters 4 and 5).

The Political Ecology of Infrastructure

Political ecologists have long shown how hydraulic infrastructures structure conditions of possibility for human life (Swyngedouw 2004; Wade 1982). Infrastructures give form to our aspirations, dreams, and bodies. Infrastructures situate humans in their environments in ways that neither determine nor are determined by human agency. Instead, as Bruce Braun and Sarah Whatmore (2011) have pointed out, the human has long been brought into being *with* technologies, infrastructures, and the environments that we inhabit.[12] The politics of water supply in Mumbai cannot be accounted for only by attending to the politics effected by human actors. Water's discrete and discreet workings and flows also require that we attend to the ways in which water and its situated infrastructures, as assemblies of the human and nonhuman, have political effects.

To draw attention to the ways that the environment matters to politics is not to suggest that it has an essence, a soul, or an intention that is political—an a priori politics that acts on the politics of human agents. To do so would suggest that nonhumans have a political being that is conscious and purposive.[13] Nor is it to suggest the world of materials and environments are ontologically prior to the world of humans. Instead, persons and things are multiply constituted, brought into being and becoming political through different kinds of *relations* (Barry 2011).[14] As things (or persons) are constantly drawn into emergent (social and material) relations, the new kinds of political possibilities that might ensue are tempered by their ongoing histories of form, association, and relation. Their emergent politics challenge human-centric accounts of agency and action.[15]

For instance, consider the prodigious leakages of Mumbai's water, and attempts to control it (see chapter 5). When Mumbai's water flows in ways that challenge city engineers' efforts to detect or measure leakage, this is not because the pipes have an inherently political form that "resists" a human-centered politics of measurement and control. Instead, the pipe is an accretion of human and nonhuman relations that make it extremely difficult and inconvenient for engineers to regulate leakage. This is not to say humans aren't responsible for water flows in the city's water infrastructure. Indeed it is easy to find humans responsible for water distribution in Mumbai. The knowledges and ignorances of water flows emerge from a particular set of humanist arrangements of law, engineering, and infrapolitics.

Yet, I wish to argue that these ignorances are also formed through a series of nonhuman relations between water, steel, and soil—the torrential monsoon; the crumbling materialities of aging, rusting pipes; the submergence of pipes in wetlands that allow for hidden flows to continue without being noticed; and the malleability of water lines to safely permit (unlike gas pipelines) unauthorized points of access. These gaps and leaks are not just wasteful; they are also productive of subjects and their politics in the city.

If water leaks through these accretions despite engineers' efforts to manage it, this is not just because of human intention or ignorance or because water is a singular thing that opposes accurate measurement. Nor do I mean to excuse engineers from the responsibility of managing leaking pipes and using them to distribute water equitably to populations. I only highlight here the political effects of human and nonhuman assemblages to suggest we need extend and expand our repertoire of agents and actors that matter to our accounts of water distribution in everyday life. Taken together, the subterranean amalgams of water, humanity, and steel that constitute the city's water infrastructure have political effects that are both material and meaningful. They make leakage unknowable. They carry and deliver an excess of relations that make it difficult for humans to plan, control, or appropriate the future without a sufficient consideration of the politics and histories congealed in the city's water pipes.

The Novelty of Maintenance

Infrastructures confound attempts to distinguish between discursive and material sites of rule on the one hand, and the social and the material practices of the city on the other. To maintain the amalgams of imaginations, social practices, and technical forms that constitute infrastructures is to constantly work with unstable relations of materiality, sociality, and meaning that are formed with them. It is to work in social worlds that are constantly changing even as they are being formed and distributed through infrastructure networks. As such, maintenance (or the breakdown that sometimes precedes it) is not exceptional but a regular event in the life of infrastructure. The necessity and ubiquity of maintenance not only reveals how infrastructures

FIGURE 17. Workers at the site of a break in a 137-year-old water main in the Greenwich Village neighborhood of New York, January 16, 2014. Photo by Ozier Muhamad / *New York Times* / REDUX.

are always falling apart. It also draws attention to the ways in which infrastructures are a critical site for the workings and reworkings, of materiality, hope, authority, and imagination in the present. As engineers actively decide which infrastructures to leave be, which pipes to upgrade, and which ones to replace with new lines, maintenance is a critical site for social reproduction and distributional justice—an unstable site in which the emancipatory potential of old and new infrastructures is negotiated, contested, and formed.[16]

Maintenance is vital to infrastructures as they age, not just in Mumbai but all over the world. Infrastructures have seldom been frictionless channels—surfaces or conduits that permit flow. Instead, as a wealth of studies on infrastructures in Mumbai and elsewhere has begun to show, infrastructures are perforated, leaky, crumbling networks that require considerable work to keep working.[17] Steven Jackson (2014) reminds us that "we live in a fractal and falling apart world," where repair and maintenance are not exceptional events but constant features of our social and technically enabled lives. That most of Mumbai's residents can depend on a daily supply of water is testament to the social and technological labor of thousands of officers, engineers, city councilors, and workers who work every day to make sure water continues to be distributed in the city.

Like the pipes Patankar sought to fix when we traveled together to the field, the daily work of maintaining and managing water lines demonstrates the importance of unsteady, prosaic, incremental improvisations in producing large infrastructure networks (Graham 2010; Graham and Thrift 2007). The tentative and necessary work of maintenance—work engineers sometimes describe dramatically as "fire-fighting"—is the necessary yet often ignored requirement to keep infrastructures in operation, distributing the things they were designed to carry.

Despite the ideas of stasis and stability that it evokes, maintenance is more than a set of predictable repertoires of restoring relations between bodies and things—of "returning" infrastructures to their original working state. As connections become blocked, pipes leak, or diverse populations are cut off from services, maintenance work is a dynamic and constant exercise of creativity and innovation. In every moment of every day, maintenance depends on constantly changing laws, moralities of government, technologies of regulation, and social practices that form infrastructures. As a result, Gupte, Patankar, and other engineers seldom used standardized protocols to fix leakages. They were constantly using situated knowledges, materials, and tools to repair the network. As they improvised solutions to reconnect some households while leaving others be, their work revealed maintenance to be a dynamic and political process producing new technologies and renewed publics. They showed how maintenance is a temporal, hyperinterested form of labor that recomposes infrastructures with the means, rationalities, and technologies of the dynamic, ever-shifting present. It promises and often (re)produces new social beings and technical forms layered upon the already existing subjectivities and materialities of government (Fisch 2013).

For infrastructures to continue delivering the things they ought to be distributing, it is not just pipes but also social relations that require maintenance (see Elyachar 2010; Simone 2004b). In Jogeshwari, religious festivals, prize ceremonies, prayer ceremonies, and even NGO rights trainings and workshops provide occasions and events through which diverse kinds of relations are carefully made and maintained. Often called "cultural programs," these events also provide locations and occasions for new kinds of relations to be formed. For example, the cultural program to celebrate Women's Day did more than furnish judges (the anthropologist included) with delicious food (see chapter 4). These events produce new forms of subjectivity and new kinds of obligations that are layered like the infrastructures to which they are attached. Such unsteady assemblies of different social subjectivities permit residents to make relations and claims on more powerful others.[18] The flows of water or other resources that sometimes result do not produce forms of equality that have long been the hallmark of progressive politics. Yet they provide another tentative, fickle, valuable, and precious route for marginalized others to be included in and make claims to the city's programs, dreams, and regimes of distribution.

Neoliberal Reform

Amid anxieties about a coming water crisis on the one hand, and animated by desires to make Indian cities world class on the other, federal, state, and municipal officials in India have been participating in transnational projects to implement neoliberal reforms of urban water networks. Yet during the time I was doing fieldwork in 2007–8, Srinivas Chari, a proponent of water reforms, suggested that while there had been attempts of reform in over forty-four towns and cities in India, not one of these efforts had failed to produce significant controversy. Indeed, as an attention to the different controversies around water reforms places as diverse as Manila, Jakarta, Johannesburg as well as the towns of England and Wales shows, these disputes are not particular to Mumbai.[19] Why are urban water reforms so controversial? Ethnographies of water reforms in these cities have begun to provide some answers.

I have shown how attempts at reform in Mumbai encountered a variety of social and material difficulties embedded in everyday workings of the city's water infrastructures. As is suggested by its etymology—*reform*— consultants and other experts seeking to implement reforms of Mumbai's water network did not have the luxury of creating a new water system (with new rules). When the WDIP consultants sought to propose new sets of relations between water, pipes, people, and their political and social imaginations, they needed to do so while accounting for the extant form of water infrastructures and the diverse moralities, imaginations, and practices of political subjects and experts that these infrastructures have been producing in the city.[20] As the consultants sought to imagine and produce new relations (between persons, things, and water) through the city's water infrastructures, they encountered a set of social and material difficulties they were unable to sufficiently apprehend, reorder, and reform.

This book details how the reform project was challenged and compromised by the diverse political authorities that form (and know) the system (see chapter 2), the expectations and demands of city residents that water—a vital good necessary to live—be distributed by the state despite the uncertainties embedded in the city's water infrastructure (see chapter 4), and finally, the inability of consultants and experts to perform an authoritative audit of the unknown flows of water that structure it (see chapter 5). As such, the WDIP ran into controversy not just socially and politically but also technically for a range of reasons that compromised the reform project.

Even though settlers were actively marginalized in the existing infrastructure, many continued to insist that water remain the responsibility of the city water department. Few demanded its privatization. Settlers in Mumbai saw water supply as a fundamental responsibility and reason of the state. They asked, what is the use of government if it cannot provide water? They constantly evaluated the morality of state officials based on their disposition around water services. Unlike the new regimes being proposed that sought to decenter the relations that constitute the city's public system, its present form provided a known and knowable route through which settlers could access water. They were anxious about the new uncertainties a different paradigm would bring. Recognizing their classed location in the city, settlers wondered whether they would be even more marginalized by an as-yet-unknown, privately managed, "water tight" infrastructure of distribution.[21]

As it is reproduced in everyday life, Mumbai's extant water infrastructure—its pumps, valves, engineers, city councilors, plumbers, and social workers—is a system of relations that provides many locations at which residents can make hydraulic claims. Relative to private systems, public systems are more tolerant of both excess and leakage. Leakage and excess are not just "waste" here but, as Timothy Luke (2010) has shown, are also the very conditions that make public infrastructures durable.[22] It is precisely because public water infrastructures are filled with excess (workers, technology, and water), and leakage, that they are a persistent and pernicious form that produces life in the city. The water system in Mumbai accommodates settlers *because* it is more forgiving of leakage. As such, it is more easily put to uses beyond those for whom it has been designed.

If an attention to the everyday life of Mumbai's water infrastructure draws attention to the generativity of leakage and also to the work of settlers aspiring to live in the city, it also delineates the limits of ongoing debates that animate the privatization of water services. Too often, these debates juxtapose public and private systems in simplified and dichotomous terms.[23] On the one hand, proponents of neoliberal reform suggest that amid increasing water insecurity, private systems are more efficient and able to fairly distribute water to marginal populations. In opposition, rights activists (in Mumbai and several other parts of the world) have argued that water is a fundamental and vital resource and a right of citizenship (see chapter 4). While such ideological debates (popular in both policy literature and also political praxis) are potent, this book demonstrates at least two problems with the forms these debates take.

First, such debates overlook the ways in which the assumptions of public and private distribution systems are not necessarily borne out in the field.[24] Take the assumption that public systems are starved of resources and expertise and, as a consequence, are unable to make investments in network maintenance or afford to extend the system to settlers. Mumbai's water department budgets reveal neither that it is weak, financially speaking, nor that neoliberal rationalities or technologies of distribution would be more efficient, profitable, or cost effective. Mumbai's water department is already tremendously profitable, mostly *because* it does not use water meters to bill some residents for water (see chapter 5).[25] Its engineers are most qualified to maintain, operate and extend water infrastructures in the city. Yet, as an attention to the everyday practices of settlers also shows, publics do not get water as a right in Mumbai's public system. Mumbai's water department regularly refuses to extend water infrastructures in the settlements despite having the finance and expertise to do so.[26]

Second, an attention to the everyday life of water infrastructures demonstrates that these are seldom public *or* private but often both. Public and private institutional regimes (property rights), organizational forms (asset management organizations), and resource governance paradigms (water rates, etc.) may form the same water system (Bakker 2010). As water systems are continuously extended over decades in the city, they frequently gather different governmental regimes and rationalities, producing different public *and* private bodies along the way. Mumbai's water infrastructure is an assemblage of public–private relations that collects and moves rain water from agrarian publics in Shahpur to private homes and businesses in the city. It is produced by state water subsidies for residents, a public water department that often uses private contractors to do its maintenance work, as well as a set of institutional regimes that uphold and enable the formation of private property rights in the city and the primacy of state authority.

Normative models of the public and the private also overlook the very ways in which ideas, bodies, and materials are always partially, simultaneously, and differentially formed as public *and* private by water infrastructures. For instance, public city water engineers see the city's residents as customers of the water utility, customers that need to show they pay their water bills if they wish to call upon the maintenance activities of state officials. Nevertheless, the hydraulic customer is not "always right." Settlers need to establish themselves as good, pliant subjects of the hydraulic system. Hydraulic infrastructures, as such, are completely entangled with questions of political membership, private property, and social belonging in the city.

While hydraulic infrastructures are an important site for the making of citizens and persons, they are not the only sites at which cities and citizenship are constituted and claimed. As Thomas Blom Hansen and Oskar Verkaaik point out, "No city can be fully known, as it is one of modernity's most powerful empty signifiers—too multi-layered and overflowing in histories and meanings to be fully captured by a single narrative or name" (2009, 8). Multiply mobilized, the city is composed of many social, political, and physical infrastructures—housing, energy, media, roads, for example. These infrastructures matter to residents in different ways and they produce political subjectivities in different ways.[27]

By drawing attention to the uncertainties and peculiarities of Mumbai's water infrastructure in this book, I do not wish imply that they (or their infrastructures) work smoothly anywhere else. In fact, it is precisely because cities in the Global North are also regularly governed by infrastructure breakdown and uncertainty that work in postcolonial cities is critical. Following hurricanes that flood subways, electricity grids that collapse, highway tunnels that leak, or seas that rise, we are reminded in the United States, as in India, that infrastructures are always moments in processes that gather unstable relations of nature, materials, and humans; they are formed by relations that always escape political control by slipping into dynamic regimes of the unknown and the not knowable. As we live in the unknowable and unstable environments of our climate-altered planet—environments in which we are often governed by ignorance—it is increasingly important to ask: How do people live amid environmental and technological uncertainty? How do urban populations recompose their lives amid precarious infrastructures and their mundane, unexceptional breakdowns? Here, the discrete, differential, and very ordinary water infrastructures in the cities of Mumbai might be less a marker of people in the past. Instead, as a mundane condition of the present, these infrastructures ask us—as they do the city's residents—to gather our tools and quietly, modestly carve out new terrains of livability for the future.

Notes

PREFACE

1. As David Mosse points out, "the relationship between water and society is as complex an historical, sociological and regional problem as any that can be imagined. Any contribution can hardly fail to be humbled by the fundamental questions invoked and the weight of antecedent interdisciplinary scholarship" (2003, 1). In their review article, Ben Orlove and Steven Caton (2010) suggest that the generativity of social studies of water has to do with its ability to traverse (and therefore connect) our political, social, and biological lives.

2. Instead of using the now problematized terms of *slum* and *slumdweller* (see Desai 2003; Echanove and Srivastava 2009; Ghannam 2002); in this book I use the *settlement* and *settler* to identify particular *kinds* of urban objects (homes) and subjects (residents) that are made prior to state recognition. I elaborate my reasons for doing so in the introduction of this book.

3. Arjun Appadurai has argued that emergency narratives stifle thinking and, moreover, reproduce unequal power relations. In his study of housing activists in Mumbai, he demonstrates how they refute emergency modes of organizing and instead practice a "politics of patience" that allows different voices to be heard and gathered (2002, 30).

4. In a provocative special issue on urban resilience, Bruce Braun and Stephanie Wakefield (2014) have suggested that the environmental apocalypse is not in our imminent future. Instead, they suggest that for many people in the world it is already a present reality. We are already dwelling in it (see also Braun 2014).

5. Accordingly, several NGOs in Mumbai now host programs through which ordinary residents can research, document, and tell their stories in and of the city. Pukar, an NGO based in Mumbai, resources and supports the research interests of hundreds of youth every year. "Youth fellows" are given the tools to tell their stories, of love and work, of mills and caste, of ecologies and gender in the city. A cofounder of Pukar, Appadurai has recently argued that it is critical that such research be carried out and the opportunity to narrate the city not be the privilege of the specialist alone. Research needs to be "deparochialized," Appadurai argues, because it "is vital for the exercise of informed citizenship" (2006). A different NGO, Yuva, has focused more on the making of news. They produce *Hamari Awaaz*, a video news bulletin that is made by youth living in different settlements.

6. Drawing on the work of Marilyn Strathern (2004) and Ursula Le Guin (1996), Donna Haraway (2014) has encouraged us to populate and destabilize our stories and retell them as gatherings of experience. "It matters what stories tell stories," she suggests,

insisting that what is needed now are not heroic storytellers (or ethnographers) but an effort to apprehend the worlds we know unstably and collectively with others.

7. Loosely translated, the Nakshatra are the twenty-seven lunar mansions that have long been used by astronomers in India to measure the calendar year. The monsoon is marked by the time when one of ten Nakshatra are directly overhead.

8. Here I draw on Dipesh Chakrabarty's (2009) essay, "The Climate of History," which has insisted that climate change promises to forever alter humanist pretensions of discrete social and environmental domains, and as such collapse enlightenment distinctions between natural history and social history.

INTRODUCTION

1. I begin with an account of the numbers that compose Mumbai's water system consciously, because this is how the system is often represented by engineers to the city's journalists and researchers.

2. See Chakrabarty (2007) and Coelho (2006) for more about the politics of shouting in postcolonial India

3. *Tai* is a kinship term signifying big sister in Marathi. With the exception of the filmmaker residents that I worked with in Jogeshwari, I have given pseudonyms to those who are not public figures in order to protect their identity.

4. Through an account of river restoration in Nepal, Anne Rademacher (2011) shows how settler populations too have desires and aspirations for greening their urban environments. These aspirations complicate accounts that identify the greening of cities as a bourgeois project.

5. If the blockage (or leakage) was located on the household side of the meter, it would be Alka tai's family that would be responsible for repairs. On the other hand, if it was located prior to the meter, it would be the formal responsibility of the city government.

6. My interest in the ordinary here emerges not only with recognition of Alka tai's family's extraordinary accomplishments but also with the work of Asef Bayat (1997). Bayat has urged an attention to the everyday political praxis through which marginalized lives are rendered more stable, through a "quiet encroachment of the ordinary" (Bayat 1997, 61; see also Anjaria 2011; Ghannam 2002).

7. Scholars of informality working in Mumbai and South Asia more generally have made signal contributions by describing the everyday processes through which marginalized residents have established themselves in the city (see McFarlane 2008; Ananya Roy 2003; Ananya Roy and AlSayyad 2004). Newer work has extended the analytics of informality by demonstrating how it is not merely in the domain of the marginalized but also key to the work of bureaucrats, state officials, and real estate developers as well (Baviskar and Sundar 2008; Bear 2015; Ananya Roy 2005).

8. See Bjorkman (2015), Echanove and Srivastava (2009), Ghannam (2002), and Ghertner (2015) for nuanced readings on how the category of "slum" often erroneously conflates living conditions, legality, built form, and moral virtue into a single unit of "slum" housing deemed to be unsuitable for civil life.

9. See, for instance, Raj Kapoor's *Shree 420* (1955), Anurag Kashyap's *Black Friday* (2004), and Danny Boyle's *Slumdog Millionaire* (2009).

10. See, e.g., Suketu Mehta's *Maximum City* (2004), Mike Davis's *Planet of Slums* (2006), Robert Neuwirth's *Shadow Cities* (2006), and Katherine Boo's *Behind the Beautiful Forevers* (2012).

11. See Desai (2003), Echanove and Srivastava (2009), and Ghannam (2002).

12. I recognize the terms *settlers* and *settlement* have fraught histories, particularly because they are usually used to identify the unauthorized and often violent process of constructing colonial settlements in the settler societies of Israel, Australia, and the United States.

13. Bruce Braun (2005) asks why nonhuman natures remain static and passive in accounts of urban water. Arguing that the properties of water also influence urban politics, Braun suggests that human geographers pay closer attention to these "more-than-human" relations.

14. See also J. K. Gibson-Graham (1996), who has drawn attention to the gendered scripts through which capitalism is known. They urge that we do not take the narrative of capital as complete and totalizing. More recently, Anna Tsing (2015) suggests we see capitalism as "patchy" and always needing an outside to colonize.

15. Vinay Gidwani has made a powerful critique of Chakrabarty's argument here, suggesting that his dualist rendering of capitalist histories continues to locate Europe as the center from which capitalist projects emanate (Gidwani 2008).

16. Feminist geographers have pointed to the gendered metaphors through which capitalism has been narrated and urged that we refuse their power (see Gibson-Graham 1998; Hart 2002). For work arguing for an attention to the contingent expansion of capitalist life, see Mitchell (2002) and Tsing (2015).

17. See Gandy (2002), Hamlin (1998), and Joyce (2003).

18. See Mitchell (2002) and Mukerji (2010) for accounts of the rise of engineering in nineteenth-century Egypt and France, respectively.

19. Caroline Humphrey (2005) has urged us to recognize how ideology appears in and is produced by material structures. Here I draw attention to the ways in which infrastructures give material form to liberal ideologies, and might explain why infrastructures have returned as a key site of governmental action in these more neoliberal times. By governments around the world, infrastructures are seen to be a suitable site for state action, one that creates the grounds for, but does not intervene in, the workings of the market (see Collier 2011).

20. As such, infrastructures are also a key site for the administration of structural violence on variously disenfranchised groups (Rodgers and O'Neill 2012).

21. I suggest this may be the case not just in Mumbai but in many other postcolonial cities around the world.

22. As scholars of citizenship have noted, subjects—like the urban poor in Mumbai—might be formal citizens, entitled to the guarantees of citizenship, and still not receive its guarantees (Appadurai 2002; Holston and Appadurai 1996). On the other hand, subjects who are not formal citizens—such as illegal immigrants—might still receive the substantive distributions of citizenship (Holston 2008; Sassen 2003).

23. See Appadurai (2002), Clarke (2013), V. Das (2011), Holston (2008), Lazar (2013), Ong (1996, 2006), and Thomas (2011).

24. There is a rich literature in anthropology on the relation between national citizenship and cultural difference. See, for instance, Clarke (2013), Herzfeld (1992), Ong (1996), Rosaldo (1994), and Zérah and Landy (2013).

25. In this section, I am thinking of recognition as has been theorized by Elizabeth Povinelli (2002). As I describe in chapter 2, recognition is an ambivalent event, which calls on settlers to perform their subjectivity in particular ways so as to call on the state's care. On the other hand, once settlers are "seen by the state" as such, they are also liable to the exercise of its disciplinary apparatus.

26. See Ferguson (1999) for more on the nonlinear relations between political membership, time, and modernity.

27. Note that hydraulic infrastructures reveal and delineate different processes of urban citizenship relative to land- and property-based accounts. While the recognitions of property have long been central to establishing citizenship in the city (D. Harvey 2008; Holston 2008; Joyce 2003), including obtaining water services, an attention to the everyday life of water infrastructures reveals how the event of tenurial security is not sufficient to guarantee hydraulic citizenship in the city.

28. In their article "Beyond 'Culture,'" Akhil Gupta and James Ferguson (1992) argue against a reading of culture as being isomorphic with space, and instead urge an attention to how communities are constituted through meaningful inscriptions and interconnections made in space.

29. Julie Chu (2014) has urged an attention to the political work of disrepair (see also Graham and Thrift 2007).

30. South and Southeast Asian scholarship has been particularly attentive to the ways in which water infrastructures are generative of state institutions and political relations. See, e.g., Geertz (1972), Gilmartin (1994), Hardiman (1996, 2002), Lansing (1991), L. Mehta (2005), Mosse (2003), Schwenkel (2015), and Whitcombe (1972). In more recent years, urban political ecologists have shown how water networks are constitutive of the political field in the city (Carroll 2012; Gandy 2002, 2014; Kaika 2005; Kjellén 2006; Loftus 2012; Meehan 2014; Sultana and Loftus 2012; Swyngedouw 2004; Swyngedouw and Heynen 2013).

31. Foucault (2008) described the rise of biopolitical government in Europe (particularly France). Extending and complicating his account of Europe as the center of this form of rule, Ann Laura Stoler (1995) and Peter Redfield (2005) have since demonstrated how these techniques of government were first produced and improvised through relations with its colonial subjects.

32. While Foucault refers to technologies of power in his work, he was less lucid about how material technologies "make a difference" in his work (Bennett 2010). In part, this may be because, as Michael Behrent (2013) argues, Foucault's use of the term *technology* has had less to do with material technologies and more to do with signifying a particular art of managing populations and the self through instruments like the map, the census, and the survey. This is not to say that Foucault neglected the power of material objects in his work. He took care to remind his readers that material artifacts are "rigorously indivisible" from the ideas that form them, where neither the material nor the ideational is primary in the first instance (Foucault 1984, 253; see also Larkin 2008). Nevertheless, matter tends to remain passive in these accounts (Barad 2003; Lemke 2014). It often articulates with, but seldom objects to or remains outside of, the political formations from which it is sought to be drawn. See also Mitchell (2011).

33. See Boyer (2014, 2015) for the relation between energy and biopolitics.

34. See, for instance, Coleman (2014) and Degani (2013) for the kinds of political subjectivity and hopes for the future effected by electricity in India and Tanzania, respectively. On the other hand, see Larkin (2008) and Sundaram (2010) for an attention to how the media infrastructures that electricity enables produce different kinds of social and political forms of connection and circulation.

35. In theorizing infrastructure as accretion, I am mindful of the work of Franz Boas, who theorized culture as an accretion (Boas 1974), and also of more recent work by Donald Moore (2005), who urged an attention to historically "sedimented" social practices in Zimbabwe.

36. Sarah Whatmore (2006) reminds us that the recent turn to materiality is, in fact, a "materialist return." As I evoke hydraulic networks to theorize political and social forms of cities and citizenship, I am conscious of the past–present legacies of materialist scholarship, particularly in the field of environmental studies. Early explorations of nature–society relations have shown how political systems are made and consolidated by powerful groups controlling the resources of already existing landscapes.

37. Karl Wittfogel worked with mechanistic formulations of hydraulic systems to describe the formation of "hydraulic societies" (see also Strang 2016). In his landmark tome, *Oriental Despotism* (1957), Wittfogel theorized how these were ruled by authoritarian "despots" in the "Orient" through the management and control of irrigation structures— particularly large-scale irrigation and flood control projects. Wittfogel's rendering of social order (and also social others) borne out of controlling "nature" has been powerful and troubling, to scholars of both India and of environmental studies more generally. For instance, Janet Abu-Lughod (1991) has questioned whether the hydraulic systems he characterized in South India were either despotic or centralized. On the other hand, Donald Worster (1992) takes a different approach. In his work on California, there is nothing "oriental" about hydraulic societies. Either way, Wittfogel's work on hydraulic societies is troubling because it suggests that material conditions (of water scarcity or abundance) are what structure social order in the first instance (see also Geertz 1972). Here, I depart from Wittfogel to describe a different hydraulic regime, one that, while durable, has diverse locations of control, authority, and leakage.

38. The uncertainty I describe here is not just a material uncertainty of when water will "come" but also a political uncertainty of who is in control of water and its diverse kinds of pipes, valves, and politics. I suggest uncertainty to be an outcome of processes that are simultaneously material and political (cf. Thompson, Warburton, and Hatley 1986).

39. Noting the peculiar invisibilities of infrastructure, Susan Leigh Star (1999) famously noted how infrastructures are often invisible until they break down. It is when infrastructures break down, Star argues, that their tenuous relations become visible. Taking up her provocation, geographers have demonstrated how both breakdown and infrastructural visibility are ubiquitous and particularly noticeable in cities of the Global South (Graham 2010; Graham and Thrift 2007; McFarlane 2008), where multiple infrastructural regimes jostle for prominence (Furlong 2014). The tangle of electric and television cables, water pipes, drums, and buckets visibly materializes the contentious state of technology and authority in these cities. Yet while these infrastructures are indeed apparent, less clear is the relationship between visibility and breakdown in these locations. First, these knotty

visible assemblages are often, in fact, working in these locations. Second, as "concrete semiotic and aesthetic vehicles oriented to addressees" (Larkin 2013, 329), roads and energy infrastructures are often built to be especially spectacular—to demonstrate the power and technological prowess of nation-states, corporations, or other institutions to deliver the visions and appearances of modernity (P. Harvey and Knox 2015; Schwenkel 2015). What the hypervisibility of infrastructure in the South (and indeed in many other locations) reveals instead is the lack of any easy correspondence between visibility and breakdown.

40. Heidegger (1977) has reminded us that we are thrown into worlds that are not of our making, worlds that are already formed by technology. These silently, and often invisibly, produce the very conditions of possibility for corporeal, social, and institutional life.

41. See Limbert (2010) for an account of the temporalities of energy production. See McKay (2012) for a description of how subjects make claims to state resources using different temporal frames.

42. For research on water infrastructures, see Bjorkman (2015), Ranganathan (2014), and von Schnitzler (2013). Hannah Appel (2012a, 2012b), Andrew Barry (2013), Leo Coleman (2014), and Timothy Mitchell (2011) have generated critical insights through their work on energy infrastructures. For housing, see Fennell (2015) and Schwenkel (2013). Penelope Harvey and Hannah Knox (2015) and Jeremy Campbell (2012) have researched roads in Latin America. Through her research on the Nile and his research on the Panama Canal, Jessica Barnes (2014) and Ashley Carse (2012) have demonstrated how infrastructures produce disconnections and rescale geographies.

43. As theorists have pointed out, infrastructures have been used as a heuristic device (by social scientists and politicians alike) to measure and map the progress and development of nations (see Graham 2010; Gupta 2015).

44. See Dossal (2010), Gandy (2002), and Hamlin (1998).

45. Based on fieldwork with apartheid infrastructures in Johannesburg, Antina von Schnitzler (2013) has demonstrated how infrastructures separate, differentiate, and preclude the formation of publics as much as they connect them (see also Harvey and Knox 2015).

46. See Dossal (1991), Gandy (2014), and Zérah (2008).

47. There is, however, some research into how water connections were extended into the working-class *chawls* in the early twentieth century (Chandavarkar 2007; Hazareesingh 2000).

48. In critiquing neoliberalism, scholars sometimes presume that the postcolonial state has a history of durable public services that is only now being undone.

49. There is now a well-established literature that examines the relation between documents and citizenship. See Cody (2009), V. Das (2011), Gupta (2012), Hull (2012), McKay (2012), and Tarlo (2001).

50. See V. Das (2011), Hull (2012), and Tarlo (2001) for critical scholarship that attends to the relation between documents and citizenship.

51. I use Barry's (2013) theorization of the political situation to draw attention to the ways that the political terrain is made through a negotiation of invisible and visible relations. Amita Baviskar and Nandini Sundar (2008) critique Chatterjee's assertion that the subjects of political society use moral claims, social connections, and cash to demand en-

titlements. Instead, they argue that members of powerful and more marginalized groups *alike* deploy these relations in everyday life.

52. Work that assumes the liberal subject sometimes assumes the normativity of nuclear households as a unit of governmental intervention. Nevertheless, "the household" and the community do not exist a priori but are constantly being made through hydraulic and other infrastructures.

53. In her work on the privately owned public toilets in the Ghanian city of Temba, Brenda Chalfin has demonstrated how infrastructures are productive of publics—here a "commonwealth of waste" (2014, 2016; see also Marres 2012). Reminding us that these publics are dynamic formations that are being un/made by infrastructures everywhere, Catherine Fennell's (2015) study of public housing in Chicago develops a materialist conception of sympathy to theorize how public infrastructures are brought into being.

54. Here I use Homi Bhabha's (2012) framing of the "not quite" to describe how infrastructures in the Global South are seen through a neocolonial gaze (in the North and South alike) as outcomes of processes of mimicry, a mimicry that attempts to overcome yet only reinscribes national difference between nations deemed to be developed and developing. The visibility of infrastructures in the South has been a commonplace way to distinguish them from those in the North, where scholars in s&TS have argued that infrastructures are visible until they break down (see Star 1999; Star and Ruhleder 1996). I question the neat association between functionality and visibility by drawing attention to contested infrastructural practices in Mumbai (see also Barnes 2014; Carse 2014). In so doing, I follow scholars of Mumbai's infrastructures who have questioned the normative expectations of infrastructural invisibility implicit in earlier accounts, pointing to the ways in which colonial histories and postcolonial politics make infrastructures a highly visible mediation of technology and politics (see Bjorkman 2015; Gandy 2014; McFarlane 2008). Yet this is not to say that the invisibility of infrastructures in the Global North be taken as given. Historians of technology, working primarily on infrastructures in Europe and the United States, have shown how the invisibility of working infrastructures is a precarious achievement that needs extraordinary work (see Barry 2013; Coutard 1999; Hughes 1983; Starosielski 2015). For more on the relation between visibility, power, and infrastructure, see also Appadurai (2015), Finkelstein (2015), Gupta (2015), and Larkin (2013).

55. American newspapers now regularly report infrastructure breakdowns. See Belson (2008), Davison (2011), McGeehan, Buettner, and Chen (2014), Murley (2011), and Schaper (2014).

56. For more on the NURM, see Banerjee-Guha (2009), S. Benjamin (2008), and Ranganathan, Kamath, and Baindur (2009).

57. See Bakker (2007, 2010) for a lucid account of why this staged contest of public versus private systems is also theoretically insufficient.

58. Just as infrastructure—transport, banking, currency—underpins commerce, James Scott argues, "infrapolitics provides much of the cultural and structural underpinning of more visible political actions" (1990, 184; see also Hansen and Verkaaik 2009). While Scott foregrounds the social relations of infrapolitics, in this book I extend his formulation to also consider the politics of the hidden, underground materials of the city's water infrastructure. These connections are not only differentially visible and political, acted

upon by human agents. The city's water infrastructure is also a vital participant in its political life, often acting in ways outside or beyond those desired by its government.

59. See Elyachar (2010) for a similar account of how residents in Cairo seek to fix their water connections through such "phatic labor" (see also Simone 2006).

60. There is by now sufficient research documenting these important shifts in Indian cities. For more recent accounts, see Bjorkman (2015), Doshi (2012), Ghertner (2015), Goldman (2011), Harris (2013), and Ranganathan (2014).

61. I have focused on these processes elsewhere (see Anand 2006; Anand and Rademacher 2011).

62. Here, the works of Jonathan Shapiro Anjaria (2016), Solomon Benjamin (2008), and Liza Weinstein (2014) have been notable exceptions.

63. Tess Lea (2015) has cautioned against the coherent narratives of much ethnography when she warns that these deny the fragmented, multiple, and partial realities in which we live.

CHAPTER 1. Scare Cities

1. For an excellent political ethnography on the Shiv Sena, see Hansen (2001). See also Katzenstein, Mehta, and Thakkar (1997) for an account of the institutional histories that accounted for its rise in Mumbai.

2. While conducting fieldwork, I found engineers and politicians often making the city's problems visible through mystifying numbers (Prakash 2010) and ritual incantations bemoaning the absence of suitable, sufficient infrastructure (Appel 2012b).

3. Of course, this is not what the Shiv Sena is only known for in the city. It has one of the most organized women's wings that regularly sponsors welfare and social service events in the city, including programs to donate school uniforms, clothes, and so on (Bedi 2007, 2016; Roy 2009). It also sponsors a number of livelihood generation projects in the city (Solomon 2015).

4. Urban research based in cities of the Global South proliferated in the early 2000s. Much of this scholarship explored the makings of citizenship by attending to questions of land and housing (see Appadurai 2002; S. Benjamin 2008; Doshi 2012; Ghertner 2016, Holston 2008; Hull 2012; Meehan 2014; Tarlo 2000; Weinstein 2014; Zeiderman 2016). More recently, scholars began to explore questions of urban membership and citizenship through studies of water in the postcolonial city (see Bjorkman 2015; Coelho 2006; Kooy and Bakker 2008; Meehan 2014; Ranganathan 2014; von Schnitzler 2013).

5. For more on the productive life of scarcity, see also Alatout (2008), Bakker (2000), Birkenholtz (2009), Giglioli and Swyngedouw (2008), L. Mehta (2005), and United Nations Development Programme (2006).

6. Accordingly, Linton and Budds (2014) have urged us to see the water cycle as a "hydrosocial cycle."

7. I use the term *technopolitics* following Larkin (2013) and Mitchell (2002) to signal ways in which political relations are formed and reproduced through technological assemblages.

8. While historians have largely focused on colonial and postcolonial South Asia beyond its cities, careful accountings of Mumbai through the nineteenth and twentieth

centuries can be found in a series of three volumes on the city edited by Sujata Patel and Jim Masselos (2003) and Sujata Patel and Alice Thorner (1995, 1996).

9. As detailed in the previous interlude, Bombay's prolific growth in this period was inextricably linked to its rise as a central node in the opium trade with China and the cotton trade with the British Empire during the late nineteenth century. The temporary interruption of the American cotton trade during its civil war (1861–65) and the opening of the Suez Canal (1866) made Bombay a vital node in the cotton trade during this period (Hazareesingh 2001).

10. At the time, Salsette lay beyond the limits of the colonial city. In the time since, it has been incorporated into the city.

11. In his history of liberalism and the city, Patrick Joyce suggests that colonial urban government of Indian cities was conservative, contradictory, and limited (2003, 250). Municipal government was circumscribed in colonial India, and colonial officials did not seek to govern persons but communities, many of whose leaders were more frequently nominated by the British than elected.

12. Larkin (2013) has drawn our attention to the ways in which infrastructures do not just carry things but also "address" publics. For more on the disjunctures between liberal and colonial modes of address through infrastructure provision, see Gandy (2014) and Zérah (2008).

13. See Gandy (2002), Hamlin (1998), and Joyce (2003).

14. For more on the histories of town planning in colonial India, see Dossal (1991), Kidambi (2007), Klein (1986), Nair (2005), and Srinivas (2015).

15. See Balibar (1988), Chatterjee (2004), and Mamdani (1996).

16. Thus, Vihar was completed in 1860, Tulsi in 1879, Tansa in 1925, Modak Sagar in 1957, Upper Vaitarna in 1973, Bhatsa in 1981, and the Middle Vaitarna in 2012. New dams are currently being designed and planned at Pinjal, Gargai, and on the Daman Ganga River. Taken together, the Pinjal and Gargai dams will submerge seventeen villages and an additional 2,850 hectares of forestland (SANDRP 2014).

17. Writing in the 1980s, political ecologists drew special attention to how states are made through discourses of ecological crisis (see Blaikie 1985; Blaikie and Brookfield 1987; Saberwal 2000; Thompson, Warburton, and Hatley 1986).

18. To derive per capita water demand, the report draws on three other studies that recommend and predict how much water residents in cities like Mumbai should and might use. Here, too, the report vacillates between arbitrarily fixing the demand at 150 and 240 liters per person day (LPCD). Based on these diverse "targets" of water supply, the committee fixes the allocation of water that should be planned for in the city: "considering all these aspects, it is preferred to plan development work for the next 30 years' water supply on the basis of a flat rate of 240 LPCD, as has been actually observed in Greater Bombay" (Bombay Municipal Corporation 1994, 3–8).

19. I examine the leakage figures and their political effects in more detail in chapter 5.

20. Here I draw on Teresa Caldeira's (2000) work in São Paulo to suggest that narratives of water scarcity (like narratives of crime in her work) organize and structure the lived experiences of everyday life in the city.

21. I am indebted to scholars of state formation who have demonstrated how states are made through projects to control environmental resources at the margins (Escobar 1995;

Ferguson 1994; Gupta 1995; Li 1999, 2007; Mitchell 2002; Scott 1998; Sivaramakrishnan 2002; Tsing 2005).

22. Following the pioneering work of Amartya Sen (1981), scholars of water have shown how scarcity is both discursively produced and an effect of the distributive politics of states (Alatout 2008; Barnes 2014; Birkenholtz 2009; Hardiman 2007; L. Mehta 2005; Otero et al. 2011).

23. As such, an attention to water infrastructures destabilizes the centrality of political independence in our histories of the city. The postcolonial city continues to extract water from marginalized populations in the ever-receding urban periphery through a mobilization of scarcity statistics, much as the colonial city did prior to 1947.

24. The name and acronym of the city's municipal administration has, like the name of the city itself, has been changing over the years. As a result both residents of the city and the municipal employees today call the city and the city administration several different names including the BMC (or the Bombay Municipal Corporation, the Brihanmumbai Municipal Corporation), the MCGM (or the Municipal Corporation of Greater Mumbai), or Mumbai Mahanagar Palika in Marathi. This instability is also manifest in the city's own publications (see, e.g., Brihanmumbai Municipal Corporation 1999, Municipal Corporation of Greater Mumbai 2001). The naming controversies of the city conceal a fraught debate over the city's identity (see Hansen 2001). In maintaining this instability throughout the book, I intend to keep this controversy open and unresolved.

25. The engineer here is referring to the historic rainfall on July 26, 2005, when parts of the city received 94.4 centimeters (37 inches) of rain in a twenty-four-hour period. As a result of this rainfall and a steady destruction of the city's wetlands over the preceding decades, over a fifth of the city's area was flooded and thousands of people were killed in the region (Government of Maharashtra 2006).

26. In actual practice, however, the city water department does maintain, access, and use certain bore wells. This water is often delivered by municipal trucks to areas underserved by the city's water infrastructure.

27. Newspapers often identify well water operators as the water tanker "mafia" (see newspaper reports in the *Mid-Day*, September 16, 2009; *Mumbai Mirror*, November 12 and 17, 2009; see also Graham et al. 2014). In these reports, the term *mafia* designates a black box of informal practices that are not adequately described or defined.

28. Despite knowing neither the number of wells in the city nor how much water these wells provide, these engineers claim that the city's underground water can meet only 6 percent of the city's water needs.

29. See, for instance, Baviskar (1995), D'Souza, Mukopadhyay, and Kothari (1998), A. Kothari and Bhartari (1984), L. Mehta (2005), Arundhati Roy (2001), and World Commission on Dams (2000).

30. Work in urban geography that focuses on the resources that enable the metabolic city is a notable exception. For instance, see work by Gandy (2002), Heynen, Kaika, and Swyngedouw (2006), and Linton (2010).

31. See, e.g., McCully (2001), L. Mehta (2005), Reisner (1987), and Whitcombe (1972). There is also a rich literature on irrigation projects in colonial India that demonstrates how such initiatives gave form to the colonial state at the cost of several other hydraulic traditions/practices (see D'Souza 2006; Gilmartin 1994; Hardiman 2002).

32. See, e.g., Bapat and Agrawal (2003), Bjorkman (2015), and Shaban and Sharma (2007). Work by Swyngedouw (2004) and Gandy (2002) are exceptions in this regard.

33. Here I am drawing on the work of Donna Haraway (1991) and Matthew Gandy (2005) to reflect on how the urban body emerges as always-already distinguished and differentiated through the production of water infrastructure.

34. See, e.g., Barnes (2014), Carse (2014), Cronon (1991), and Thomas (2012).

35. This was the year prior to the dry monsoon of 2009 that I describe in the previous section.

36. See Reisner (1987) for a similar history of Los Angeles.

37. With some exceptions, rural residents who live near the pipelines are given formal access to the network and are billed for this access. Engineers told me that they were permitted access so that they would not damage or pilfer water from the water mains, and cause far greater losses as a result.

38. In making this claim, I follow the work of David Nugent (2004) and Akhil Gupta (1995), who have urged an attention to the everyday practices of government.

39. These figures were provided to me by the deputy hydraulic engineer (Planning) in 2008, when I asked him how the waters of the Bhatsa were allocated.

40. For more on the histories and the politics of the Shiv Sena, see Hansen (2001) and Katzenstein, Mehta, and Thakkar (1997).

41. See Brihanmumbai Municipal Corporation (BMC) MCGM et al. (2001, 2006).

INTERLUDE. Fieldwork

1. Mary Louise Pratt (1986) has eloquently commented on the fraught practice of the ethnographer's arrival story. Arrival stories, for Pratt, serve to authorize and set apart the ethnographer from the subjects of her ethnography. Arrival stories of this sort are some-what more convoluted (and perhaps more necessary) for the "native" ethnographer. I tell a version of this story not only to unsettle the idea of the native ethnographer as being of the place (and people) subjected to ethnography, but also to blur the boundaries between the practices of research, of kinship, and of citizenship.

CHAPTER 2. Settlement

1. The demolitions were especially brutal because only months before, the political party in office, seeking reelection, had promised to regularize these settlements and make them eligible for water services.

2. See Ghannam's (2002) work on Cairo; D. Harvey's (2003) work on Paris; Holston's (1989) book on Brasilia; N. Smith's (1996) work on New York; and Tarlo's (2000) work on Delhi.

3. For an excellent recent book on the relation between aesthetics and the makings of the world-class city, see Ghertner (2015). Steven Gregory (1998) reminds us that the project of world-class city making is never complete, and needs constant development work. Thus, the newer efforts to remake Indian cities are only the most recent iterations of an older historical process (see Anand 2006; Baviskar 2011; S. Benjamin 2008; Doshi 2012; Kalia 1999, 2004; Mazzarella 2003; McFarlane 2008; Nijman 2008, 2009; Ananya

Roy 2009; D. Roy 2009; K. Sharma 2005 for the history of these efforts in different cities).

4. See also Holston (2008), Patel and Masselos (2003), Patel and Thorner (1996), and Ren (2011).

5. For some time now, structural, dualistic accounts have been especially powerful in characterizing and theorizing inequality in cities in the Global South. Popular books on the city (M. Davis 2006; Neuwirth 2006), scholars of urban planning (Dwivedi and Mehrotra 1995), urban development reports (such as the *Mumbai Human Development Report*), newspaper reports, and urban geographers (Banerjee-Guha 2009; D. Harvey 2008) commonly describe and theorize cities of the South in dichotomous terms. These newer works have a family resemblance in their accounting of power with older treatises such as Wittfogel's (1957) study of "Oriental despotism."

6. There is a generative genealogy for this work. See, for instance, Hansen and Verkaaik (2009), Schneider and Schneider (1976), and Scott (1977).

7. Chatterjee (2005) is careful to suggest that the relations of political society do not lie outside the state but run right through it—involving junior officials, engineers, and administrators, as well as elected political representatives and their political parties. Nevertheless, Chatterjee and scholars following him propose that the practices of political society are enduring and seldom transition to the politics of citizenship.

8. Here I am thinking in particular of the work of Abdou Maliq Simone (2014) and Asef Bayat (2010), who have demonstrated how a quiet yet anticipatory politics is productive of urban life for many disavowed by its exclusive rules.

9. There has been significant scholarship documenting this process. See, for instance, Barry (2001, 2013), Gandy (2014), and Mitchell (2002, 2011).

10. Of course, as historians of liberal citizenship have shown, these projects of equality came with their own class and gender exclusions (see, e.g., Holston 2008).

11. For more on this process, see Dossal (2010), Gandy (2014), Hamlin (1998), and Hazareesingh (2001).

12. This is not to say that the liberal political subject has existed as such in the metropole. As work on political machines in North American cities in the mid-twentieth century reveals, liberal government has long been in battles to overcome diverse forms of association in cities in both the colonial and the postcolonial world (Golway 2014; see also S. Benjamin 2008; M. Davis 2006; Holston 2008; Lamarchand 1977; Scott 1977).

13. The gendered category of patronage obfuscates the way that women also conjure political authority in the city. Tarini Bedi (2016) has published a lucid and provocative account of political "matronage" in the womens' wing of the Shiv Sena.

14. See Mol (2002) and Simone (2004a, 2004b).

15. See Dossal (2010), Holston (2008), and Joyce (2003).

16. This was the case not just in Jogeshwari but in Mumbai more generally (see K. Sharma 2000).

17. In Jogeshwari, the production of Premnagar as a Muslim "pocket" adjoining Marathi settlements was also facilitated by the Shiv Sena, which in the 1990s steadily began "recognizing" the tenancy of Marathi residents' living structures as tenants to (mostly) Muslim landlords in Jogeshwari.

18. "Tribal" groups, including the Warli and Mahadev Koli, continue to live in and adjacent to Sanjay Gandhi National Park in Borivali (see Zérah and Landy 2013). For a careful study of the particular history and practice of classifying social groups as "indigenous tribes" in India, see Bayly (1996) and Skaria (1999).

19. Here I am indebted to the work of Farha Ghannam (2002), who has urged an attention to the lives of those inhabiting resettlement colonies decades after the event of demolition and resettlement (see also Tarlo 2000).

20. Literally meaning "brother," residents of the city often use the term to address other men of a similar age. *Bhai* is also used colloquially to identify/address big men that often have links to the mafia in the city.

21. This history of differentiated and diffuse sovereignty in the settlements has a long history and continues to this day (Hansen and Verkaaik 2009).

22. The pagdi system is a durable form of tenancy, peculiar to Mumbai, in which the tenant pays eleven months up front. It is difficult to evict those living in buildings from their tenancy if they are paying pagdi.

23. The TADA was a notorious law promulgated in 1985 by the central government. Under it, people could be imprisoned for long periods without a trial, and confessions under torture were permissible in court. A vast majority of TADA detainees were Muslims.

24. This is not to say that Yusuf bhai did not have narratives of and around corruption in the city. Corruption talk is both potent and prolific in the Indian polity (Gupta 2012). Here, I show that Yusuf did not use the terms of corruption in describing his actions but instead used the language of relations (*rishta*).

25. Unlike in many other parts of the world, in India such practices are not as much the monopoly of powerful elites. Relative to other countries (like the United States), the poor and middle class use personal relations in this way as much as do the wealthy.

26. There has been a renewed attention to the relations of friendship in theorizing political life. This literature has highlighted the possibility of relations of political inclusion amid relations of difference—politics that does not seek to evade or neutralize prejudice or difference (see, e.g., Derrida 2005; Devji 2005).

27. As an appointee of the colonial government, the office of the municipal commissioner was instituted precisely to control the demands of elected officials in colonial Mumbai (Kidambi 2007).

28. For example, the current councilor from Meghwadi grew up in its settlements and became the most powerful political leader there. As a democratically elected king, he dispenses favors and justice to the settlement's residents and workers, recommending students for admission to schools and colleges on the one hand, and organizing mobs to humiliate teachers and other state officers for not performing their duties on the other.

29. For more on the histories and differentiating effects of slum policy, see Bardhan et al. (2015), Chatterji and Mehta (2007), P. K. Das (2003), Doshi (2012), and Mukhija (2003).

30. At the time of fieldwork, the cutoff date was 1995. It has since been moved forward to 2000.

31. Notification of a given property as a slum area makes the claims of property owners more precarious, in part, because they would be liable to pay for these improvements in arrears in the event they sought to exercise their rights to the land.

32. Authorized structures sit on land that is the most difficult to appropriate. The BMC has to embark on the process of land acquisition, and any package the BMC offers has to also include the cost of the structure. Residents living in tolerated structures used to be entitled to an equivalent area of land in case of displacement. Now, because the BMC has trouble identifying land for resettlement, it is giving 225-square-foot apartments to inhabitants of these structures in case their land is needed for public purposes. Like those living in tolerated structures, those in protected structures are also eligible for rehabilitation.

33. The cutoff date is currently 2000. See Bardhan et al. (2015) for a helpful genealogy of the cutoff date and slum policies more generally. As a result of state policy, the cutoff date has been consistently and repeatedly revised over the years. Unlike the colonial period, postcolonial government officials are now compelled to be, or at least seem to be, accountable to the demands and petitions of voters living in settlements. Requiring their votes to be elected to political office, the manifestos of political parties routinely promise to extend the cutoff date in every election.

34. The difficulty of distinguishing eligible residents from ineligible ones is not found in Mumbai alone. See Hull (2012) for an account of this process in Islamabad.

35. Here I have found Povinelli's (2002) work on the fraught politics of recognition among autochthonous Australians very instructive. For careful accounts of how residents gather state documents to make claims on the state, see V. Das (2011), Hetherington (2011), and Hull (2012). See also Simone's (2010) work on anticipation as a politico-temporal practice of urban life.

36. The ability to get one state document requires citizens to have in their possession other state documents. For instance, the food ration card is often required of residents as a "proof of address," to be used despite the fact that the card itself displays a message indicating that it is an entitlement of citizenship and cannot, in turn, be used as a proof of address.

37. See Corbridge et al. (2005) for an account of these practices in different parts of India.

38. Because of the low cost of water, as well as bills and billing concerns, those living in the settlements are not eligible to apply for a water connection on their own. They are required to apply in a group of ten or so, with one person nominated as secretary.

39. Once assembled, the application begins its journey in the bureaucracy: from the desk of the junior engineer to the sub-engineer to the assistant engineer at the ward office, and then across the city to the executive engineer and the deputy hydraulic engineer, who would give his approval before passing the application back "down" for the junior engineer to implement. In contrast to regular connections to authorized structures, the procedure for such "standpost connections" is designed to take time and requires someone or something to "motivate" the passage of the file to the most senior echelons of the water department and back (see Hull 2003). Even those with genuine documentation often require a facilitator who has knowledge of how the state works and is interested enough to follow the application (see Auyero 2000; Hansen and Verkaaik 2009). Most frequently, this person is a plumber (see chapter 5).

CHAPTER 3. Time Pé (On Time)

1. City water engineers and administrators have suggested that the capacity of these private water tanks aggregated across the city have a net storage capacity that exceeds the total daily supply of water in the city. While there is no way to verify their claims, it is worth considering how private water tanks are a "force" to reckon with in the city. See Meehan (2014).

2. Since I first drafted this chapter, there has been an emergent body of work that attends to the way that infrastructures produce shared experiences of time among social groups. See Appel (2012b), Barak (2013), Gupta (2015), and Hetherington (2014).

3. In talking with city engineers, I heard different norms that were being put in place at different times (e.g., I sometimes heard they designed connections so that slum dwellers get 45 LPCD and building residents receive 90 LPCD; see also Bjorkman 2015). That these quantities are always shifting, depending on the engineer, neighborhood, and time of year, is itself indicative. Regardless, those living in settlements are always allocated significantly less water than those living in buildings.

4. Thus, while engineers overestimate the population when calculating the undifferentiated city's water demand (see introduction), they underestimate the population when calculating distribution requirements for settlements.

5. As water enters the reservoir, its levels rise, increasing the water pressure in the pipes downstream. As water is released into the pipes, the reservoir levels are drawn down, decreasing the water pressure.

6. In conversations with his colleagues and seniors, Patankar also described our journey as being "in the field."

7. The city is beholden to the daily work of chaviwallas for its everyday water supply. See Bjorkman (2015) for an account of how the city shut down in 2000 when its municipal workers went on strike.

8. As a valve turns, the flow of water changes within moments, producing constantly shifting pressure levels throughout the system. The rapidly shifting pressures and flows generated by the intermittent system are hard to measure and control, even for the electronic SCADA (Supervisory Control and Data Acquisition) pressure monitors.

9. I am indebted to Carol Greenhouse for a close reading and stimulating set of observations that have helped animate this section.

10. This was also the reason that most people washed and swept the ground outside their homes.

11. See Banerjee-Guha (2009), M. Davis (2006), Harvey (2008), and Neuwirth (2006).

12. As I discussed in chapter 2, eligibility for city water is contingent on a whole range of documents that settlers are required to provide during the application process.

13. Ranging between US$300 and US$2,000 for these improvements, the amounts of money required were significant. Yet with their household structure safe from state demolitions and their husbands and grown children working at jobs with reliable incomes, many were willing to invest capital to better their water situation.

14. Literally meaning "aunt" in Marathi, *mausi* is an honorific term that is often used to address older women in Mumbai.

15. Mumbai resident and filmmaker Govindi Gudilu has created a wonderful short about these water-gathering practices. Titled *4:30 p.m.*, the film is part of the collection *Ek Dozen Paani* (2008) and is accessible at http://www.youtube.com/ekdozenpaani.

16. Adjacent to the city's national park, the area is home to panthers and other wild animals that have attacked children in recent times.

17. See Durga Gudilu's film *Yaadé* (2008) for an account of these practices in the recent past.

18. Kathleen O'Reilly (2006) has shown how water work is gendered as women's work in rural Rajasthan.

INTERLUDE. Flood

1. Take, e.g., the song "Rim Jhim" featured in the Bollywood film *Manzil* (1979), which routinely plays on the radio during the monsoons.

2. Alex Nading (2014) and Ashley Carse (2014) have productively illustrated the emergent ecologies of mosquitoes and canal economies in Nicaragua and Panama by examining the articulations of nature-cultures and infrastructure.

3. See also Ranganathan (2015) for an account of flood infrastructures as assemblages in Bangalore.

4. Unlike what is connoted by the term in the United States or Europe, suburbs in Mumbai's city neighborhoods are densely populated areas (like Jogeshwari) where most of the city's residents live. They are so called because they were more recently incorporated into the city (largely between 1944 and 1968).

5. See Carse (2012) for an account of how nature is sometimes read as infrastructure's infrastructure.

CHAPTER 4. Social Work

1. There is a rich literature on this topic in both political science and anthropology. See Auyero (2000), Boissevain (1974), Lamarchand (1977), and Zhang (2001). For work that is especially focused on India, see Anjaria (2011), Gupta (2012), Wade (1982), and Witsoe (2013).

2. In his work with derivative traders working in financial markets in Japan, Hirokazu Miyazaki (2013) has drawn attention to the work of arbitrage—a trading strategy that profits from discrepancies in prices of economically related assets. Arbitrage is not a resolution of price discrepancies between different economic markets, Miyazaki suggests, but instead a mediation of *knowledge gaps* between markets—between people who know (financiers) and do not know (investors). Arbitrage is a trading strategy that keeps financial markets working by traders managing and mediating relations of incomplete knowledge and difference. It is because of arbitrage, Miyazaki explains, that markets are able to work even as they make profits for arbitrage experts. As plumbers manage and mediate access to water in Mumbai, plumbers and social workers perform acts of political arbitrage, mediating knowledge gaps and subjectivities to keep political systems working in the city.

3. Here I am drawing on the work of Noortje Marres (2012) to suggest an attention to materially mediated publics. In chapter 1, I demonstrate how these material publics are

not independent of but rather formed through and with discursive hydraulic publics and counterpublics in the city (cf. Warner 2002).

4. Residents in Mumbai's settlements and NGO sector frequently draw distinctions between CBOs, which are local, place based, and provisionally supported in the community, and NGOs, which often work in many neighborhoods and frequently receive institutional funding from philanthropic (often transnational) donors.

5. Here I draw Appadurai's attention to locality into conversation with Haraway's work on situated knowledges. As Appadurai has famously shown, localities are produced through relational work across different scales (local, national, global; see Appadurai 1996, 2002). This work is productive of "situated knowledges" that residents and community leaders frequently mobilize in making life possible in the city (Haraway 1991). For Haraway, situated knowledges are interpretive positions and depend on the chosen positions of both the observer and the object (1991, 198). Such "partial locatable critical knowledges" (191) can and must be in conversation with critical interpretation among fields of interpreters and decoders (196). Their truth depends on the extent to which audiences can be convinced of their claims.

6. As anyone with a (biological and/or social) family has recognized, relations can demand consuming and competing forms of loyalty. Vishnu and other social worker friends I had in the settlement were frequently asked to formally join political parties and were given prominent places in rallies and commemorations. These invitations were not only a recognition of their good work but also an attempt to incorporate their work as enabled by the party, and to cultivate their loyalty in delivering votes at election time.

7. See Bedi (2016) for a wonderful ethnography of the Shiv Sena Womens Wing. See also Auyero (2000) for an account of these practices in Argentina.

8. Activists and organizers working in the settlements frequently identified the workers of CBOs and NGOs as those working in the "social field."

9. See also Bjorkman (2015).

10. A large Indian conglomerate, Reliance, had recently taken over electricity distribution. Since, settlers had been complaining vociferously about the larger bills that accompanied this transition. A year later, in the summer of 2009, Shiv Sena activists attacked Reliance Energy's head office to protest the high electricity rates ("Reliance Office Attacked by Suspected Shiv Sena Men," IBN Live, June 30, 2011, accessed January 30, 2012, http://www.news18.com/news/india/shiv-sena-attack-317907.html).

11. See Englund (2006), Paley (2001), and Riles (2000) for nuanced and careful accounts of the ways in which NGOs negotiate the fields of politics in their work.

12. In fact, elected representatives at all levels of government (city, state, and federal) seldom work on or think about policy. They vote largely following the instructions of *their* leaders (often called "high commands"). See Banerjee (2008) and Scott (1977).

13. This division of labor is familiar to those working in social movements in India. For example, in her book on the movement against the Narmada Dam, Baviskar (1995) describes how tribal members of the movement felt that they could not lead the movement.

14. In the words of one of the city's hydraulic engineers, "There is a water shortage and we have to balance the water. One day we give short supply here, the next day over there."

15. Friends in the settlement jokingly recounted one time when an election candidate had put a pipeline in the settlement, promising that water would flow through it if he was elected. When he was defeated in the election, he uprooted his pipe and took it away! See also Bjorkman (2015).

16. For instance, while talking about the surprising success of his party in the federal elections, Ismail stated that he was proud his constituency delivered two thousand more votes to his party than in the previous election. He claimed that this was due to its good works in the area. "People have noticed" his performance, he said, alluding to the fact that the party leadership was pleased with the results of his work.

17. The amount that each councilor is sanctioned for local area development projects is an index of their power in the city council. Whereas all councilors were allocated twenty-five lakh rupees (US$50,000) in 2007, the head of the municipal standing committee was able to access eight crore rupees (US$1.6 million) (Suryawanshi 2008).

18. This is not to say that the engineers' office does not intimidate settlers. Rather, by approaching the engineer in a group and not being as known to him, settlers were able to mobilize the discourse of rights more than if they went alone.

19. Compromised legal achievements also played a role. Having been part of the city for over fifteen years, Sundarnagar is now recognized by the city administration.

20. For a history of these relations, see Chandavarkar (2007) and Hazareesingh (2000).

21. These claims, as scholars have pointed out, are both powerful and not fully sufficient to ensure a fair distributive regime (see Bakker 2007, 2010; Page 2005; von Schnitzler 2008).

22. Activists and protestors are often belittled as children by city councilors. For an account of why revealing the public secret is so scandalous, see Zerubavel (2006).

23. Discontent with the injustice that had occurred, the NGO activists, together with youth groups in the settlements, went to the police station to file charges against the councilor's men who had intimidated and assaulted them. The next day, the activists were informed that the accused, together with the chief hydraulic engineer and the councilor of their ward, had filed countercharges against them for "unlawful assembly" (at a public meeting). As activists rushed from pillar to post to post bail, they were reminded that even a public consultation has certain rules, exclusions, and behaviors that are deemed dangerous and out of place by the city's civil authorities.

24. On a related note, urban residents are not seen by the state as singular, individuated subjects. Just as the state is diffuse, multiple, and plural and is given form through a bundle of heterogeneous practices (Abrams 1988; Gupta 1995; Mitchell 1991), so too is the subject multiply configured. For instance, residents in the settlements of Andheri might depend more on relations of patronage to get access to schools than they do hospitals. As Sandhya tai explained when describing her work in the settlement, several settlers would often go to private schools or hospitals if they could afford them, preferring to be consumers of the private service over those offered by the state.

INTERLUDE. River/Sewer

1. See Sarita Polmuri's meditative documentary *Mithi Nadi* (2008) on the toxicities that rivers are subjected to.

CHAPTER 5. Leaks

1. See Illich (1985) for a description of the difference between water and H_2O. See Scott (1998) and Rose and Miller (1992) for more on government at a distance.

2. Still recovering from the very public opposition to and subsequent collapse of water privatization projects it had supported in Delhi and Bangalore, the World Bank and its consultants repeatedly tried to reassure people that the project in Mumbai was about "improvement" and not privatization. State officials, engineers, residents, and even the odd anthropologist were told not to call this study *privatization*.

3. See, for instance, Braun and Whatmore (2011), Haraway (1991), and Latour and Weibel (2005).

4. Of course, this is an extremely difficult process as regulators attempt to price water appropriately to make it significant enough to conserve but not out of reach of anyone's daily needs. Andrea Ballestero (2015) has drawn attention to the fraught ethical and technical processes through which regulators attempt to derive a humanitarian and yet financially viable price for water in Costa Rica.

5. In fact, it is precisely because constant supply regimes were argued to be more profligate that London initially stalled efforts to convert its system from an intermittent to a 24/7 one (Hillier 2011).

6. See Bornstein (2014).

7. Following international standards, consultants bring the causes of water loss into view by qualifying leakages as real/physical or apparent/social and speculating (based on estimations of consumption) what the quantities of these leakages were.

8. See Mathews (2008), Petryna (2002), and Proctor and Schiebinger (2008) for careful theorizations of the politics and powers of ignorance.

9. I would like to thank Shaylih Muehlmann and Natasha Myers for drawing my attention to this.

10. During the first decade of the twenty-first century, new water accounting protocols urged urban water utilities to ensure that as much water as possible was "visible" and billed by the water utility (a source of revenue for the water department), and not "wasted" as leakage (Kingdom, Liemberger, and Marin 2006). Accordingly, consultants in Mumbai embarked on procedures to try and identify and measure water loss by its physical and social causes.

11. For instance, a report by the International Water Association begins with a section on the importance of *reliable* metering, noting that meters themselves "require careful management" and are prone to a host of problems including encrustation, deterioration with age, and unreliable flow rates (Lambert and Hirner 2000). At times, particulate blockage can increase water pressure through the meter, causing elevated readings (Castalia Strategic Advisors 2007). In intermittent systems, meters also read and register air flowing through them, a common occurrence at the start of the daily water supply. Finally, meters are read by humans, who are a source of both deliberate and accidental error. Engineers would complain that meter readers seldom went to the field to read water meters, preferring instead to generate consumption figures in the comfort of their offices. Yet, because meters were unreliable, engineers were unable to enforce good reading practices on their workers. Even when engineers would scrutinize bills generated by

the billing department, they were unsure of when an unusual reading was due to excessive (or minimal) water use, a faulty meter, or an errant (or bribed) meter reader.

12. See Anand (2015) for more on this controversy.

13. Here I draw on the work of Bruno Latour, who has urged that we disassemble constitutive distinctions between humans and nonhumans, nature and culture, subject and object in theorizing social and political life. For Latour, things, laws, insects, bacteria, and people are all actants; they emerge through relations with others in networks and act through these relations. Latour argues that actants are objects that have effects on other things through relations—they make a difference (Bennett 2010; Harman 2009). As such, Latour refuses to prioritize humans as being above or beyond nonhumans with which they are in relations. Instead, as humans and nonhumans emerge through relations with each other, it becomes difficult to consider human action/agency in a different register than other kinds of action effected by nonhumans. All these effects, Latour argues, may be theorized as political effects.

14. To the extent that dam building could be identified as a singular project, this could only be done after the different relations between human and nonhuman forces had been stabilized to produce the dam (Latour 1996).

15. See Barad (1996), Bennett (2011), Haraway (1991), Latour (2005), and Schrader (2010).

16. Katie Meehan has drawn on the work of scholars in object-oriented ontology to suggest that infrastructures are forceful, "capable of creating, policing, and destroying the very contours of existence" (Meehan 2014, 216).

17. James Laidlaw (2010) points out that rather than existing as a fundamental essence that inheres and emerges in situations, agency is an "aspect of situations," an effect that emerges out of how we arrange and narrate stories of responsibility in everyday life.

18. For instance, in his recent work, Appadurai has critiqued actor–network theory and Bruno Latour for overlooking the way in which it dilutes questions of human responsibility. While Appadurai is open to considering a world structured by multiple non/human agencies, he asks how responsibility may be adjudicated in words where agency is "democratically distributed to all sorts of *dividuals*" (Appadurai 2015, 234).

19. John Law (1987) has argued that the stability of engineered forms emerges out of a relation between their heterogeneous elements. By focusing on the emerging power of Portuguese ships in the fifteenth century, Law describes how the "heterogeneous engineers" of Europe drew together not only elements of ship design and technological innovations of the magnetic compass. Their success was also contingent on their ability to successfully accommodate specific temporality and directionality of the trade winds (see also Latour 1996).

20. I borrow the idea of encompassment from Ferguson and Gupta (2002), who urge against seeing certain scales of rule (like the global) as "encompassing" others.

21. Engineers recounted to me how older city employees could find leakages using just a sounding rod and a cone. They would place the cone on the rod near a spot that had leakage and listen for the sounds of leakage. Engineers spoke of how the art was being lost among the newer employees.

22. See Gupta (2012), Herzfeld (1992), and Holston and Appadurai (1996).

23. "Water gutter passage. That is the work of councilors," a councilor's PA told me one day. By speaking of the different urban development projects that state and federal elected representatives handled, he suggested a layered state and its differently constituted publics.

24. Indeed, even when I was at the BMC's offices, I noticed several applications came with endorsements from representatives of political parties.

25. Nevertheless, there are problems with these normative approaches. By no means are these practices particular to India, or even to the developing world as the category of corruption suggests. Indeed, such relational practices are ubiquitous in different parts of the world. For instance, they are very familiar (and even legal) in work for corporations, lobbyists, and the interests of elected representatives in Washington, DC. This category of corruption frequently focuses on the exchange of (illicit) money that accompanies these acts.

26. Lobbyists and councilors are similar in that they offer not money but special relations to powerful officials—ways of distinguishing their client's claim from those multiple claims of the faceless, anonymous public.

27. As Gupta (2012) points out, higher-level bureaucrats have a margin business, extracting large rents from few well-to-do clients. Maqbool's work is a volume business, accepting and working with small rents he charges to many small clients.

CHAPTER 6. Disconnection

1. Ferguson engages Julia Kristeva's idea of abjection to theorize the ways in which people throughout the African continent are being disconnected by regimes of international trade and finance from any claims to global membership. See Ferguson (1999) and Kristeva (1982).

2. See, for instance, Baviskar (2003a), Bush (2009), McGregor (2008), and Reddy (2015).

3. By attending to the social differentiations emergent from infrastructure management, this work is in conversation with Gandy (2004), Kooy and Bakker (2008), McFarlane and Rutherford (2008), Star (1999).

4. This is a phenomenon in not just Jogeshwari but other Indian cities as well. See Desai and Sanyal (2012), Gupta and Sharma (2006), and Hansen (2001).

5. Chakrabarty (2007) describes how, for subaltern groups, "shouting" at administrators in postcolonial India is an established form of redress.

6. See Bjorkman (2015) and Coelho (2006) for similar accounts of engineers demanding accountability in Mumbai and Chennai, respectively.

7. Mike Davis makes this point about Los Angeles in his book *City of Quartz* (1990). See also Coelho (2006).

8. As scholars and engineers point out, settlements are congested in Mumbai because they are the primary supply of housing for the city's serving classes. In the absence of any affordable housing, people have little choice but to buy or rent one-room homes in settlements. As Patel, the retired city engineer, pointed out to me, the "root cause" of settlements in Mumbai was the failure of the city development plan to zone, provision, and provide affordable housing for the lower-middle classes and the poor. Muslim settlements

are even more "congested" because of the difficulty Muslims have had in acquiring a home in most other parts of the city (Appadurai 2000). The problem became even more intransigent following the demolition of the Babri Masjid and the ensuing violence in neighborhoods like Jogeshwari in 1992 and 1993 (Hansen 2001). Cutting across class, neighbors, developers, and landlords are unwilling to rent, lease, or sell homes to Muslim families, even those with the money to buy a home. As Muslims try to establish homes any place that they can, settlements such as Premnagar have grown dramatically in size (and not in area) over the past two decades. The congestion that has ensued becomes the ground for their further marginalization when engineers avoid working in "congested areas."

9. In 2006, as Bal Thackeray grew older and the Shiv Sena more invisible, his charismatic nephew split with the Sena and formed his own party, the Maharashtra Navnirman Sena (MNS). Eerily, the nephew's first notable political act was to revive a political campaign against Bihari and Uttar Pradeshi migrant workers in the city. With his message circulating on the twenty-four-hour news cycle, I read frequent reports of how the younger Thackeray's party workers beat up taxi drivers, prospective railway employees, and vendors from North India in several parts of the city between February and October 2008. Supporting his party workers' actions, Thackeray ridiculed and warned against those who come to the city to work, insisting, loudly and in Marathi, that the city's work be preferentially allotted to the "natives" of Maharashtra state, and to those who speak its language. Spewing inflammatory rhetoric against outsiders, he challenged the state to act against him for speaking up for the Marathi people. As journalists granted him interviews and the state government wrung its hands, Thackeray's political power grew with every act of violence.

10. Troublingly, the road between the Marathi settlements and Premnagar was often called "the border," separating the Muslims from the Hindus.

11. In the course of doing fieldwork in Mumbai, I worked hard to understand how Hindu engineers, bureaucrats, and indeed many others I lived with harbored mistrust of Muslims as a religious group, while sustaining and even cherishing relations with Muslims they knew. These disjunctures point to both the possibilities and limits of a "politics of friendship" (Devji 2005) that lives with a politics structured by ethnic, religious, or economic difference.

12. Here I recall Mary John and Satish Deshpande (2008) and Baviskar and Sundar's (2008) observations in which they point out that the efficacy of political society may not extend to groups that cannot mobilize sufficient demographic pressure at the ballot box.

13. City engineers knew that Premnagar's population was several times greater than what was officially reported by the census in 2001. Yet they expressed an inability to design the network for its actual population and used the smaller, registered population in their calculations.

14. On urban infrastructure, see Gandy (2004, 2008), Graham (2010), McFarlane (2008), and Simone (2004b, 2006). On citizenship and the state, see Gupta (1995), Mitchell (1991), Ferguson (1999), and Holston (2008).

15. In contrast, the Municipal Corporation is requiring that new developments, at least on paper, make arrangements for rainwater harvesting infrastructures in their conceptualization, design, and construction.

16. See, for instance, Forsyth (2003), Sivaramakrishnan (2002), and Vayda and Walters (1999).

1. See Spike Lee's film *When the Levees Broke* (2006), Goldberg and Hristova (2008), and Gregory (1998) for an account of histories of state marginalization through infrastructures in the United States.

2. Flint native and filmmaker Michael Moore has been stridently urging accountability for the residents of Flint, demanding that the governor of Michigan be arrested for his willful neglect and oversight (see Michael Moore, "How Can You Help Flint?," accessed February 1, 2016, http://michaelmoore.com/DontSendBottledWater/).

3. See Fennell (2015) and Gregory (1998).

4. Here, I do not mean to suggest that structural violence emerges from inaction. As Gregory (1998) and Gupta (2012) demonstrate, it emerges through specific actions and cultivated dispositions, where some populations are let be, and let die. Yet I wish to suggest that the violence embedded in the decision to continue to supply Flint's residents with toxic water, while insisting on its safety, is different because it is an act that proposes to protect and make people live even as it is poisoning them slowly.

5. See also Lea and Pholeros (2010), L. Mehta (2005), and Swyngedouw (2004, 2015). Of course, the values and regimes that residents attach to piped water are not ahistorical phenomena. The expectations of and aspirations for piped water were brought into being not before but as Mumbai's hydraulic infrastructure was built and reformed over the last 150 years by the city government.

6. In early 2016, the mayor of the city of Detroit approved a plan to shut off thousands of household connections for the nonpayment of water bills.

7. See Boyer (2014), Chakrabarty (2009), Haraway (2014), and Tsing (2015).

8. Tsing (2015) has urged that we attend to the patchy landscapes of the Anthropocene.

9. In fact, constituting most of a human's body weight, water is the very matter of human life.

10. I draw on this idea of friction from the work of Tsing (2005).

11. Life not only has meaning, Didier Fassin reminds us, but is also matter. The materialism Fassin gestures to "is not simply, in the Marxian sense, that of the structural conditions which effectively largely determine the conditions of life of the members of a given society; it is also, in Canguilhem's sense, that of the very substance of existence, its materiality, its longevity and the inequalities that society imposes on it. To accept this materialistic orientation," Fassin suggests, "is not a merely theoretical issue. It is also an ethical one. It recognizes that the matter of life does matter" (Fassin 2011, 193).

12. See also Braun (2014) for an account on how technologies and infrastructures are especially vital mediants for urban life.

13. Scholars have often identified the lack of intentionality and purpose to argue that things cannot be political. Nevertheless, if humans can be political without intention (e.g., in their personal life or in their pursuit of their private interests), then it is apparent that intentionality or purpose cannot be the marker of what does/does not constitute the political field.

14. As Andrew Barry (2011) has pointed out in his remarkable work about metals and metallurgy, politics as such always emerges as plural—through diverse relations and

between different arrangements of humans and nonhumans. Of course, this is not to suggest that either persons or things that are being drawn into relations are singular. Human bodies, water, and many others are plural assemblages of several different kinds of living and nonliving forms (Mol 2002).

15. Politics, as feminist scholars have shown, does not require intentionality or consciousness to be political (Barad 1996; Bennett 2010; Haraway 1991). Following this work, I draw attention to the ways in which politics emerges through relations between human and nonhuman worlds regardless of our ability to adjudicate the consciousness, soul, or intentionality of nonhuman others.

16. As working infrastructures produce expectations and breakdowns in everyday life, state (or state-like) authorities are called to account for these moments of rupture. Authorities and subjects alike have learned the rituals and routines to replace and repair infrastructures. New pipes provide a precious opportunity to visibly demonstrate good works to political constituents, even as the contracts and approvals these require allow councilors to personally benefit. As such, they demonstrate how infrastructures are a fundamental site for political claims and an important locus to examine the workings of the political. See von Schnitzler (2013) for an account of this process in South Africa.

17. See Graham and McFarlane (2015) and Graham and Thrift (2007).

18. See Appadurai (2002) for a description of how toilet festivals were productive of new relations and subjectivities between the government and the governed.

19. See, for instance, Bakker (2003) for protests against privatization in England and Wales, Cheng (2015) for an account of reforms in Manila, Kooy and Bakker (2008) for work on Jakarta, and von Schnitzler (2008) for Johannesburg,

20. Brian Larkin has urged we more carefully consider the political aesthetics of infrastructural forms together with the "tactile way[s] of living" these enable. He urges us to consider the ways in which infrastructures express histories as they "act on people to produce new experiences of the world" (Larkin 2015).

21. Settlers desire water connections not only because these deliver water. The connections also provide documents with which the settlers can (eventually) claim and improve their homes in the city (Das 2011). In Mumbai, as in many other places, the water bills that accompanied legal connections were also vital documents they needed to make their precarious homes in the city more durable.

22. In his work on electricity, Luke (2010) has pointed out that the ability of infrastructures to withstand peak demand or natural disaster is related to the degree of redundancy (of both water and workers) that forms the infrastructure. The greater the degree of redundancy (or overcapacity), the more the infrastructure can cope with an unexpected event.

23. See, for instance, Barlow and Clarke (2001) and Shiva (2002).

24. Bakker (2010) and Sangameswaran, Madhav, and D'Rozario (2008).

25. Consultants for the WDIP as well as reformers in other national and international fora insist that full-cost pricing for water through water meters would make water utilities more financially viable and able to invest in infrastructure maintenance and expansion works. Yet, in Mumbai, universal metering would in fact make the already very well endowed water department *less* financially viable. A significant share of its revenue comes from water and sewerage taxes on older buildings. Changing these revenue paradigms to volumetric models would reduce the revenues of the water department.

26. In fact, department circulars I came across while doing fieldwork entreated engineers to use the surplus funds of the water department. Nevertheless, these funds were seldom fully utilized either to maintain the city's water pipes or to extend them to more marginal settlers.

27. A study of Mumbai's energy infrastructures, for instance would produce a different account of how the city and citizenship are made. The everyday maintenance of electric grids instantiates different assemblies of the imagination, materials, laws, and practices than those of water infrastructures (see Coleman 2008). As such, electric infrastructures congeal a range of diverse values, moralities, and oppositions.

References

Abrams, Philip. 1988. "Notes on the Difficulty of Studying the State." *Journal of Historical Sociology* 1 (1): 58–89.

Abu-Lughod, Janet. 1991. *Before European Hegemony: The World System A.D. 1250–1350.* New York: Oxford University Press.

Agarwal, Anil, and Sunita Narain, eds. 1997. *Dying Wisdom: Rise, Fall and Potential of India's Traditional Water Harvesting Systems.* New Delhi: Centre for Science and Environment.

Alatout, Samer. 2008. " 'States' of Scarcity: Water, Space, and Identity Politics in Israel, 1948–59." *Environment and Planning D: Society and Space* 26 (6): 959–82.

Althusser, Louis. 1970. "Part II: The Object of Capital." In *Reading Capital,* by Louis Althusser and Etienne Balibar. New York: New Left Books.

———. 1971. "Ideology and Ideological State Apparatuses (Notes towards an Investigation)." In *Lenin and Philosophy, and Other Essays,* 127–86. New York: Monthly Review Press.

Anand, Nikhil. 2006. "Disconnecting Experience: Making World Class Roads in Mumbai." *Economic and Political Weekly* 41 (31): 3422–29.

———. 2011. "Pressure: The Polytechnics of Water Supply in Mumbai." *Cultural Anthropology* 26 (4): 542–63.

———. 2015. "Leaky States: Water Audits, Ignorance, and the Politics of Infrastructure." *Public Culture* 27 (2 76): 305–30.

Anand, Nikhil, and Anne Rademacher. 2011. "Housing in the Urban Age: Inequality and Aspiration in Mumbai." *Antipode* 43 (5): 1748–72.

Anjaria, Jonathan Shapiro. 2006. "Urban Calamities: A View from Mumbai." *Space and Culture* 9 (1): 80–82.

———. 2011. "Ordinary States: Everyday Corruption and the Politics of Space in Mumbai." *American Ethnologist* 38:58–72.

———. 2016. *The Slow Boil: Street Food, Rights, and Public Space in Mumbai.* Stanford, CA: Stanford University Press.

Appadurai, Arjun. 1996. *Modernity at Large: Cultural Dimensions of Globalization.* Minneapolis: University of Minnesota Press.

———. 2000. "Spectral Housing and Urban Cleansing: Notes on a Millennial Mumbai." *Public Culture* 12 (3): 627–51.

———. 2002. "Deep Democracy: Urban Governmentality and the Horizon of Politics." *Public Culture* 14 (1): 21–47.

———. 2006. "The Right to Research." *Globalisation, Societies and Education* 4 (2): 167–77.

———. 2015. "Mediants, Materiality, Normativity." *Public Culture* 27 (2 76): 221–37.

Appel, Hannah. 2012a. "Offshore Work: Oil, Modularity, and the How of Capitalism in Equatorial Guinea." *American Ethnologist* 39 (4): 692–709.

———. 2012b. "Walls and White Elephants: Oil Extraction, Responsibility, and Infrastructural Violence in Equatorial Guinea." *Ethnography* 13 (4): 439–65.

Aretxaga, Begoña. 2003. "Maddening States." *Annual Review of Anthropology* 32:393–410.

Ashar, Sandeep, and Sharad Vyas. 2007. "Demand Will Water Down Supply." *Daily News and Analysis*, March 6.

Auyero, Javier. 2000. *Poor People's Politics: Peronist Survival Networks and the Legacy of Evita*. Durham, NC: Duke University Press.

Awachat, Anil. 1975. "Violence of the Chawls." *Economic and Political Weekly* 10:469–70.

Bailey, F. G. 1963. *Politics and Social Change: Orissa in 1959*. Berkeley: University of California Press.

Bakker, Karen. 2000. "Privatizing Water, Producing Scarcity: The Yorkshire Drought of 1995." *Economic Geography* 76 (1): 4–27.

———. 2003. *An Uncooperative Commodity: Privatizing Water in England and Wales*. Oxford Geographical and Environmental Studies. New York: Oxford University Press.

———. 2007. "The 'Commons' versus the 'Commodity': Alter-globalization, Anti-privatization and the Human Right to Water in the Global South." *Antipode* 39 (3): 430–55.

———. 2010. *Privatizing Water: Governance Failure and the World's Water Crisis*. Ithaca, NY: Cornell University Press.

Balibar, Étienne. 1988. "Propositions on Citizenship." *Ethics* 98 (4): 723–30.

Ballestero, Andrea. 2015. "The Ethics of a Formula: Calculating a Financial–Humanitarian Price for Water." *American Ethnologist* 42 (2): 262–78.

Banerjee, Mukulika. 2008. "Democracy, Sacred and the Everyday." In *Democracy: Anthropological Approaches*, edited by J. Paley, 63–95. Santa Fe, NM: School for Advanced Research Press.

Banerjee-Guha, Swapna. 2009. "Neoliberalising the 'Urban': New Geographies of Power and Injustice in Indian Cities." *Economic and Political Weekly* 44 (22): 95–107.

Bapat, Meera, and Indu Agarwal. 2003. "Our Needs, Our Priorities: Women and Men from the Slums in Mumbai and Pune Talk about Their Needs for Water and Sanitation." *Environment and Urbanization* 15 (2): 71–86.

Barad, Karen. 1996. "Meeting the University Halfway: Realism and Social Constructivism without Contradiction." *Feminism, Science and the Philosophy of Science*, edited by Lynn Nelson and Jack Nelson, 161–94. Boston: Kluwer Academic Publishers.

———. 2003. "Posthumanist Performativity: How Matter Comes to Matter." *Signs: Journal of Women in Culture and Society* 28 (3).

Barak, On. 2009. "Scraping the Surface: The Techno-Politics of Modern Streets in Turn-of-Twentieth-Century Alexandria." *Mediterranean Historical Review* 24 (2): 187–205.

———. 2013. *On Time: Technology and Temporality in Modern Egypt*. Berkeley: University of California Press.

Bardhan, Ronita, Sayantani Sarkar, Arnab Jana, and Nagendra R. Velaga. 2015. "Mumbai Slums since Independence: Evaluating the Policy Outcomes." *Habitat International* 50 (December): 1–11.

Barlow, Maude, and Tony Clarke. 2001. *Blue Gold: The Global Water Crisis and the Commodification of the World's Water Supply.* Ottawa: Octopus Books.

Barnes, Jessica. 2014. *Cultivating the Nile: The Everyday Politics of Water in Egypt.* New Ecologies for the Twenty-First Century. Durham, NC: Duke University Press.

Barry, Andrew. 2001. *Political Machines.* London: Athlone Press.

———. 2011. "Materialist Politics: Metallurgy." In *Political Matter: Technoscience, Democracy, and Public Life*, edited by Bruce Braun and Sarah Whatmore, 89–118. Minneapolis: University of Minnesota Press.

———. 2013. *Material Politics: Disputes along the Pipeline.* Chichester, UK: Wiley-Blackwell.

Baviskar, Amita. 1995. *In the Belly of the River: Tribal Conflicts over Development in the Narmada Valley.* New Delhi: Oxford University Press.

———. 2003a. "Between Violence and Desire: Space, Power, and Identity in the Making of Metropolitan Delhi." *International Social Science Journal* 55 (175): 89–98.

———. 2003b. "For a Cultural Politics of Natural Resources." *Economic and Political Weekly* 38 (48): 5051–55.

———, ed. 2007. *Waterscapes: The Cultural Politics of a Natural Resource.* Ranikhet, India: Permanent Black.

———. 2011. "Cows, Cars and Rickshaws: Bourgeois Environmentalists and the Battle for Delhi's Streets." In *Elite and Everyman: The Cultural Politics of the Indian Middle Classes*, edited by A. Baviskar and R. Ray, 391–418. Delhi: Routledge.

Baviskar, Amita, and Nandini Sundar. 2008. "Democracy versus Economic Transformation?" *Economic and Political Weekly* 43 (46): 87–89.

Bayat, Asef. 1997. "Un-Civil Society: The Politics of the Informal People." *Third World Quarterly* 18 (1): 53–72.

———. 2010. *Life as Politics: How Ordinary People Change the Middle East.* Stanford, CA: Stanford University Press.

Bayly, Chris. 1996. *Empire and Information: Political Intelligence and Social Communication in North India, 1780–1870.* Cambridge Studies in Indian History and Society 1. Cambridge: Cambridge University Press.

Bear, Laura. 2015. *Navigating Austerity: Currents of Debt along a South Asian River.* Anthropology of Policy. Stanford, CA: Stanford University Press.

Bedi, Tarini. 2007. "The Dashing Ladies of the Shiv Sena." *Economic and Political Weekly* 42 (17): 1534–41.

———. 2016. *The Dashing Ladies of the Shiv Sena: Political Matronage in India.* Albany: State University of New York Press.

Behrent, Michael C. 2013. "Foucault and Technology." *History and Technology* 29 (1): 54–104. doi:10.1080/07341512.2013.780351.

Belson, Ken. 2008. "Plumber's Job on a Giant's Scale: Fixing New York's Drinking Straw." *New York Times*, November 23.

Benjamin, Solomon. 2005. "Touts, Pirates and Ghosts." In *Bare Acts*, edited by Monica Narula et al., 242–54. Sarai Reader 5. Delhi: Sarai Programme, CSDS.

———. 2008. "Occupancy Urbanism: Radicalizing Politics and Economy beyond Policy and Programs." *International Journal of Urban and Regional Research* 32 (3): 719–29.

Benjamin, Walter. 1969. *Illuminations*. . New York: Schocken Books.

Bennett, Jane. 2005. "The Agency of Assemblages and the North American Blackout." *Public Culture* 17 (3): 445–66.

———. 2010. *Vibrant Matter: A Political Ecology of Things*. Durham, NC: Duke University Press.

Bergson, Henri. 1921. *Time and Free Will: An Essay on the Immediate Data of Consciousness*. Library of Philosophy. New York: Macmillan.

Bhabha, Homi. 2012. *The Location of Culture*. Hoboken, NJ: Taylor and Francis.

Biehl, João, and Peter Locke. 2010. "Deleuze and the Anthropology of Becoming." *Current Anthropology* 51 (3): 317–51.

Birkenholtz, Trevor. 2009. "Irrigated Landscapes, Produced Scarcity, and Adaptive Social Institutions in Rajasthan, India." *Annals of the Association of American Geographers* 99 (1): 118–37.

Bjorkman, Lisa. 2014. "Becoming a Slum: From Municipal Colony to Illegal Settlement in Liberalization-Era Mumbai." *International Journal of Urban and Regional Research* 38 (1): 36–59.

———. 2015. *Pipe Politics, Contested Waters: Embedded Infrastructures of Millennial Mumbai*. Durham, NC: Duke University Press.

Blaikie, Piers, and Harold Brookfield. 1987. *Degradation and Society*. London: Methuen.

Boas, Franz. 1974. *The Shaping of American Anthropology, 1883–1911: A Franz Boas Reader*. Edited by George W. Stocking Jr. New York: Basic Books.

Boissevain, Jeremy. 1974. *Friends of Friends: Networks, Manipulators and Coalitions*. Oxford: Blackwell.

Boo, Katherine. 2012. *Behind the Beautiful Forevers*. New York: Random House.

Bornstein, David. 2014. "The Art of Water Recovery." *New York Times*, July 10.

Bourdieu, Pierre. 1977. *Outline of a Theory of Practice*. Cambridge: Cambridge University Press.

Bowker, Geoffrey C. 1994. *Science on the Run: Information Management and Industrial Geophysics at Schlumberger, 1920–1940*. Cambridge, MA: MIT Press.

Boyer, Dominic. 2014. "Energopower: An Introduction." *Anthropological Quarterly* 87 (2): 309–33.

———. 2015. "Anthropology Electric." *Cultural Anthropology* 30 (4): 531–53.

———. 2017. "Revolutionary Infrastructure." In *Infrastructures and Social Complexity: A Companion*, edited by Penelope Harvey, Casper Bruun Jensen, and Atsuro Morita, 174–86. New York: Routledge.

Braun, Bruce. 2005. "Environmental Issues: Writing a More-Than-Human Urban Geography." *Progress in Human Geography* 29 (5): 635–50.

———. 2014. "A New Urban Dispositif? Governing Life in an Age of Climate Change." *Environment and Planning D: Society and Space* 32 (1): 49–64.

Braun, Bruce, and Stephanie Wakefield. 2014. "Inhabiting the Post-Apocalyptic City." *Society and Space* 32 (1). Commentary for the special issue "A New Apparatus: Technology, Government and the Resilient City."

Braun, Bruce, and Sarah Whatmore. 2011. "The Stuff of Politics: An Introduction." In *Political Matter: Technoscience, Democracy, and Public Life*, edited by Bruce Braun and Sarah Whatmore, ix–xl. Minneapolis: University of Minnesota Press.

Brenner, Neil. 2013. "Theses on Urbanization." *Public Culture* 25 (1 69): 85–114.

Brihanmumbai Municipal Corporation, H. E. Department, and Chief Engineer (Sewerage Operations). 2001. *Water Charges Rules (Effective from 01.02.2001)*. Mumbai.

———. 2006. *Water By-Laws*. Hydraulic Engineer's Department. Mumbai.

Bröckling, Ulrich, Susanne Krasmann, and Thomas Lemke. 2011. *Governmentality: Current Issues and Future Challenges*. New York: Routledge.

Bryson, Valerie. 2007. *Gender and the Politics of Time: Feminist Theory and Contemporary Debates*. Bristol: Policy.

Burchell, Graham. 1996. "Liberal Government and the Techniques of the Self." In *Foucault and Political Reason: Liberalism, Neo-liberalism and Rationalities of Government*, edited by Andrew Barry, Thomas Osborne, and Nikolas Rose, 19–36. London: UCL Press.

Burra, Sundar. 2005. "Towards a Pro-Poor Framework for Slum Upgrading in Mumbai, India." *Environment and Urbanization* 17 (1): 67–88.

Bush, Ray. 2009. " 'Soon There Will Be No-One Left to Take the Corpses to the Morgue': Accumulation and Abjection in Ghana's Mining Communities." *Resources Policy* 34 (1–2): 57–63.

Caldeira, Ken, Govindasamy Bala, and Long Cao. 2013. "The Science of Geoengineering." *Annual Review of Earth and Planetary Sciences* 41: 231–56.

Caldeira, Teresa Pires do Rio. 2000. *City of Walls: Crime, Segregation, and Citizenship in São Paulo*. Berkeley: University of California Press.

Callon, Michel. 1989. "Society in the Making: The Study of Technology as a Tool for Sociological Analysis." In *The Social Construction of Technical Systems: New Directions in the Sociology and History of Technology*, edited by Wiebe E. Bijker, Thomas P. Hughes, and Trevor J. Pinch, 83–106. Cambridge, MA: MIT Press.

Calvino, Italo. 1972. *Invisible Cities*. San Diego: Harcourt Brace.

Campbell, Jeremy M. 2012. "Between the Material and the Figural Road: The Incompleteness of Colonial Geographies in Amazonia." *Mobilities* 7 (4): 481–500.

Carroll, Patrick. 2012. "Water and Technoscientific State Formation in California." *Social Studies of Science* 42 (4): 489–516.

Carse, Ashley. 2012. "Nature as Infrastructure: Making and Managing the Panama Canal Watershed." *Social Studies of Science* 42 (4): 539–63.

———. 2014. *Beyond the Big Ditch: Politics, Ecology, and Infrastructure at the Panama Canal*. Infrastructures series. Cambridge, MA: MIT Press.

Castalia Strategic Advisors. 2007. "K-East Water Distribution Improvement Project." Customer Service and Technical Report. Wellington, India.

Central Public Health and Environmental Engineering Organisation. 1999. *Manual on Water Supply and Treatment*. 3rd ed. Ministry of Urban Development. New Delhi.

Chakrabarty, Dipesh. 2000. *Provincializing Europe: Postcolonial Thought and Historical Difference*. Princeton, NJ: Princeton University Press.

———. 2007. " 'In the Name of Politics': Sovereignty, Democracy, and the Multitude in India." *Public Culture* 19 (1): 35–57.

———. 2009. "The Climate of History: Four Theses." *Critical Inquiry* 35 (2):197–222.

Chalfin, Brenda. 2014. "Public Things, Excremental Politics, and the Infrastructure of Bare Life in Ghana's City of Tema." *American Ethnologist* 41 (1): 92–109.

———. 2016. " 'Wastelandia': Infrastructure and the Commonwealth of Waste in Urban Ghana." *Ethnos: Journal of Anthropology*. Accessed July 25, 2016. http://www.tandfonline.com/doi/abs/10180/00141844.2015.1119174.

Chandavarkar, Rajnarayan. 2007. "Customs of Governance: Colonialism and Democracy in Twentieth Century India." *Modern Asian Studies* 41 (3): 441–70.

Chatterjee, Partha. 2004. *The Politics of the Governed: Reflections on Popular Politics in Most of the World*. New York: Columbia University Press.

———. 2005. "Sovereign Violence and the Domain of the Political." In *Sovereign Bodies: Citizens, Migrants, and States in the Postcolonial World*, edited by Thomas Blom Hansen and Finn Stepputat, 82–100. Princeton, NJ: Princeton University Press.

———. 2008. "Democracy and Economic Transformation in India." *Economic and Political Weekly* 43 (16): 53–63.

Chatterji, Roma, and Deepak Mehta. 2007. *Living with Violence: An Anthropology of Events and Everyday Life*. New York: Routledge.

Cheng, Deborah. 2015. "Contestations at the Last Mile: The Corporate–Community Delivery of Water in Manila." *Geoforum* 59:240–47.

Chitale, Madhav. 1997. "Conflict for Water." *Water Supply* 15 (1): 1–8.

Chu, Julie Y. 2014. "When Infrastructures Attack: The Workings of Disrepair in China." *American Ethnologist* 41 (2): 351–67.

Clarke, Kamari M. 2013. "Notes on Cultural Citizenship in the Black Atlantic World." *Cultural Anthropology* 28 (3): 464–74.

Cody, Francis. 2009. "Inscribing Subjects to Citizenship: Petitions, Literacy Activism, and the Performativity of Signature in Rural Tamil India." *Cultural Anthropology* 24 (3): 347–80.

Coelho, Karen. 2006. "Tapping In: Leaky Sovereignties and Engineered Dis(Order) in an Urban Water System." In *Turbulence*, edited by Monica Narula et al., 497–509. Sarai Reader 6. Delhi: Sarai Programme, CSDS.

Coleman, Leo. 2008. "Delhi in the Electrical Age: Technologies of Rule and the Rites of Power in India's Capital, 1903–2006." PhD diss., Princeton University.

———. 2014. "Infrastructure and Interpretation: Meters, Dams, and State Imagination in Scotland and India." *American Ethnologist* 41 (3): 457–72.

Collier, Stephen J. 2011. *Post-Soviet Social: Neoliberalism, Social Modernity, Biopolitics*. Princeton NJ: Princeton University Press.

Comaroff, Jean, and John L. Comaroff. 2011. *Theory from the South, or How Euro-America Is Evolving toward Africa*. Boulder, CO: Paradigm Publishers.

Corbridge, Stuart, et al. 2005. *Seeing the State: Governance and Governmentality in India*. New York: Cambridge University Press.

Coutard, Olivier. 1999. *The Governance of Large Technical Systems*. New York: Routledge.

Cronon, William. 1991. *Nature's Metropolis: Chicago and the Great West*. New York: W. W. Norton.

Das, P. K. 2003. "Slums: The Continuing Struggle for Housing." In *Bombay and Mumbai: The City in Transition*, edited by Sujata Patel and Jim Masselos, 207–34. New Delhi: Oxford University Press.

Das, Veena. 2011. "State, Citizenship, and the Urban Poor." *Citizenship Studies* 15 (3–4): 319–33. doi:10.1080/13621025.2011.564781.

Davis, Jennifer. 2003. "Corruption in Public Service Delivery: Experience from South Asia's Water and Sanitation Sector." *World Development* 32 (1): 53–71.

Davis, Mike. 1990. *City of Quartz: Excavating the Future in Los Angeles*. Haymarket Series. London: Verso.

———. 2006. *Planet of Slums*. London: Verso.

Davison, Janet. 2011. "City Water Leaks Wasting Millions of Tax Dollars." Canadian Broadcasting Corporation News, November 23. Accessed June 30, 2016. http://www.cbc.ca/news/canada/city-water-leaks-wasting-millions-of-tax-dollars-1.1048035.

Dawson, Ashley, and Brent Hayes Edwards. 2004. "Global Cities of the South." *Social Text* 22 (4): 1–7.

De Boeck, Filip. 2015. "'Divining' the City: Rhythm, Amalgamation and Knotting as Forms of 'Urbanity.'" *Social Dynamics: A Journal of African Studies* 41 (1): 47–58.

Degani, Michael. 2013. "Emergency Power: Time, Ethics, and Electricity in Postsocialist Tanzania." In *Cultures of Energy: Power, Practices, Technologies*, edited by Sarah Strauss, Stephanie Rupp, and Thomas Love, 177–92. Walnut Creek, CA: Left Coast Press.

Derrida, Jacques. 2005. *Politics of Friendship*. Translated by George Collins. New York: Verso.

Desai, Renu. 2003. "Producing Urban Informality in Mumbai: Policy, Politics, and Practice in Jari Mari and Shantiniketan." Master's thesis, University of California at Berkeley.

Desai, Renu, and Romola Sanyal. 2012. *Urbanizing Citizenship: Contested Spaces in Indian Cities*. Delhi: Sage.

Devji, Faisal. 2005. "A Practice of Prejudice: Gandhi's Politics of Friendship." In *Muslims, Dalits, and the Fabrication of History*, edited by Shail Mayaram, M. S. S. Pandian, and Ajay Skaria, 78–98. Delhi: Permanent Black.

Doshi, Sapana. 2004. "The Rise of an Imperial Urban Water Complex: 'Sanitary' Bombay 1850–1890." Master's thesis, University of California at Berkeley.

———. 2012. "The Politics of the Evicted: Redevelopment, Subjectivity, and Difference in Mumbai's Slum Frontier." *Antipode* 45 (4): 844–65.

Dossal, Mariam. 1991. *Imperial Designs and Indian Realities: The Planning of Bombay City, 1845–1875*. New York: Oxford University Press.

———. 2010. *Theatre of Conflict, City of Hope: Mumbai, 1660 to Present Times*. New Delhi: Oxford University Press.

D'Souza, Rohan. 2006. "Water in British India: The Making of a 'Colonial Hydrology.'" *History Compass* 4 (4): 621–28.

D'Souza, Rohan, Pranab Mukhopadhyay, and Ashish Kothari. 1998. "Re-evaluating Multi-purpose River Valley Projects: A Case Study of Hirakud, Ukai and IGNP." *Economic and Political Weekly* 33 (6): 297–302.

Dwivedi, Sharada, and Rahul Mehrotra. 1995. *Bombay: The Cities Within*. Bombay: India Book House.

Echanove, Matias, and Rahul Srivastava. 2009. "Taking the Slum Out of 'Slumdog.'" *New York Times*, February 21.

Ehrlich, Paul. 1968. *The Population Bomb*. New York: Ballantine Books.

Elyachar, Julia. 2010. "Phatic Labor, Infrastructure, and the Question of Empowerment in Cairo." *American Ethnologist* 37 (3): 452–64.

Englund, Harri. 2006. *Prisoners of Freedom: Human Rights and the African Poor*. Berkeley: University of California Press.

Escobar, Arturo. 1995. *Encountering Development: The Making and Unmaking of the Third World*. Princeton Studies in Culture/Power/History. Princeton, NJ: Princeton University Press.

Fabian, Johannes. 1983. *Time and the Other: How Anthropology Makes Its Object*. New York: Columbia University Press.

Farooqui, Amar. 2006. *Opium City: The Making of Early Victorian Bombay*. Gurgaon, India: Three Essays Collective.

Fassin, Didier. 2011. "Coming Back to Life: An Anthropological Reassessment of Biopolitics and Governmentality." In *Governmentality: Current Issues and Future Challenges*, edited by Ulrich Bröckling, Susanne Krasmann, and Thomas Lemke, 185–200. New York: Routledge.

Fennell, Catherine. 2015. *Last Project Standing: Civics and Sympathy in Post-Welfare Chicago*. Minneapolis: University of Minnesota Press.

Ferguson, James. 1994. *The Anti-Politics Machine: "Development," Depoliticization, and Bureaucratic Power in Lesotho*. Minneapolis: University of Minnesota Press.

———. 1999. *Expectations of Modernity: Myths and Meanings of Urban Life on the Zambian Copperbelt*. Berkeley: University of California Press.

———. 2015. *Give a Man a Fish: Reflections on the New Politics of Distribution*. Lewis Henry Morgan Lectures. Durham, NC: Duke University Press.

Ferguson, James, and Akhil Gupta. 2002. "Spatializing States: Toward an Ethnography of Neoliberal Governmentality." *American Ethnologist* 29 (4): 981–1002.

Finkelstein, Maura. 2015. "Landscapes of Invisibility: Anachronistic Subjects and Allochronous Spaces in Mill Land Mumbai." *City and Society* 27 (3): 250–71.

Fisch, Michael. 2013. "Tokyo's Commuter Train Suicides and the Society of Emergence." *Cultural Anthropology* 28 (2): 320–43.

Forsyth, Tim. 2003. *Critical Political Ecology: The Politics of Environmental Science*. New York: Routledge.

Foucault, Michel. 1984. "Space Knowledge and Power." In *The Foucault Reader*, edited by Paul Rabinow, 239–56. New York: Pantheon Books.

———. 1988. "Social Security." In *Politics, Philosophy, Culture: Interviews and Other Writings, 1977–1984*, edited by Lawrence D. Kritzman. New York: Routledge.

———. 1991. "Governmentality." In *The Foucault Effect: Studies in Governmentality*, edited by Graham Burchell, Colin Gordon, and Peter Miller, 87–104. Chicago: University of Chicago Press.

———. 1995. *Discipline and Punish: The Birth of the Prison*. New York: Vintage Books.

————. 2008. *The Birth of Biopolitics: Lectures at the Collège de France, 1978–79*. Edited by Michel Senellart. New York: Palgrave Macmillan.

Fuller, Chris. J., and John Harriss. 2001. "For an Anthropology of the Modern Indian State." In *The Everyday State and Society in Modern India*, edited by Chris J. Fuller and Véronique Bénéï, 1–30. London: Hurst and Co.

Furber, Holden. 1965. *Bombay Presidency in the Mid-eighteenth Century*. New York: Asia Publishing House.

Furlong, Kathryn. 2011. "Small Technologies, Big Change: Rethinking Infrastructure through STS and Geography." *Progress in Human Geography* 35 (4): 460–82.

————. 2014. "STS beyond the 'Modern Infrastructure Ideal': Extending Theory by Engaging with Infrastructure Challenges in the South." *Technology in Society* 38:139–47.

Gandy, Matthew. 2002. *Concrete and Clay: Reworking Nature in New York City*. Cambridge, MA: MIT Press.

————. 2004. "Rethinking Urban Metabolism: Water, Space and the Modern City." *City* 8 (3): 363–79.

————. 2005. "Cyborg Urbanization: Complexity and Monstrosity in the Contemporary City." *International Journal of Urban and Regional Research* 29 (1): 26–49.

————. 2008. "Landscapes of Disaster: Water, Modernity, and Urban Fragmentation in Mumbai." *Environment and Planning A* 40 (1): 108–30.

————. 2014. *The Fabric of Space: Water, Modernity, and the Urban Imagination*. Cambridge, MA: MIT Press.

Ganesh, N. 2010. "Water Woes: Why Mumbai Will Not Go Dry." Rediff.com, January 13.

Gaonkar, Dilip Parameshwar, and Elizabeth A. Povinelli. 2003. "Technologies of Public Forms: Circulation, Transfiguration, Recognition." *Public Culture* 15 (3): 385–97.

Geertz, Clifford. 1972. "The Wet and the Dry: Traditional Irrigation in Bali and Morocco." *Human Ecology* 1 (1): 23–37.

Ghannam, Farha. 2002. *Remaking the Modern: Space, Relocation, and the Politics of Identity in a Global Cairo*. Berkeley: University of California Press.

Ghertner, D. Asher. 2012. "Nuisance Talk and the Propriety of Property: Middle Class Discourses of a Slum-Free Delhi." *Antipode* 44 (4): 1161–87.

————. 2015. *Rule by Aesthetics: World-Class City Making in Delhi*. New York: Oxford University Press.

Gibson-Graham, J. K. 1996. *The End of Capitalism (As We Knew It): A Feminist Critique of Political Economy*. Cambridge, MA: Blackwell.

Gidwani, Vinay. 2008. *Capital, Interrupted: Agrarian Development and the Politics of Work in India*. Minneapolis: University of Minnesota Press.

Giglioli, Ilaria, and Erik Swyngedouw. 2008. "Let's Drink to the Great Thirst! Water and the Politics of Fractured Techno-natures in Sicily." *International Journal of Urban and Regional Research* 32 (2): 392–414.

Gilmartin, David, 1994. "Scientific Empire and Imperial Science: Colonialism and Irrigation Technology in the Indus Basin." *Journal of Asian Studies* 53 (4): 1127–49.

Goldberg, David, and Stefka Hristova. 2008. "Blue Velvet: Re-dressing New Orleans in Katrina's Wake." *Vectors: Journal of Culture and Technology in a Dynamic Vernacular*. Accessed July 25, 2016. http://www.vectorsjournal.org/projects/index.php?project=82.

Goldman, Michael. 2011. "Speculative Urbanism and the Making of the Next World City." *International Journal of Urban and Regional Research* 35 (3): 555–81.

Golway, Terry. 2014. *Machine Made: Tammany Hall and the Creation of Modern American Politics*. New York: Liveright.

Government of Maharashtra. 2006. *Fact Finding Committee on Mumbai Floods: Final Report*. Mumbai: Government of Maharashtra.

———. 2015. "Sanjay Gandhi National Park Borivali, Mumbai." Maharashtra Forest Department. Accessed January 6, 2016. http://www.mahaforest.nic.in/place_detail .php?lang_eng_mar=Mar&placeid=7.

Graham, Stephen. 2010. *Disrupted Cities: When Infrastructure Fails*. New York: Routledge.

Graham, Stephen, and Simon Marvin. 2001. *Splintering Urbanism: Networked Infrastructures, Technological Mobilities and the Urban Condition*. New York: Routledge.

Graham, Stephen, and Colin McFarlane. 2015. *Infrastructural Lives: Urban Infrastructure in Context*. New York: Routledge.

Graham, Stephen, and Nigel Thrift. 2007. "Out of Order: Understanding Repair and Maintenance." *Theory, Culture and Society* 24 (3): 1–25.

Greenhouse, Carol. 1996. *A Moment's Notice: Time Politics across Cultures*. Ithaca, NY: Cornell University Press.

Gregory, Steven. 1998. *Black Corona: Race and the Politics of Place in an Urban Community*. Princeton, NJ: Princeton University Press.

Gudilu, Durga. 2008. *Yaadé*. In *Ek Dozen Paani*, edited by Nikhil Anand, Shaina Anand, and Ashok Sukumaran. India: Aagaz, Akansha Sewa Sangh, CAMP, and Nikhil Anand. Digital video. http://www.youtube.com/ekdozenpaani.

Gudilu, Govindi. 2008. *4:30 p.m.* In *Ek Dozen Paani*, edited by Nikhil Anand, Shaina Anand, and Ashok Sukumaran. India: Aagaz, Akansha Sewa Sangh, CAMP, and Nikhil Anand. Digital video. http://www.youtube.com/ekdozenpaani.

Gupta, Akhil. 1995. "Blurred Boundaries: The Discourse of Corruption, the Culture of Politics, and the Imagined State." *American Ethnologist* 22 (2): 375–402.

———. 2012. *Red Tape: Bureaucracy, Structural Violence, and Poverty in India*. Durham, NC: Duke University Press.

———. 2015. "Suspension." Theorizing the Contemporary, *Cultural Anthropology* website, September 24, 2015. Accessed July 25, 2016. http://www.culanth.org/fieldsights /722-suspension.

Gupta, Akhil, and James Ferguson. 1992. "Beyond 'Culture': Space, Identity, and the Politics of Difference." *Cultural Anthropology* 7 (1): 6–23.

———. 1997. "Discipline and Practice: 'The Field' as Site, Method and Location in Anthropology." In *Anthropological Locations: Boundaries and Grounds of a Field Science*, edited by Akhil Gupta and James Ferguson, 1–46. Berkeley: University of California Press.

Gupta, Akhil, and Aradhana Sharma. 2006. "Globalization and Postcolonial States." *Current Anthropology* 47 (2): 277–307.

Hacking, Ian. 1990. *The Taming of Chance*. Ideas in Context. Cambridge: Cambridge University Press.

Hamlin, Christopher. 1998. *Public Health and Social Justice in the Age of Chadwick: Britain, 1800–1854*. Cambridge History of Medicine. Cambridge: Cambridge University Press.

Hansen, Thomas Blom. 1999. *The Saffron Wave: Democracy and Hindu Nationalism in Modern India*. Princeton, NJ: Princeton University Press.

———. 2001. *Wages of Violence: Naming and Identity in Postcolonial Bombay*. Princeton, NJ: Princeton University Press.

———. 2005. "Sovereigns beyond the State: On Legality and Authority in Urban India." In *Sovereign Bodies: Citizens, Migrants, and States in the Postcolonial World*, edited by Thomas Blom Hansen and Finn Stepputat, 169–91. Princeton, NJ: Princeton University Press.

Hansen, Thomas Blom, and Oskar Verkaaik. 2009. "Introduction—Urban Charisma: On Everyday Mythologies in the City." *Critique of Anthropology* 29 (1): 5–26.

Haraway, Donna. 1991. *Simians, Cyborgs, and Women: The Reinvention of Nature*. New York: Routledge.

———. 2014. "Anthropocene, Capitalocene, Chtulucene: Staying with the Trouble." Lecture delivered at UC Santa Cruz, May 9. Accessed January 31, 2016. https://vimeo.com/97663518.

Hardiman, David. 1996. "Small Dam Systems of the Sahyadris." In *Nature, Culture, Imperialism: Essays on the Environmental History of South Asia*, edited by David Arnold and Ramachandra Guha, 185–209. Delhi: Oxford University Press.

———. 2002. "The Politics of Water in Colonial India." *Journal of South Asian Studies* 25 (2): 111–20.

———. 2007. "The Politics of Water Scarcity in Gujarat." In *Waterscapes: The Cultural Politics of a Natural Resource*, edited by Amita Baviskar, 40–64. New Delhi: Permanent Black.

Harman, Graham. 2009. *Prince of Networks: Bruno Latour and Metaphysics:* Prahran, Vic.: Re.press.

Harris, Andrew. 2013. "Concrete Geographies: Assembling Global Mumbai through Transport Infrastructure." *City* 17 (3): 343–60.

Hart, Gillian. 2002. *Disabling Globalization: Places of Power in Post-Apartheid South Africa*. Berkeley: University of California Press.

Harvey, David. 2003. *Paris, Capital of Modernity*. New York: Routledge.

———. 2008. "The Right to the City." *New Left Review* 53 (September–October): 23–40.

Harvey, Penelope, and Hannah Knox. 2015. *Roads: An Anthropology of Infrastructure and Expertise*. Expertise: Cultures and Technologies of Knowledge. Ithaca, NY: Cornell University Press.

Hazareesingh, Sandip. 2000. "The Quest for Urban Citizenship: Civic Rights, Public Opinion, and Colonial Resistance in Early Twentieth-Century Bombay." *Modern Asian Studies* 34 (4): 797–829.

———. 2001. "Colonial Modernism and the Flawed Paradigms of Urban Renewal: Uneven Development in Bombay, 1900–25." *Urban History* 28 (2): 235–55.

Heidegger, Martin. 1977. *The Question Concerning Technology*. New York: Garland.

Herzfeld, Michael. 1992. *The Social Production of Indifference: Exploring the Symbolic Roots of Western Bureaucracy*. New York: Berg.

Hetherington, Kregg. 2011. *Guerrilla Auditors: The Politics of Transparency in Neoliberal Paraguay*. Durham, NC: Duke University Press.

———. 2013. "Beans before the Law: Knowledge Practices, Responsibility, and the Paraguayan Soy Boom." *Cultural Anthropology* 28 (1): 65–85.

————. 2014. "Waiting for the Surveyor: Development Promises and the Temporality of Infrastructure." *Journal of Latin American and Caribbean Anthropology* 19 (2): 195–211.

Heynen, Nik, Maria Kaika, and Erik Swyngedouw. 2006. *In the Nature of Cities: Urban Political Ecology and the Politics of Urban Metabolism*. New York: Routledge.

Hillier, Joseph. 2011. "The Rise of Constant Water in Nineteenth-Century London." *London Journal* 36 (1): 37–53.

Holston, James. 1989. *The Modernist City: An Anthropological Critique of Brasília*. Chicago: University of Chicago Press.

————. 2008. *Insurgent Citizenship: Disjunctions of Democracy and Modernity in Brazil*. Princeton, NJ: Princeton University Press.

Holston, James, and Arjun Appadurai. 1996. "Cities and Citizenship." *Public Culture* 8 (2): 187–204.

Hughes, Thomas Parke. 1983. *Networks of Power: Electrification in Western Society, 1880–1930*. Baltimore: Johns Hopkins University Press.

Hull, Matthew S. 2003. "The File: Agency, Authority, and Autography in an Islamabad Bureaucracy." *Language and Communication* 23:287–314.

————. 2012. *Government of Paper: The Materiality of Bureaucracy in Urban Pakistan*. Berkeley: University of California Press.

Humphrey, Caroline. 2005. "Ideology in Infrastructure: Architecture and Soviet Imagination." *Journal of the Royal Anthropological Institute* 11 (1): 39–58.

Illich, Ivan. 1985. H_2O and the Waters of Forgetfulness: Reflections on the Historicity of "Stuff." Dallas: Dallas Institute of Humanities and Culture.

Jackson, Steven. 2014. "Rethinking Repair." In *Media Technologies: Essays on Communication, Materiality, and Society*, edited by Tarleton Gillespie, Pablo Boczkowski, and Kirsten Foot, 221–40. Cambridge, MA: MIT Press.

Jain, Srinivas. 2014. "The Myth of Mumbai's Water Crisis." NDTV, July 19. Accessed May 13, 2015. http://www.ndtv.com/mumbai-news/myth-of-mumbais-water-crisis-590792.

Jensen, Casper Bruun. 2016. "Pipe Dreams: Sewage Infrastructure and Activity Trails in Phnom Penh." *Ethnos: Journal of Anthropology* 2016:1–21. doi: 10.1080/00141844.2015.1107608.

John, Mary, and Satish Deshpande. 2008. "Theorising the Present: Problems and Possibilities." *Economic and Political Weekly* 43 (46): 83–86.

Joyce, Patrick. 2003. *The Rule of Freedom: Liberalism and the Modern City*. London: Verso.

Kaika, Maria. 2005. *City of Flows: Modernity, Nature, and the City*. New York: Routledge.

Kalia, Ravi. 1999. *Chandigarh: The Making of an Indian City*. New Delhi: Oxford University Press.

————. 2004. *Gandhinagar: Building National Identity in Postcolonial India*. Columbia: University of South Carolina Press.

Kandviker, Ajit P. 1978. "Economics and Politics of Grass." *Economic and Political Weekly* 13 (47): 1927–29.

Kaplan, Robert. 1994. "The Coming Anarchy." *Atlantic Monthly*, February.

Katzenstein, Mary F., Uday Singh Mehta, and Usha Thakkar. 1997. "The Rebirth of Shiv Sena: The Symbiosis of Discursive and Organizational Power." *Journal of Asian Studies* 56 (2): 371–90.

Kaviraj, Sudipta. 2003. "A State of Contradictions: The Post-colonial State in India." In *States and Citizens: History, Theory, Prospects*, edited by Quentin Skinner and Bo Stråth, 145–63. Cambridge: Cambridge University Press.

Khan, Naveeda. 2006. "Flaws in the Flow: Roads and Their Modernity in Pakistan." *Social Text* 24 (489): 87–113.

Kidambi, Prashant. 2007. *The Making of an Indian Metropolis: Colonial Governance and Public Culture in Bombay, 1890–1920*. Burlington, VT: Ashgate.

Kingdom, Bill, Roland Liemberger, and Philippe Marin. 2006. *The Challenge of Reducing Non-Revenue Water (NRW) in Developing Countries—How the Private Sector Can Help: A Look at Performance-Based Service Contracting*. Water Supply and Sanitation Sector Board Discussion Paper 8. Washington, DC: World Bank.

Kjellén, Marianne. 2006. "From Public Pipes to Private Hands: Water Access and Distribution in Dar es Salaam, Tanzania." PhD diss., Stockholm University.

Klein, Ira. 1986. "Urban Development and Death: Bombay City, 1870–1914." *Modern Asian Studies* 20 (4): 725–54.

Kobayashi, Kazuo. 2013. "Indian Cotton Textiles in the Eighteenth-Century Atlantic Economy." *Africa at LSE* (blog), June 27. http://blogs.lse.ac.uk/africaatlse/2013/06/27/indian-cotton-textiles-in-the-eighteenth-century-atlantic-economy/.

Kooy, Michelle, and Karen Bakker. 2008. "Technologies of Government: Constituting Subjectivities, Spaces, and Infrastructures in Colonial and Contemporary Jakarta." *International Journal of Urban and Regional Research* 32 (2): 375–91.

Kothari, Ashish, and Rajiv Bhartari. 1984. "Narmada Valley Project: Development or Destruction." *Economic and Political Weekly* 19 (22/23): 907–20.

Kothari, Miloon, and Nasreen Contractor. 1996. *Planned Segregation: Riots, Evictions and Dispossession in Jogeshwari East, Mumbai/Bombay, India*. Mumbai: Youth for Unity and Voluntary Action.

Kristeva, Julia. 1982. *Powers of Horror: An Essay on Abjection*. European Perspectives. New York: Columbia University Press.

Kundu, Debolina. 2014. "Urban Development Programmes in India: A Critique of JnNURM." *Social Change* 44 (4): 615–32.

Kundu, Debolina, and Dibyendu Samanta. 2011. "Redefining the Inclusive Urban Agenda in India." *Economic and Political Weekly* 46 (5): 55–63.

Laidlaw, James. 2010. "Agency and Responsibility: Perhaps You Can Have Too Much of a Good Thing." In *Ordinary Ethics: Anthropology, Language, and Action*, edited by Michael Lambek, 143–64. New York: Fordham University Press.

Lamarchand, René. 1977. "Political Clientelism and Ethnicity in Tropical Africa: Competing Solidarities in Nation-Building." In *Friends, Followers, and Factions: A Reader in Political Clientelism*, edited by Steffen W. Schmidt, James C. Scott, Carl Landé, and Laura Guasti, 100–122. Berkeley: University of California Press.

Lambert, Allan, and W. Hirner. 2000. *Losses from Water Supply Systems: Standard Terminology and Recommended Performance Measures*. London: International Water Association.

Lansing, J. Stephen. 1991. *Priests and Programmers: Technologies of Power in the Engineered Landscape of Bali*. Princeton, NJ: Princeton University Press.

Larkin, Brian. 2008. *Signal and Noise: Media, Infrastructure, and Urban Culture in Nigeria*. Durham, NC: Duke University Press.

———. 2013. "The Politics and Poetics of Infrastructure." *Annual Review of Anthropology* 42 (1): 327–43.

———. 2015. "Form." Theorizing the Contemporary, Cultural Anthropology website, September 24. Accessed July 25, 2016. https://culanth.org/fieldsights/718-form.

Latour, Bruno. 1987. *Science in Action: How to Follow Scientists and Engineers through Society.* Cambridge, MA: Harvard University Press.

———. 1996. *Aramis, or The Love of Technology.* Cambridge, MA: Harvard University Press.

———. 2005. *Reassembling the Social: An Introduction to Actor-Network-Theory.* Clarendon Lectures in Management Studies. New York: Oxford University Press.

Latour, Bruno, and Peter Weibel, eds. 2005. *Making Things Public: Atmospheres of Democracy.* Cambridge, MA: MIT Press.

Law, John. 1987. "Technology and Heterogeneous Engineering: The Case of Portuguese Expansion." In *The Social Construction of Technological Systems: New Directions in the Sociology and History of Technology,* edited by Wiebe E. Bijker, Thomas P. Hughes, and Trevor J. Pinch, 111–34. Cambridge, MA: MIT Press.

Lazar, Sian. 2013. *The Anthropology of Citizenship: A Reader.* Hoboken, NJ: Wiley-Blackwell.

Lea, Tess. 2015. "What Has Water Got to Do with It? Indigenous Public Housing and Australian Settler-Colonial Relations." *Settler Colonial Studies* 5 (4): 375–86.

Lea, Tess, and Paul Pholeros. 2010. "This Is Not a Pipe: The Treacheries of Indigenous Housing." *Public Culture* 22 (1): 187–209.

Le Guin, Ursula K. 1996. "The Carrier Bag Theory of Fiction." In *The Ecocriticism Reader: Landmarks in Literary Ecology,* edited by Cheryll Glotfelty and Harold Fromm, 149–54. Athens: University of George Press.

Lemke, Thomas. 2014. "New Materialisms: Foucault and the 'Government of Things.'" *Theory, Culture and Society* 32 (4): 3–25.

Lewis, Clara. 2009. "Civic Body Learns It Has More Wells Than It Knew Of." *Times of India,* July 8.

Li, Tania Murray. 1999. "Compromising Power: Development, Culture, and Rule in Indonesia." *Cultural Anthropology* 14 (3): 295–322.

———. 2007. *The Will to Improve: Governmentality, Development, and the Practice of Politics.* Durham, NC: Duke University Press.

Limbert, Mandana E. 2010. *In the Time of Oil: Piety, Memory, and Social Life in an Omani Town.* Stanford, CA: Stanford University Press.

Linton, Jamie. 2010. *What Is Water?: The History of a Modern Abstraction.* Vancouver: UBC Press.

Linton, Jamie, and Jessica Budds. 2014 "The Hydrosocial Cycle: Defining and Mobilizing a Relational-Dialectical Approach to Water." *Geoforum* 57: 170–80.

Loftus, Alex. 2006. "Reification and the Dictatorship of the Water Meter." *Antipode* 38 (5): 1023–45.

———. 2012. *Everyday Environmentalism: Creating an Urban Political Ecology.* Minneapolis: University of Minnesota Press.

Luke, Timothy. 2010. "Power Loss or Blackout: The Electricity Network Collapse of August 2003 in North America." In *Disrupted Cities: When Infrastructure Fails*, edited by Stephen Graham, 55–68. New York: Routledge.

Maharashtra Water Resources Regulatory Authority Act. 2005. *Law, Environment and Development Journal* 1 (1): 80. Accessed January 31, 2016. http://www.lead-journal.org /content/05080.pdf.

Malthus, Thomas. 1798. *An Essay on the Principle of Population*. London: J. Johnson.

Mamdani, Mahmood. 1996. *Citizen and Subject: Contemporary Africa and the Legacy of Late Colonialism*. Princeton, NJ: Princeton University Press.

Marres, Noortje. 2012. *Material Participation: Technology, the Environment and Everyday Publics*. New York: Palgrave Macmillan.

Masco, Joseph. 2016. "The Age of Fallout." *History of the Present: A Journal of Critical History* 5 (2) 137–68.

Mathews, Andrew. 2008. "State Making, Knowledge, and Ignorance: Translation and Concealment in Mexican Forestry Institutions." *American Anthropologist* 110 (4): 484–94.

Mathur, Anuradha, and Dilip Da Cunha. 2001. *Mississippi Floods: Designing a Shifting Landscape*. New Haven, CT: Yale University Press.

———. 2009. *Soak: Mumbai in an Estuary*. New Delhi: Rupa.

Mauss, Marcel. 1925. *The Gift*. New York: W. W. Norton.

Mazzarella, William. 2003. *Shoveling Smoke: Advertising and Globalization in Contemporary India*. Durham, NC: Duke University Press.

McCully, Patrick. 2001. *Silenced Rivers: The Ecology and Politics of Large Dams*. London: Zed Books.

McFarlane, Colin. 2008. "Sanitation in Mumbai's Informal Settlements: State, 'Slum,' and Infrastructure." *Environment and Planning A* 40 (1): 88–107.

———. 2011. *Learning the City: Knowledge and Translocal Assemblage*. Malden, MA: Wiley-Blackwell.

McFarlane, Colin, and Jonathan Rutherford. 2008. "Political Infrastructures: Governing and Experiencing the Fabric of the City." *International Journal of Urban and Regional Research* 32 (2): 363–74.

McGeehan, Patrick, Russ Buettner, and David Chen. 2014. "Beneath Cities, a Decaying Tangle of Gas Pipes." *New York Times*, March 23.

McGregor, JoAnn. 2008. "Abject Spaces, Transnational Calculations: Zimbabweans in Britain Navigating Work, Class and the Law." *Transactions of the Institute of British Geographers* 33 (4): 466–82.

McKay, Ramah. 2012. "Documentary Disorders: Managing Medical Multiplicity in Maputo, Mozambique." *American Ethnologist* 39 (3): 545–61.

Meehan, Katie M. 2014. "Tool-Power: Water Infrastructure as Wellsprings of State Power." *Geoforum* 57 (November): 215–24.

Mehta, Lyla. 2005. *The Politics and Poetics of Water: Naturalising Scarcity in Western India*. New Delhi: Orient Longman.

Mehta, Suketu. 2004. *Maximum City: Bombay Lost and Found*. New York: Alfred A. Knopf.

Meillassoux, Claude. 1981. *Maidens, Meal, and Money: Capitalism and the Domestic Community*. New York: Cambridge University Press.

Menon, Meena, and Neera Adarkar. 2004. *One Hundred Years One Hundred Voices: The Millworkers of Girangaon; An Oral History*. Calcutta: Seagull Books.

Mhaske, Pandurang. 2008. "City Stands on Shaky Grounds." DNA, September 17.

Mintz, Sidney. 1985. *Sweetness and Power: The Place of Sugar in Modern History*. New York: Viking.

Mitchell, Timothy. 1991. "The Limits of the State: Beyond Statist Approaches and Their Critics." *American Political Science Review* 85 (1): 77–96.

———. 2002. *Rule of Experts: Egypt, Techno-politics, Modernity*. Berkeley: University of California Press.

———. 2011. *Carbon Democracy: Political Power in the Age of Oil*. London: Verso.

Miyazaki, Hirokazu. 2013. *Arbitraging Japan: Dreams of Capitalism at the End of Finance*. Berkeley: University of California Press.

Mol, Annemarie. 2002. *The Body Multiple: Ontology in Medical Practice*. Durham, NC: Duke University Press.

Moore, Donald S. 2005. *Suffering for Territory: Race, Place, and Power in Zimbabwe*. Durham, NC: Duke University Press.

Moore, Sarah. 2008. "The Politics of Garbage in Oaxaca, Mexico." *Society and Natural Resources* 21 (7): 597–610.

Morrison, Kathleen. 2015. "Archaeologies of Flow: Water and the Landscapes of Southern India Past, Present, and Future." *Journal of Field Archaeology* 40 (5): 560–80.

Mosse, David. 2003. *The Rule of Water*. Delhi: Oxford University Press.

Muehlmann, Shaylih. 2012. "Rhizomes and Other Uncountables: The Malaise of Enumeration in Mexico's Colorado River Delta." *American Ethnologist* 39 (2): 339–53.

Mukerji, Chandra. 2010. "The Unintended State." In *Material Powers: Cultural Studies, History and the Material Turn*, edited by Tony Bennett and Patrick Joyce, 81–101. London: Routledge.

Mukhija, Vinit. 2003. *Squatters as Developers: Slum Redevelopment in Mumbai*. Burlington, VT: Ashgate.

Municipal Corporation of Greater Mumbai. 1994. *Report of the Expert Committee (Water Planning) on Bombay's Future Water Resources and Improvement in Present Water Supply Scheme*. Mumbai: Executive Engineer, Water Works Planning and Research.

———. 2008. "Leak burst data," K-East WDIP.

———. 2010. *Mumbai Human Development Report*. New Delhi: Oxford University Press.

Municipal Corporation of Greater Mumbai, and Hydraulic Engineers Department. 1999. *Master Plan for Water Supply of Mumbai (for Its Growth by the Year 2021)*. Mumbai: Executive Engineer, Water Works Planning and Research.

Municipal Engineers Association, Mumbai, and Brihan Mumbai Licenced Plumbers Association. 2006. *Mumbai's Water: Glorious History of BWW*. Mumbai: Sukhdeo Kashid.

Munn, Nancy. 1992. "The Cultural Anthropology of Time: A Critical Essay." *Annual Review of Anthropology* 21:93–123.

Murley, Susanna. 2011. "Is NYC Regularly Losing 30 Percent of Its Water?" *Huffington Post,* June 22.

Murphy, Michelle. 2006. *Sick Building Syndrome and the Problem of Uncertainty: Environmental Politics, Technoscience, and Women Workers.* Durham, NC: Duke University Press.

Nading, Alex M. 2014. *Mosquito Trails: Ecology, Health, and the Politics of Entanglement.* Berkeley: University of California Press.

Nair, Janaki. 2005. *The Promise of the Metropolis: Bangalore's Twentieth Century.* New Delhi: Oxford University Press.

NDTV. 2015. "26 July: The Day Mumbai Stopped." NDTV online. Accessed November 1, 2015. http://www.ndtv.com/photos/news/26july-2005-the-day-mumbai-stopped-11000.

Neuwirth, Robert. 2006. *Shadow Cities: A Billion Squatters, a New Urban World.* New York: Routledge.

Nijman, Jan. 2008. "Against the Odds: Slum Rehabilitation in Neoliberal Mumbai." *Cities* 25 (2): 73–85.

———. 2009. "A Study of Space in Mumbai's Slums." *Tijdschrift voor economische en sociale geografie* 101 (1): 4–17.

Nugent, David. 2004. "Governing States." In *A Companion to the Anthropology of Politics,* edited by David Nugent and Joan Vincent, 198–215. Malden, MA: Blackwell.

———. 2006. "Comments on Globalization and Postcolonial States." *Current Anthropology* 47 (2): 301.

———. 2010. "States, Secrecy, Subversives: APRA and Political Fantasy in Mid-20th-Century Peru." *American Ethnologist* 37 (4): 681–702.

Ong, Aihwa. 1996. "Cultural Citizenship as Subject-making: Immigrants Negotiate Racial and Cultural Boundaries in the United States." *Current Anthropology* 37, no. 5 (1996): 737–62.

———. 2006. *Neoliberalism as Exception: Mutations in Citizenship and Sovereignty.* Durham, NC: Duke University Press.

O'Reilly, Kathleen. 2006. " 'Traditional' Women, 'Modern' Water: Linking Gender and Commodification in Rajasthan, India." *Geoforum* 37 (6): 958–72.

Orlove, Ben, and Steven Caton. 2010. "Water Sustainability: Anthropological Approaches and Prospects." *Annual Review of Anthropology* 39 (October): 401–15.

Otero, Iago, Giorgos Kallis, Raül Aguilar, and Vicenç Ruiz. 2011. "Water Scarcity, Social Power and the Production of an Elite Suburb: The Political Ecology of Water in Matadepera, Catalonia." *Ecological Economics* 70 (7): 1297–1308.

Page, Ben. 2005. "Paying for Water and the Geography of Commodities." *Transactions of the Institute of British Geographers* 30 (3): 293–306.

Paley, Julia. 2001. *Marketing Democracy: Power and Social Movements in Post-dictatorship Chile.* Berkeley: University of California Press.

Pandian, Anand. 2008. "Pastoral Power in the Postcolony: On the Biopolitics of the Criminal Animal in South India." *Cultural Anthropology* 23 (1): 85–117.

Patel, Sujata, and Jim Masselos. 2003. *Bombay and Mumbai: The City in Transition.* New Delhi: Oxford University Press.

Patel, Sujata, and Alice Thorner. 1995. *Bombay: Mosaic of Modern Culture*. Bombay: Oxford University Press.

———. 1996. *Bombay: Metaphor for Modern India*. Bombay: Oxford University Press.

Petryna, Adirana. 2002. *Life Exposed: Biological Citizens after Chernobyl*. Princeton, NJ: Princeton University Press.

Polanyi, Karl. 2001. *The Great Transformation: The Political and Economic Origins of Our Time*. Boston: Beacon.

Polmuri, Sarita. 2008. *Mithi Nadi*. In *Ek Dozen Paani*, edited by Nikhil Anand, Shaina Anand, and Ashok Sukumaran. India: Aagaz, Akansha Sewa Sangh, CAMP, and Nikhil Anand. Accessed July 25, 2016. http://www.youtube.com/ekdozenpaani.

Polmuri, Supriya. 2008. *Prashna*. In *Ek Dozen Paani*, edited by Nikhil Anand, Shaina Anand, and Ashok Sukumaran. India: Aagaz, Akansha Sewa Sangh, CAMP, and Nikhil Anand. Accessed July 25, 2016. http://www.youtube.com/ekdozenpaani.

Poovey, Mary. 1998. *A History of the Modern Fact: Problems of Knowledge in the Sciences of Wealth and Society*. Chicago: University of Chicago Press.

Povinelli, Elizabeth. 2002. *The Cunning of Recognition: Indigenous Alterities and the Making of Australian Multiculturalism*. Durham, NC: Duke University Press.

Prakash, Gyan. 2010. *Mumbai Fables*. Princeton, NJ: Princeton University Press.

Pratt, Mary Louise. 1986. "Fieldwork in Common Places." In *Writing Culture: The Poetics and Politics of Ethnography*, edited by James Clifford and George Marcus, 27–50. Berkeley: University of California Press.

Proctor, Robert N., and Londa Schiebinger, eds. 2008. *Agnotology: The Making and Unmaking of Ignorance*. Stanford, CA: Stanford University Press.

Rademacher, Anne. 2011. *Reigning the River: Urban Ecologies and Political Transformation in Kathmandu*. Durham, NC: Duke University Press.

Rahnema, Majid. 1992. "Participation," in *The Development Dictionary*, edited by Wolfgang Sachs, 155–76. Hyderabad: Orient Longman Limited.

Rane-Kothare, Anita. 2012. "Caves of Mumbai." Talk at the Observer Research Foundation, May 31. Accessed March 14, 2015. https://www.youtube.com/watch?v=sTH-FnHfR7U.

Ranganathan, Malini. 2014. "Paying for Pipes, Claiming Citizenship: Political Agency and Water Reforms at the Urban Periphery." *International Journal of Urban and Regional Research* 38 (2): 590–608.

———. 2015. "Storm Drains as Assemblages: The Political Ecology of Flood Risk in Post-Colonial Bangalore." *Antipode* 47 (5): 1300–1320.

Ranganathan, Malini, Lalita Kamath, and Vinay Baindur. 2009. "Piped Water Supply to Greater Bangalore: Putting the Cart before the Horse?" *Economic and Political Weekly* 24 (33): 53–62.

Rao, Nikhil. 2013. *House, but No Garden: Apartment Living in Bombay's Suburbs, 1898–1964*. Minneapolis: University of Minnesota Press.

Rao, Shashank. 2007. "Take a Leak: New Zealand Company's Pilot Report on Public Culture Privatisation of Water Supply Is Rejected Twice because BMC Was Not Satisfied with Its Estimate of Water Leakages." *Mid-Day*, June 2.

Reddy, Rajyashree N. 2015. "Producing Abjection: E-waste Improvement Schemes and Informal Recyclers of Bangalore." *Geoforum* 62 (June): 166–74.

Redfield, Peter. 2005. "Foucault in the Tropics: Displacing the Panopticon." In *Anthropologies of Modernity: Foucault, Governmentality, and Life Politics*, edited by Jonathan Xavier Inda, 50–79. Malden, MA: Blackwell.

Reisner, Marc. 1987. *Cadillac Desert: The American West and Its Disappearing Water*. New York: Penguin Books.

Ren, Xuefei. 2011. *Building Globalization: Transnational Architecture Production in Urban China*. Chicago: University of Chicago Press.

Riles, Annelise. 2000. *The Network Inside Out*. Ann Arbor: University of Michigan Press.

Robinson, Jennifer. 2002. "Global and World Cities: A View from Off the Map." *International Journal of Urban and Regional Research* 26 (3): 531–54.

———. 2011. "Cities in a World of Cities: The Comparative Gesture." *International Journal of Urban and Regional Research* 35 (1): 1–23.

Rodgers, Dennis, and Bruce O'Neill. 2012. "Infrastructural Violence: Introduction to the Special Issue." *Ethnography* 13 (4): 401–12.

Rosaldo, Renato. 1994. "Cultural Citizenship and Educational Democracy." *Cultural Anthropology* 9 (3): 402–11.

Rose, Nikolas. 1999. *Powers of Freedom: Reframing Political Thought*. Cambridge: Cambridge University Press.

Rose, Nikolas, and Peter Miller. 1992. "Political Power beyond the State: Problematics of Government." *British Journal of Sociology* 43 (2): 173–205.

Roy, Ananya. 2003. *City Requiem, Calcutta: Gender and the Politics of Poverty*. Minneapolis: University of Minnesota Press.

———. 2004. "The Gentleman's City: Urban Informality in the Calcutta of New Communism." In *Urban Informality: Transnational Perspectives from the Middle East, Latin America, and South Asia*, edited by Ananya Roy and Nezar AlSayyad, 147–70. Lanham, MD: Lexington Books.

———. 2005. "Urban Informality: Toward an Epistemology of Planning." *Journal of the American Planning Association* 71 (2): 147–58.

———. 2009. "The 21st-Century Metropolis: New Geographies of Theory." *Regional Studies* 43 (6): 819–30.

Roy, Ananya, and Nezar AlSayyad. 2004. *Urban Informality: Transnational Perspectives from the Middle East, Latin America, and South Asia*. Lanham, MD: Lexington Books.

Roy, Arundhati. 2001. *The Greater Common Good*. Mumbai: India Book Distributors.

Roy, Dunu. 2009. " 'World Class': Arrogance of the Ignorant." *Hardnews* (blog), August 3. Accessed January 15, 2016. http://www.hardnewsmedia.com/2009/08/3133.

Rushdie, Salman. 2008. *The Enchantress of Florence: A Novel*. London: Jonathan Cape.

Saberwal, Vasant. 2000. "Environmental Alarm and Institutionalized Conservation in Himachal Pradesh, 1865–1994." In *Agrarian Environments: Resources, Representation and Rule in India*, edited by Arun Agrawal and K. Sivaramakrishnan, 68–85. Durham, NC: Duke University Press.

Sangameswaran, Priya, Roopa Madhav, and Clifton D'Rozario. 2008. "24/7, 'Privatisation' and Water Reform: Insights from Hubli-Dharwad." *Economic and Political Weekly* 43 (14): 60–67.

Sassen, Saskia. 2003. "The Repositioning of Citizenship: Emergent Subjects and Spaces for Politics." *CR: The New Centennial Review* 3 (2): 41–66.

Sawant, Pooja, and Tapasvi Kaulkar. 2008. *26/7*. In *Ek Dozen Paani*, edited by Nikhil Anand, Shaina Anand, and Ashok Sukumaran. India: Aagaz, Akansha Sewa Sangh, CAMP, and Nikhil Anand. Digital video. http://www.youtube.com/ekdozenpaani.

Schaper, David. 2014. "As Infrastructure Crumbles, Trillions Of Gallons Of Water Lost." National Public Radio. Accessed June 30, 2016. http://www.npr.org/2014/10/29 /359875321/as-infrastructure-crumbles-trillions-of-gallons-of-water-lost.

Schmidt, Steffan. 1977. *Friends, Followers, and Factions: A Reader in Political Clientelism*. Berkeley: University of California Press.

Schneider, Jane, and Peter Schneider. 1976. *Culture and Political Economy in Western Sicily*. Studies in Social Discontinuity Series. New York: Academic Press.

Schrader, Astrid. 2010. "Responding to *Pfiesteria piscicida* (the Fish Killer) Phantomatic Ontologies, Indeterminacy, and Responsibility in Toxic Microbiology." *Social Studies of Science* 40 (2): 275–306.

Schwenkel, Christina. 2013. "Post/Socialist Affect: Ruination and Reconstruction of the Nation in Urban Vietnam." *Cultural Anthropology* 28 (2): 252–77.

———. 2015. "Spectacular Infrastructure and Its Breakdown in Socialist Vietnam." *American Ethnologist* 42 (3): 520–34.

Scott, James. 1969. "The Analysis of Corruption in Developing Nations." *Comparative Studies in Society and History* 11 (3): 315–41.

———. 1977. "Patron–Client Politics and Political Change in South East Asia." In *Friends, Followers, and Factions: A Reader in Political Clientelism*, edited by Steffen W. Schmidt, James C. Scott, Carl Landé, and Laura Guasti, 123–46. Berkeley: University of California Press.

———. 1990. *Domination and the Arts of Resistance: Hidden Transcripts*. New Haven, CT: Yale University Press.

———. 1998. *Seeing like a State: How Certain Schemes to Improve the Human Condition Have Failed*. Yale Agrarian Studies Series. New Haven, CT: Yale University Press.

Sen, Amartya. 1981. *Poverty and Famines: An Essay on Entitlement and Deprivation*. Oxford: Oxford University Press.

Shaban, Abdul, and R. N. Sharma. 2007. "Water Consumption Patterns in Domestic Households in Major Cities." *Economic and Political Weekly* 42 (23): 2190–97.

Shaikh, Shali. 2008. *Pyasa Premnagar*. In *Ek Dozen Paani*, edited by Nikhil Anand, Shaina Anand, and Ashok Sukumaran. India: Aagaz, Akansha Sewa Sangh, CAMP, and Nikhil Anand. Accessed July 25, 2016. http://www.youtube.com/ekdozenpaani.

Sharif, Ismail. 2008. *Rishta*. In *Ek Dozen Paani*, edited by Nikhil Anand, Shaina Anand, and Ashok Sukumaran. India: Aagaz, Akansha Sewa Sangh, CAMP, and Nikhil Anand. Accessed July 25, 2016. http://www.youtube.com/ekdozenpaani.

Sharma, Kalpana. 2000. *Rediscovering Dharavi*. New Delhi: Penguin Books.

———. 2005. "Forget Shanghai, Remember Mumbai." *The Hindu*, February 21.

Shiva, Vandana. 2002. *Water Wars: Privatization, Pollution, and Profit*. Cambridge, MA: South End Press.

Simone, AbdouMaliq. 2004a. *For the City yet to Come: Changing African Life in Four Cities*. Durham, NC: Duke University Press.

———. 2004b. "People as Infrastructure: Intersecting Fragments in Johannesburg." *Public Culture* 16 (3): 407–29.

————. 2006. "Pirate Towns: Reworking Social and Symbolic Infrastructures in Johannesburg and Douala." *Urban Studies* 43 (2): 357–70.

————. 2010. *City Life from Jakarta to Dakar: Movements at the Crossroads.* Global Realities. New York: Routledge.

————. 2014. *Jakarta: Drawing the City Near.* Minneapolis: University of Minnesota Press.

Simone, AbdouMaliq, and Achmad Uzair Fauzan. 2013. "Majority Time: Operations in the Midst of Jakarta." *Sociological Review* 61 (S1): 109–23.

Sivaramakrishnan, K. 2002. *Modern Forests: Statemaking and Environmental Change in Colonial Eastern India.* Stanford, CA: Stanford University Press.

Sivaramakrishnan, K., and Arun Agrawal. 2003. "Regional Modernities in Stories and Practices of Development." In *Regional Modernities: The Cultural Politics of Development in India,* edited by K. Sivaramakrishnan and Arun Agrawal, 1–61. Stanford, CA: Stanford University Press.

Skaria, Ajay. 1999. *Hybrid Histories: Forests, Frontiers, and Wildness in Western India.* Delhi: Oxford University Press.

Smith, Mitch. 2015. "A Water Dilemma in Flint: Cloudy or Costly?" *New York Times,* March 24.

————. 2016. "Michigan: Emergency Declared over Flint's Water." *New York Times,* January 6.

Smith, Neil. 1996. *The New Urban Frontier: Gentrification and the Revanchist City.* London: Routledge.

Solomon, Harris. 2015. " 'The Taste No Chef Can Give': Processing Street Food in Mumbai." *Cultural Anthropology* 30 (1): 65–90.

South Asian Network on Dams, Rivers and People (SANDRP). 2014. "Pinjal and Gargai Dams: Affecting Tribal Areas, Tansa Sanctuary, Western Ghats; Shall We Still Go Ahead?" Blog, January 16. Accessed January 23, 2016. https://sandrp.wordpress.com /2014/01/16/pinjal-and-gargai-dams-affecting-tribal-areas-tansa-sanctuary-western -ghats-shall-we-still-go-ahead/.

Srikrishna Commission. 1998. *Report of the Srikrishna Commission Appointed for Inquiry into the Riots at Mumbai during December 1992 and January 1993.* Mumbai: Government of Maharashtra.

Srinivas, Smriti. 2015. *A Place for Utopia: Urban Designs from South Asia.* Seattle: University of Washington Press.

Star, Susan Leigh. 1999. "The Ethnography of Infrastructure." *American Behavioral Scientist* 43 (3): 377–91.

Star, Susan Leigh, and Karen Ruhleder. 1996. "Steps toward an Ecology of Infrastructure: Design and Access for Large Information Spaces." *Information Systems Research* 7 (1): 111–34.

Starosielski, Nicole. 2015. *The Undersea Network.* Durham, NC: Duke University Press.

Stoler, Ann Laura. 1995. *Race and the Education of Desire: Foucault's "History of Sexuality" and the Colonial Order of Things.* Durham, NC: Duke University Press.

————. 2004. *Partial Connections.* Walnut Creek, CA: AltaMira Press.

Strang, Veronica. 2004. *The Meaning of Water.* New York: Berg.

————. 2016. "Infrastructural Relations: Water, Political Power and the Rise of a New 'Despotic Regime.' " *Water Alternatives* 9 (2): 292–318.

Strathern, Marilyn. 1988. *The Gender of the Gift: Problems with Women and Problems with Society in Melanesia*. Studies in Melanesian Anthropology. Berkeley: University of California Press.

———. 1991. "Partners and Consumers: Making Relations Visible." *New Literary History* 22 (3): 581–601.

———, ed. 2000. *Audit Cultures: Anthropological Studies in Accountability, Ethics, and the Academy*. New York: Routledge.

Subramanian, Ajantha. 2009. *Shorelines: Space and Rights in South India*. Stanford, CA: Stanford University Press.

Sultana, Farhana, and Alex Loftus. 2012. *The Right to Water: Politics, Governance and Social Struggles*. New York: Earthscan.

Sundaram, Ravi. 2010. *Pirate Modernity: Delhi's Media Urbanism*. Asia's Transformations. New York: Routledge.

Suryawanshi, Sudhir. 2008. "Waikar Gets Rs 8 cr of BMC Fund Pie." *Mumbai Mirror*, March 13.

Swyngedouw, Erik. 2004. *Social Power and the Urbanization of Water: Flows of Power*. Oxford: Oxford University Press.

———. 2015. *Liquid Power: Contested Hydro-Modernities in Twentieth-Century Spain*. Cambridge, MA: MIT Press.

Tarlo, Emma. 2000. "Welcome to History: A Resettlement Colony in the Making." In *Delhi: Urban Space and Human Destinies*, edited by Véronique Dupont, Emma Tarlo, and Denis Vidal, 51–74. New Delhi: Manohar.

———. 2001. "Paper Truths: The Emergency and Slum Clearance through Forgotten Files." In *The Everyday State and Society in Modern India*, edited by C. J. Fuller and Véronique Bénéï, 68–90. London: Hurst and Co.

Taussig, Michael. 1999. *Defacement: Public Secrecy and the Labor of the Negative*. Stanford, CA: Stanford University Press.

Thomas, Deborah A. 2011. *Exceptional Violence: Embodied Citizenship in Transnational Jamaica*. Durham, NC: Duke University Press.

Thomas, Kimberley 2012. "Water under the Bridge? International Resource Conflict and Post-Treaty Dynamics in South Asia." *South Asia Journal* 5:11–28.

Thompson, E. P. 1967. "Time, Work-Discipline, and Industrial Capitalism." *Past and Present* 38 (December): 56–97.

Thompson, Michael, Michael Warburton, and Tom Hatley. 1986. *Uncertainty on a Himalayan Scale: An Institutional Theory of Environmental Perception and a Strategic Framework for the Sustainable Development of the Himalaya*. London: Ethnographica.

Tindall, Gillian. 1982. *City of Gold: The Biography of Bombay*. London: Temple Smith.

Trouillot, Michel-Rolph. 1995. *Silencing the Past: Power and the Production of History*. Boston: Beacon.

Tsing, Anna. 2005. *Friction: An Ethnography of Global Connection*. Princeton, NJ: Princeton University Press.

———. 2015. *The Mushroom at the End of the World: On the Possibility of Life in Capitalist Ruins*. Princeton, NJ: Princeton University Press.

United Nations Development Programme. 2006. *Human Development Report 2006: Beyond Scarcity; Power, Poverty and the Global Water Crisis*. New York: Palgrave Macmillan.

Vayda, Andrew, and Bradley Walters. 1999. "Against Political Ecology." *Human Ecology* 27 (1): 167–79.

Verdery, Katherine. 1996. *What Was Socialism, and What Comes Next?* Princeton Studies in Culture/Power/History. Princeton, NJ: Princeton University Press.

von Schnitzler, Antina. 2008. "Citizenship Prepaid: Water, Calculability and Techno-Politics in South Africa." *Journal of Southern African Studies* 34 (4): 899–917.

———. 2013. "Traveling Technologies: Infrastructure, Ethical Regimes, and the Materiality of Politics in South Africa." *Cultural Anthropology* 28 (4): 670–93.

Wade, Robert. 1982. "The System of Administrative and Political Corruption: Canal Irrigation in South India." *Journal of Development Studies* 18 (3): 287–328.

Warner, Michael. 2002. "Publics and Counterpublics." *Public Culture* 14 (1): 49–90.

Waters, Colin, et al. 2016. "The Anthropocene Is Functionally and Stratigraphically Distinct from the Holocene." *Science* 351 (6269). doi: 10.1126/science. aad2622.

Weinstein, Liza. 2014. *The Durable Slum: Dharavi and the Right to Stay Put in Globalizing Mumbai*. Globalization and Community. Minneapolis: University of Minnesota Press.

Whatmore, Sarah. 2006. "Materialist Returns: Practising Cultural Geography in and for a More-Than-Human World." *Cultural Geographies* 13 (4): 600–609.

Whitcombe, Elizabeth. 1972. *Agrarian Conditions in Northern India*. Berkeley: University of California Press.

Winner, Langdon. 1999. "Do Artifacts Have Politics?" In *The Social Shaping of Technology*, edited by Donald MacKenzie and Judy Wajcman, 28–40. Buckingham, UK: Open University Press.

Witsoe, Jeffrey. 2011. "Corruption as Power: Caste and the Political Imagination of the Postcolonial State." *American Ethnologist* 38 (1): 73–85.

———. 2013. *Democracy against Development: Lower-Caste Politics and Political Modernity in Postcolonial India*. South Asia across the Disciplines. Chicago: University of Chicago Press.

Wittfogel, Karl. 1957. *Oriental Despotism: A Comparative Study of Total Power*. New Haven, CT: Yale University Press.

Wolf, Eric. 1982. *Europe and the People without History*. Berkeley: University of California Press.

Woolgar, Steve, and Geoff Cooper. 1999. "Do Artefacts Have Ambivalence? Moses' Bridges, Winner's Bridges and Other Urban Legends in S&TS." *Social Studies of Science* 29 (3): 433–49.

World Commission on Dams. 2000. *Dams and Development: A New Framework for Decision-Making; The Report of the World Commission on Dams*. London: Earthscan.

Worster, Donald. 1992. *Rivers of Empire: Water, Aridity and the Growth of the American West*. Oxford: Oxford University Press.

Zeiderman, Austin. 2013. "Living Dangerously: Biopolitics and Urban Citizenship in Bogotá, Colombia." *American Ethnologist* 40 (1): 71–87.

————. 2016. *The Endangered City: The Politics of Security and Risk in Bogotá.* Durham, NC: Duke University Press.

Zérah, Marie-Hélène. 2008. "Splintering Urbanism in Mumbai: Contrasting Trends in a Multilayered Society." *Geoforum* 39:1922–32.

Zérah, Marie-Hélène, and Frédéric Landy. 2013. "Nature and Urban Citizenship Redefined: The Case of the National Park in Mumbai." *Geoforum* 46 (May): 25–33.

Zerubavel, Eviatar. 2006. *The Elephant in the Room: Silence and Denial in Everyday Life.* New York: Oxford University Press.

Zhang, Li. 2001. *Strangers in the City: Reconfigurations of Space, Power, and Social Networks within China's Floating Population.* Stanford, CA: Stanford University Press.

Index

Page numbers followed by *f* indicate illustrations.

abjection, 203, 230, 259n1; of Premnagar
settlers, 24, 193–95, 214–15, 214–16; race
and class and, 224; water quality and,
213–14
Abu-Lughod, Janet, 243n37
actants, 163, 258n13
agency, 124, 258n17; human and nonhuman, 170–73, 230, 258n13, 258n18;
women's, 125
Agrawal, Arun, vii
Akbar Birbal stories, ix–x
Alatout, Samer, 39
Althusser, Louis, 123
Andheri, 73, 80, 256n24
anthropocene, 225, 261n8
Appadurai, Arjun, 239n3, 239n5, 255n5,
258n18, 262n18
arbitrage, 133, 254n2
Arputham, Jockin, 65–66, 68
Asha: founding, 134–35; leaders and
members, 133–34, 143; programs and
events, 131–32, 132f, 149; socio-political
affiliations, 138–39, 155, 156–57

Ballestero, Andrea, 237n4
Bandrekar Wadi, 200–202
Banerjee, Mukulika, 145
Barad, Karen, 168
Barnes, Jessica, 32, 229
Barry, Andrew, 188, 244n51, 261n14
Baviskar, Amita, 214, 244n51, 255n13,
260n12

Bayat, Asef, 240n6, 250n8
Behrent, Michael, 242n32
belonging: cultures of, 217; documents of,
153; social, 6, 8, 64, 112, 237; urban, 10,
16, 32, 149, 157, 213–14
Bennett, Jane, 163, 171–72
Bhabha, Homi, 245n54
bhai, term usage, 251n20
Bhatsa Dam, 48f, 52–55
bills, water, 118, 236, 252n38, 257n11, 261n6;
computerized system for, 103; of
Premnagar residents, 198–99, 210, 217;
for proof of residence, 88–89, 262n21;
rates, 166
biopolitics, 11, 104, 242n31
blockage, water, 4, 12, 240n5, 257n11
Borivali National Park, 74, 95, 142, 159,
251n18
Bourdieu, Pierre, 112
Braun, Bruce, 230, 239n4, 241n13
Brihanmumbai Municipal Corporation
(BMC): administrators, 82–83;
Building Proposal Department, 86;
demolitions, 65–66, 79–80, 249n1;
incorporation, 74, 129; leakage figures,
165; naming controversy, 248n24;
political affiliation, 201; production of
abjection, 195; water connections, 91,
118, 185, 259n24; water consumption
study, 43; water reforms, 140, 149–53;
water supply schedules, 98; well water
and, 46, 212

British colonization, 25, 26f, 27, 33–35, 70, 247n11
Burra, Sundar, 84

Caldeira, Teresa, 247n20
Callon, Michel, 32
canals, 53–54
capitalism, 6, 122, 241n14, 241n16
Carse, Ashley, 254n2
Chakrabarty, Dipesh, 6, 240n8, 241n15, 259n5
Chalfin, Brenda, 245n53
Chary, Srinivas, 163–64
Chatterjee, Partha, 15–16, 67–68, 70, 250n7
chaviwallas (key people), 253n7; job to turn on valves, 1, 101–6, 108; photos of, 2f, 104f
citizenship: colonial model of, 35; documentation, 87–89, 252n36; formal, 8–9, 72, 241n22; hydraulic, 7, 8–10, 58, 148–49; infrastructures of, 93, 217; liberal and neoliberal, 14–15, 72, 89, 93, 250n10; practices of, 81, 185; as a process, 213; property and, 242n27; rights, 58, 67, 134, 139, 145, 236; settler, 16, 23, 57, 65–66; urban, 58, 64, 72, 194, 214, 225, 261n5; water connections and, 15, 244n47
city: colonial, 14, 27, 33–35, 247n10, 248n23; government, 46, 83–86, 132, 144, 156, 240n5, 261n5; inequalities, 67, 250n5; liberal/illiberal, 6–7, 15, 23, 225; modern, 34–35, 69, 237; planning, 66–68, 249n3; politics, 59, 68, 156, 216, 231; scale and, 34, 98; world-class, 249n3. See also postcolonial cities
civil society, 72, 149, 194; NGOs and, 143; political society and, 15–16, 67–68, 93, 156–57
climate change, 24, 225–27, 229, 240n8
colonialism. See British colonization
community based organizations (CBOS), 150, 155; definition, 255n4; public organization, 140–41; socio-political connections, 149, 155. See also Asha

connections, water: applications for, 89–92, 118, 252n39, 259n24; citizenship and, 15, 244n47; city councilors and, 144–49; costs, 116, 119, 253n13; for different built structures, 86–87; difficulties, 113–15, 144; fixing, 179–81, 233; shared, 16–17, 98, 108–9, 116–118, 117f; social class and, 15, 244n47; unauthorized or illegal, 182–84, 203, 209–12, 216. See also leakages; meters, water; pipes; plumbers
contaminated water, 45, 213–14; Flint River, 223–25
Contractor, Nasreen, 86
corruption, 77–78, 105, 185–86, 251n24, 259n25
councilors: city administration and, 83; control of water system, 184, 259nn23–24; housing development and, 84; influence over engineers, 183–84, 185; plumbers and, 185–86; political loyalties and, 146–48; protests and, 151–54, 256nn22–23; settler relations, 91–92, 157; social worker relations, 154–56; water connection applications and, 144–45; water policy and, 140–41, 255n12
Crawford, J. H. G., 34
cultural politics, 195, 214–15
cultural programs, 139, 233
cyborg waterscapes, 47, 48f

dairy farms, 74–75, 76
dams: construction, 34–35, 170, 258n14; dangers of, 47; management and maintenance, 49–52; in Mumbai history, 36–37, 247n16; water levels in, 39
Davis, Mike, 31
demolitions, 65–66, 74, 249n1; policies, 84; protests and violence over, 73
disconnections, water, 13, 33, 194, 203
displacement, 47, 55, 76, 80, 252n32
distribution, water: consultants, 234, 262n25; engineer responsibilities for, 101, 172, 177, 187; and human life,

227–29, 231; in Jogeshwari, 20; material politics of, 41; measurements, 166–68; plans, 1, 12, 37; privatization of, 18–19, 22, 140, 214, 235–36; unequal, 41–43, 47, 152, 172, 227. See also connections, water; water supply schedule

drains, 111, 128, 129; rivers as, 159

drinking water, 53, 54, 58, 213, 219; toxic, 223–25

East India Company, 25, 34–35, 70

Economic Times, 39

Ehrlich, Paul, 31

electricity, 171, 262n22, 263n27; connections, 114–15; privatization of, 140, 255n10

emergency narratives, viii, 239n3

engineers: billing and metering and, 166–67, 198–99, 237, 258n11; city councilors and, 183–84; colonial, 35; control of water system, 187–88; dam projects and, 36; heterogeneous, 173, 258n19; lack of qualified, 173–74; leakages and, 24, 163–68, 172–73, 179–82; in Shahpur, 49–51; underground water and, 44–46, 177–79, 248n28; view of Muslims, 195, 260n11; water connections and, 90–92, 148–49, 252n39, 256n18; water scarcity and, 40–42; water supply management, 35, 43–44, 100–101, 107–8, 253nn3–4, 255n14

ethnographer-subject relationship, 61–64, 249n1

ethnography, viii, 61, 226, 246n63, 249n1

Fassin, Didier, 261n11

Fatehpur Sikri, x

Fennell, Catherine, 245n53

Ferguson, James, 194, 229, 242n28, 259n1

fieldwork, 61–64

films, viii, 261nn1–2; Ek Dozen Paani (Gudilu), 191, 254n15; Pyasa Premnagar (Shaikh), 210; The Question (Polmuri), ix; 26/7 (Sawant and Kaulkar), 128

fire hydrants, 106

Flint, Michigan, 223–25, 261n2

floods: of July 2005, 106, 128–30, 135, 219, 248n25; management, 50–51

food rations, 80

Foucault, Michel: on biopolitics, 11, 242n31; on governmentality, 228; on technologies of power, 104, 242n32

friendship, 205–6; politics of, 72, 260n11; relations of, 78, 93, 251nn25–26; of settlers and state officials, 79–81, 229

Gandy, Matthew, 33, 249n33

Geddes, Patrick, 35, 81

gender, 122, 124–26, 241n14, 241n16

Gibson-Graham, J. K., 241n14

Global North, 17–18, 225, 237, 245n54

Global South: city inequalities, 67, 250n5; infrastructures, 17, 245n54, 261; social class, 62; urbanization, 31, 246n4

Gore, Mrinal, 81–84

Gregory, Steven, 249n3, 261n4

groundwater. See underground water

Gupta, Akhil, viii, 94, 195, 242n28, 259n27, 261n4

Hansen, Thomas Blom, 136, 237

Haraway, Donna, 239n6, 249n33, 255n5

Harvey, David, 31

Hazareesingh, Sandeep, 35

Heidegger, Martin, 244n40

Hetherington, Kregg, 172

Hindustan Times, 159–60, 219

hinterlands, 49

housing: affordable, 259n8; proof of residency, 87–90, 252n36; safety of, 194; types, 86–87; water supply and, 100

human and nonhuman relations, 32, 58, 163, 258n14; agency, 171–73, 258n13, 258n18; flow of water and, 169–70, 230–31; plural assemblages of, 261n14; politics and, 188, 230–31, 262n15

Humphrey, Caroline, 241n19

informality, 4, 240n7; city planning and, 66–68; state authority and, 76–77, 79
infrapolitics, 20, 231, 245n58
infrapower, 136, 139
infrastructures: breakdown of, 17–18, 24, 225, 227, 237, 262n16; citizenship and, 237, 242n27; colonial/postcolonial, 14–15, 25, 26f, 27–28; energy, 227; invisibility/visibility of, 13, 17, 228, 243n39, 245n54; liberal ideology and, 6–7, 69–70, 241n19; maintenance of, 231–33; media, 227, 243n34; Mumbai's hydraulic history of, 33–36, 261n5; nature-cultures and, 127, 129, 254n2; planetary, 226–27; as political and social structures, 13–14, 163, 244n43; public vs. private, 18–20, 235–36, 245n53; transportation, 127; urban, 69, 159–60. See also electricity
Inquilab Nagar, 113, 116
International Women's Day, 131–32, 233
irrigation, 52–54, 243n37

Jackson, Steven, 232
Jawaharlal Nehru National Urban Renewal Mission (NURM), 18
Jogeshwari: caves, 74, 95; flooding, 135; history and location, 73–75; public water connections, 23; settler and state relations in, 79–81; spring water, 191–92, 192f; state authority in, 76–78; water demand, 115; water distribution, 20
Joyce, Patrick, 69, 247n11

Kanheri caves, 74, 95
Kaplan, Robert, 276
K-East ward: leakages in, 167, 169, 173–74, 174f; water improvement project, 19, 140, 162; water supply schedule, 101, 102f
Kothari, Miloon, 86
Kristeva, Julia, 259n1

labor, 191–92, 232–33; of chaviwallas, 102–5; division of, 109–13, 124, 135, 255n13
Laidlaw, James, 258n17

Larkin, Brian, 13, 246n7, 247n12, 262n20
Latour, Bruno, 258n13, 258n18
Law, John, 258n19
Lea, Tess, 246n63
lead poisoning, 224, 261n4
leakages: accountability for, 170; detection technologies, 175, 258n21; engineer responsibilities, 172–73, 179–82; flow of water and, 168–69, 172, 230–31; ignorance over, 182–83, 231; managing and fixing, 173–75, 179–82, 187; materiality of, 13, 182, 188; measuring, 165–68; public water system and, 235; state power and, 187–88, 189; subterranean, 44, 174, 176; totals, 162, 165; 24/7 water projects and, 24, 164; valves and, 106
Le Guin, Ursula, 239n6
liberal government, 7, 69–71, 104, 228, 250n12
life, human: distributions of, 228–29, 231; infrastructures and, 225–26, 230; matter and, 261n11; politics of, 228, 261n13; water and, 219–21, 227, 261n9
Luke, Timothy, 235, 262n22

Maharashtra Navnirman Sena (MNS), 47, 260n9
Maharashtra Water Resources Regulatory Authority Act (2005), 54
mahila gath (Women's Group), 131, 140, 145, 148, 155
Mahim Creek, 219
Malthus, Thomas, 31
Marathi people, 201–2, 208–9, 250n17, 260nn9–10
marginalization, 6, 47, 49, 248n23, 260n8, 261n1; informality and, 68, 240n7; political society and, 15–16; of settlers, 107, 194, 202, 229, 235
Marres, Noortje, 254n3
materiality: of citizenship, 8; of hydraulic societies, 243n37; of infrastructures, 8, 10, 11–12, 176, 228, 231–32; of leakages,

13, 182, 188; "return" to, 243n36; uncertainty of, 243n38

mausi, term usage, 253n14

Mauss, Marcel, 214

measurement: for leakages, 165–68; technologies of, 168, 170; for water levels, 39. *See also* quantities, water

Meehan, Katie, 258n16

Meghwadi: slum status, 2; water network, 206–7, 207*f*, 211; water pressure in, 2–3

Meillassoux, Claude, 122

meters, water, 236, 262n25; estimates, 198; prepaid, 151, 153; rates, 166; shared, 117; un/reliability of, 169, 257n11

migrants, 30–31, 55–57, 260n9

millworkers, 75–76

Ministry of Urban Development, 18–19, 24, 43, 164, 167

Mitchell, Timothy, 170

Mithi River, 23, 129, 159–60, 219–20

Miyazaki, Hirokazu, 254n2

monsoons, 39, 240n7, 254n1; city dependence on, 32–33, 107; deficient, 46; floods and flood management, 50–51, 106, 128–30, 248n25

Mosse, David, 239n1

Mumbai: congested areas, 201–2, 259n8; history and geography, 25, 26*f*, 27–28, 33–34; liberal governance, 7, 14–15; structural inequalities, 62–63; suburbs, 128–30, 254n4; water demand and population, 29–30, 34, 36–39, 42–44, 57–58, 247n18; water sources, 49–50, 54–55, 57; water types in, 23, 220

Mumbai Hydraulic Engineering Department: founding, 33; surplus funds, 263n26; water distribution plan, 1, 37; water programs, 84. *See also* engineers

Muslims, 73, 195, 209, 259n8; abjection of, 24, 194, 215, 230; discrimination toward, 202–3, 260n11

Nading, Alex, 254n2

nakshatra, ix, 240n7

Nehru, Jawaharlal, 74

neoliberalism, 22, 103, 227; governance in Mumbai, 7, 14; postcolonialism and, 15, 244n48; water reforms and, 234

newspapers, 19, 32, 55, 248n27; Flint water story, 223–24; leakage stories, 166–67; Mithi River story, 159–60; water scarcity stories, 33, 36–37, 39–40, 44

New York City, 176, 232*f*

nongovernmental organizations (NGOs), 131, 138–39, 255n4; activists/workers, 141–43, 150, 155, 233, 256n23; public organization, 140–41. *See also* Vikas

Nugent, David, 162, 215, 249n38

pagdi system, 77, 251n22

patronage, 71, 78, 79, 250n13, 256n24; citizenship and, 72, 156; political, 91–92, 93, 137, 138. *See also* friendship

personhood, 71, 109, 122, 124, 157, 216; gendered forms of, 100, 113

phenomena, 168, 261n5

pipes: cleaning, 17; costs, 207; fixing, 179–81; leaching, 224–25; measuring water in, 168–69; photos, 42*f*; pump connections to, 196–97; technologies, 175; valves, 101–6, 104*f*, 181. *See also* leakages

planners, 66–68, 249n3

plumbers, 90, 91, 254n2; city councilors and, 17, 185–86; costs of/to, 207, 210–11; knowledge of water system, 203, 204, 206–7; settler relations, 17, 185–86; unauthorized water connections made by, 182–83, 209–12, 216

police, 77, 80, 105, 131–32, 220

policy: city councilors and, 140–41, 255n12; on slums, 84–85, 252n33; water, 54

political ecology, 23, 216, 227, 230

political economy, 214, 217

political parties, 30, 47, 56, 58; banners, 137, 138*f*; development funds, 147, 256n17; settler relations with, 92, 141–43; social organization affiliations with, 136–39; volunteer loyalty and, 146–48, 256n16. *See also* Shiv Sena political society: civil society and, 15–16, 67–68, 93, 156–57; efficacy of, 260n12; practices of, 72, 250n7

political subjectivity, 71–72, 132, 156, 237, 250n12; conflicts, 133–34

politics: of agency, 230; of citizenship, 225, 250n7, 261n5; city/urban, 32, 59, 68–69, 82, 156, 216, 231, 241n13; cultural, 195, 214–15; democratic, 188; of friendship, 63, 72, 250n26, 260n11; of human belonging, 6; of infrastructure, 8, 163, 187, 245n54; of life, 228–29; materiality and, 41, 172, 187; NGOs and, 143, 156; as plural in form, 71, 261n14; of rights, 16; technology and, 10, 12, 245n54; of water distribution, 41, 47; of water time, 125. *See also* technopolitics

population growth, 31, 34, 247n9; water supply and demand and, 36–39, 247n18

postcolonial cities, 67, 73, 94, 237, 248n23; abjection and, 214, 230; liberalism and, 7, 15, 36, 70–71; water demand and, 42

Povinelli, Elizabeth, 242n25, 252n35

Prakash, Gyan, 27

Pratap Nagar, 101

Pratt, Mary Louise, 249n1

Premnagar: abjection of settlers, 24, 193–94, 214–15; electoral constituency, 208; engineer attitudes toward, 200–203, 208–9, 211–12; housing, 75, 260n8; Muslim residents, 73, 202–3, 250n17; population, 260n13; resettlement, 74–76; social life, 205; unauthorized water connections, 209–11, 217; water network, 206–7, 207f, 216; well water, 45, 193, 212–14, 216

pressure, water: controlling and monitoring, 106, 175, 253n8; higher elevation and, 199; in Meghwadi, 2–3; problems, 113, 116, 119; reservoirs and, 101, 253n5; uneven, 1, 9–10

prices, water, 164, 257n4

privatization, 198; of electricity distribution, 140, 255n10; management consultants, 161; opposition to, 19, 140, 149,

257n2; of water distribution, 18–19, 22, 140, 214, 235

protests: domestic violence, 132f, 134; marches, 81–83; for more water, 1; Revolt of 1857, 35; water reform, 150–54, 154f, 157, 256n23

Public Private Infrastructure Advisory Facility (PPIAF), 19

public water systems, 18–20, 235–36; engineers and, 24; personal-political practices of, 184–86

Pukar, 239n5

pumps, 116, 196–97, 199–200

qualities, water, 32, 46, 220; of leakage, 162; as magical, 219

quantities, water, 29, 32; allocated by resident type, 100, 253n3; as approximations, 161, 176; calculations for, 166; from dams, 54; rationing, 107; for urban residents, 42–44

Rademacher, Anne, 240n4

Rane-Kothare, Anita, 95

Redfield, Peter, 70, 242n31

reforms, water, 22; controversy and opposition to, 140, 150–54, 154f, 157, 256n23; neoliberalism and, 234–35; proposals and consultations, 24, 134, 149–50

Reliance, 255n10

reservoirs, 101, 199, 253n5

Roy, Ananya, 68

Roy, Arundhati, 55

Rushdie, Salman, x

safety, water, 46–47, 223–25

Sahar village, 103

Salsette, 25, 26f, 34, 247n10

Sanjay Gandhi National Park, 74, 95, 142, 159, 251n18

scarcity: discourses, 33, 56, 57–58; in Mumbai, 36–37, 40–41, 229; political and social anxieties of, 32, 39, 40, 56, 125; silencing of, 41–42; state institutions and, 39–40, 248n22; water leakage and, 165

Schnitzler, Anita von, 244n45
science and technology studies (STS), 11,
    170, 245n54
Scott, James, 81, 245n58
Sen, Amartya, 229, 248n22
settlers: access to water, 12, 20, 43, 75, 85,
    235–36; community organizations and,
    133, 134, 149; leaders, 76–77, 251n21;
    politicians and, 136–37, 144–47, 256n15;
    recognition as citizens, 16, 65–66;
    rights, 141–43, 156–57; social move-
    ments, 81–83; state documents and,
    87–89, 94, 252n36; survival instincts,
    80; term usage, vii, 5, 239n2, 241n12;
    visibility of, 155; water connections for,
    15, 16, 72, 89–92, 98
sewage, 129, 159, 213
Shahpur, 51–52; access to water, 52–53, 58;
    rainfall, 46; water management, 49–51
Sharma, Aradhana, 195
Shiv Sena, 55–56, 86, 211, 246n3, 260n9;
    political position, 30; social organ-
    izations and, 137, 138; supporters, 73,
    195, 206, 208, 250n17
Shiv Tekadi, 101
silences, 41–42, 47, 57
Simone, Abdou Maliq, 250n8
sinkholes, 23, 174–75
situated knowledges, 136, 233, 255n5
Sivaramakrishnan, K., vii
Slum Areas Act, 84–86, 87
slum dwellers. See settlers
slums: city declaration of, 85–87, 252nn31–
    33; definition, vii, 5, 239n2, 240n8;
    demolition or clearance of, 65–66, 75,
    81, 249n1; preconceptions of, 4–5; pro-
    test marches, 82–83; rehabilitation or
    improvement, 76, 84–86, 252nn31–32;
    water connections in, 85, 113–14, 144
social class, 15, 37, 62, 143, 244n47
social mobility, 118
social relations, 10, 22, 133, 157, 233, 245n58;
    access to water and, 108–9; fieldwork
    and, 63; of settlers and state officials,
    78. See also friendship; patronage

social workers, 254n2, 255n8; civil and
    political affiliations, 135–39, 255n6;
    networks, 134, 137; settler relations, 133,
    134–35
springs, 191–92, 192f
squatters. See settlers; slums
Star, Susan Leigh, 29, 243n39
state formation, 162, 188, 247n21
state officials, 77–79, 80–81. See also
    councilors
Stoler, Ann Laura, 70, 242n31
storage tanks, 3, 9, 98, 110f
stories and storytelling, vii–x, 21, 224,
    239nn5–6, 249n1
storm water, 45, 129–30
Strathern, Marilyn, 71, 239n6
subterranean water. See underground
    water; wells
Sujal Mumbai, 150
Sundar, Nandini, 244n51, 260n12
Sundarnagar, 86, 144, 148, 256n19

tai, term usage, 240n3
tanker water, 45, 248n27, 253n1
Tansa Dam, 36, 44, 48f, 52
technologies, 104, 236, 244n40; impro-
    vised, 227, 233; leakage, 175, 188, 258n21;
    material, 11, 173, 242n32; of measure-
    ment, 168, 170; political, 14; "private,"
    197, 199
technopolitics, 13, 32, 99, 171, 188, 246n7
tenancy, 72, 85, 88, 115–16
Terrorist and Disruptive Activities Act
    (TADA), 77, 251n23
Thackeray, Bal, 29, 260n9
Thackeray, Raj, 203, 260n9
Thane district, 54
Thompson, E. P., 121–22
time: clock, 122; social relations of, 98–99,
    108–9; state management of, 99, 106–8;
    for turning pipe valves, 102–5; water
    collection and, 120–21, 191–92, 196–97;
    water supply schedules and, 100–101,
    102f, 122–24; women or gender and,
    109–13, 121–22, 124–26

Times (India), 46
trade, 27, 247n9, 254n2
Trouillot, Michel-Rolph, 41
Tsing, Anna, 226, 241n14, 261n5
tunnels, water: Mumbai's, 44; New York's,
176, 225

underground water, 45, 47, 194, 216; leakage, 44; Mumbai's network, 177–79,
178*f*. *See also* wells
urbanization, 31, 68, 246n4
urban revitalization, 3, 65–66, 240n4; river
renewal, 159–60

Vaitarna Dam, 36, 48–49, 52, 54, 247n16
Verdery, Katherine, 99
Verkaaik, Oskar, 136, 237
Vihar Dam, 34–35
Vikas: activists, 141–43, 152–53; training,
134, 144–45, 148
violence: domestic, 132*f*, 134; from inaction, 224, 261n4; Jogeshwari riots,
73, 260n8; toward migrants, 30, 203,
260n9; during protests, 153–54

Waikar, Ravindra, 29–30, 58
Wakefield, Stephanie, 239n4
washing, 110–13, 111*f*, 253n10
water access: for agriculture and rural
needs, 51–55, 249n37; higher elevation
and, 199–200; inequalities, 1–2, 43; in
Mumbai history, 33–35; in Premnagar
settlement, 196; rights to, 19, 57; state
and, 10, 12; for urban residents, 42–44;
for working-class households, 15,
244n47. *See also* water supply schedule
water-collecting practices, 118–21, 120*f*,
191–92, 254n15; restrictions or limita-
tions, 123, 124, 196–97

Water Distribution Improvement Project
(WDIP), 19, 140, 162, 235; consultants,
234, 262n25
water harvesting systems, 45, 95–96,
260n15. *See also* water-collecting
practices
water lines: connections, 146, 183, 210–11;
leakage, 41; legal and illegal, 200*f*, 203;
pumps on, 200; shared, 108, 116–17, 117*f*,
196; sizes, 12, 206
Water Rights Campaign, 22, 140, 142,
150, 152
water supply schedule: concept of time
and, 98–100, 122–24, 253n2; demand
for timeliness in, 125–26; by neighborhood zone, 1, 97–98, 100–101, 102*f*,
253n3; recalibration and changes to,
106–8, 163; for turning on pipe valves,
101–6; 24/7 system, 122, 163–64, 178,
257n5
wells, 46–47, 96, 168, 248nn26–28;
in Premnagar, 45, 193, 212–14, 216
Whatmore, Sarah, 230, 243n36
Wittfogel, Karl, 12, 243n37, 250n5
Wolf, Eric, 160
women: labor, 109–13, 124; savings
groups, 135, 138, 144; time concepts
and, 121–22, 125–26; water collection
and, 124–25; Women's Day cele-
brations, 131–32
World Bank, 24, 81, 84, 122; water audit,
167, 170; water reform programs, 19,
140, 149, 151, 162, 257n2
Worster, Donald, 243n37

xenophobia, 56, 201, 203, 260n9

youth, viii, 206, 239n5; groups, 113,
140–42; in protests, 151–55, 256n23

Made in the USA
Las Vegas, NV
28 October 2021